Please return/renew this item by the last date shown. Books may also be renewed by phone or internet.

💻 www3.rbwm.gov.uk/libraries

☎ 01628 796969 (library hours)

☎ 0303 123 0035 (24 hours)

www.rbwm.gov.uk

Royal Borough
of Windsor &
Maidenhead

WOMEN OF THE VATICAN

WOMEN
OF THE
VATICAN

FEMALE POWER IN A MALE WORLD

Lynda Telford

AMBERLEY

For Linda Halliday, without whose expertise, encouragement, support, photographs, good company, and enthusiasm the visits to La Bella Roma would have been work rather than pleasure, and yes, I did have the map upside down! Mia Grata.

First published 2020

Amberley Publishing
The Hill, Stroud
Gloucestershire, GL5 4EP

www.amberley-books.com

British Library Cataloguing in Publication Data.
A catalogue record for this book is available from the British Library.

ISBN 978 1 4456 8623 3 (hardback)
ISBN 978 1 4456 8624 0 (ebook)

Typesetting by Aura Technology and Software Services, India.
Printed in the UK.

Contents

1

Early Struggles

It has been said 'scandal does not define an institution'[1] but sometimes, without the impetus of an occasional scandal to fix the institution in the mind, its history may begin to fade from popular memory as the centuries pass. At the very least, the record may become the province and preserve of an elite.

Many scandals regarding the papacy are apocryphal, or have become much distorted over the centuries. It is often difficult to reconcile the original story with its later, fictional, additions. Nor can it be assumed that a man who has found himself, rightly or wrongly, embroiled in a scandal, cannot in other matters still be considered to be a good, or worthy, man. The best of men may prove to be liable to some weakness in their private lives, despite a desire for probity in their public ones.

There were, however, many who desired, and kept, the Supreme Office of Pontiff, whose general behaviour became notorious and quite incompatible with the position and authority they held. It is sometimes a matter of amazement, even amusement, to observe what lengths men were prepared to go to, to obtain such a position. Few men elected to the papacy could remain entirely untouched by it. The power for good is there, just as the immense influence is also there, and if some of those fortunate enough to be elected to the office allowed themselves to become dazzled by it, it is hardly surprising.

The unique position of pontiff could place a man above kings and princes, and make them subject to his will. He had the power to raise up other men, to create a faction for his support.

Whatever one's personal beliefs, the papacy is a major part of the fabric of the history of Europe, as well as in the wider world. During the larger part of the last 2,000 years there can be few places untouched by it, or its decisions.

It must also be remembered that the scandalous, the greedy, the generally 'larger than life' personalities will always command a greater share of fame – or notoriety – than the quieter characters, whose work is steady and whose lifestyle is beyond reproach. There were, of course, popes and members of the Sacred College who dedicated themselves to a life of service and personal sacrifice. But there were also many whose aims were social and worldly, rather than vocational and religious.

By the 11th century, Rome was led by thirteen powerful families who had climbed to the top of the pile with determination backed by force. These were headed by the Frangipani, who had made a fortress within the ancient Colosseum and controlled the Forum area. The Corsi had built a fortified house within the ancient Tabularium (Public Record Office) on Capitol Hill. The Pierleoni were based on Isola Tiburina (Tiber Island) and had made a fortress in the Theatre of Marcellus, and the Crescentii had the best stronghold of all, within the Castel Sant'Angelo, then known as the Castel dei Crescentii.

These families began to consider the papacy their own prerogative. They were determined to install one of their own on the throne of St Peter, or at least help to decide who was to wear the papal tiara. Bribery was rife, and votes could easily be bought. Even murder was not dismissed as a method of removal for a pope, or papal candidate, who was likely to be inimical to family interests. These 'front-runner' candidates are still known as 'papabile' or 'pope to be'.

The history of Christianity is popularly begun by the work of St Peter. We know that Peter – arguably the first of the holy fathers – was also an actual father of children. He was a married man, which was the norm for an adult male at the time. The woman whose name is most closely connected with him is St Petronilla, reputedly his daughter, who was revered as a virgin martyr. This lady, much venerated in Europe, is often represented holding the keys of St Peter, with which she received the newly dead into Heaven. Whether or not she was St Peter's biological daughter, or merely a spiritual one, she had the firm recommendation of the early Christians, and was believed to have been close to him.[2]

Her grave was on the Via Ardeatina, along with Saints Nereus and Achilleas, also martyrs. A marble sarcophagus containing her reputed remains was discovered in the chapel dedicated to her in the 'old' St Peter's Basilica, and the Liber Pontificalis (the Book of Pontiffs) describes the inscription to 'Aureae Petronillae Filiae Dulcissimae' (the golden Petronilla, the sweetest daughter.)[3] A daughter of St Peter is certainly mentioned, and Abbot John, in his 6th-century list, puts her with the martyrs who suffered in Rome at the beginning of the Christian era.

She was reputed to have been very beautiful, so much so that Peter locked her away from the attentions of men. A noble named Flaccus wanted to marry her but was refused, and legends say that the girl starved to death. She died while still young, and when her coffin was opened for later renovations, she was incorrupt, with flowers in her hair.[4] There is, in St Peter's, a painting of the 'Burial of St Petronilla' after an original by Guercino, (Giovanni Francesco Barbieri), which is now in the Capitoline Gallery in Rome. Petronilla also has the distinction of a statue on the right hand colonnade in St Peter's Square.

It seems that Christ was never the advocate of priestly celibacy that later church writers argued he was. Physical 'purity' was not required of any priest before 1139 and marriage was then the norm. Once celibacy became a requirement it was frequently and openly ignored. In the Apocryphal Gospels (St Thomas) Christ is reputed to have said: 'When, as little children, you remove your clothes without shame. When you make the two become one, when you make male and female into a single unity, then you will enter the Kingdom.' In Matthew, Christ is reported as saying:

> Have ye not read, that He which made them at the beginning, made them male and female... For this cause shall a man leave father and mother and cleave to a wife, and they shall twain be one flesh.[5]

Of course Christ, as every other Jewish male, would have been expected to marry, though the Bible remains silent on the subject.

Modern writers have tended to assume that he would have followed the traditions of his time.[6] While these newer theories may appear blasphemous to those brought up in the Christian tradition, they are viable in general terms, given the belief system then. It was obligatory for a Jewish father to find a suitable wife for his son, and Mishnaic Law states 'an unmarried man may not be a Teacher', which would have excluded any man practising celibacy from assuming the Rabbi role as Christ did.

The Gospel of Thomas says that Jesus 'often shared the couch of Salome' and the Coptic 'Book of the Resurrection of Christ' (attributed to the disciple Bartholomew) says that when Mary Magdalene went to the tomb, she was accompanied by 'Salome, who tempted Him'. Therefore, the later religious leaders who were equally 'tempted' may well have been following an older tradition more closely than they realised.[7]

Some of the later Catholic writers claim that St Peter was a widower, but there is no evidence of this, and the theologian Clement of Alexandria wrote that Peter had a wife who visited Alexandria with him. Similarly, St Paul, who was to shape the sexual teachings and behaviour of the later church, asks in his first letter to the Corinthians, 'Have I not the right to have a Christian wife about with me, like the rest of the Apostles?' He also said, 'If you marry, you do not sin' and cautioned against any prolonged continence.[8] Although other pronouncements seemed to lean the other way, saying in his first epistle to the Corinthians: 'It is well for a man not to touch a woman.' Perhaps his marriage had proved unhappy, leading to a change of opinion? The Gnostic Gospels certainly suggest that they had a more broadminded approach. Then, the demands of an unnatural celibacy would often prove extremely difficult for many to adhere to, spoiling either their lives or the ministry of men otherwise drawn to the priesthood.

This not only ran counter to the early church, with its natural family structure, but merely served to hide natural urges and create a false situation, where the bastard children of priests who had some influence could be easily referred to as nephews and nieces, and be well provided for. This culminated in the notorious 'cardinal-nephews' of the Renaissance, many of whom were the actual children of the popes who raised them to rank and wealth, often at a very early age. This advancement was not only to give the offspring security, but to create a support network for the pope himself, encouraging nepotism and allowing factions to flourish. This was to the general detriment of the Sacred College, resulting in a general lack of trust towards powerful religious figures.

Once early Christianity reached Rome, it came up against its first real brush with the concept of religious celibacy, except for the notoriously strict Essene Sect. Professor John Barton in his history of the Bible pointed out that:

> There were various groupings in the 1st century CE among Palestinian Jews: Pharisees, Sadduces, scribes and Essenes, to name just four... Essenes, according to Josephus, Philo and the Roman writer Pliny the Elder, led a somewhat ascetic life, involving many purification rituals and, at least for some, celibacy.

('At least for some' – a reminder that the teachings of the Catholic church, including those on sexual relations, were formulated over centuries and did not spring fully formed from the Gospels.)

The Roman Vestal Virgins were a very exclusive and very small group of holy women, drawn from the highest nobility. Only ever six in number at one time, they were chosen as young children to serve the Sacred Flame of Vesta, which could never be allowed to die out. This group of women each served for thirty years, with their dowries invested for them by the State. The dowries could be state-provided if their families could not afford them, for many Roman families were status-proud but purse-poor. This money would accumulate nicely during the woman's term of service, providing her with honourable and comfortable retirement, still only in early middle age.

Their constant virginity during their time of duty was important for the security and well-being of Rome itself. Any lapse of purity of their part was severely punished, although a Vestal could not officially be killed by the state. Her lover certainly would be, as an example to others, and the erring Vestal would be locked into an underground chamber, with a limited amount of bread and water, to reflect on her stupidity in the short time left to her. It dealt with the problem of punishing a sacred woman without the state having her blood on its hands. Though a retired Vestal was legally allowed to marry, few did so, as it was considered extremely unlucky. Few men were prepared to risk the wrath of the Gods, despite the temptation of the high-born woman and her comfortable pension, once she left the Domus Vestae.[9]

Contrarily, side by side with this abstract idea of celibacy was the ever-present image of the phallus. The lucky erect penis still gives the modern visitor the impression that every second house must have been a brothel! Not the case, of course, as these images were found everywhere, sometimes even worn as jewellery, and were a far more effective indication of Rome's prevailing sexual attitudes than the idea of a few Vestals valiantly fighting a rearguard action in defence of beleaguered virginity.

This concept was always to have a rather ambivalent place in Roman thought. Virginity was certainly something to be treasured, even revered, but preferably for someone else. The average citizen went merrily on his way, hoping that the continuing purity of the city's Vestals would be an umbrella, to shield the more commonplace people from harm, even while they enjoyed sexual freedom denied to the Vestals, who were going about their daily rituals almost alongside them.

Sexual restraint was not then particularly highly regarded as an entity in itself. The earlier Republic had certainly attempted to be strait-laced in its attitudes, and women found themselves with correspondingly less personal freedom. They were always subject to the Paterfamilias, the father, who technically had the right of life or death over them. By the end of the Republican era he was less likely to kill an erring wife or daughter for sexual peccadilloes, though before then it had been far from unusual. His authority over his household had been absolute. Interestingly, the lead pipes carrying Rome's water so brilliantly, unfortunately resulted in lower fertility for Rome's men, though they could not have been aware of this. As the Roman nobility tended to produce fewer children, it was desirable that all Roman men became fathers. At the five-year census, any married man who had no children would be encouraged to divorce his barren wife and find another, as the family was failing in its duty to the state to provide future soldiers and administrators.

This was in accord with the earliest Judeo-Christian way of life, where the head of the family was not only in a position of authority over its members, but was also held responsible for their good behaviour, lest the family be shamed before its priests and neighbours. These ideas would later be lost in the general laxity of the Empire, when the power of women grew along with their sexual freedom.

During the time of Messalina, wife of the Emperor Claudius, such ideas of responsibility for dependants were cast aside. She was his third wife, many years his junior, and quickly became bored with him, though they had managed to produce two children together. The son, Britannicus, would later be poisoned by his stepbrother, Nero,[10] son of Claudius's fourth wife Agrippina the Younger, and the girl Claudia Octavia was forced to marry her stepbrother Nero. He eventually divorced her after becoming involved with Poppaea Sabina and later ordered Octavia's death. This was accomplished by opening her veins to allow her to bleed to death, though when it took too long, the eighteen-year-old girl was beheaded. A terrible end for a girl whose only fault was her unfortunate ancestry.[11]

Messalina herself was a nymphomaniac, who is reputed to have competed with the famous prostitute Scylla to see which of them could service the most men in one night. Messalina won. Her husband, though totally unable to control her, was long-suffering, only acting against her when she foolishly plotted against him with one Godius Silius, and went so far as to marry her co-conspirator. She was executed on her husband's order, who then declared that he would not remarry – though he did – to an even worse wife, who supposedly poisoned him. The later rulers of Rome, venal though they were, couldn't compare with their forerunners.[12]

The earliest Christians suffered from the same struggles, and even Peter, 'The Rock', was tarnished by his public denouncement of his Master. In later life he also ran away from Rome, and was turned back by a vision of Christ, which, when asked where He was going, (the 'Quo Vadis?' of the swords and sandals epics), was told that Christ was returning to be crucified again, in place of Peter. A church now stands on the spot, and Peter did indeed turn back to face the fate awaiting him in Rome.

Paul of Tarsus, a Roman citizen, and the man who would be most concerned with the spread of the controversial new religion, never met Jesus, though he did know Peter. It appears that they did not get on well. Respect for the man chosen to be the foundation of the new church may have been mandatory, but respect for the man himself, with his uncertain ministry and lack of confidence, was less easy to feel. St Paul prided himself on once having a face-to-face confrontation with Peter at Antioch.[13] He quoted their argument extensively, always making clear his belief that Peter was too prone to give in to criticism, such as he'd faced from the Jewish hard-liners. Paul also liked to emphasise his own daring in having stood up to Peter. This was one of the first recorded disputes between potential Christian church leaders, though there would be plenty more. Dissension and factions would make Rome into a battleground for warring families and individuals who were, ostensibly, on the same side.

Neither Peter nor Paul would live much longer after their meeting. By the second century it was believed that Nero had had them both killed, although there is no evidence of the dates of their martyrdoms. It was the belief that both these saints had lived in Rome that helped to make it the natural centre for the new religion. They are both believed to have spent some time imprisoned in the notorious Tullianum, near the Forum, and below the Carcer. This prison was in Roman times accessible only by a ladder from a hole in the roof. There are indications that they were put to death some time in the mid-60s, and the existence of their monuments was mentioned by a cleric around 200 AD, with later building work uncovering a pagan cemetery on Vatican Hill. In 1965 Pope Paul VI declared that bones found in a shrine under St Peter's Basilica were those of Peter. Some pointed out that many criminals had also been buried in that area, though it may well have been the site of Peter's execution.[14]

In 2017 pots from the Roman era were found in an ancient church in the Trastevere area of Rome. The church of Santa Maria in Cappella (consecrated in 1090) had been closed for thirty-five years due to structural problems and during work close to the early medieval altar a slab was lifted to reveal the pots. Inscriptions on the lids claim that the bone fragments inside were not only from St Peter himself, but also Popes Cornelius, Callixtus, Felix, and four other Christian martyrs. It has been suggested that they may have been removed from the Basilica for safety by Pope Urban II in the late eleventh century, during a time of schism within the church. They are now undergoing analysis.[15]

This new discovery is a continuation of the confusion and controversy which has bedevilled the church since the first signs of friction between Peter and Paul. Although Lactantius wrote that Nero 'crucified Peter and slew Paul' there is no further evidence of the death of the apostle, or his place of burial, except for the belief that he was beheaded.[16] The Acts of Paul (an apocryphal work written about AD 160) and first mentioned by Tertullian agree with this.[17] Incidentally, Tertullian found the work heretical, because it encouraged women to preach and baptise. Both were denied to females as soon as the Christian church was fully established.

The early church was still jostling for its place among several other religions, and had not formed standardised beliefs. The cult of the Egyptian Goddess, Isis/Aset, was very popular throughout the Empire, for example. This particular religion was in fact so popular that it very nearly eradicated the newly emerging Christianity before it got off the ground. The devotional vote went to the Mother Goddess rather than the Christ. This devotion to her was to last a very long time, with her worship at Philae (founded in 380 BC) only ending in the 6th century AD.[18] Isis/Aset then re-emerged as the template for the Virgin Mary.

Other cults were almost as difficult to uproot, with important Easter celebrations (usually at the same time as the Jewish Passover) being performed in different areas at different times. Some people even wanted to celebrate Easter every Sunday! The argument continued for centuries, and showed the need for one central leader to eradicate the disharmony. This appeared to be achieved around the mid-150s AD with Anicetus, who may have ordered the construction of the first shrines on Vatican Hill and the Via Ostiensis. He drew up a list of 'Bishops' to give some semblance of legitimacy to the Christian religion.

By the time of Victor (189–198) one man had emerged who intended to bring the others into line. In an effort of unification, he 'picked a fight' with the people who were still happily celebrating Easter at the same time as Passover, instead of the week after, as he preferred.[19] When agreement couldn't be reached, he excommunicated all those who would not toe the line, in the first real show of papal authority. His high-handed methods eventually failed, but showed that the idea of jurisdiction centred on Rome was gaining ground.

In the late second century, the burial ground on the Appian Way was bought and the Catacombs of San Callisto would then house a 'Crypt of the Popes' where Bishops of Rome could be buried together. It was intended to create continuity and focus. The complex occupies around ninety acres, with a twelve-mile long network of galleries on four levels more than twenty metres deep. Here would eventually be buried many martyrs, many ordinary Christians, and sixteen of the earliest of the popes.

This was not only on the Appian Way, but close to what would become the church of 'Domine, Quo Vadis?' as if to emphasise the humiliation of the church's first leader, Peter, having been shamed by his Saviour, who was prepared to face execution a second time because his chosen deputy could not face it once. The church has what are reputed to be the footprints of Christ, which are copies of originals kept in the Basilica of San Sebastiano, where Peter and Paul were believed to have been originally interred.

From the earliest days, the church pursued a policy of accumulation of wealth, on the premise that the ministry could not be expanded if the mother-church was poor.

Not everyone approved of this, and Pope Calixtus (217–222) was murdered by a mob who resented the increasing numbers of Christians in an already overcrowded area. There were also objections to the 'old' gods being neglected and dishonoured. Riots became commonplace, and in AD 250 the Emperor Decius started an offensive against Christianity. In a parody of what would one day be the norm, but in reverse, the Christians were obliged to honour the traditional Roman gods. Those who refused suffered for their intransigence. Pope Fabian himself (236–250) was arrested and later died of the treatment he received while imprisoned.[20] Many Christians complied with the Emperor's demands – becoming a martyr for one's faith does not appeal to everyone – and so many Christians turned up to show allegiance to the gods that many were turned away and told to return another day.

Pope Fabian's example was emulated by Pope Sixtus II (257–258) who was arrested while preaching in the cemetery of Praetextatus.[21]

He surrendered to the authorities to prevent reprisals among his congregation but was beheaded, along with his deacons.

Once Constantine became Emperor, things began to change. He was a worshipper of Sol Invictus, but at the Battle of Milvian Bridge in AD 312 he attributed his victory to having seen a 'cross of light' in the sky. Although he defeated his rival Maxentius, he had no personal change of heart, and continued to worship the sun god. The future of the Christian religion was certainly secured, but as a political exercise rather than from personal conviction.

Pope Damasus (366–384) is accounted a saint, despite being involved in some very unsavoury exploits. Pope Liberius died in AD 366, resulting in riots, and Damasus had a rival named Ursinus, who had actually already been consecrated, so Damasus employed thugs to murder the supporters of Ursinus and deposed him. Unfortunately, he was still harassed by the resentful Ursinus, who then had him officially accused of adultery.

Damasus had a good deal of charm, and used much of it to convert Rome's upper-class women, though he claimed he did so in order that their husbands would follow them into the church.[22] He became notorious for his love of luxury and criticised for extreme ostentation – his churches were described as being 'gleaming with gold'. He persuaded St Jerome to translate the testaments into Latin, thereby making it the principal language of the church, but St Basil referred to him as 'irritating' and said he 'found him impossible to work with' also referring to the Pope as 'arrogant'.

Damasus was responsible for the first chronological list of popes, and gathered information about the many people, including martyrs, who were buried in the catacombs. He may have been well over eighty when he died, but came from a long-lived family – his mother was well over ninety at her death, and had been vowed to celibacy for sixty years.[23] Damasus would certainly not be the last pope with a taste for ostentation, nor the last one who enjoyed the company of women. Ammianus Marcellinus wrote of him:

Bearing in mind the ostentation of life in Rome, I do not deny that those who are desirous of such a thing should use vituperation and exert themselves to the full in order to obtain what they seek. Since, when they get it, they will be free from care to such an extent that they will be enriched from the offerings of married women, ride seated in carriages, clothe themselves with meticulous care and serve banquets so lavish that their dinner parties outdo the feasts of kings.[24]

St Jerome had written to him in AD 376 declaring 'though your Eminence alarms me, your kindness draws me to you.'

From his death in AD 384, there were no less than seven other popes by AD 440. It was a time of great disturbance in Rome, which was sacked by the Visigoths in AD 410. The Empire had, by that time, been divided into the Eastern and Western parts, with Ravenna the seat of the western, while the eastern emperor had his seat in Constantinople. Despite being so far away, the eastern ruler still had a good deal of influence on what happened in Rome. Pope Leo I (440–461) had Attila the Hun to contend with, though he managed to persuade him to withdraw outside the walls of Rome. Leo was the first pontiff to be given the honour of a burial within St Peter's Basilica.

St Augustine (354–430) and Bishop of Hippo, was accounted one of the most influential of the church fathers, but he had a very rocky start. He was born a Roman citizen, in Africa, and his family was Christian but he did not consider himself to be a Christian, to the great grief of his mother, and he lived an extremely hedonistic lifestyle. He said, 'My nature was foul and I loved it! I loved my own errors – not that for which I erred – but the error itself.' He was later to decide that 'human nature is naturally inclined towards sin.'

At the age of seventeen he was part of a gang of youths involved in every vice, and he took a mistress with whom he lived for the next fifteen years. She gave birth to his son, Adeodatus (372–388) but in AD 385 he separated from her in order, so he said, to improve his image, as he had decided to betroth himself to a ten-year-old girl. He would have to wait another two years, at least, before she was old enough to marry him legally, so he occupied himself in the meantime with regular visits to prostitutes. He admitted that he was 'in love with loving, like water I boiled over, heated by my fornications.' By the time his betrothed was old enough to become his wife, he had changed his mind again, deciding this time to become a priest. Even then, he was aware of his limitations, praying 'God, give me chastity – but not yet!'

Despite an apparent shift in opinion, where he remonstrated with several sinners, he still had trouble with his own celibacy. He declared 'nothing is so powerful, in drawing downwards the spirit of a man, than the caresses of a woman, and that physical intercourse which is the part of marriage.' He thundered against any attempt at contraception, calling it 'a poison of sterility' and regarding any woman who tried to limit her family as being 'her husband's harlot'. Yet even as an older man, he still feared his own sexuality, refusing to allow even his sister (who was a nun) to visit him without a chaperone, for fear that seeing any female close by, he would be overcome by lust!

In AD 440 Pope Sixtus III (390–440), a correspondent of St Augustine's and seemingly suffering from the same problem, was actually tried for the seduction of a nun. His accusers were unable to substantiate the charge as the woman would not speak, although in an attempt at defence, he quoted the story of the woman caught in adultery. This was taken to be a tacit confession of his wrongdoing.

Pope Leo I (440–461) used sexual corruption to expand the church's political power. The Emperor Valentinian III was a licentious man, and his mother Galla Placidia, would do anything the Pope asked. She encouraged her son in his excesses, so that she and the Pope could have a free hand in running what was left of the Roman Empire. She at one point pledged her daughter's virginity to God, only to find that the girl was already pregnant. The unfortunate daughter was then sent to a convent anyway, though more as a punishment than as a vocation. Leo I was a stickler for virginity (except in his own life) and made the strange pronouncement that a woman needed to be 'tested for virginity' for sixty years before she could take the veil and become a nun. He did allow bishops to keep their wives, provided they treated them only as sisters, and he was the first Pope to claim the right to put heretics to death – loosely considered to be anyone who disagreed with him. He abhorred the Manichaean sect, then Christianity's main rival, and wanted to hear certain specific things during the questioning of its followers, mainly sexual details. These were often obtained under torture, using brutal methods to achieve the results he wanted. This probably said rather more about his own fantasies than those of his victims.

Pope Vigilius (537–555) was so determined to become the pontiff that he allowed himself to become nothing more than a puppet of the eastern rulers, Justinian and Theodora. He possibly considered that the end justified the means.

Theodora, though never actually living in Rome, was still a woman who wielded enormous power, as the Eastern Empire then held sway over the western. Her husband, the Emperor Justinian, had hoped to unite the stronger Eastern Empire with the weakened remains of the Roman. Theodora had a fascinating history, being born to parents living on the periphery of the circus, and she grew up to be a performer of sorts, and a part-time prostitute. From this humble beginning she became a courtesan, rising to a position of wealth and notoriety. When Justinian succeeded his uncle as Emperor in AD 527, she caught his eye but her lifestyle had to change. She became a reformed character, though even that was insufficient, for he wished to marry her and had to change the law to enable him to do so. Theodora as Empress became highly autocratic, and Procopius said of her

> No one dared to intercede for any person who had displeased her. Neither passage of time nor surfeit of punishment, nor any act of supplication, nor threat of death ... would persuade her to lay aside any part of her rage. In short, Theodora was never known to reconcile herself with anyone who had ever given her offence, even after they had left the land of the living. The child of the dead man would inherit the Empress's hatred, just as he inherited anything else belonging to his father, and he bequeathed it to the third generation.[25]

Theodora appeared to keep her husband's regard, despite the difficulties. It is said that he remained very jealous of her relationships with other men, to the extent that when he heard that she had been secretly meeting with a young man, he had him arrested. Hearing of the arrest, Theodora acted in an attempt to save the victim but was not in time, finding that the youth had already been tortured and killed. She then confessed to Justinian that he was not a lover but her son, born during her time as a courtesan.

Theodora used the experiences of her life to sometimes ease the lot of other women, once she had personal power. She helped to close brothels and cracked down on forced prostitution. She opened a convent where ex-prostitutes were able to support themselves and made rape punishable by death. She also ended the killing of wives if they were found guilty of adultery, as well as expanding the rights of women in matters of property ownership and divorce. She helped to prevent the exposure of unwanted children, usually females, and gave women some guardianship rights over their own children, which had previously been the exclusive property of their fathers.

Despite the assessment of her character, already given by Procopius, he admitted that she was 'naturally inclined to assist women in their misfortune.' Theodora died of cancer at the age of forty-eight in June of 548 and Justinian was known to be distraught at her loss.[26]

While the eastern rulers were establishing a firm foundation, the roller-coaster of the west went on. The relationship between east and west had thawed a little, but Benedict I (575–579) had to wait almost a year to receive imperial confirmation of his consecration as Pope. Rome faced famine, floods and plagues, along with the depredations of the Lombards and the resurgence of heresy in Africa. Only by the beginning of the seventh century had it achieved a position of prestige again. Though still living under the shadow of Constantinople, it was beginning to edge away from eastern control. This, unfortunately, did not guarantee any better behaviour from the men wishing to take over the papal throne. There was schism in Rome throughout the tenth century, with popes being elected and dethroned in rapid succession.

Benedict VIII was still a layman when he became Pope, and was remarkable for being tonsured, ordained, and enthroned all in the one day – as were his successors, who happened to be his brother and nephew. By that time, the Roman people had become so accustomed to corruption of various kinds that though they might be wearied, they were never actually surprised by it.

Technically, any baptised male was then eligible for election to the papacy, so it wasn't quite as bad as it sounds. In modern times, despite another technicality, which allows for a pope to be chosen 'by acclamation', the reality is that a cardinal is chosen from among the other members of the College of Cardinals.

Pope Leo IX (1049–1054) was a more saintly man, unwilling to accept the burden offered to him, but he turned out to be one of the good popes, and astonished everyone by his energy. Unfortunately, even saintliness doesn't please everyone, and in this case the King of France was less than pleased when the Pope proclaimed a Holy War against the Normans.

Pope Alexander II (Anselmo de Baggio) was a man whose reign proved of importance to England, for he gave the Normans his blessing for their invasion of it. He later tried to claim that he had merely confirmed their victory at Hastings in 1066 once it was an accomplished fact, to lessen his involvement in the conquest of an erstwhile free people. However, William de Poitiers was certain that the Pope had not only blessed the invasion before it set out but had also given the Normans a ring as a token of his support and a standard of St Peter to carry into England with them. These obvious indications of papal support were later instrumental in guaranteeing the full submission of the English church to the Normans. William of Poitiers was justified in his claim that the Pope had interfered in the matter, saying 'Strange, for a man who was supposedly committed to peace, and general brotherhood,' though those terms were probably more loosely interpreted.

Pope Gregory VII (Ildebrando di Soana) who was elected in 1073, was a reformer. He decided that the election of a pope was a matter which concerned the members of the Sacred College only, limiting the interference of outsiders and affirming papal authority. He made new rules for the inmates of the Vatican to live by, foremost among them being a rigorous enforcement of celibacy. He was to spend years in conflict with the Holy Roman Emperor Henry IV, who was excommunicated by him no fewer than three times. It was only later, when his strict regime proved successful in reforming the morals of those around him, that he was hailed as one of the greatest of popes. He was canonised as a saint by Benedict XIII in 1728. But however appropriate his reforms may have seemed during and just after his reign, by the early twelfth century the general behaviour in the Vatican had again deteriorated alarmingly.

At the election of Teobaldo Boccapecci as Celestine II in 1124 there was again chaos. He is counted as being an anti-pope as he was immediately forced off the papal throne, literally, when the supporters of a rival faction objected to his election. Roberto Frangipani, along with a body of troops, broke into the church and at sword point forced the papal vestments onto their own man, one Lamberto Scannabecchi. He was enthroned immediately, taking the name of Honorius II. After several days of rioting in the city, Honorius managed to establish himself and began a six-year reign. Celestine, the defeated candidate, was obliged to resign officially, then retire. There was a tradition that the deposed pope had celebrated his elevation too early by presenting the cathedral in Citta di Castello with a beautiful sculptured silver altar frontal, or antependium. There is no record whether the grateful recipients were required to give it back.[27]

In 1154 the only English pope, Nicholas Breakspear, became Adrian IV. He had been noticed and approved of by the saintly Pope Eugenius a few years earlier. Eugenius declared that he 'found the English were admirably suited to perform any task that they turned their hands to, and thus were to be preferred to all other races. Except, that is, unless their natural frivolity got the better of them.'

Unfortunately, Pope Adrian did not seem to have much natural frivolity, or even basic good humour. One Arnold of Brescia had been troubling him for some time. Arnold called on the church to renounce all ownership of property; a move naturally not much approved of. While the previous pope had merely ignored his fanciful ideas, Adrian IV decided to act more firmly, but was perhaps overreacting by laying all Rome under an Interdict. It was considered to be an act of breathtaking courage – or perhaps foolhardiness – that a foreign pope, who had been in office only for a few weeks, would dare to close all the churches in Rome. This brought the city to a religious standstill. To make things far worse, Easter was approaching, and the most important festival in the church's calendar could not be ignored. To the ever pragmatic citizens of Rome it was an incomprehensible idea to turn away from the city all the pilgrims who normally flocked there at that time, bringing their spending money with them.

For several days there was stalemate, with Arnold of Brescia and his supporters grimly hanging on, but by the middle of Holy Week the people of Rome, impelled by financial concerns, marched on the Capitol and expelled Arnold from Rome. Pope Adrian was then able to celebrate Easter as usual at the Lateran Palace, and the citizens were able to make a profit from the pilgrims.

Adrian died in 1159 after a rather troubled reign, which included Frederic Barbarossa invading Italy. The Pope's sarcophagus can still be seen in St Peter's Basilica, and in 1607 it was opened to reveal the body of the English Pope. He was described as being 'an undersized man, wearing a large emerald on his hand, and with Turkish slippers on his feet'.

In 1159, after the burial of Adrian, thirty cardinals assembled in Conclave to elect his successor. All but three of them voted for Cardinal Roland of Siena, who was duly elected Pope. However, Cardinal Octavian of the powerful Crescentii family, one of the few who disagreed with the decision, made his presence felt. Just as the new Pope was being robed, (as Alexander III), Cardinal Octavian sprang at him, snatched the robe from him, and attempted to put it over his own head. It was taken from him, but a servant of his was ready with another, with which he dressed himself. Unfortunately, in his haste, he had put the robe on back to front! There then followed an undignified scuffle, described at the time as 'scarcely believable confusion'. The original Pope's supporters (after all, he had just been almost unanimously elected), were trying to tear the robe from the usurping Octavian's back, and were being stoutly resisted. So much so that he ended up with the robe's fringes entangled around his neck. He then broke free of them and made a dash for the papal throne, sitting on it defiantly and holding on grimly while others did their best to try to drag him off. Throughout the scuffle, he shouted continually that he was the new pope, and was calling himself Victor IV.

He then jumped off the throne and ran through the Basilica, followed by his gang of armed sympathisers. He eventually met a clutch of terrified minor clergy trying to hide away from the rampaging pope and his gang. These men were forced at sword point to 'acclaim' him, under threats against their lives, which they hastily did. This allowed Victor to declare himself to be the legal pope, as he was officially 'Pope by Acclamation'. Legally, this could override the results of any legitimate election.

The three valid methods of choosing a pope were by scrutiny, by compromise, or by acclamation, also called 'quasi-inspiration'. This last method consisted of the candidate being proclaimed by popular consent and was looked on as a decision proceeding directly from the Holy Spirit.[28] Whether or not the forced acclamation from a small group of clergy in fear of their lives could be described as 'popular consent' bothered Victor not at all.

Due to this apparent acceptance of him, however forcibly achieved, nothing further could be done for a time, leaving the legally elected pope to take refuge in a tower within the Vatican, fearing reprisals from Victor's men. It soon became clear that Victor was a friend of the Empire and had the Emperor's powerful backing, but his support in Rome began to dwindle after a short while and the citizens wanted their original choice back. He was rescued from his tower and carried in triumph to the Lateran Palace. Unfortunately, with the Empire and the Crescentii family against him, Alexander found the papacy hard going, and he realised that he would be unable to rule peaceably. He tried to excommunicate the antipope Victor, who merely excommunicated him in retaliation, so Rome descended into schism for the second time in thirty years.

Both of the competing popes spent time outside of Rome during the next few years, as their fortunes veered back and forth. This went on until 1165 when the 'real' pope, Alexander, was requested to return. Pope Victor had by then been living for some time at Lucca, where he had successfully supported himself be becoming a bandit! He seemingly found nothing incongruous in a man claiming to be pope actually becoming a common robber. He died shortly after Alexander's restoration and the original pope was then able to return to Rome and attempt to rule. Unfortunately, there were by then several other 'antipopes' who elected themselves and each other for years to come, bringing the Papacy into disrepute and making the citizens of Rome even more cynical regarding Papal politics. The citizens did eventually become so tired of the situation, which was badly affecting the lucrative tourist trade, that they cleared the other claimants out of the city, allowing Alexander to finally take up his position properly.

The end of the thirteenth century brought Innocent III to the papal throne (Lotario dei Conti di Segni, 1198–1216.) He was one of the most powerful popes, compelling all princes to obey his decisions and starting crusades against those who refused to accept his orders. The Albigensian Crusade alone was responsible for the deaths of around 100,000 people in Southern France.[29] Innocent also inaugurated the Fourth Crusade, which backfired and led to the sacking of Constantinople in 1204, leading to much increased hostility between the eastern and western churches.

Innocent IV (Sinibaldo Fieschi 1243–1254) decided that he had the right to exert his authority over everyone on earth, whether they were Christian or not, civilised or not, whether they had ever heard of him or not. He became the first instigator of the Inquisition.[30] After the death of Pope Nicholas IV in 1292, the papacy was vacant for two years. This meant no decisions could be reached. It sometimes took extreme measures to bring the cardinals to heel and make them choose the next pontiff. To prevent dilatoriness, they could be confined in hot, uncomfortable quarters, on a minimal diet, to persuade them to make their choice quickly. Even this was not always successful when powerful family factions opposed each other, and cardinals could easily be intimidated – or bribed – by one side or the other. If the Papal Tiara went to a man inimical to oneself could mean many years of hostility from the future pope.

Pope Boniface VIII[31] had these difficulties when he was opposed by the Colonna family. They were so determined to unseat him that they questioned the validity of the previous pope's abdication in an effort to make Boniface's election invalid. Boniface was eventually to have long-standing arguments with the King of France, Philip IV, and also with the writer Dante Alighieri, who, in his *Divine Comedy* consigned the Pope to the Eighth Circle of Hell. Dante's levels of punishment were: First Circle – virtuous pagans; Second Circle – Lust; Third Circle – Gluttony; Fourth Circle – Greed; Fifth Circle – Anger; Sixth Circle – Heresy; Seventh Circle – Violence; Eighth Circle – Fraud; Ninth Circle – Treachery. There was even a painting of Pope Boniface, buried upside down, with his legs and feet sticking out of the ground and on fire, suffering in the company of other fraudulent popes.

He was to institute the first of the Holy Years, which are still held, and which became hugely profitable due to the immense numbers of pilgrims descending on Rome. They brought with them cash offerings, which often amounted to such large sums that clerics were stationed outside the Church of St Paul-Outside-the-Walls, armed with rakes, to enable them to scoop up all the coins left behind by pilgrims in the hope of them being exchanged for blessings. The first used of the phrase 'raking it in' perhaps?

The history of the Vatican was in these years so suffused with greed and self-seeking that it is a wonder that many of the popes were not made to suffer on several levels of the 'Inferno' in turn.

When Clement V became pope in 1305, he began the 'Babylonian Captivity' of papal rule away from Rome by establishing his court at Avignon. This culminated in the confusion of having more than one pope at once, as the official ones were ruling from France, while others, who subsequently took over in Rome, either elected or electing themselves, becoming 'antipopes.'

Clement V was also to become famous for his persecution of the Knights Templar. In this he was aided by the King of France. The persecution was power- and finance-based rather than a religious matter, and was to bring about the utter destruction of the Order and the murder of the Grand Master, Jacques de Molay, in March 1314.[32]

Before he was executed by being burned at the stake, the Grand Master cursed both the King of France and Pope Clement. He cried that they would both be 'summoned to appear before the judgement of God, within a year, to answer for their crimes'. The Pope died before the month was out and the King of France was killed six months later in a hunting accident. This convinced many people that the Grand Master and the Templars had been innocent of the crimes of which they had been accused, and had faced with enormous courage the tortures they had undergone. It was another reason to hate the memory of the pope, who had already earned the dislike of the people by making no less than five of his relatives into cardinals and giving them substantial grants of money, causing financial problems at the Vatican. While in power, he had attempted to ease these money problems (entirely of his own making) by extreme parsimony. This had sifted downwards to such an extent that it was said at the time that anyone wishing to see the pope would have to bribe everyone, even the man on the door. His sudden death was not mourned.

By the end of the thirteenth century the papacy was increasingly ruled by the advancement of those 'papal families' whose power and determination to hold onto that power would ensure that they and their supporters would dominate the Vatican throughout the Renaissance period. Their wealth and influence would become notorious, and their methods of acquiring it, and attempting to maintain their grip on it when it was wrested from others, would easily follow the worst traditions of the early papacy's frictions and factional hostilities.

But these were just the men. Despite the regular calls for celibacy, and the living of what was termed 'a regular life', there were always women at the very heart of the Roman power machine. Women who were using the men who were ostensibly using them, women often of intelligence and courage, not merely sex objects, but often women whose desire for wealth and influence was just as strong as that of the men who were Rome's figureheads. These men often could not function at all without the other half of the world's population, the mothers, the sisters, the sisters-in-law, the mistresses and the daughters. The common women also served, swarming in and around the Vatican in defiance of all rules and in contravention of the regular prohibitions against them. Women who blithely ignored the misogyny of the few men who could manage to live without them.

These women were likely to be reviled, sometimes hated, looked down on, abused, accused of harlotry, of greed, of fraud, of usury, of nepotism and of spreading every kind of vice, disease, temptation and corruption. They were thought to be a nuisance and an appalling interference in an area where no female had any business to be, yet they are just as interesting, often as amazing, and frequently as diverse, as the men they served, amused, supported, and sometimes disgraced. Their interference was often considered to be a stain on the papacy itself, and an abomination within the sacred enclave of holiness that it was supposed to represent. Yet they brought to it a different perspective, a softening, and a sense of ease and pleasure that would otherwise have been lacking in many of the otherwise austere lives they touched. That they also brought difficulties, children, expenses, and sometimes even a sense of guilt, was inevitable. Though they were by no means hidden, their presence would always be considered slightly shameful, and the men who associated with them, who were vastly in the majority, would found their own families with them, and without them the world would have lost several future popes.

In considering the activities of some of these women, the behaviour of the popes themselves needs to be borne in mind. Could the women have actually been any worse?

Corruption and Power: Marozia and Others

As for women, and everything to do with them, it was as if there were no women in the world. This absolute silence, even between close friends, about everything to do with women, was one of the most profound and lasting lessons of my early years in the priesthood.

Pope John XXIII, *Journal of a Soul*[1]

St Augustine of Hippo, who admitted cheerfully to enjoying the fornication of his youth, and to still being capable of being tempted towards it when he grew older, tried in his later life to curb his sexual transgressions. He wrote: 'Insist of the work of the flesh only in such measure as is necessary for the procreation of children. Since you cannot beget children in any other way, you must descend to it against your will, for it is the punishment of Adam.'[2]

These later pronouncements are typical of the older man, advising others to deny themselves the pleasures of the flesh in which he had so freely indulged in earlier years. The contrast between his earlier writings and those of John XXIII are obvious, and it is clear that Pope John was trained from his earliest years to not think about women at all.

But what virtue is there is having to pretend that half the world's population does not exist? What triumph over the will can there be for a man who has never been tempted? Why must it be assumed that every female with whom one is likely to come into contact is going to be not only a source of temptation, but of vice? Surely it is better to have had some experience of human relationships, platonic or otherwise, to enable one to understand the pressures and problems other people have to undergo? Living in a bubble, protected from all 'occasion of sin' does not help anyone to learn to handle people or have any meaningful interaction with them. Nor does it help to overreact, to imagine that all innocent relationships are bedevilled by the sin of lust, waiting to strike at any moment.

History shows us that the vast majority of the early popes had already had some sexual experience, and many continued this after they were elected. Understanding the personal relationships, the familial relationships, and even the sexual relationships of the people with whom one is likely to come into contact can only assist a leader to help his people. To know and be able to understand the emotional bonds, what the dependence between people feels like, the passions and the problems, the need to have children and to protect and nurture them. Without this knowledge, any man in authority may serve his people, but is not fully able to advise and guide as he should.

This is evident even now in some of the more conservative-minded cardinals, who still consider the idea of contraception anathema, yet do not have to feel the responsibility and desperation of trying to feed a large family when poor. Nor do they have to watch a wife grow old before her time, worn down by childbearing and the demands of several young children. The fact that most people now simply make such choices for themselves, in defiance of church rules, is a loss for the church, and with a more enlightened attitude the churches could have remained at the centre of life. Men of religion in the early church did have the opportunity to learn these lessons for themselves, not at third hand. It must be remembered that clerical celibacy was not a requirement until 1139, and that even after that date, the taking of concubines, as opposed to actual wives, continued unabated.[3]

It should also be borne in mind that, when clerical marriage was forbidden, the church lost many good men, good leaders of their communities, who refused to cast off their wives. For those who did remain in the priesthood, brothels catering for clerics opened. This became a far greater scandal than the taking of respectable wives had ever been, and there was an attempt to deal with it by the introduction of a 'tax', upon payment of which a cleric was entitled to have one housekeeper living under his roof, without questions being asked.[4]

When Aelia Galla Placidia (wife of the western Roman Emperor Constantius III) pledged her daughter's virginity to God, only to find that the girl was already pregnant, the girl was hurriedly sent away to a convent out of sight. But it seems that her confinement was not absolute. It is said that she managed to send a message to Attila the Hun, promising him half of Italy as her dowry if he would ride to her rescue. Apparently, he was tempted by the promise of the gain of such territory, even if he were less enticed by the prospect of a wife already pregnant by another man. However, he did set out with the intention of rescuing her. He was persuaded by Pope Leo I to turn back once he reached the outskirts of Rome. Presumably, the girl then had to stay where she was, to suffer the consequences of her 'sin'. What happened to the father? Did he run away, aware of the danger once the result of his seduction became obvious? Was he killed by her vengeful family, in retaliation for the shaming of the girl? We are never likely to find out, as history is so often tantalisingly silent on such details.

The Empress Galla Placidia had already had a life of drama. She had been forced into her second marriage, to Constantius, by her brother Honorius, and this brother's affection for her was apparently so strong that it caused scandalised comment and even eventually prompted her to leave Rome. Even if plain fornication might be considered a fact of life, the idea of brother and sister incest was always held in abhorrence in Rome, which is not to say it didn't happen, merely that it was strongly disapproved of. Despite her great power in Rome, and her long regency on behalf of her son, any such suggestion would be a terrible scandal and would have ruined her. She did, however, always maintain great influence over the then Pope, Boniface I. She urged him to renounce his alliance with the Vandals, begging that he should 'not permit the Empire of the Romans to lie under the hand of the Barbarians'. She was to die in Rome in AD 450 after a lifetime of great prominence in political affairs. Fortunately, her death took place just five years before her son, Valentinian III, was assassinated at the age of thirty-five (in AD 455). His killing had been arranged by Petronius Maximus, who was taking his revenge for the rape of his wife by Valentinian. The murdered Emperor's wife, Licinia Eudoxia, and their two daughters, were shipped off to Africa, when the Vandals sacked Rome in 455 AD.[5]

Unfortunately, Valentinian had never been able to rule his Empire with a fraction of the ability or common sense shown by his mother.

This early evidence of the rule of women, even at the highest level, is an example of the presence of females at all levels in the lives of the men vowed to religion. Due to the imposition of the rule of celibacy, it drove decent women into a false position, turning wives into concubines and their legitimate children into bastards. This was intentional, as concubines and their bastards, having no rights in law, therefore had no inheritance, and the church needed to take no responsibility for them.

As the medieval period advanced, the position of women generally became more precarious. They were considered in law to be 'mere infants' in their understanding, largely fit for nothing but being either brood mares or playthings. That they could be both capable and wise was discounted, and any influence they might have over their menfolk began to be held as unworthy, and their opinions incompetent. It was in this atmosphere of female oppression that there grew the legend of Pope Joan.

Pope Joan (Ioannes Anglicus 855–857) was supposed to have been a young Englishwoman who entered the church in disguise following a lover. Through her ability, she rose swiftly through the ranks and was elected Pope, though the association with her lover continued throughout, and her colleagues believed her to be a male.

Her true gender was only discovered by accident when she went into labour during a religious procession, and supposedly gave birth to a child between the Colosseum and St Clement's Church! She is said to have been killed immediately and buried in the place where her shame was discovered so dramatically. Later religious processions tended to avoid the spot.

The legend is a very old one, mainly spread by Martin of Troppau, who was a Dominican monk who served as a chaplain to Clement IV in the 1260s. He wrote what was probably the first book of papal scandals, which became immensely popular due entirely to its salacious content. This work is largely responsible for the enduring legend of the female pope, and in his chronology she is supposed to have been between the reigns of Leo IV and Benedict III. There is, however, no contemporary account of her life, and no proof that she ever existed. From the first formal reference of her, in the mid-thirteenth century, she seemed to move around, and her story can be placed almost anywhere in the ninth or tenth centuries.

By the sixteenth century it had become the name of a popular card game, before the details faded from memory.

The greatest use of the story, of course, was as a general attack on women. It echoed the popular opinion that any woman, however clever or capable she might otherwise appear to be, would always sooner or later be let down by her natural appetites. It claimed that any woman would be prepared to throw to the winds all her achievements in order to satisfy her baser instincts. This story would be used again and again as an example of the unreliability and sheer foolishness of women in general.[6]

It did lead to a tradition that any new pope had to sit on a special chair with a large hole in the seat, to allow a physical examination to take place to ensure that the pope was in fact male. This story was repeated frequently, claiming that the chair had been made specially, after the Pope Joan business, to prevent any possibility of a woman ever claiming the papal throne. In reality, there were two chairs of white marble, and the holes in the seats were designed to allow water to run off the sitter, as they had originally been made for the Baths of Caracalla.

It did, however, prove rather unfortunate for Pope John VIII (872–882) who is sometimes confused with the mythical female pope. He was in fact a ruthless warrior who founded the papal navy and fortified Rome against the Saracens. He also had the dubious distinction of being eventually assassinated by his own monks, who first tried to poison him, then resorted to beating him to death when the poison failed. His unfortunate placing in the papal lists confuses him with the Pope Joan legend, and continues the fallacy that he was a cross-dresser and a closet female. Whatever type of man he may have been – and the accounts range widely from his activities as a soldier earning him respect, to the claim that his personality and private attitudes were so obnoxious that they felt obliged to inflict a violent death upon him – he was a real person. But the fictional female pope usurped his position in the popular imagination.

For almost a century the papacy had been pursuing three interrelated policies: to ease the church away from Eastern Imperial control, to free the church from the constant Lombard incursions, and to forge firm alliances with the secular powers in the west.[7] When Charlemagne died, he left his vast Frankish Empire in the hands of his two sons, Charles and Carloman, as joint rulers. Carloman died in AD 771 leaving Charles as sole ruler. He had then embarked on a career of military expansion and made claims over the church, which were just as restrictive as any suffered under the eastern rulers. Pope Leo III actually paid homage to him, a reversal of the 'natural' order, where the pope should have been considered the final authority between the secular people and God. Between the death of Leo III in AD 816 and the accession of Sergius III in AD 904 there were no less than twenty-three popes claiming the right to reign during the intervening eighty-eight years. The short and turbulent tenure of most of these reigns can have given nobody any confidence in the ability of the papacy to govern wisely, or be able to bring any harmony into the discord of Roman life; let alone any hope that the papacy could ever be in a position to guide and advise the rest of Europe.

Despite the relatively lengthy reigns of Gregory IV (827–844) and John VIII (872–882) the others came and went with dizzying rapidity, and the years 896–897 saw no less than four of them advance into, and retreat from, history very briefly. Poor Pope Boniface VI (896) managed to survive for only fifteen days! Boniface was followed by Stephen VII, who exhumed the corpse of his predecessor Formosus and put it on trial. He found the corpse guilty and had it punished, eventually having it thrown into the river. That this act of disrespect led to his own deposition, imprisonment, and death by strangulation, seemed not to disturb, or even surprise, anyone.

Into this atmosphere of carnage and confusion, Pope Leo V was elected in 903. He inherited all the turbulence of the preceding years and it is perhaps a mark of the total disorder and chaos into which Rome had fallen that an ordinary parish priest was elected, rather than one of the candidates from an aristocratic family.[8] Pope Leo V, from Ardea in the Papal States, had the problem of trying to establish a reign during the period of the 'Saeculum Obscurum', or Dark Age. He faced an antipope named Christopher who threw him into prison in September of that same year, where he was most likely murdered. The antipope then took his place and reigned until January 904, when he was in turn replaced by Sergius III.

Sergius had already been elected once, (in December 897), but had had to step down to allow the accession of John IX, who had the all-important Imperial support. Sergius got his second chance and grasped it with both hands. He considered that all previous popes from John IX onwards were plain usurpers, and set about overturning all their decrees, using violence to enforce his own. He did have the support of the Roman aristocracy, and in particular that of the family of a woman named Marozia.

Marozia – also known as Mariozza or Mariuccia – was born around 890 AD. In that year her parents, Theodora and Theophylact, moved from Tusculum to take up residence in Rome, about fifteen miles away. They had another daughter, older than Marozia, also named Theodora.

Theophylact was a capable man, and in time became a senator, a judge, and a duke, responsible for the Roman militia as well as the papal finances. His wife, Theodora, was also held in enough respect for her to be given the title of Senetrix. However, these successes and honours did not satisfy Theodora's greed for power. She hoped to be able to establish a dynasty, so that she and her family could rule Rome in perpetuity.[9] Theodora and her husband were dealing with a Pope who was a relative (Theophylact's cousin), yet was to be treated very carefully, a man for whom violence and even murder held no fears. He had already been suspected of ordering the deaths of both his immediate successors and had fathered several illegitimate children. He had earned himself a reputation for being 'efficient and ruthless'.[10] His reign would eventually be described a 'dismal and disgraceful', as even when a Cardinal, Sergius had acquired a reputation for cruelty. The arrangement made between Theodora and Sergius would include the sexual services of their daughter Marozia, who was then fifteen years old. The girl, who was reputedly very beautiful, apparently had no qualms about becoming the Pope's concubine, and her presence in the Pope's most private moments would guarantee that her parents could consolidate their position, and with the backing and favour of Sergius they could begin to exercise real power in Rome.

Marozia not only quickly became Sergius' mistress, but a mother, bearing him a son named John. While Marozia kept the Pope occupied, her parents controlled the Papal court. Marozia had another child, a daughter who was also confusingly named Theodora, after her grandmother and aunt, and all the ladies of the family would come to be described as 'shameless strumpets, neither daughter being of much better reputation than the mother'.[11]

Marozia and her sister Theodora helped to rule the pope, who was then thirty years Marozia's senior. The experience of wielding power over the older man was something she not only enjoyed but would never forget. It would encourage her ambitions and foster a determination to use any means possible to acquire and hold on to power. Marozia was given the titles of 'Senetrix' and 'Patricia' of the city of Rome. Even with Marozia and her sister as his mistresses, it does not appear that Sergius was even faithful to the family. The historian Cesare Baronius[12] wrote that the Pope was fond of having sex with young girls, and was 'the slave of every kind of vice, and the most wicked of men'. Baronius was a Cardinal and the Vatican librarian, and his assessment of Pope Sergius is damning. Sergius reigned for only just over seven years, but the family who had used his position as a stepping stone to power for themselves had no intention of relinquishing it.

Normally, the death of a pope resulted in battles of succession, but the senior Theodora averted these by arranging that her nominee should take office as Pope Anastasius III. Through this man she expected her family's prominence to continue, but he only lived for two years, obliging her to install Lando, an aristocratic Lombard, in his place. He was to reign for even less time, a mere six or seven months, (August 913 to March 914) giving Theodora the task of finding yet another man to suit her purpose. Fortunately, she already had one in mind.

Neither of the two previous popes had been men of a holy lifestyle, and of Lando it had been said that 'though an anointed bachelor, he consumed the greatest part of his life among lewd women, and was at last himself consumed, after only a few months!' But Lando had had a bastard son, another John, and a grown man, who was already rising to prominence in the church. Marozia's mother, Theodora Senior, had already fallen in love with him, and he had been made Bishop of Bologna, then Archbishop of Ravenna. She planned to keep her lover close to home, by arranging for him to be elected as the next pope after his father's death, and Lando's son did indeed become Pope John X in 914. The affair between Theodora and John X is not accepted by all. Johann Peter Kirsch wrote in *The Catholic Encyclopedia* Volume 8:

This statement is, however, generally and rightly rejected as a calumny. Liutprand wrote his history some fifty years later, and constantly slandered the Romans, whom he hated. At the time of John's election Theodora was advanced in years, and is lauded by other writers (e.g. Vulgarius).

Liutprand, Bishop of Cremona, related that Marozia had not been in agreement with this move of her mother's. The election of John X was to cause friction between the mother and daughter, while the mother continued as his mistress after his election. Her position with him also ensured that she remained the real power behind the papal throne, which was something that Marozia wanted for herself.[13]

Liutprand called the connection 'this monstrous crime' and fulminated against the senior Theodora for continuing to act as the pope's advisor as well as his mistress. She was loudly condemned by him as being a common harlot, and his opinion of her daughters was certainly no better. He called Theodora 'a shameless whore, who exercised power over the Roman citizens, as if she were a man'. He was one of the people responsible for spreading the story that Marozia was the mother of a son by her father's cousin, Sergius III. It was true, and that son would eventually become Pope John XI.

Theodora's patronage of John X was to be a long-lived connection, and more useful than her previous ones. John was industrious, and able to work in harmony with her husband. Together they created a menage-a-trois that resulted in a coalition of Italian rulers, under the papacy itself.

Theodora still had Marozia on her hands, and though the girl resented her mother's re-emergence and her own subsequent loss of status, she was still beautiful and still young enough to be of value. She was then twenty-two years old, and had an establishment on the Isola Tiburina, the small island in the River Tiber in Rome. There she entertained many young men, both nobles and prelates, who lived extremely decadent lives and kept mistresses, enjoying every luxury. Into this scene came Alberic, Marquis of Camerino. He was a German, whose army had proved vital to the Italian allies and the new coalition. As Marozia's husband he could continue to be useful and also be able to support and protect the family. Theodora considered him to be an ideal candidate for Marozia, but the apparent harmony between the mother and her resentful daughter was not to last very long.[14]

In 924, when Alberic managed to repel a Saracen attack, the scheming Marozia had turned his success to her own credit. Her relationship with him was already beginning to fail, and she had eagerly embarked on a series of open affairs with other men. Marozia persuaded Alberic to attack Rome, hoping to oust her mother, but while the coup failed and Alberic was eventually killed at Orte, later in 924 Marozia had borne a son to him, and was already more than capable of establishing herself and taking her revenge. She had no intention of being dependent on the goodwill of only one man, with the ever-present risk that she might herself be discarded. To prevent this, she envisaged something on the lines of the plans her parents had made, of a hereditary line, but not as mere nobles. What Marozia had in mind was to establish a hereditary papacy! This was to be beholden to only her, and her own son John was intended to be its first incumbent.

Theodora Senior and her husband Theophylact were by that time both dead. Their achievements had been great. Despite all the difficulties, they had carved out a place for themselves and their family, and Theodora particularly had succeeded brilliantly in controlling the men who held power and were close to her. They, in their turn, had treated her with obvious respect, and had shared and promoted her interests. They had given her their trust.

Marozia was left as the head of the powerful family they had created, but she had no intention of sharing her power with her late mother's lover the Pope. She married Guy of Tuscany, the brother of Pope John's military ally, then with her new husband's help she laid siege to the Vatican. Amazingly, they were encouraged in this attack on the Pope by the Roman citizens, and eventually John was captured at the Lateran Palace. He was imprisoned in Castel Sant'Angelo and Rome was soon to find that it was no longer under papal control, but that of Marozia.

Liutprand again had plenty to say on the matter, claiming that the Pope was killed by being smothered with a pillow, or perhaps strangled. Marozia appeared to have no regrets at all in ordering the death of the man her mother had loved. Her only concern was to hold the papacy in her hands, ready for the time when her son by Pope Sergius would be old enough to be elected.

The murdered Pope John was promptly replaced by Pope Leo VI. He was already elderly and only reigned for five or six months.

Liutprand again claimed that Marozia had him murdered, by poison this time, and there is said to be some mystery about his rapid demise. He was then replaced by Stephen VII in 928 (sometimes referred to in the chronology as Stephen VIII). This pope managed to hold on to his life and his position for approximately two years, and when he died in 931, Marozia considered that the time had come for the reigns of the puppet popes to stop. She was ready to make her move to put her own son on the papal throne, even though he was still only in his early twenties. She had her wish, and in February or March of 931 he was elected pope, taking the title John XI.

Marozia must have believed at that point that all her plans were coming to fruition. She no doubt looked forward to a lifetime of controlling both church and state through her son and hopefully of establishing that line of 'family' popes she was working for.

At first, Pope John seemed to be doing well. He supported the Cluniac Order of reforming monks founded in 909, dedicated to halting the decline in monastic discipline.[15] With her son on the papal throne, Marozia evidently decided that she no longer needed her husband, and would have a freer hand without him. Although she had had a daughter with him, and he had helped her to overthrow John X, he disappears from history around 929. His fate is uncertain and there is no actual evidence that he was killed, but the people whom Marozia found surplus to requirements tended to be disposed of quickly.

She intended to make a new marriage, and the man she chose to be her third husband was the half-brother of her first one, Alberic. He was named Hugh of Arles and had recently been elected King of Italy, which increased Marozia's status still further by making her a queen. The fact that he already had a legal wife was no obstacle to either party, and Marozia's son, the Pope, granted Hugh a dispensation without question, leaving him free to marry Marozia. Hugh was, of course, already Marozia's brother-in-law and therefore within the forbidden degree of consanguinity, but nothing was to be allowed to interfere with her marriage to him, so John XI not only allowed his mother's new marriage but actually officiated at it, and attended all the festivities afterwards.

Despite the many sycophants in attendance, not everyone was pleased with the new marriage. Marozia's other son, the half-forgotten Alberic II, was growing by then into an astute and determined young man.

He stood up during the celebrations to denounce his mother, and her marriage to his uncle. Insults were then traded between Alberic and Hugh that would not be easily forgotten, and would eventually lead to tragedy. Alberic shouted at Marozia that she was a 'treacherous and unloving mother' and cried out publicly 'the majesty of Rome has sunk to such depths that she now obeys the orders of harlots!' He went on 'Could there be anything viler than that the city of Rome should be brought to ruin by the impurities of one woman?'[16]

It is obvious that there was no love lost between the members of the unruly family, and Alberic may have suffered some jealousy at the way his mother had constantly favoured John, to his own detriment. What does surprise is that he did not immediately meet an unfortunate end by reason of his embarrassing tirade, as both Marozia and Hugh were known to be quick-tempered and ruthless in dealing with opposition. John also, the young Pope, cannot have been pleased to hear what Alberic had said, with its accusations of papal complicity and corruption.

John's true character had already shown itself in his easy acceptance of the marriage, which in the eyes of the church was illegal. He had begun to indulge himself in a lifestyle so dissolute that, along with the behaviour of his mother and other female relatives, caused that period of papal history to be known as 'The Great Pornocracy'.

Rome, however, was always ready to riot against its rulers, and had already begun to turn against the family's authority, helped by word spreading of what Alberic had said regarding his mother, brother, and the new husband at the wedding feast. Incited by Alberic, the mob stormed the castle and Hugh, forgetting his martial image and also his new wife, managed to scramble down the walls on a rope. He fled, leaving Marozia and her son John to face the crowds of irate citizenry alone.

They were easily captured and both imprisoned, though Alberic proved too wise to kill either of them out of hand. Pope John XI was left with only ceremonial duties to perform, losing all real power, and died either in December 935 or January of 936, after the first scandal had died down. He had reigned for a little less than five years.[17] Marozia, though spared her life, was to prove the more unfortunate. Alberic was fully aware that it would do his reputation no good at all to have his mother killed openly, but he considered her far too dangerous ever to be released. She was imprisoned in the Castel Sant'Angelo (once the mausoleum of the Emperor Hadrian), which was at that time by far the the most seure place of imprisonment Rome could offer.[18]

Alberic, however, was no angel, despite his stance of respectability at his mother's wedding. He had already fathered a bastard son, who would one day become Pope John XII, and who would be said to have included among his many mistresses 'one of his father's own concubines, Stephana, a widow named Anna, and the widow of Ranier'. The taking of one of his father's mistresses was also considered practically incestuous, and an act of great depravity.[19] Nevertheless, in his role as Rome's ruler, Alberic was more successful and was to stay in power for twenty-two years. He held enough influence to be able to appoint the next five popes. One of these, Marinus II (942–946) was not considered worthy of his position, being described as 'begat of a common woman and the son of a necromancer', which was tantamount to being the son of a devil-worshipper.[20]

Finally, it appeared that pity was being shown towards Marozia. She had been incarcerated for over five years, and was then almost fifty years old. She bore little resemblance to the venal and beautiful temptress whose slightest wish had once been law in Rome. It was said that a bishop was sent to visit Marozia in her prison, after the ban of excommunication originally been made against her was lifted. The Bishop was instructed to 'exorcise any evil that the woman may still have had in her, with the intention that she should be in a state of grace before being executed'. She was still considered far too dangerous ever to be released. Marozia was actually the prisoner of the Pope, not the civil authority. On a second visit the Bishop reputedly saying to her: 'Marozia, daughter of Theophylact, are you among the living? I Bishop John Crescentius of Protus, command you to speak.'

Marozia replied 'I am living my lord bishop, I am living.' Then, after a long pause, she begged 'For all my sins, forgiveness!'

The Bishop then read out the warrant he had brought with him: 'Inasmuch as you, Marozia, did from the beginning and at the age of fifteen years, conspire against the rights of the See of Peter in the reign of the Holy Father Pope Sergius, following the example of your satanic mother Theodora...'

The warrant continued with accusations that Marozia had intended to take over the whole world, by the means of ruling the papacy through her descendants, beginning with her son Pope John XI and 'that she had dared, like Jezebel of old, yet again to take a third husband'. She was, in the warrant, held responsible even for the evil life of her grandson, Pope John XII, though she had been held in prison throughout his nine-year reign. This grandson was the son of Alberic II and seemed to have inherited his family's failings in full measure. The charges regarding him continued:

> Your grandson, Pope John XII, perjured himself, breaking his oath to the Great Emperor. He stole the treasury of the Popes and fled to Rome's enemies, and was deposed by the Holy Synod, to be replaced by Leo VIII. Then this apostate returned to Rome, cut off the nose and tongue and two fingers of the Cardinal-Deacon, flayed the skin of Bishop Otger, cut off the head of the Notary Azzo and also beheaded sixty-three of Rome's clergy and nobility. During the night of 14th May 964, while having illicit and filthy relations with a Roman matron, he was surprised in the act of sin by the woman's angry husband. In his just wrath, he smashed his skull with a hammer, and thus liberated his evil soul to the grasp of Satan.[21]

Exciting though all this certainly is, the suggestion that these charges were read out to Marozia before her own death is apocryphal. Leo VIII is believed to have died in May 964, and whether the details of his death are as given or not, Marozia could not have been held responsible for his behaviour, as she had already been killed, probably in 937. The chroniclers of the time not only enjoyed a juicy story as much as anyone else, but probably really did consider Marozia culpable, owing to the appalling example she gave to her children. Her family was considered to have had a taint that made all its members eager to indulge themselves in every sin. The story goes on to say that 'once the warrant was read out in full, an executioner entered the room, and suffocated Marozia with a cushion, for the wellbeing of Holy Mother Church, and the peace of the Roman people.'

Liutprand of Cremona summed up the family and the matriarch: 'A certain shameless strumpet called Theodora ... at some time sole monarch of Rome – shame upon us to say the words – exercised power in the most manly fashion. She had two daughters,

Marozia and Theodora and these damsels were not only her equals, but could even surpass her in all the exercises that Venus loves!'

Marozia's influence was to continue after her death. John XII's brother Gregory and also Pope Benedict VIII (1012–1024) were her great-grandsons, and Benedict IX (1032–1048) was her great-great grandson. Pope John XIII was her nephew, the son of her sister Theodora, so her ambition to create a hereditary papacy was almost achieved. Edward Gibbon noted the score: '...her bastard son, two grandsons, two great-grandsons, and one great-great-grandson all became popes, a rare geneaology.' Marozia and her mother were described as 'vainglorious Messalinas, filled with fleshly lust and cunning in all forms of wickedness. They governed Rome and prostituted the chair of St Peter for their minions and their paramours.'[22]

They were certainly considered to have been appalling women, although one wonders how they might have been judged had they been male. The record of the popes themselves at that time was disgraceful, and Theodora and Marozia behaved just as the men did. That was the main problem. Not merely that such excesses and cruelties had become the norm within the Vatican, but that women were giving the orders, arranging elections of popes, and even committing murders. These things had been rife for centuries, and what the commentators (and Alberic II) deplored, though his own descendants were to prove no better, was that females had usurped the male prerogative of controlling the papacy and Rome itself.

Evidence for this assumption lies in the remark made by Liutprand of Cremona, when he criticised Theodora and Marozia saying 'they exercised power in the most *manly* fashion.' It was not the use of power itself that was the crime, it was that it was being wielded by women that could not be tolerated. However, the men in the lives of these women had been happy to go along with them, realising that they had a ruthlessness and efficiency equal to their own.

They had stepped away from the expected place for women, they were not meek, not pious or obedient, and were therefore considered sinful because they acted outside male control. They would be followed by many other women, who were equally able to make their presence felt and have their orders obeyed.

The Notorious Queen: Joanna of Naples and Onwards

Joanna was born in 1326, the eldest surviving child of the heir to the Kingdom of Naples, which was then the most important sovereignty in Italy. Her father was Charles, Duke of Calabria, the heir of her grandfather, Robert, King of Naples. Joanna's mother was Marie de Valois, the daughter of Charles III de Valois, a younger son of the King of France.

Thirty-six years on, Giovanni Boccaccio in his *Famous Women*, would say of her: 'Joanna, Queen of Sicily and Jerusalem, is more renowned than any other woman of her time, for her lineage, for her power, and for her character.'

In 1266, when Joanna's great-great-grandfather Charles of Anjou had established a claim of sovereignty over the area, it had included the island of Sicily. The connection between Naples and Sicily would continue, at least theoretically, even though the people of Sicily had rebelled against Charles's harsh rule in 1282 and invited the King of Aragon to rule them instead. Throughout Joanna's lifetime, and for a long while to come, the Kingdom of Naples would still be known as the Kingdom of the Two Sicilies.[1]

Charles of Aragon, the founder of the Angevin dynasty, was the youngest brother of Louis IX, King of France, who was later canonised as St Louis. Joanna's great-great-grandmother was Beatrice, Countess of Provence, one of a famous family of sisters who had all become queens.[2] It was an impressive lineage.

Joanna was the fourth child of Charles and Marie's family, but two older sisters (Eloisa and Maria) and one brother (Charles Martel) had predeceased her, so that at her birth she became second in line to the throne, after her father. He was to die on 9 November 1328, leaving his wife pregnant with another daughter, who would also be named Marie, and his heir Joanna, only two years old. Unfortunately for any sense of continuity in Joanna's life, her mother would also die two years later.

After Joanna's father died, her grandfather had problems to face regarding the succession. He had a choice between Joanna, his granddaughter, or various nephews. He chose Joanna, due to his great love for his late son. As the official heiress presumptive, she was proclaimed Duchess of Calabria in September 1333, and became Princess of Salerno in 1334.[3]

The next most important step was to betroth the young heiress to a suitable husband. In order to reconcile his brother's descendants to the fact of the little girl's premier position, he arranged a marriage between Joanna and Andrew, the six-year-old younger son of his nephew Charles of Hungary. Through his father, this boy had his own claim to the crown of Naples. No time was wasted, and the marriage contract was signed on behalf of the two children in November 1332. The actual marriage would take place at Santa Chiara Basilica on 26 September 1333, Joanna being around five years old and her husband six.[4]

Since the death of her mother, Joanna had been brought up by her grandparents, King Robert and Queen Sancia. Everything she would come to believe in as an adult was learned at their court, at the Castel Nuovo. They were both charismatic figures, and the Castel Nuovo was largely a palace of pleasures. There Joanna would be prepared, mainly by her step-grandmother, soaking up the intricacies of religion, literature and the responsibilities of her royal position, to ready her for her future.

Robert the Wise was a man of great reputation, and was much admired in Europe for his devotion to learning as well as an ability to expand his territories at the expense of his neighbours. He was capable of managing such diverse areas as Naples and Provence, as well as writing over 300 sermons in Latin.

Robert's life had been fraught with difficulties, beginning when his father Charles the Lame (later King Charles II of Naples) lost a battle for Sicily and was captured by the King of Aragon.

It was arranged that his three younger sons (Louis aged fourteen, Robert aged ten and Raymond Berengar aged seven) would take his place as hostages until a treaty was arranged. They were to suffer a form of imprisonment and deprivation for several years until a settlement was finally reached. This had to be moved along by the pope, who then crowned Charles the Lame as King of Sicily. Part of the deal included Robert's older brother Louis marrying King James II of Aragon's sister Violante. Robert had learned to rely on Louis during the years of captivity, but during that time Louis had taken a vow of celibacy. His feelings of aversion towards women were so strong that he could not even bring himself to kiss his mother, when they were finally reunited after his seven years' separation. It was hopeless to expect that he would make any woman a decent husband, let alone manage to produce the necessary children, so the bride was transferred to Robert instead.[5]

On returning to Naples, he and Violante found that the eldest brother, the heir, had died of illness, along with his wife. They had had a son, but King Charles was deeply concerned that a small child ruled by his advisors could not possibly keep the territories safe. He knew Naples would need a strong ruler, and Louis was next in line. However, his deep religious feeling would not allow him to accept the position, and again, his continuing aversion to women would ensure that there would be no heirs from him, so that honour also went to Robert.

Violante died after only five years of marriage, leaving two sons; Louis, who also died in 1310, and Charles, who would become Joanna's father. Robert remarried to Sancia of Majorca. Joanna's formative years would be directed by this formidable woman, who was devoted to the Franciscan Order, especially the Poor Clares. She taught Joanna to speak Latin fluently, as well as giving her a good education in all other matters she might need for her future. She asked permission of the Pope that several members of the order could live with her at Castel Nuovo, and she was allowed two. She would also frequently petition the Pope to allow her to divorce her husband and become a nun, which was just as frequently refused. She had always been far more of a nun than a wife, despite her long but childless marriage to Robert. The Pope had, in the past, repeatedly told her to give more of her attention to her husband, but at the same time he felt obliged to chastise Robert for his flagrant infidelities, though in the circumstances they were perhaps understandable.[6]

Joanna's life was not all piety and lessons. She was surrounded by the royal entourage and the social whirl it created, and was able to enjoy the luxuries of the court. One of the people who would become important in her life was Catherine de Valois, the widow of Robert the Wise's younger brother, Philip Prince of Taranto. Philip had divorced his first wife on a trumped-up charge of adultery in order to marry Catherine, mainly because she was the sole heir to the Empire of Constantinople.

Charles of Valois (younger brother of King Philip IV of France) had married Baldwin II's granddaughter, who inherited the old Emperor's claim. She died, taking her claim out of his hands, for it was then inherited by her daughter Catherine. Catherine was married to Philip of Taranto when she was only ten years old in order to secure her claim for the family.

When Joanna first met Catherine she was twenty-eight years old and recently widowed. She was also highly intelligent, shrewd, lively, and determined to make good her claim of being Empress of Constantinople to pass it on to her sons. These boys, Robert, Louis and Philip, were still very young. Catherine was everything that Queen Sancia was not, being sophisticated and worldly, keen on all pleasures. She quickly became involved with various lovers, especially one Niccolo Acciaiuoli, who was not only attractive, charming and handsome, but also had a great ability with finances. Catherine made him her counsellor and tutor to her children.[7] She was a charismatic figure, but her hedonistic lifestyle caused resentment towards her from other people less well placed.

Joanna's closest female friendship was with her nurse, Philippa the Catanian, who had been with the family for thirty years. This woman was married to an Ethiopian, Raymond of Campagno, who had once been a slave, but had risen through ability to become a commander of the army. Boccaccio was to remark sourly that the 'African soldier joined the bed of the Sicilian washerwoman.'[8] Joanna became very close to them both and gave them her trust. Because of this they were able to rise in status, 'finding themselves the owners of towns, estates, villas, horses, numerous servants, rich clothes and all kinds of goods in abundance', according to Boccaccio. Despite his dislike, they were usually held in respect for their industry and reliability. They had three sons and one daughter, and proved themselves invaluable to the royal family, with Philippa being appointed Guardian to Joanna, the heir.

This relationship gave Joanna the security and continuity she needed, though some of the nobility continued to be jealous. Boccaccio in particular made frequent sharp remarks about the devotion they showed to their children, saying, 'You would think that they were the children of a king, rather than of a slave.'[9] He also said 'nothing great, serious or arduous was accomplished, unless it was approved of by Robert, Philippa, or Sancia.'

The marriage of Joanna and Andrew of Hungary was pushed forward by the Pope in this atmosphere of luxury and political intrigue. Pope John XXII had for years discounted the claims of the King of Hungary, Carobert (the eldest son of Charles Martel, the original heir to the throne of Naples). When Carobert's throne had been usurped and he was banished to Hungary, as a consolation prize, his resentment flourished. The pope ignored him, but then gradually changed his mind. He later saw that if Carobert's son Andrew should marry Joanna, it would settle the old argument and the future offspring of the couple would inherit both territories.

The immense wealth of Carobert was probably the deciding factor. Pope John XXII was well known to be a miser, and 'one who appreciated the value of a gold florin'.[10] He had already increased his income greatly by raising taxes and fines. When he finally died the papal clerks would be astonished at the amount of treasure, comprising gold plate, precious gemstones, and gold coins, were found in the papal vaults.[11]

Naturally enough, the King of Hungary cherished fond ideas that his son Andrew would become King Consort of Naples when he married Joanna, but that was not at all the idea of the court of Naples. They saw the boy merely as a sire for the breeding of the next generation. They never intended to give him any real power, and expected Hungary to be satisfied with the empty title without any of the influence usually associated with it. Hungary had fondly imagined that the marriage would solve the long-running dispute, but Naples saw it only as a minor concession, that the boy's bloodline should be used to strengthen Joanna's own, not that the Hungarian claim should take over. In any case, there were other claimants, not least the children of Catherine de Valois and her late husband the Prince of Taranto. There was also an illegitimate son of Robert the Wise (with one of his wife's ladies in waiting) after all attempts on Sancia's virtue had failed. This young man was known as Charles of Artois.

Joanna's grandfather, frustrated and unhappy in his domestic life with Sancia, had turned to learning for his satisfaction. The examination of Petrarch at the Castel Nuovo in March 1341, to certify that the scholar was sufficiently qualified for the office of Poet Laureate in Rome, was a hugely important cultural event. For three full days Robert questioned the scholar before the ruling council and the university, an examination that the scholar had no difficulty in answering. Joanna was fifteen when this intellectual investigation took place. It was the time when she might have been expected to consummate her marriage to Andrew, although it was already obvious that it would not be a love match.

On 16 January 1343, nearing the end of his life and by then too weak to leave his bed, Robert the Wise dictated his will. He confirmed Joanna as his successor and as his sole heir, both to Naples and whatever was left of the Kingdom of Jerusalem. It was emphasised that if Joanna died childless, the inheritance would pass to her sister Maria, not to her husband Andrew of Hungary. In fact, the young man was specifically excluded from playing any governing role at all.

The will called for a council, led by Sancia, to rule until Joanna reached her majority, which had been confirmed as being on her twenty-fifth birthday. There was no time for anyone to question the wisdom of these provisions, or to press for some reinstatement of the Hungarian claim, for after just four days Robert the Wise died, and the terms of his will became inviolable.[12]

Joanna built her grandfather a splendid tomb, but she wasn't blind to the way his will had left her and Naples exposed. If the Hungarians should raise an army in defence of Andrew's position, there was nobody capable of leading Naples' response. Joanna's sex, plus the stipulation that every decision had to go through the council, would slow down any possibility of practical gathering of troops and swift action. The council did back her in her appointment of Hugo del Balzo, the Count of Avellino, as her ambassador to the papal court. As a new queen, she would have to do formal obeisance to the Pope for her kingdom, and Balzo was ordered to be her surrogate for this. She would also need to be crowned, and he was also instructed to ask the Pope, by then Clement VI, to allow Andrew to be crowned King. This did not mean that she intended to give him any actual authority, but hoped that the face-saving honour might ease the difficult situation.

There was, of course, another route to power in Naples, and that was through Joanna's sister Maria, who was her heir and very valuable in the marriage market. Robert had wanted Maria to marry the heir to the French throne, but that would have caused further factional dispute, and it was finally decided that this potentially dangerous young woman should be married to her cousin Charles of Durazzo. The dispensation for this marriage arrived with astonishing speed, given the normal pace of papal business, only six weeks after the death of Robert the Wise. This may have convinced Joanna that her move to stabilise the kingdom had papal approval, but the marriage was still not particularly popular at the court in Naples. Charles took the lead by removing Maria to a property of his own, where he married her and made sure that the nuptials were consummated immediately, to prevent any future claim that the union was invalid.[13]

Naturally, other relatives with prior or closer claims to have a part in the future ruling of the court were scandalised at the surreptitious marriage and Charles soon had to defend his property against attack. Soon all Naples was facing war, and Joanna realised that the hurried marriage had been a very bad idea. She attempted to reject it, complaining to the Pope about Charles and refusing her sister the usual dowry. She insisted that the marriage be annulled. Other rulers became involved, each with an eye on their own claims, and the Pope was obliged to protest that he had granted the dispensation 'for that union on account of the benefit to be expected from it'. Further letters from the irate Joanna prompted the Pope to advise her to forgive the newly married couple, but soon Maria was pregnant, so Joanna had no alternative but to recognise the legality of the marriage.[14]

Although Maria's hasty marriage had caused problems, there were worse ones to come. Only a couple of weeks after the recognition of Maria's union, four hundred Hungarian noblemen, knights and courtiers paraded into Joanna's capital, led by her formidable mother-in-law, Elizabeth, the Dowager Queen of Hungary.[15]

The Hungarian queen was disturbed not only by the political climate in southern Italy, but by the fact that Robert's will had not been revised by the Pope in Andrew's favour, despite many pressures and promises. She was aware that her son occupied a very awkward position in Naples, and even when Andrew rode out to meet his mother, Joanna did not accompany him. Instead, she remained just inside the capital at Somma, wearing her crown and dressed in her full robes of state, to show her personal sovereignty as the Hungarians approached.

It soon became clear that Andrew seldom saw Joanna, and there is some indication that he even had to ask permission to enter his wife's bedroom. Though Joanna referred to her husband as 'the king', Andrew had never been officially crowned, had no connection at all with the government, and even no control over his own household. He was still young and unsure of himself, and had grown up entirely in Joanna's shadow. His mother did not accept the arrangement as Andrew apparently did, and she was determined to alter it.

She sent a large cash bribe to the papal court, then residing at Avignon, which was intended to persuade the Pope to crown her son. The Pope suggested that a legate should visit Naples to take charge of affairs. This idea horrified Joanna, who had no intention at all of allowing the Pope to interfere in such a way. She also faced the problem of the failure of the medieval super-companies at this time, such as the Bardi and the Peruzzi, who had controlled much of Italy's wealth, just when the wealth of the Hungarians was being made abundantly clear to her, undermining her position.[16]

Businesses had always failed from time to time, but the size and scope of the Lombard dealings was unprecedented. Nobody could have believed in 1343 how long or how deep the financial downturn would be. Though the Bardi and the Peruzzi along with the Acciaiuoli family had for a long time kept their financial heads above water skilfully, they would still fail at the start of Joanna's reign and she would be blamed, however unfairly, for the resulting difficulties.

These difficulties would be seen by the Hungarians as an opportunity and they would use their considerable resources to continue to press for a coronation for Andrew and for his rights as a king.

Joanna's position was exacerbated by the decision of her step-grandmother, Queen Sancia, to finally take her religious vows and leave the court. It was what she had always longed for. The Pope had dissolved Naples' ruling council and Sancia took that as her opportunity to retire from the world. Only Joanna's old nurse, Philippa, would remain of the secure foundation that had once supported her.

The Pope finally compromised and agreed to give Andrew the title of king and the coronation his mother wanted. But these honours meant nothing without the actual power, which was not on offer. On 3 February 1344 Pope Clement specified in a letter to Joanna that although Andrew would be crowned with her, the Kingdom of Naples still belonged to her alone, as the rightful heir of King Robert, 'just as if she was a man' and he made things clear to the Hungarians that if Joanna died without an heir of her own, then the throne would go to her sister Maria.[17]

This unwelcome news coincided with the return of Joanna's mother-in-law Elizabeth, who was amazed at the level of animosity shown to them by the native courtiers and she was even informed by the Hungarian members of Andrew's household that there had been plots against his life. She wrote again to the Pope, who by that time was thoroughly tired of her demands and would do no more, so she determined to take her son home to Hungary with her. Joanna, to avoid further scandal, was obliged to plead with her not to do that, aided by Catherine de Valois, who also foresaw further scandals looming. Andrew was seventeen years old but was still being treated as a child, and though Elizabeth finally allowed herself to be persuaded, she continued to press the Pope regarding he son's rights. This was despite the fact that her continuing demands were causing a good deal of resentment and even putting her son's life at some risk.

Pope Clement's Legate, Cardinal Aimeric de Chatelus, arrived in Naples only two weeks after Elizabeth of Hungary had again left. It was to be his task to try to tame the factions at court, and receive vows of obedience from Joanna and Andrew. Joanna had to take an oath of obedience to the Pope in a public ceremony before the whole court, which she found humiliating. The relationship, already strained, between Naples and the papal court, could only worsen. In a short time the Cardinal-Legate was writing to the Pope asking to be transferred elsewhere.

The Pope refused his request, but gave him the right to raise taxes on the clergy and to sell favours, both temporal and spiritual, as he should wish. The next stage was the transfer of power, in which Joanna would officially recognise the church's authority over her realm, and the actual government would then pass to the Cardinal-Legate. Joanna fell ill that summer, postponing the ceremony until August. While she was incapacitated, Andrew stepped forward and to everyone's surprise seized the initiative. He released the notorious Pipini brothers from prison and actually knighted them.[18] As these men had been accused of every type of crime imaginable, his sudden patronage of them caused not merely amazement but horror. Though the Hungarian faction seemed to have acquired three dangerous and intimidating followers, everyone else was terrified. The brothers proceeded to behave much as they always had, 'living luxuriously, riding in state, holding jousts and appearing in the presence of the queen and Andrew with loftier banners than their own.' This was observed and reported by Domenico da Gravina.

It appeared that Andrew was determined to show everyone who still opposed him that they might expect retribution. He began to employ threats, even towards Joanna, and quickly became hated.

The appearance of the papal legate took the immediate pressure off Joanna, giving her a little more personal freedom, even though Andrew's apparent friendship with the Pipini brothers had undermined her position. Boccaccio suggested that it was at this time that she took a lover named Robert of Cabannis. This is a move that Joanna would regularly be accused of throughout her lifetime, irrespective of the husbands she also acquired. In this case the highly unsatisfactory nature of her marriage to Andrew may mitigate for her. If she did take a lover at this time, it should be remembered that she was only eighteen years old, and that her marriage was a loveless disaster.

Other chroniclers were to suggest the names of other men with whom she was supposed to be involved, but they may be apocryphal. As Boccaccio said, 'Where there is the least familiarity, of any sort, with a man, disgrace easily stains the most honourable woman.'

Aimeric was in Naples at that time, and Joanna must have been aware that she was being spied on, but Aimeric had said that her extravagance was threatening the church's income from Naples. The Pope reacted to this by cancelling every grant made by the queen since Robert the Wise had died. This was followed by another decree listing people who were accused of 'provoking mischief between the queen and her lord and master' and this list included her closest friends. These were so dangerous that a proviso was sent to the Cardinal-Legate suggesting that he leave Naples before the decrees were to be made public. He would be relieved of his position, and his successor would have to deal with the fallout from them.

However, Joanna was still able to resume some level of normality in her dealings with Andrew, and in April it was announced that the queen was pregnant.[19] Though there had been rumours of infidelity, it was generally accepted that the child was fathered by Andrew. The pregnancy, though bringing a new and disruptive element into the political status quo, by promoting Andrew's position as the father of the next heir, also confirmed that Joanna was fertile, which in turn strengthened her position as queen.

Unfortunately, it also made it more difficult to go on refusing Andrew's rights. It would be a vindication of the marriage, and she knew that her in-laws would be back to take advantage of it, and she was right. As soon as the news reached them, they sent a series of bishops and lawyers to Naples, in attempts to propel Andrew into power.

Clement's new Nuncio arrived in May, and finally returned the rule of Naples into Joanna's hands. She then found that Aimeric had posted the Bull rejecting all Joanna's gifts on pain of excommunication. She was in no mood to accept any further papal interference, so simply ignored the Pope's instructions. Clement, however, was beginning to favour the Hungarian cause, and this was to push Joanna into a new alliance with Philippa the Catanian and some of her other supporters. The Nuncio's announcement that Joanna and Andrew would be crowned together in a formal ceremony in the following September, suggesting as it did that Andrew would share Joanna's power, only forced the already difficult situation even further out of control.[20]

Joanna and Andrew moved to the summer palace at Aversa, famous for its pleasant gardens. They intended to stay there until it was time for the coronation, when their two households would make the short journey back to Naples. Joanna was then six months pregnant and wished to avoid the heat of the city as long as possible.

At that point, the pope changed his mind yet again. He sent letters to Joanna and to Andrew, confirming that he considered Joanna to be 'sole ruler' again. Andrew was chastised for his immature behaviour and his coronation was again made conditional upon him recognising his wife's sovereignty. He was forbidden, under pain of excommunication, from interfering in his wife's authority, before or after the ceremony.

During this very confusing time, Joanna had continued to administer government from Aversa, seeing delegations from the capital nearly every day. But Andrew had nothing to occupy him and it was merely a holiday for him during which he enjoyed himself in the surrounding countryside. On 18 September he spent the afternoon watching dances being performed outside the castle, and Joanna was already asleep when he returned to their apartment.[21]

While preparing for bed, Andrew was informed that a courtier waited to see him. Believing the messenger, he hastily dressed and followed the man onto a gallery, to be met there by a group of armed men. Before he could react, he was seized and the door bolted behind him, preventing his escape. There was a fierce struggle but Andrew was unarmed and outnumbered, and he was soon subdued. Some of the men were holding his mouth so that he could not cry out, so firmly that the marks of their gauntlets showed on his face after his death. A rope was brought and he was strangled with it, then dragged to the adjacent balcony, where he was flung over, with the rope wrapped about his neck. Some other men standing below in the garden dragged on his legs to make sure that he was dead.

An official report of the crime filed later at the papal court, stated that 'others tore out his hair, dragged him and threw him into the garden. Some say that they swung him as if hanging him over the said garden, some also got him under the knees, and that this likewise left external traces.'

They had intended to bury him to hide the evidence of the crime, and cut the rope holding his corpse which had suspended him over the balcony. But the thud of his body hitting the ground awakened his nurse, Isabelle the Hungarian, who had been with him since his childhood. She surprised the murderers before they had time to conceal his body, and she raised the alarm. On hearing her screams, the attackers rushed off into the night. The papal crime report continues: 'It was before related to us, that they had intended to throw him into a deep well, and thereafter give out that he had left the country... this they would have carried out, if his nurse had not come quickly upon the scene.'

The rest of the castle was thoroughly searched, but no murderers were found. At that point, the queen was woken by her servants and informed that her husband had been killed. One has to wonder why she was not wakened earlier, by the noise of the scuffle, the shouts and perhaps even screams? The balcony where all this took place was situated between the bedrooms of the king and queen, and so comparatively close to where Joanna was said to be sleeping. Opinions are divided regarding the queen's role in Andrew's death and although she officially expressed disgust at the murder, her friends were widely considered to be suspects in it.

The Hungarian faction naturally wanted to sensationalise the murder as much as they could. It was far more shocking for the queen to be assigned a leading role in the conspiracy to murder, and one must remember that the chroniclers always tend to be storytellers. However, historians still argue about the level of the queen's personal involvement.

Andrew was buried in the Cathedral of Naples, in the chapel of St Louis, next to the remains of his paternal grandparents. Joanna ordered a daily mass to be said in her husband's memory. Amazingly, within forty-eight hours, one of the alleged assassins was then caught in Aversa. It was Tommasso Mambriccio, who had been Andrew's chamberlain. He was to be questioned closely, so much so that he died under torture, which may have been intended. The queen continued to maintain her innocence to the end of her life, both of murdering her husband and of conspiring in the murder of her husband. In the circumstances she must have known that suspicion would automatically fall onto her, whether she was guilty or not. One letter telling of the news has survived, addressed to the 'nobles, statesmen and Governing Council of the Republic of Florence' and dated 22 September, sent from Aversa:

An unutterable crime, a prodigious iniquity, a sin inexpiable, hateful to God and horrifying to mortality, perpetrated with inhuman ferocity and the shedding of innocent blood, by the hands of miscreants, has been committed on the person of our hitherto Lord and Husband.[22]

Pope Clement offered to take over the enquiry into Andrew's death and Joanna could hardly refuse, though she would probably have preferred not to have papal agents again looking into everything that went on in Naples. Despite her advanced pregnancy, there was a petition from Robert of Taranto, her cousin, suggesting the two of them should marry. Joanna was already aware of her sudden vulnerability, as a woman now without a protector. She knew that she had to put Robert off, but had to move slowly, and fortunately the Pope's administration, which had also received a similar petition, moved even more glacially. Before she had to show her hand she went into labour on 25 December 1345 and was eventually delivered of a healthy son. This birth helped to establish her line, and give to Naples a little added security. The child was to be named Charles Martel.

Joanna knew that she would indeed need the backing of another husband, one likely to be able to cope with the internal politics of Naples. In 1347 she would marry Louis, Prince of Taranto. He was known for his prowess at arms and could presumably defend her and her child, and he was one of those men with whom her name had earlier been linked.

Louis' brother Robert, who had enforced the writing of the petitions of marriage, was still not prepared to give up the idea that he should marry her himself, despite her marriage to Louis. The long delays of the church in investigating the death of Andrew had allowed wild rumours to spread, which in turn led to both accusations of complicity and rioting. Clement VI was struggling with the factional politics of Naples, and tried to bring the murderers to justice, but was overwhelmed by events elsewhere in Europe. Not only was Louis' brother Robert still making himself unpleasant, but Andrew's mother again spurred the Pope into action, demanding justice for her son. The Pope was obliged to warn her not to attempt to invade Naples, under threat of being put under an Interdict.[23]

Louis the Great, the elder brother of Andrew, arrived with Hungarian troops at Benevento in January of 1340, intending to invade, and Joanna had to leave Castel Nuovo, leaving behind her young son in the care of his household. Louis of Taranto also fled in another galley, finally rejoining Joanna in Avignon where they intended to meet with the Pope. Andrew's child, who had been left with the household servants, was taken back to Hungary by his uncle, where he died in 1348, aged only two years. Before leaving Naples, Louis the Great executed Charles of Durazzo, who was Joanna's cousin and brother-in-law, by having him beheaded in the same place where Andrew had been attacked.

Joanna was in dire need of two things, which only the Pope could supply. The first was a papal dispensation regarding her marriage to Louis, which the couple had failed to obtain prior to their wedding as was usual, and the second was the Pope's exoneration (some might have called it rather closer to absolution) for the death of Andrew.

Before any such exoneration could be given, Joanna would have to go through the indignity of an enquiry, almost a trial, before the Pope, who had undertaken the investigation into Andrew's murder. This would not be merely a formality. Joanna had received permission to speak on her own behalf to refute the Hungarian allegations of involvement, but despite the difficulties she managed to beguile her audience. The Pope was impressed, and Joanna was obviously glad to have his support.

After the queen had given her evidence, the Pope and cardinals conferred. They decided that she was 'not only innocent, but above the suspicion of any guilt', as Costanzo was to report. He also said, 'She spoke at length, with good grace, and with eloquence, and brought forth many good reasons for her defence.' The Pope was pleased with her and with her husband, and he showed his approval by presenting them with the Golden Rose, a valuable ornament encrusted with pearls and jewels, which was traditionally bestowed on the fourth Sunday of Lent as a mark of special papal favour. The Pope also then issued a Bull formally legitimising Joanna's marriage to Louis. Joanna's first daughter, sired by Louis, was born at Avignon.

Amazingly then, to appease Hungarian sensibilities, the Pope actually agreed to another trial for Joanna, still accused by her in-laws of the death of Andrew, with the proviso that if she were found guilty she would lose her kingdom, which would then be inherited by Maria. This is an interesting point, as the King of Hungary was at that point hoping to marry Maria, so it would make a very satisfactory outcome for Joanna to be found culpable and to have Maria inherit the kingdom as his wife. However, if Joanna were to again be found to be innocent, the King of Hungary would be required to give up all further attempts against Naples, which would be returned to Joanna. She certainly did not fear the second investigation and inquest. She had been given the Pope's full support during the first. The second also ended as she had expected, with the Hungarians being obliged to hand back Naples to her and her new husband Louis of Taranto. It was finally time for them to return home.

Joanna's second daughter with Louis, named Francoise, was born in 1351 and shortly afterwards Louis received from the Pope the formal recognition of his co-rulership with Joanna. Unfortunately, things would turn sour between the married couple, and Louis of Taranto would eventually wrest all power from Joanna, leaving her a sovereign in name only. His name was to precede hers on all documents and their marriage became very unhappy. Neither of their two daughters would live to survive their parents, a tragic end to what had started so promisingly.

Matteo Villani said of their relationship, 'He honoured the queen little, whether this was his fault – and his responsibility was great – or that of the queen, he often beat her as one would a lowly woman, to the great shame of the crown.' Joanna, in a letter to Innocent VI of December 1353 complained that she was 'humiliated and anguished' by the behavior of her husband. She said that he cheated on her and had fathered at least three children by other women. Though Louis was a capable commander, and faced many attacks and uprisings during his marriage to Joanna, he was generally disliked. One chronicler wrote of him that he had '...caused great corruption in all the kingdom'. When Louis died in 1362 Petrarch, who was familiar with the Court at Naples, said of him that he was '...violent and mendacious, prodigal and avaricious, debauched and cruel'. He also said that Louis had been 'a person who neither knew how to make his subjects love him, nor needed their love.'[24]

The year after the death of Louis, Joanna married for the third time, her new husband being James IV, the titular King of Majorca. He was the son of James III of Majorca and his wife Constance of Aragon. He was born in 1336 and was imprisoned by his uncle, Peter IV of Aragon, after his father had been killed trying to regain his kingdom. It was said that he had been 'kept in a cage' in Barcelona until 1362, when he escaped taking refuge in Naples.

Joanna married him in 1363, at Castel Nuovo but, aware of the problems with her previous marriage, she wisely kept him away from governmental matters. Unfortunately, it was still to become another unsuccessful marriage and they had no children, indeed, it was reported that they were rarely together. James had dreams of one day regaining Majorca and took part in the Battle of Najera in 1367, but was stricken with illness. He was then captured by Henry II of Castile and held as a prisoner until Joanna was obliged to ransom him. He returned to Naples, but only briefly, before setting off again for another attempt at his restoration, but defeated again, he fled to Castile, where he died at Soria in January 1375.

Still apparently not tired at the thought of marriage, Joanna gamely tried yet again, marrying her fourth husband in 1376. To be fair to her, she was still without an heir, and was trying to solve this problem for her country. She had tried to arrange the marriage of her niece Margaret of Durazzo to her first cousin Charles of Durazzo, but the proposed match met with strong opposition. Joanna was determined to undermine Charles's position as her potential heir by producing a healthy child of her own, so her fourth choice was Otto, the Duke of Brunswick and Grubenhagen, who had earlier defended her rights in Piedmont. Although Otto was only to be a prince-consort, the union was bound to offend Charles of Durazzo, who saw the kingdom as his by right of inheritance, and he approached Joanna's old enemy Louis the Great of Hungary.

During this time, the Western Schism developed, resulting in the election of two popes, Urban VI (Bartolomeo Prignano) in Rome, and Clement VII (Cardinal Robert of Geneva) who reigned in Avignon. Urban VI was a supporter of the enemies of Joanna, so she naturally gave her support to Clement in Avignon. In May of 1380 Urban then declared her to be a heretic and her kingdom forfeit, officially taking it from her control and bestowing it on none other than Charles of Durazzo.

In exchange for assistance, Joanna countered this by adopting Louis I of Anjou as her heir. This prompted Charles of Durazzo to invade Naples in November of 1380 leading an army composed largely of Hungarian troops. The designated heir, Louis, did not intervene quickly enough, and Joanna had to entrust Otto with the defence of Naples, but he had very few troops at his disposal, and Charles was able to enter Naples and besiege Joanna at Castel Nuovo. Without adequate help she had no choice but to surrender and was captured and imprisoned, firstly at Castel dell'Ovo and later in the fortress of Nocera.

Joanna's captivity was extremely unpleasant, being under the supervision of the Hungarians, particularly one Palamede Bozzuto, who had been appointed by Charles. Bozzuto treated her brutally, despising her for her support of Pope Clement. She was given poor food which could be denied to her altogether at the whim of her tormentor, and only had one lady to attend her, with three servants. Even the rings she wore on her fingers were forcibly taken from her.

Louis of Anjou, still officially her heir, finally moved at the head of a large army, intending to mount a rescue of the queen. He passed through Turin and Milan, and by September of 1352 he was close to Rome – but unknown to him he was too late, and Joanna was already dead.[25] She had been moved to the fortress of San Fele near to Muro Lucarno, and was killed there on 27 July 1382. She was fifty-four years old. Charles of Durazzo inevitably claimed that her death was natural, but he was not believed. Sources unanimously claimed that the queen had been murdered. Thomas of Niem, the secretary to Pope Urban, stated that she had been cruelly strangled while kneeling at her prayers. Marie of Blois, the wife of Joanna's heir Louis of Anjou, claimed that the queen had been bound hand and foot before being smothered between two mattresses. Other sources said that she was smothered with pillows. Her body was taken to Naples, where it was put on display for several days as proof that she was dead.

She had been excommunicated by Pope Urban (though not by Pope Clement) so she could not receive Christian burial. This caused problems and it was reported that her body was eventually thrown into a deep well in the grounds of the Santa Chiara Church, where her remains were to lie for centuries. It was a disgraceful end for a queen, given that when she was excommunicated by Urban there had been two popes who did not agree on the ban and were in opposition to each other. It is anyone's guess, even now, which was the 'legal or rightful' one, or even which was the more worthy man.[26]

As with the ill treatment and violence the woman had had to suffer, which was clandestine and remote in location, her murder was taken for granted. There seemed to be no reprisals ever sought and nobody was ever held to account for it, despite her royal status. She had always been a religious woman, yet had died brutally and without any of the consolations of the church she had always supported. She was denied any form of funeral and her remains were treated with appalling disrespect considering her position. For this, Pope Urban has to take responsibility, as it was certainly well within his power to lift the ban he had placed her under. The excommunication had been made for political rather than religious reasons and once she became a prisoner she had the right to expect to be able to receive religious consolation, and for the sacraments to be available to her at her death. Pope Urban chose not to allow her these privileges.

Two months after she was killed, Louis of Anjou invaded the kingdom. He finally fought Charles at Benevento in 1383 and eventually the kingdom would be split, with Charles ruling from the capital, and Louis ruling from Apulia. Louis the Great died only a couple of months after Joanna was murdered, leaving a ten-year-old daughter, Maria, as Queen. Charles of Durazzo returned to Hungary, always with an eye to the main chance, and with his usual disregard for the niceties he took the throne from the young heiress and had himself crowned King of Hungary in 1385. Some kind of justice was served. He was only able to reign there for thirty-nine days, being assassinated at the order of Louis' widowed queen, Elizabeth.

There is still no monument to Queen Joanna of Naples at the Church of Santa Chiara, as the ban placed on her by Pope Urban VI (himself a disputed pope) was never lifted.[27] It seems to be a most unfitting end for a queen, venal or not. She was a woman who held together a large dominion, from Provence to Italy, which was to fracture after her death. Despite the calumnies attached to her name, she had never failed to care for the poor and the sick, and had built hospitals and churches, protected trade and promoted peace. She had ruled for thirty years in a time of great turmoil, when plague and famine blighted the second half of the fourteenth century, and she certainly deserved better than she received. She has the right to be remembered as the last great sovereign of the Angevin tradition.[28]

Pope Clement VII of Avignon (1378–1417), who owed his position to Joanna's support of him, praised her publicly.

Of all the illustrious women of this world, Joanna, radiant rose among thorns, enfolded us, the whole Roman church and her subjects, in an amazingly sweet scent. She passed on from the misery of this world to the Beatitude of God's kingdom, where she lives and reigns, and where, despising and mocking her adversaries, she recovers the sceptre that has been taken from her hands, and receives her crown among the saint martyrs.

Enea Silvio Piccolomini

Enea Silvio Piccolomini was born in 1435, one of the eighteen children of an old Sienese family. He was initially secretary to the cardinals attending the Council of Basel, and was sent on a mission to Scotland to persuade King James I to invade England. His journey, particularly the sea voyage, was so fraught with difficulties that he vowed he would walk barefoot to the nearest shrine of the Virgin, if he survived it.

When the storms abated, he was relieved to find that the nearest shrine was only a few miles away. He duly trudged from Dunbar to Whitekirk to fulfil his vow, but found that he quickly lost all sensation in his feet. This gradually returned, but from then on he was to suffer from severe arthritis for the remainder of his life. To the English, it may have seemed to be a fitting punishment, not only for his interference in their affairs, but also for his less than flattering remarks about them, which he would put down in his later Commentaries:

Their cities have no walls, the houses are usually constructed without mortar, and the roofs are covered with turf. In the country doors are covered only with ox hides. The common people, who are poor and rude, stuff themselves with meat and fish, and only eat bread as a luxury. The men are short and brave, and the women are fair and charming, and very easily won! Women think less of a kiss than in Italy they would of the touch of a hand ... there is nothing the Scottish like better to hear, than some abuse of the English.

If that were indeed the case, he certainly gave them plenty to go on, for after travelling into England he continued to write his opinions of his hosts:

After knocking at the door of a farmhouse, I had dinner there with the host and the parish priest. Many relishes and chickens and geese were served, but no bread or wine. All the men and women of the village came running to see the strange sight, as one would marvel at Ethiopians or Indians, and so they gazed at us in amazement, asking where we came from and whether we were Christians.

When the meal ended, the host and the priest went away, saying they were taking refuge in a tower some way off, for fear of the Scots, 'who when the river was at a low ebb, often crossed at night to make raids on them'. He besought the men to stay, but the women thought that the enemy could do them no wrong, 'for they do not count being outraged as a wrong.'

After some time had passed, two young women showed him to a chamber 'strewn with straw' and showed plainly 'that they planned to sleep' with him. He claimed he 'repulsed the protesting girls ... and remained alone among the heifers and goats.'[29]

If he refused the girls on that occasion, he did not always do so. He was then a layman and along with some other literary gifts he had a talent for writing erotic poetry and pornographic stories, one of which became the best-selling book of the fifteenth century, known as *The Tale of the Two Lovers*, which he wrote in 1444. It is full of erotic imagery and centres around a married woman and a servant of the Duke of Austria (Lucretia and Euryalus). Euryalus at one point exclaimed 'Love conquers all, let us yield to love!'

The author of that work certainly followed his own advice, and spent his early and middle years fathering several bastards.

In his 'secret memoirs' Piccolomini was to mention a lover named Elizabeth, who was a Breton. He was not merely a bewildered young man at that time, but a career diplomat of almost forty years of age. She was married, but he 'begged her for three days to sleep with him' until she relented.

He was later overjoyed to hear that she had conceived their son, and he wrote with delight to his father telling him the news. Unfortunately, his father was less enthusiastic to have to welcome another illegitimate child into the family, and Enea wrote to him again, protesting his natural pleasure at the event.

> You write that you do not know whether to be glad or sorry that the Lord has given me a child. I see only cause for gladness and none for sorrow. For what is sweeter to mankind than to beget in one's likeness and continue one's stock? What on earth is more blessed than to see your children's children? For my part, I am delighted that my seed had borne fruit, and some part of me will survive when I die. I thank God who has made this woman's child a boy, so that another little Enea will play about my father and mother and give his grandparents the comfort that his father should have supplied. For if my birth was a pleasure to you, who begat me, why should my son not be a pleasure to me? Perhaps you will say it is my offence that you mourn, because I begot this child in sin? I do not know what idea you have of me. Certainly you, who are also flesh, did not beget a son made of stone or iron. You know what a cock you were and I am also no eunuch, nor to be put in the category of cold-blooded. Nor yet am I a hypocrite, who wants to be seen as better than I am. I confess my error, for I am no holier than David the King, nor wiser than Solomon.[30]

The remark that Piccolomini's father would 'know' the child, suggests that he would be brought up by his grandparents. One wonders what happened to the mother in this, as her husband surely cannot have shared the joy of her lover at the birth of a bastard child? Unfortunately, she receives no further mention, as if the proof of Piccolomini's virility is enough in itself, and the woman who shared his indiscretion was of no importance.

Piccolomini was unrestrained in his writing but it is still extraordinary that he would send to his parents such a letter when he was busy working his way towards a career in the church. He and other writers frequently quarrelled among themselves, accusing one another of being homosexuals. The historian Gregorovius estimated that Piccolomini fathered twelve illegitimate children in all.[31]

In later life he claimed to be reformed, but he was never a happy celibate. He only too quickly referred to his lecherous youth, not only with pleasure, but with regret at its loss. He was ordained in 1446, became Bishop of Trieste in 1447, and Bishop of Siena in 1450. He was made a Cardinal in 1456, such is the speed of advancement when one befriends a pope, in this case Eugenius IV. In 1458 Piccolomini was elected to the papacy, becoming Pope Pius II.

He still kept his eye on the ladies, becoming enamoured of Queen Charlotte of Cyprus who went to Rome to beg him to help her when she lost her throne to her illegitimate half-brother. In his memoirs he speaks of her 'sparkling eyes' and her colouring, which he describes as being 'somewhere between blonde and brunette', far more than he does of her political problems. He said that she was 'not without charms' and recounted that she had kissed his feet 'very lovingly'. He certainly denied her nothing when she resided in Rome, and gave her first the Convertendi Palace in Trastavere, then later a large house in the Piazza Scossacavalli. Though there is no evidence that they became lovers, the Pope's descriptions of her, always flattering and fulsome, show clearly that he was smitten. She was to die in Rome in 1487 and her funeral was paid for by Innocent VIII. She was buried in St Peter's Basilica in the Chapel of St Andrew and St Gregory.

Pope Pius II, Piccolomini, wrote that 'matrimony had been forbidden to priests for good reasons, but there were much better reasons to restore it! ... it is much better for priests to marry, for many would be saved by the conjugal state...' He also said that Rome was the only city in the world to be run by bastards, and he should know.[32]

He tried, and failed, to organise a crusade, and earned something of a reputation as a humanist owing to his apparent opposition to slavery, but his opposition to that state was only in respect of the slaves who had been newly baptised as Christians. He wrote an exhaustive refutation of Islam, essays on the care of horses, some descriptions of Europe and Asia, along with a large quantity of speeches and letters. His main claim to fame still rests on his Commentaries, an erotic comedy named Chrysis, and his salacious novel 'The Story of Two Lovers' which seem to be rather unsuitable subjects upon which to base the literary output of a Pope. He died in 1464 after a reign of only six years.

Queen Catherine of Bosnia

Queen Catherine was the wife of King Stephen Thomas, married in 1446. They had two children, a son Sigismund, and a daughter Catherine. She also had stepchildren, particularly the heir Stephen Tomesevic, with whom she did not get on well. Her husband died in 1461 and she became Dowager Queen. She had converted to Catholicism from the (heretical) Bosnian Church during her marriage and had built many churches.

The relationship with Stephen, the new king, continued to be poor and caused internal strife, which was a greater problem as the country was already greatly weakened by Ottoman advances. This caused Stephen to settle his differences with her, giving her the Dowager's rights. Catherine's own brother argued with their father and brought in the Turks for support, and Mehmet the Conqueror moved into Bosnia to take over control. The royal family was obliged to flee, and Catherine's children were both captured and forced to become Muslims, while Catherine herself and King Stephen's wife Maria managed to escape, but King Stephen was caught and executed.

In 1467 Catherine sailed to Italy, where Pope Paul II granted her a pension. She tried, and repeatedly failed, to get back her children, and the Pope did his best to support her in her despair. He eventually moved her to a house near San Marco Evangelista di Campidoglio and encouraged her gradually to take back her life. She eventually became prominent in Roman society, without ever giving up hope that her family would be reunited. The later Pope,

Sixtus IV, would eventually give her a large property close to the Tiber to be her home for her lifetime.

The papacy of this period took very seriously the responsibility it held towards royal persons who had converted to Catholicism, and suffered as a result. It was to provide safety and a home in Rome for several of Europe's royalties, and their followers, over the centuries, and many of these people behaved without gratitude in response to what often proved to be a very long lasting and expensive support network.

Queen Catherine was to finally have an entourage of forty knights who accompanied her to St Peter's Basilica to celebrate the New Year of 1475. She enlisted the help of Ludovico Gonzaga, Marquis of Mantua, to negotiate with the Sublime Porte, in an attempt to get back her children and also asked for help over time from Galeazzo Maria Sforza, the Duke of Milan. All the negotiations came to nothing, as her children had been brought up in a different religion and another culture and had been married abroad. Even had she managed to see them, they would not have known her. She was never to meet them again.

In 1478 she made vows and took minor Franciscan Orders, then made her will and expressed a wish to be buried by the altar of Santa Maria in Aracoeli in Rome. She named Pope Sixtus and his successors as guardians of the Bosnian crown and was buried as requested, though her tombstone was moved in 1590 from the floor before the altar to a position on the wall, where it remains.[33]

Queen Charlotte of Cyprus

Queen Charlotte was the daughter of John II of Cyprus and succeeded to the throne at his death in 1458, aged only fourteen years. She was crowned at St Sophia Cathedral in October 1458. Her right to her throne would be challenged by her illegitimate half-brother James, and she never had more than a tenuous hold over her kingdom, owing to his opposition and influence. She became Princess of Antioch in 1456 (the same year in which she married her first husband, when she was only twelve years old). Her father had chosen for her husband John of Portugal, but their marriage lasted for only a year before John died. Her second husband, Louis of Savoy, Count of Geneva, married her in 1457, a union which had been arranged by the Genoese, who promised her assistance against her usurper half-brother James.

In 1460 James captured Famagusta and Nicosia with the help of Egypt and Charlotte and her husband Louis were blockaded at Kyrenia for three years before being able to escape and fleeing to Rome in 1463. James was then formally crowned King of Cyprus.

In Rome, Charlotte would live under the affectionate protection of Pope Pius II, who described her as 'a woman of twenty-four, middle height, bright eyes, complexion between dark and fair, with smooth speech which flows like a torrent, after the manner of the Greeks. She wears French costume, and has delicate manners, becoming her royal blood.' Her first language was indeed Greek, but she could also write in French and Italian, and passably in Latin. She was bright, attractive, and outspoken.

In Rome she formed a small Greek court, and later, with papal help, would move to Rhodes to try to regain her kingdom of Cyprus. In November 1483 she would again be received at the Vatican by Pope Sixtus IV and would be 'seated at an equal height and dignity' with him. She lived for a time at a house on the Piazza Scossacavalli in the Borgo, which the Vatican had previously made available to Queen Catherine of Bosnia.

During her exile, she adopted a son, Alfonso of Aragon, who was an illegitimate child of Ferdinand II of Naples. In 1485 she ceded her claim to her cousin's son, Charles I of Savoy, who was next in line of succession, in exchange for an annual pension of 4,300 florins. She died in Rome on the 16 July 1487 aged only forty-three and was buried in St Peter's, with her funeral expenses being paid for by Pope Innocent VIII.[34]

Pope Paul II

Pietro Barbo, Paul II, was to follow Pius II. He would prove to be an extremely vain man, fond of ceremony and public show. He prided himself of possessing little culture, yet his real achievement was the building of the Palazzo Venezia in Rome.

To indulge his love of lavish spectacle, he decreed that Jubilee Years should be held every twenty-five years rather than every half century, so that he could enjoy one. He had what amounted to a mania for collecting beautiful things, including handsome young men.

He was to abolish the College of Secretaries attached to the Vice-Chancellery, and suppressed the Roman Academy, forbidding Roman children to study Pagan poets, fearing that the classics would corrupt them.[35] He attempted to pacify the King of Bohemia, with whom Pius II had quarrelled, but failed there too, and ended by having to excommunicate him and trying to persuade the King of Hungary to go to war with him.

He believed himself to be extraordinarily handsome (though his extant portraits do not confirm that), and enjoyed parties and admiration. He was to become a famous promoter of sports and carnivals, so long as Rome's Jewish community could be persuaded to pay for his indulgences. He was to have a papal tiara made for himself, which was said to 'outweigh a palace in its worth' being covered in multi-coloured jewels of great worth. His cardinals would begin to refer to him, rather contemptuously, as 'Our Lady of Pity' owing to his ability to burst into tears at the least provocation. He would use this easy facility of tears as a weapon, and a means of getting his own way when opposed or he thought he was losing an argument.

He was a nephew of Pope Eugenius IV and had originally been trained to be a merchant, but at his uncle's election changed his career. His extravagant generosity made him popular with those who befriended him, and when he was standing for election as pope he said he would buy a villa for every cardinal who voted for him, to escape the summer heat of the city. When he did become pope, he intended to be named Pope Formosus, which meant 'handsome' but was persuaded against it. He was eager to appoint new cardinals to strengthen his power base, but liked to create them *in pectore* (without publicly revealing their names), which became one of several areas of contention with the College of Cardinals.[36]

After his death, his successor Pope Sixtus IV, and a group of cardinals inspected his treasure trove, and found 300,000 ducats'-worth of pearls, plus gold and jewels worth another 300,000 ducats. There was also a diamond that alone was worth 7,000 ducats. He died in 1471, aged fifty-four years, in slightly suspicious circumstances. After a day when he seemed perfectly well, he retired to bed. His chamberlain later went in, only to find the Pope foaming at the mouth. He rushed off to find help, and when he returned the Pope was dead. Some believed that he had had a stroke, some said a heart attack, while others blamed everything from his inordinate love of melons to his exertions with one of his male lovers. It had been a reign full of contradictions, show and spectacle, but without any real substance.[37]

Sixtus IV

Francesco della Rovere became Pope in 1471 and was a noted patron of the arts, who would build the Sistine Chapel and create the Vatican Archives. Unfortunately, he was also notable for his nepotism and Stefano Infessura would say of him that 'he was another lover of boys, and sodomites, who awarded bishoprics and nominated cardinals, in exchange for the sexual favours of handsome young men.'[38]

He did create an unusually large number of new cardinals, nominating twenty-three during his pontificate. This built the usual solid power base of supporters, with the intention that they could continue his policies after his death. Two of these protégés would also become popes – Giuliano della Rovere as Julius II and Battista Cibo as Innocent VIII.

None of these rather sadly scandalous and largely ineffectual men who ruled during the early part of the Renaissance would be able to compete in determination or lasting fame, with a girl child who was born in 1463. She would become a woman of high intelligence, an enquiring and logical mind, and an unfailing courage, and would earn both affection and respect. She would prove to be a capable commander and a worthy adversary, whose life would touch the lives of popes, and would place her as a friend, and later as a fierce opponent, of the Vatican. She would be remembered in a way that most of her male contemporaries, always eager for glory, would greatly envy. Though she started life merely as an illegitimate daughter of the great House of Sforza, she would become its most famous ambassador.

The Tigress: Caterina Sforza

Caterina was born in Milan in 1463, the illegitimate daughter of Galeazzo Maria Sforza, heir to the Duchy, and his mistress Lucrezia Landriani, who was married to one of his courtiers. He was the always-useful compliant husband, as Lucrezia and Galeazzo Sforza had at least four children together. Galeazzo was known to be a womaniser, and had had two wives plus several mistresses over the years, so he had several 'families' to provide for. He was known also to have a cruel streak, and had made many enemies. He was reputed to take some pleasure in devising tortures for those who offended him.

However, Caterina would always be very proud of her bloodline and shared her father's determination and courage. She kept the Sforza name all her life, despite having three husbands of her own, and would have agreed with her fearsome sire that all children were of value to an important family, whether legitimate or not. Her mother continued to take an interest in her, and was watchful during the crucial moments of her daughter's life even during her final years; but Caterina's all-important education was in the hands of her father's family and she was raised amidst the refinement and luxury of the Milanese court.

Caterina grew up bold, with a desire from the earliest age to be 'her own person'. She became a quick and forceful child, with an enquiring mind, and had the usual love of hunting and dancing, those amusements of the aristocracy, but her interests would also stretch to include alchemy, which was a rather more unusual occupation for a female scion.

The Sforza family had risen to nobility and power through the sword, the only way in a clutch of separate principalities that struggled against each other in medieval Italy.[1] By the late fifteenth century many of the leading families had lost power. In Rome, for example, the continual struggles had left two families at the top of the heap, always watchful to establish their own control: the Colonna, who were acolytes of the Emperor Charles V, and the Orsini, who were close allies of the de' Medici family of Florence. Caterina's father, Galeazzo Maria, continued his father Francesco's municipal development, as well as holding firmly onto power during his ten-year reign. Milan under Francesco had set up one of the first printing presses, and made other sophisticated technological advances. It also kept up its fertile farmlands and produced everything from silks to armour, to service both the luxury and military trades, which existed side by side.[2]

When Galeazzo took over Milan, Caterina was three years old. Together with the rest of her father's court she went to live in the castle of Porta Giovia where she enjoyed not only luxury but a first-class education, growing up alongside the Duke's legitimate children. There was little difference between the education of the male and female children, and she would learn Latin and would eventually have access to the famous ducal library, containing over a thousand books, many of which were illuminated and of great value.

She read Boccaccio's *Illustrious Women*, who ranged from Eve to Joanna of Sicily. This Queen was reputed to have employed Caterina's great-grandfather Muzio Attendolo as a bodyguard, but was also said to have added him to her list of lovers.[3] Caterina, in her protected childhood, cannot have imagined that she, too, would merit inclusion into books about uncommonly capable, even warlike, women.

The Sforza's emphasised the training of their female children in use of weapons and in riding, not only for pleasure and for hunting. Caterina's contemporary in Spain, Isabella of Castile, would have had a similar upbringing, and this gave the girls an advantage in adulthood, when the problems of living in a war-torn society would surround them. To the Sforzas, the young women they raised would need every skill, including control of their emotions, fearlessness, discipline, and patience, alongside the usual literary and feminine ones.

Fifteenth-century Milan was already a centre for the most luxurious goods, clothing and jewellery, as well as more practical needs such as weapons. Here men such as Tommaso Missaglia could develop new designs to improve freedom of movement in armour while fighting, and include new ways of protecting the wearer from developments in firearms. The other side of the city's fame was in producing the most exquisite silk brocades, and the distinctive 'dagging' of the edges and hems of clothing. This was first used in Milan, and became almost an art form there. Caterina would become known not only for her natural beauty, but also for her fashionable style, her elegance, and this in a court already filled with beautiful and stylish women.

Her first experience of state visits would come in 1471, when the Milanese court made a journey to Florence, to see Lorenzo de' Medici. The trip was designed to impress and so much was spent on clothing that onlookers were dazzled.[4] Lorenzo (known as The Magnificent) was not a king, nor even a duke, but he lived as one. His home boasted an even larger library than the Sforzas owned, and he kept scholars in his household. The friendship between the Sforza and de' Medici families healed a rift from a century earlier, and the visitors were welcomed, but the Medici household also had sumptuary laws, prohibiting the spending of too much money on finery. Florence preferred to spend its undoubted wealth in the streets, where great buildings were being erected, and on life-sized sculptures, which were intended to make more lasting memorials. They also produced entertainments, such as Mystery Plays, where children could dress as angels and flew through the air. If the Sforzas had expected to outshine the Medici with their extravagant clothing, the Medici managed to surprise them with their own achievements and privately considered the Milanese to be wasteful.[5]

Caterina's childhood came to an end in her tenth year, when, after returning from a visit to Florence, Galeazzo Maria contracted smallpox and became very ill. All his heirs were still children, and his wife Bona prepared herself to be Regent for her son, taking immediate action to protect the dukedom for the heir, Gian Galeazzo, who was only two years old. She wrote to her brother-in-law Louis XI of France, requesting his support.[6]

But the precautions proved premature, for despite all expectations, Galeazzo recovered. He then embarked on a transformation for

Milan, intending that it should be able to compete with other courts, in art, architecture, and especially in music. Printing was fostered in an effort to catch up with the intellectual ambience of Florence. Galeazzo had also seen the Gonzaga castle in Mantua on his journeys, and realised that a defensive building could also be magnificent. In 1472 he started the cycle of decorative paintings in Porta Giovia and his great hall was to have hunting scenes including family portraits. Another ambition was to create the finest choir in Europe and he sent for the best musicians and singers. He even lured a few away from the King of Naples, which left Ferdinand *cum la bocca molto amara*, with a bitter taste in his mouth.

He also began certain political actions that would later reverberate in Caterina's own life.[7] In Romagna, the small fiefdom of Imola had been in a state of unrest, with revolts against the ruling Manfredi family. Imola was in a strategic position between north and south and had fertile and productive farms. It had also been ruled by the Milanese and by the Pope, but at that time both Venice and Florence wanted it. Galeazzo Sforza took Imola by force in 1471, adding it to his own territory and ousting the Manfredi. Many other rulers expressed their outrage at the bold move, including Lorenzo the Magnificent.

Pope Paul had died, and the new Pope was Sixtus IV. His election had been supported by the Duke of Milan, and Sixtus showed himself to be friendly. The Sforza had planned an extravagant Christmas celebration, inviting Ludovico Gonzaga of Mantua, Pino Ordelaffi of Forli, Giovanni Bentivoglio of Bologna and the new Pope's rather dissolute nephew Girolamo Riario, who was Count of Bosco. Riario was then thirty years old, the son of the Pope's sister Bianca, by a lowly born man. Many looked down on Riario's lineage, and it was true that he had only been a customs officer until his uncle became pope.

Once that happened, he suddenly became a captain in the papal army. Machiavelli would later claim that 'he sprang from a very vile and base condition.'[8] Whatever he was, he might be useful and Duke Galeazzo planned to betroth him to the eleven-year-old Constanzia Fogliani, the daughter of his uncle Corrado Fogliani and Gabriella Gonzaga.

Gabriella, who had originally been in favour of the match, changed her mind when Riario arrived, because he demanded an immediate sexual union with Constanzia, once the betrothal was confirmed. Gabriella insisted that he would have to wait until the girl was fifteen, another four years, and negotiations were begun to try to find some compromise.[9] The actual physical consummation of the match was considered necessary in many cases to make the marriage fully legal, and prevent one of the parties having a change of mind. Gabriella finally allowed Constanzia to be 'put to bed' with Riario, without any actual sexual contact, but in front of witnesses, in order to make the betrothal secure. This was not satisfactory to all parties and eventually Galeazzo offered his own daughter, Caterina, to be Riario's bride, despite her being only ten years old to his thirty. The marriage contract was formalised on 17 January 1473 and Galeazzo made no demur at the idea of his daughter losing her virginity at such a young age. Caterina's own opinion was not asked for. A week later the Duke reported that 'Count Girolamo leaves this morning to return to his Holiness the Pope ... he slept with his wife again, and is very happy and content.'[10]

The Pope felt obliged to issue a Papal Bull to deal with the matter of the bride being so much under the legal age for marriage, but everyone else seemed far more concerned with her dowry of 10,000 ducats. Expensive wedding gifts of gowns and brocades sewn with pearls were given to Caterina by Riario. They had been intended for Constanzia but that no longer mattered, once he and Caterina were legally married. Of course, the real key to all the rush, and the bridegroom's determination that the marriage should never be overturned, was not the immature person of the bride, or even her dowry, but Imola. The bridegroom's brother, Cardinal Pietro Riario, a charming, worldly man and very successful with women, was delighted to be able to purchase Imola for Milan for the sum of only 40,000 ducats, and Girolamo became Count of Imola. The Cardinal was to die shortly afterwards, aged only twenty-seven, and Girolamo was quickly able to claim his huge fortune too, as well as his position at the papal court. The new Countess of Imola, by then aged eleven, was sent away to grow up. She did not see her husband again for three years.

She spent that time at her father's court, continuing her studies. She heard nothing of her husband during that time, but he had been busy with several mistresses and had sired a son (obviously illegitimate) named Scipione. He did not bother to visit Imola, but he did begin to make enemies. In Milan, also, the Duke was alienating his allies. He had not called a council meeting for twenty-five years and when he did it was only to demand money to fund his extravagant lifestyle. He had once boasted that his 'greatest sin was lust', hence the several 'families' of children he was obliged to provide for. In 1474 he became infatuated by Lucia Marliani, who was nineteen years old. She was already married to a man named Raverti, a merchant, who happily accepted 4,000 ducats to step aside and Lucia was then given a house, and an annual allowance. The Duke's only stipulation was that Lucia should 'not have any carnal bond with any other person', which included her husband.[11]

By 1475, Lucia had been made into a countess, and any idea of trying to keep the Duke's infatuation a secret was then pointless. Apart from her allowance, she received many valuable gifts, and he once even paid 12,000 ducats for one brooch for her. The people were becoming restive due to the Duke's increasingly despotic behaviour, and by Christmas his death was being plotted. The conspirators were praying for help in ridding Milan of the tyrant, and Andrea Lampugnano, Carlo Visconti and Girolamo Olgiati hoped that after the Duke was dead all their debts would be cleared – a common fallacy to expect things to prosper after an assassination. Visconti's involvement in the plot was a surprise, as he was the ducal chancellor and a member of the council. However, he wanted to avenge the Duke's seduction of his sister, and the subsequent loss of family honour.

On 26 December Bona asked her husband not to attend Mass at the church of St Stephen, but he ignored her plea and also refused to wear his steel breastplate under his clothing. At the church, Andrea Lampugnano approached the Duke as if he were a petitioner, but then plunged his dagger into the Duke's chest. The assassins then landed fourteen more stabbing blows and Galeazzo Maria Sforza was dead, aged only thirty-two.

If the plotters had imagined that Milan would support them, they were wrong. Lampugnano was found hiding and immediately killed. Visconti was handed over to the authorities by his disgusted family and Olgiati was captured quickly. They were all publicly quartered. Gian Galeazzo became Duke at only six years old, with his mother as Regent. She rapidly became a competent, even fearsome, head of state, which was a lesson that Caterina was not likely to forget.[12]

The widow was concerned for the Duke's stained soul and asked Pope Sixtus to absolve him, which he did, when Bona repaid the sums that Galeazzo had extorted. The Pope also noticed that Caterina, by then thirteen years old, was ready to join her husband in Rome. The legality of her marriage was again confirmed, but just to be safe, another proxy wedding was carried out.[13]

She was still very young and must have felt keenly the separation from her family and friends. She wrote letters to her stepmother and stepsisters admitting to homesickness, but Bona had already done all she could to provide for her stepdaughter's comfort and health. Caterina had a large entourage providing a magnificent parade, with towns on the route warned to give her a proper welcome. She entered Imola wearing a splendid gold brocade dress, embroidered with thousands of tiny pearls. She also wore a black silk coat, trimmed with jewels.[14]

Life at that stage must have seemed to her to be a long celebration, filled with feasts and gifts, but Imola itself was poor and rustic in comparison with Milan. Bona was delighted to hear that Caterina was welcomed, but she was concerned to hear about Taddeo Manfredi, who had been Lord of Imola in 1471, but whose grip had slipped and Galeazzo Maria had ousted him. It had been done in a gentle and courteous manner, but Manfredi was still living in Milanese territory with his son, and would always be a concern in case troublemakers tried to reinstate him.

Another problem was that Girolamo Riario had made many enemies, with the most powerful of these being another nephew of Pope Sixtus, his cousin Cardinal Giuliano della Rovere.[15] The papal court had previously advised Bona that there might be an attempt on Girolamo's life, and two men were actually arrested who claimed they had been recruited by Cardinal della Rovere.

The Pontiff changed the Riario bodyguard and kept Caterina outside Rome, suggesting that she should remain at Imola until the weather cooled, but either she was too impatient, or possibly the letter did not arrive in time. She set off for Rome, arriving there to receive further celebrations and gifts; it was by then four years since she had seen her husband.

After yet another marriage ceremony, performed by the Pope himself, Caterina and Girolamo moved into their home on the

Campo di Fiori, a residence described as 'an earthly paradise' by the Milanese Ambassador. Even Caterina, accustomed to her father's splendid court, was dazzled by the luxury of Rome. In her turn, she had generated goodwill and her influence was already at work, resulting in a cardinal's hat for her twenty-two year old uncle, Ascanio Sforza.

Rome's great wealth was not created by the production of any crops, or even luxury goods. It rested entirely on the tourist trade where the pilgrims centred on the papal court. The home in the Campo di Fiori was in a busy marketplace while Rome's other huge market was then in the Piazza Navona, only a short distance away. The Via Mercatoria, which stretched through the banking centre by the River Tiber, through the Fiori to the Piazza Venezia, was the flourishing commercial centre of the city. The Pope had had the area cleared and cleaned to help business and create confidence in his control of the city, despite the number of private armies still in existence and the need for bodyguards when travelling. However, the Ponte Sisto had recently been built, the first bridge across the Tiber since ancient times,[16] which allowed easier access to the countryside on the Janiculum Hill, where Caterina could hunt or ride in peace.

After twenty-six months of being with her husband, she had her first child Bianca in 1478. She would have six children with Girolamo – Ottaviano was born in 1479, Cesare in 1480, Giovanni Livio born at Forli in 1484, and Galeazzo Maria also born at Forli in 1485. During these years Caterina established her position as a great lady, an intermediary, able to request promotions but also attending to her family. As sister of a Duke by birth and niece of a pope by marriage, she was an important person and these were busy years for her and for her husband; and Girolamo had his own plots and schemes, which developed his hatred for the de' Medici family. They had been papal bankers, but after refusing a loan to the Pope, had lost their position to the Pazzi family. The Medici also became an obstacle for Girolamo, who wanted to found a state in Romagna, by providing troops to resist his mercenaries. The Pazzi naturally sided with Girolamo in the hope that he would help them to eliminate their rivals, the Medici. That, of course, assumed that Riario influence could not long survive the death of the then Pope.

In 1478 the plot was completed, and the Pazzi intended to assassinate the two Medici brothers in Florence. Girolamo would gather an army in Imola to prevent anyone resisting the Pazzi ruling in their place, and the Pope had already confirmed that he 'did not want the death of anyone, merely a change of government in Florence'. He described the Medici brothers, Lorenzo and Giuliano, as 'villains who have treated us badly', no doubt still smarting about the refused loan. Girolamo was convinced that the Pope would forgive whatever steps he took, but this arrogance angered the Pope, who called his nephew 'a beast'. However, Girolamo felt secure and his plotting continued.[17]

The first attempt on the lives of Lorenzo and Giuliano de' Medici was postponed when Giuliano became ill and not easily reached. When he recovered, he and Lorenzo were attacked in the Cathedral in Florence, during Mass, when Giuliano sustained a sword blow to his head and nineteen other stab wounds. Lorenzo escaped with minor injuries. The attack did not cause the Florentines to rise up against the Medici family as the plotters had hoped. On the contrary, the citizens organised a hunt for the attackers, and anyone else who might be involved, with the killers being immediately executed. The bodies were hung in the public squares and even sixteen-year old Cardinal Raffaelo Riario was seized, and kept as 'a quest' to forestall any reprisals in Rome against Florentines after the executions. This was a very serious matter, as one of the victims of the purge had been the Archbishop of Pisa.[18]

Caterina had always held Lorenzo de' Medici in high esteem and it is unlikely that she would have been a party to the Pazzi conspiracy alongside her inept husband. Rome had begun to regard Girolamo Riario with both amusement and contempt and it may be that Caterina also realised what manner of man she was bound to for life. However, her duties were clear. She was to continue producing the next generation of Riario children and trying to support her difficult husband, at least outwardly, despite her extreme youth. She was certainly successful with her primary duty and her children were born in rapid succession. Her first son Ottaviano had Cardinal Rodrigo Borgia as a godfather, and he was a pushy man, determined to advance his own career. He had amassed an enormous amount of money and had built a splendid palace to set off his treasures, and would be connected with Caterina's life from then onwards.

She was fortunate in having her children while she was young and strong. Breastfeeding was discouraged for noble women, as it had a certain contraceptive effect. Handing one's babies over to wet nurses to be fed meant that the mother could hopefully conceive again quickly. Of course, this constant childbearing before the mother had fully recovered her strength took its toll, with death in childbirth, or just after it, being one of the major hazards of a woman's life. It was also responsible for many miscarriages, when the mother, worn out by pregnancies, found that she had difficulty in carrying further children to term.[19]

The new Riario Palace was nearing completion and was one of Caterina's many responsibilities. Situated close by the Piazza Navona, it would later be known as the Palazzo della Cancelleria.[20] Though this property was in the heart of the Campus Martius, it had pleasant apartments on the upper floors and a very gracious internal courtyard, as well as a garden offering fresh air and foliage to aid relaxation.

In early 1480 Pope Sixtus IV announced plans to restore Rome's grandeur, as the city had suffered neglect since the popes had moved to Avignon in the fourteenth century. Water was bad, buildings were in disrepair, even the churches were shabby and disease was rife. When the papacy returned to Rome in 1417 it became a very slow process trying to put things right. The vital *Acqua Vergine*, the thirteen-mile water supply, which had been destroyed by invaders in the sixth century, was not rebuilt until Sixtus began his renovations. The Pope conferred his own land holding of Forli to the Riario-Sforza family in 1480, which doubled Girolamo's property. The only cloud seemingly on the horizon was that Caterina's stepmother, Bona of Savoy, had lost her position as Regent and been transferred to the Abbey at Abbiategrasso, which severed Caterina's link with the Sforza court.[21] This forced her to commit herself entirely to the Riario clan, but hostilities with Florence seemed to have come to an end and there was a respite from strife.

The Riario towns of Forli and Imola were separated by Faenza, which was a small area owned by the Manfredi clan. Obviously, connecting the two Riario territories would mean taking possession of Faenza, but the original owners of Forli, the Ordelaffis, were still angry at being deprived of their inheritance. Intrigues and plots began again, despite the townspeople of Forli being happy with the rule of the Riarios. They used Caterina in particular as a guide to the latest fashions and admired her extravagant lifestyle. She made every effort to charm them and socialise with them, but Girolamo kept more aloof and a rift between the couple began to be noticed. Caterina was invited to Milan by Ludovico Sforza, who was the new Regent for her brother, but Girolamo would not allow her to go and was 'not without anger', as she reported. He was becoming suspicious of her, and would not allow her to see her family, despite her being separated from them for several years. But he went to Rome, and Caterina was determined to go to Milan in his absence.

Girolamo's fear was that she would begin to re-identify herself with her family's interests rather than his own. He badly wanted the small area of Faenza but its owners, the Manfredi, had powerful protectors in the Este family of Ferrara. Caterina was already in contact by letters with Eleanora of Aragon, who was the wife of Ercole d'Este, but Lorenzo de' Medici remembered too well the murder of his brother and was fomenting trouble amongst the people of Forli. A conspiracy was put together to murder both Girolamo and Caterina and although this was stopped, Girolamo remained incensed that the people should want to restore the Ordelaffi rulers. The day after the assassination was supposed to have taken place, Girolamo went to Mass at Forli surrounded by 300 soldiers to remind the people that as the Pope's nephew he held power. On his return to Rome he took several of the citizens of Forli with him as hostages. Venice had refused to help him to take Ferrara from the d'Este family but had no compunction in starting a dispute of their own with Ercole d'Este over the control of the vital salt mines.[22]

When a war finally broke out between Venice and Ferrara, Girolamo was summoned to defend Rome and camped outside the city walls. It was said that he avoided endangering himself with actual combat and Caterina, whose family characteristic was boldness in battle, was disappointed with his apparent cowardice. His men were also accused of being disrespectful towards the Cathedral itself, by playing cards and dice there, using the boxes of holy relics as seats, and using obscene language and blaspheming.

The decisive battle of the salt war took place at the Campo Martio in August 1482. After dark 2,000 dead lay on the field and 360 of the enemy's nobles awaited trial in Castel Sant'Angelo. While the battle raged, Girolamo had stayed in safety within his camp, 'to guard the tents', which exposed his lack of personal courage to all of Rome. An armistice was agreed, and the Italian States celebrated a return to peace, but Girolamo was shamed and Caterina was shamed with him.

Although Caterina's marriage was proving unsatisfactory, she was in high favour elsewhere. Contemporaries reported that the Pope was very much attached to her and people began to ask for her help, for it was said that the Pope 'could deny her nothing'.[23] There were even titillating whispers bandied about regarding the Pope's close relationship with his young niece, and it did not help that Sixtus came from a lesser known family, and the status-conscious Romans scorned him for it.[24] He was a self-made man; malicious courtiers would claim that he was the son of a Ligurian fisherman. Like all the popes, noble or not, he was very keen to advance his family, as this provided the essential power base that supported his work, and help to leave behind achievements which would secure the memory of his reign.

He created a library at the Vatican with 3,500 volumes, which Caterina would have appreciated as, unlike many noblewomen, she was a voracious reader interested in many things. Only her regular pregnancies prevented her from hunting and other outdoor pleasures, which obliged her to give her free time to study instead. It was also a time of great painters, such as Botticelli, Perugino, Ghirlandaio and a young Michelangelo, all of whom worked for the Pope. Botticelli may well have used Caterina as a model for one of the Three Graces in his famous painting, *Primavera*.

Girolamo used the relatively peaceful time to extract all the money he could, being aware that the Pope could not live much longer. Girolamo then ruled Rome with his gang of thugs and was aware that who controlled the Castel Sant'Angelo would control Rome, as this stone circle was an impregnable fortress.[25] However, the age-old rivalry between the Colonna and the Orsini families kept Rome on edge. Girolamo believed that he could use their feud to his advantage, but Virgillo Orsini saw him only as a means to bring down his old enemy. In April 1482 supporters of the Orsini, assisted by Girolamo's soldiers, attacked supporters of the Colonna and a Colonna was killed. The Pope tried to restore order, but Girolamo, always warlike, insisted on the arrest of all, including Cardinal Giovanni Colonna, whom he accused of trying to kill him. Sixtus protested, but the Cardinal found himself imprisoned in Sant'Angelo.

All the pleasure had left the Vatican and discord reigned. The Pope was nearing his end and was unable to control Girolamo, who knew that his enemies would move against him as soon as the Pope was dead. In Lent of 1483 the Pope fell ill, and the College of Cardinals prepared to take back all the properties the Riarios had received as gifts. This united Girolamo and Caterina in trying to safeguard the inheritance of their children.

Instead of trying to forge alliances to help them, and in spite of the Pope's obviously failing health, Girolamo started open war in the following year by occupying Colonna lands. He provoked a violent skirmish at the Piazza Venezia during which several were killed, and tried to stab Lorenzo Colonna as he was being taken into custody. He then destroyed other Colonna possessions. Lorenzo Colonna was executed in the courtyard of the Castel Sant'Angelo within a few weeks, and when the family went to claim his body for burial it was obvious he had been severely tortured.

Caterina had stayed with the Pope, who could only watch in horror as Girolamo destroyed all his good work. Sixtus died on 12 August and the mob immediately took their revenge by tearing down the Riario's house in Rome, destroying their farm outside the city, and stealing all their possessions and livestock.

Caterina, despite being seven months' pregnant, was not helpless. While her husband was outside Rome she rode back with Paolo Orsini and boldly took control of the Castel Sant'Angelo, pointing its cannons towards the road leading to the Vatican, and was able to cut off the cardinals. She knew that they could easily dismiss Girolamo but while she held Sant'Angelo she must be taken seriously. Cardinal Raffaelo Riario, who was Camerlengo (Chamberlain of the Sacred College of Cardinals), had to arrange the Conclave to elect a new pope, and tried to soothe Caterina. She replied to his messages 'So, he wants a battle of wits with me? I have the brains of the Duke Galeazzo and I am as brilliant as he!'[26]

The cardinals were certainly afraid of the artillery commanded by her, but knew that only the election of a new pope could put an end to the violence tearing the city apart. Caterina claimed that the Pope had bequeathed control of Sant'Angelo to her family, and that she would not give it up until there was a new pontiff to take charge of it.

The College of Cardinals offered to confirm Girolamo's lordship of Imola if he would leave the city, and they would also confirm his post of Captain General of the Church, offering 8,000 ducats to him in compensation for the damage to his property. He accepted their terms, but his capitulation angered Caterina, and she prepared to resist the cardinals. Her demand for a proper parley between them set her up in opposition to her husband, who was preparing to leave Rome as agreed, and whose betrayal had weakened her.

The following night she was visited by several cardinals, who confirmed the family's possession of Imola and Forli in writing, and promised her respectful treatment if she would stand down. Heavily pregnant, and now alone, she had little choice, and left Sant'Angelo the following day, wearing an elegant gown, but also wearing a sword. As she prepared to leave for Forli it was said of her 'She was feared, because with weapons in her hands, the woman was proven to be cruel.'[27]

The Conclave elected the new Pope, Cardinal Giovanni Battista Cibo, who became Innocent VIII. He appeared to be kind, but the Florentine Ambassador reported 'He is certainly no friend to Count Girolamo.' The Pope was far more friendly towards Cardinal Giuliano della Rovere. He may have hoped that the troubles were over, but where Girolamo was, there could be no lasting peace. Lorenzo de' Medici was friendly towards the new Pope, and Girolamo found himself surrounded by hostile neighbours. The Pope had an illegitimate son of his own, Franceschetto Cibo, and Girolamo's enemies were already planning to make him the Lord of Forli and Imola in place of the Riario.

Caterina found herself no longer welcome in Rome and Girolamo invested his energies in modernising the Fortress of Ravaldino, which would not only be a fitting residence for the family, but also defensible.

There was a severe drought in Forli that summer, destroying crops and raising prices. Girolamo bought grain and sold it to the people at a discount, but even that didn't help his situation. Some of the Riario territory outside of Forli was seized by the Zampeschi brothers, and although Girolamo was eager for a fight, Caterina's common sense reminded her that the Zampeschi were backed by the Pope. She advised patience but knew it was the thin end of the wedge, as other neighbours could soon move against them. At the end of 1484 she fell seriously ill and was close to death until the New Year, but though her fierce spirit revived, she then heard that Imola had risen against the Riarios. Girolamo was able to put down the insurrection, which had been instigated by the previous ruler, Manfredi.

Caterina was ruling a much-reduced court, with philosophers and musicians replaced by soldiers. Cardinal Raffaelo Riario warned of further plots in Rome, and she found herself in poor circumstances and in a backwater, but she kept up her public life while Girolamo went about only with guards. In April 1486 plague hit the area and Caterina visited the affected areas, taking food and medicines, trying to help to tend the sick. People were amazed that the Countess would risk herself to help them, and were grateful for her practical good sense.[28]

Financial worries created further tensions within the marriage, however, and it began to founder. Caterina's sister was due to marry Maxilian I, the son of the Holy Roman Emperor, and she was invited to the wedding. Girolamo refused to let her go, claiming that her jewels were in pawn, but Caterina could easily have borrowed jewels for the occasion, as was customary. It was far more likely that Girolamo was merely demonstrating his control over her, and Caterina had already confided to Visconti, the envoy of the Duke of Milan, how bad things then were with her husband: 'The way he treats me is so bad that I envy those who have died at his hands.' She said that, as a wife, she was 'derelict, neglected and abandoned'.

Other problems grew, not only plots, but the townspeople were refusing to pay Girolamo's altered taxes, there were death threats, and the family had to move from immediate danger. The threats appeared to bring the couple rather closer together for a time, and Caterina was allowed to visit Milan, where Ludovico had created a sophisticated and vibrant city. She was obliged to leave there on hearing that Girolamo had fallen ill, and was aware that enemies were constantly watching Forli and Imola. Her husband recovered, but in a weakened state, preventing him from ruling, so Caterina had to take his place.

She began by riding to Ravaldino, despite being eight months pregnant.[29] The Castellan, Zaccheo, had taken it in exchange for several loans to Girolamo and was inimical towards Caterina. He insulted her and refused to relinquish the castle, or the city it commanded. She was obliged to retreat, but help was at hand, as the previous Castellan, Codronchi, who had been no friend to her in the past, changed his loyalties, and Zaccheo was unaware of it. He welcomed Codronchi into the castle, and was then killed by him. Hearing of Zacheo's death, Caterina rode back to Ravaldino, where she was able to negotiate with Codronchi. She took with her a new Castellan, Tommaso Feo, and regained control of the city. Stefano Infessura believed that Caterina and Codronchi had worked together, to ensure the assassination of Zaccheo.[30]

Caterina then had to face Duke Ercole d'Este of Ferrara, as he was de facto ruler of Forli. Duke Ercole tended to see women only as playthings and his attitude towards her was extremely patronising. Caterina had a farm on the border between them where she boarded soldiers and Ercole arranged a successful attack on it, claiming it was on his land. The Ordelaffi claimant to Forli then tried to exploit Girolamo's weakness by having one of the gates stormed, but Caterina's governor beat off the attack. Caterina, then fresh from childbirth, went personally to question the attackers captured, identifying the ringleaders, freeing those who were innocent, and publicly executing only the six leaders.

Girolamo, recovering a little, then went back to his fraudulent habits, demanding tributes, claiming revenues from churches, and even stealing valuable altar cloths and vestments. He reinstalled his family in the Riario Palace in Forli to keep control of the city, and though Caterina stayed firm in her loyalty towards him, she knew he was a liability.

In 1488, Pope Innocent VIII married his son Franceschetto to Lorenzo de' Medici's daughter Caterina. This alliance of two enemies meant disaster for the Riarios, and Girolamo began belated attempts to placate the local peasantry at the expense of the nobility.

Transferring taxes only caused the latter annoyance, and Ludovico Orso told him that he had made a serious mistake in alienating them, but Girolamo rounded on him angrily, accusing him of disloyalty. Orsi and his brother Checco then declared that the friendship between them and the Riarios was at an end. Still fearing Girolamo, the Orsi brothers knew they had to act first to defend themselves, so they immediately made arrangements with accomplices.

One afternoon in April 1488, after Girolamo had dined alone and was resting, they entered his room uninvited. Checco Orsi stabbed him in the chest and although Girolamo tried to flee, other accomplices rushed in and restrained him. He was then stabbed repeatedly. The townspeople, hearing the fight, gathered outside, and eventually saw Girolamo's naked body thrown over a balcony into the square below. Once sure that he was dead, the townspeople then ran into the palace and ransacked it, stealing silver plate, jewels, and furniture. Girolamo's body remained where it had fallen in the square and was then abused by the townspeople. Later it was removed to the Cathedral, where it was refused burial as the authorities feared family reprisals, and he was eventually taken to the Church of St Francis.[31]

Caterina and her six children barricaded themselves into the palace, which was then attacked by the Orsi brothers, who had taken control of the city. They forced their way into the palace and the family was taken into custody. Bishop Giacomo Saveli was sent to take charge of Forli while the succession was determined. He had detested Girolamo but insisted that Caterina and her children were to be treated with the utmost respect.

Caterina was separated from the children and taken to Ravaldino, where she was told to make her Castellan surrender. The Castellan, Feo, was loyal to the Riarios and refused to hand the fortress over to the church authorities, saying that he was entrusted with it on behalf of the new heir, Caterina's son Ottaviano. She was made to repeat her request, and one man held a spear to her side and threatened to kill her, but the prospect of immediate danger changed her tears to determination and anger, and she replied 'You may hurt me, but you cannot frighten me. I am the daughter of a man who knew no fear. You have killed my Lord, do what you want. I am, after all, just a woman!'[32]

Bishop Savelli had forbidden anyone to contact her, but the Orsis sent a priest who told her of her many sins, and those of her recently murdered husband, commanding her to surrender to the church or else share the same fate as Girolamo Riario. She and her children were then transferred a small cell in the Porta San Pietro. However, a Riario supporter, Ludovico Ercolani, was able to see her there and her guards were sympathetic towards her, so a plan could be laid.

On 16 April Ercolani saw the Bishop and gave him a message from Tommaso Feo, saying he would surrender the castle on condition the Countess paid his back wages, for which she would have to go to see him. The Bishop agreed, stipulating that the meeting would have to be in full view of witnesses. Caterina was to take only one escort with her, but as she entered the castle she amazed the spectators by turning to face them and making a very rude hand gesture towards them. She was inside the castle for three hours, while the Duke of Milan drew nearer with a relief force, and the Orsis became ever more fearful. Eventually Tommaso Feo reappeared, announcing that he had taken the Countess captive and offering to exchange her for certain noble hostages. The Bishop was immediately aware that Feo and the Countess were in league; while he was pondering his next move the Orsis took possession of Caterina's children.

They carried four-year-old Livio to where Caterina could see him, while the soldiers roared their threats at her and at the child. They expected her to give in immediately, to protect the child, but Caterina knew that she had a far better chance of fighting her enemies from within the fortress. She also knew that her children were related to the Duke of Milan, already on his way, and that he would take action if they were harmed.

This knowledge prompted her to reply to her tormentors very boldly, when she stood on the battlements and shouted her most widely quoted declaration:

'Fatelo se volete impiccatele pure davanti a me – qui ho quanto basta per fare di piu!' 'Do it if you want to, hang them in front of me – here I have enough to make more!'

Writing to Lorenzo de' Medici, Galeotto Manfredi added that she had at that point lifted her skirt and exposed her genitals to the watching crowd, clutching her pudenda to emphasise her words. (Pudenda comes from a fourteenth-century Latin expression meaning 'shameful parts.') Nobody else reported such an action and the only other person to record the more salacious version was Niccolo Machiavelli, in his *Discourses*.[33] Caterina may never have accompanied the insulting words with the vulgar gesture, but she had already by report surprised them with a rude hand gesture when she entered the castle, and if this did happen, she was already in the mood to shock.

She then turned away from the spectators and calmly went inside the castle. The Venetian Ambassador said, 'She is a Tigress, willing to eat her young to gain power.'[34] Five letters written at that time immortalise her words[35] but both Cobelli and Bernardi, who were eye witnesses, say nothing at all of the incident.[36] Both of these authors agree that her children were taken to the ramparts and threatened with violence and despite their terrified screams Caterina did not reappear. Feo, perhaps afraid that the noise would weaken her, ordered several volleys of cannon fire to drown out the screaming of her children. Again, Cobelli and Bernardi agree on this. Even Machiavelli condemned her for risking the lives of the children but by calling the bluff of her enemies she had actually saved them. In every other instance she had proved herself to be a loving mother.

Bishop Savelli returned the children to Porta San Pietro under guard, well aware that the Orsi brothers had made the situation far worse. Ludovico and Checco Orsi had to face their father and he was furious.

'You have done a bad thing and you have done it badly,' he shouted. 'When you killed the count you should have killed the whole family, for she will fight you to the death and even I – old and sick as I am – will bear the punishment!'

Days passed and Caterina ordered periodic artillery fire to keep the invaders at bay. Several townspeople defected to Ravaldino and Bishop Savelli became concerned about the Pope's stalling. Innocent VIII expressed concern about the Riario children, but he did little else. He still wanted his son to have the Forli lands, and letting the Riarios down would help him achieve this. However, the Milanese opposed him and he knew it could incite other towns into open rebellion. The Duke of Milan was close to Forli, and he did not want to make an enemy of so powerful a man, for himself or for his son, so the papal armies stayed where they were.

Bishop Savelli then said that the Riarios could move to Imola if they withdrew their claim to Forli, but the Orsi did not negotiate. The townspeople began to complain about the folly of asking help from the church and Savelli sent one of his own relatives into the city with a papal standard and carrying forged letters, to give the impression that the Pope gave his support.

During this troubled time Antonio Maria Ordelaffi offered to marry Caterina and was refused. The Pope finally made a move, appointing a Cardinal-Governor for the city and this was none other than Raffaelo Riario, Girolamo's nephew, seen as an attempt to end the dissension. The Milanese army arrived on 29 April and the Duke of Milan demanded complete restoration of the Riarios. He intended to increase his own influence in Romagna to counter the strength of Venice, and for that Caterina's regency of Forli and Imola was necessary. The Orsi made a final attempt to kill the hostage children, but they were by then fully protected by the Bishop's guards. Caterina, whose coolness and courage had been outstanding, realised that she had won.[37]

There had to be retribution for Girolamo, even though he had not been the ideal husband, but he had been Lord of Forli and Imola and the father of Caterina's children. Plotters could not be allowed to engineer his death and lay siege to Ravaldino with impunity. There had to be payment in kind. Caterina made her triumphant entry into Forli with 20,000 men of the Duke of Milan, then the reprisals had to begin; but to the townspeople's surprise she refused to allow the soldiers to sack the town.[38]

She was then hailed as the saviour of Forli, but the reasons for her action were simply pragmatic, and the Duke would not want to see his nephew's inheritance ruined. She also said that no young girls should be dishonoured: 'I care about women.' She spread the word that if her enemies were handed over, the town itself would be safe.

The Orsi left town, leaving their families behind with their father Andrea Orsi, but taking with them tens of thousands of ducats' worth of looted valuables, some belonging to Caterina. Some of it was also stolen from the Jewish moneylenders.[39]

Bishop Savelli was detained to remind the Pope not to make any further attempts to claim Riario territory. Caterina personally thanked those people who had helped her and defended her children. She then had to recover her husband's remains from the pauper's grave at St Francis, so he could be properly entombed at Forli Cathedral. Caterina stayed at Ravaldino, secure in the fortress, and summoned a new Bailiff, Matteo Barbone, entrusting him to collect together the conspirators. Those who had believed themselves safe were pulled from their beds and given the same treatment that Riario had suffered. They were hanged, castrated, disembowelled and thrown to the eager crowds, where their remains were hacked to pieces with spades. Then the Orsi were dealt with. Ludovico Checco had already fled but their eighty-year-old father, Andrea Orsi, was obliged to watch his palace destroyed and all his goods given to the Countess in reparation for her losses, before facing his own death. He was tied to a plank and dragged by a horse, with his feet raised to the horse's tail, and his head bouncing on the cobbles. The horse was galloped around the square, and by the time it had completed its third circuit, he was dead.

Caterina then sent for the terrified Orsi women, but to their great surprise, and true to her earlier declaration about her care for women, she set them free to return to their own families. Every head of a family in Forli was then read a contract outlining the duties and responsibilities of good citizens. They were required to swear on the Bible to uphold it. Only the actual conspirators were executed, horribly, to make an example of them. Caterina's swift action had ensured peace and Cobelli described her as 'merciful'.[40]

Life returned to normal, but even when the family home was restored Caterina preferred the security of Ravaldino. She was still waiting for the Pope to confirm her son as Lord of Forli, but there was a joyful reunion with Cardinal Raffaelo Riario.

Other news arrived, that Galeatto Manfredi of Faenza had been killed by his wife. She had grown tired of his continual cruel treatment of her, as well as of his long affair with the daughter of an apothecary, which had made her fear that he would have her killed. She and her accomplices tied him with ropes and stabbed him to death. For Caterina this meant that the territory between Forli and Imola was open to conquest, but the Pope confirmed the Edict that the three-year-old son of Manfredi was to be its overlord, so the opportunity to gain the land was missed. She did, however, receive confirmation of her own son's lordship, and had to be content with that.

There was a further surprise, concerning the offer of a marriage. Antonio Maria Ordelaffi again tried to press his attentions on her, though she would not consider a union with him. Nevertheless, romance was in the air, for Caterina had actually fallen in love with Tommaso Feo's brother, Giacomo. Caterina was to marry him in 1488, but secretly, to avoid losing custody of her children or the Regency she held over the lands until her son came of age. The chroniclers claimed that she was madly in love with Giacomo[41] and he was appointed Castellan of Ravaldino. Loyal friends and relations were also placed in similar positions at other Riario fortresses.

There were still conspiracies aimed at ousting Giacomo and Caterina, but all failed, even one organised by the absent Ordelaffi, who had never resigned himself to the loss of Forli.[42]

In 1492 both Lorenzo de' Medici, and Pope Innocent VIII died. It had been said of Innocent, that 'his private life was darkened by the most scandalous proceedings ... he had contracted the vice of sodomy, and his uncommon beauty when young had introduced him to Philip, Cardinal of Bologna, who served his pleasures.' It was not unusual for men to advance a career by homosexual relationships, and Innocent had also shown impartiality by producing several children. A Latin poem was not flattering:

> He begot eight sons and as many daughters, but oh! Innocent VIII, wherever you lie buried, filthiness, gluttony, covetousness and sloth will lie with thee![43]

As Pope, Innocent had always been hostile to the Riario family, and his antagonism had helped to destabilise them, both financially and politically. He was to be succeeded by Cardinal Rodrigo Borgia, as Alexander VI, which may have initially appeared to be a blessing for Caterina. Borgia had been godfather to her son and heir, and had already shown himself friendly to the family, so his accession suggested an easing of pressures.

Unfortunately, at just that time, Caterina seemed to have lost focus. She was oblivious to outside dangers, and blinded by her attachment to Feo. King Charles VIII of France, eager for expansion, believed that he had a claim to Naples. The complicated pedigrees of the European rulers meant that almost everyone was related to everyone else, leading to many such claims. Also, the sybaritic lifestyle of Pope Alexander soon became evident, so Charles thought it a good time to move across the Alps.[44] He was welcomed in Milan and moved to Pavia to meet with Gian Galeazzo, the heir to the Duchy. On his journey he heard of Gian Galeazzo's death, supposedly by poison, and suspicion soon fell on Ludovico de' Medici, but Ludovico moved very quickly indeed, and was proclaimed Duke of Milan. There was nothing at all Caterina could do about her half-brother's suspicious death.

She was bound to the papacy, as her Regency stemmed from a papal decree, and this meant that technically she was under papal control. Letters reached her, reminding her of her debt to Milan, but the Pope was supporting Naples and Caterina began to have a hard time staying neutral. Pope Alexander sent Cardinal Raffaelo Riario to persuade her to assist Naples, but to his disgust all meetings took place in the presence of Girolamo Feo. This man had certainly risen high, and seemed to be her advisor on all state matters, actually putting her in his own shadow.[45] People quickly commented on this, not being aware that they had married. Feo began to be seen as an impediment to diplomatic relations with Caterina, and she had even began to fear for his life. He handled the city's revenues, paid the soldiers, and hoped to secure their loyalty for himself.

Alexander VI was also aware of her financial problems, and that her lands did not generate a huge income. He issued a 16,000-ducat *condotta*, or course of action, in return for her support against Milan and the French. As a bonus, the fief of San Mauro, occupied by the Zampeschi family, was returned to the Riarios. Feo, inimical to Caterina's family connections, persuaded her to side with Naples, and it is a measure of how much in thrall to him she was that she agreed. Ludovico of Milan was astonished at her defection, but Caterina busied herself with providing her new allies with men and armour. It wasn't long before 2,000 French and Milanese troops arrived at Caterina's fortress of Mordano, near to Imola, demanding its surrender. Its defence was a credit to her soldiers, and they held out until the castle walls were breached. The surviving defenders were drawn and quartered, and the women hid in the church, but were carried off by the French soldiery. Corbelli refused to detail their treatment, so as 'not to further dishonour them'.[46]

It was the savagery of the French that finally woke Caterina from her daydream. She asked the Duke of Calabria for support, but he did not reply, despite being her ally. She told the people that her agreement with her allies was broken and she was putting the city under the protection of Ludovico of Milan and the French! In truth, Forli had no chance of standing against the enormous French army, but her defection meant that Florence would then have French troops almost next door. This meant that Florence would also have to capitulate, so Charles VIII was easily able to swallow up Tuscany.

It seemed clear that Caterina's relationship with Feo had made her a threat to political stability, and though the Lord of Forli, Ottaviano was then sixteen and of an age to take over, Feo seemed to stand in his way. Worse, he showed his stepson no respect, once actually slapping the boy across the face during a public argument. The Florentine Ambassador expressed his opinion of the unstable situation: 'The Countess will bury her children, her allies, and all her belongings, and she will sell her soul to the Devil, and give up her state to the Turks, before she gives up Giacomo Feo!'[47]

Caterina's personal supporters decided to deal with the matter, deploring her loss of power and hating the subsequent rise of Feo. After a family outing in August 1495, Giovanni Antonio Ghetti and some friends stopped the carriage carrying Caterina and her female children. The males of the party were riding alongside, with Feo and the bodyguards. Ghetti and his men stepped forward, taking hold of the reins of Feo's horse, and speaking in a friendly manner, but then Feo was stabbed in the back. He fell from his horse, calling Caterina's name, before dying under a storm of blows from swords and daggers. Caterina acted instantly, leaping from the carriage onto the nearest horse, and galloping to Ravaldino and safety. Feo's bodyguards had scattered, and Caterina saw Feo die as she galloped past him.

If she had behaved exactly within the letter of the law after the Siege of Ravaldino, by saving the life of anyone not directly connected with the murder of her first husband, things were very different the second time. She was to unleash staggering reprisals. Ghetti had gone to Forli, still covered with Feo's blood, to boast of the killing, expecting to be greeted as a liberator. He was amazed to realise that the Countess was neither pleased nor grateful. He and his men darted away again, but were quickly captured and brutally executed. Ghetti was 'cleaved from the crown of his head to his teeth', after which all of his extremities were severed.[48] Ghetti's wife, Rosa, once a friend of Caterina's, was inside Ravaldino with her children, and all were thrown down one of the deep wells and left to die there. A few days' later, Ghetti's five-year-old son, left in the care of a friend, was found and his throat was cut. Corbelli tried desperately to claim that Caterina did not order the deaths of the women and children, but others knew differently. The Milanese Ambassador wrote to Duke Ludovico:

> ...that which seems most detestable, she had the women killed, the wives of the two Ghetti brothers, their sons aged three and nine months, and even the nurse. All Romagna is crying to the Heavens.[49]

The Ambassador Pranchedini, though not an eye witness, said that all the people were horrified that 'the Countess had cruelly punished anyone they got their hands on, as accomplices of the two who had killed Feo.'[50]

The violence of her response to his murder showed her deep attachment to Feo, despite the friction caused by him. On the night of his death his body was recovered from the ditch into which it had been thrown. It was taken to the church of San Girolamo. Cobelli saw it personally and declared 'What shame! What cruelty! Such a beautiful face, rent like a split pomegranate.' Feo's clothes were almost torn from his body by the violence of the attack on him, and were soaked with his blood.

The following morning the drawbridge was lowered and Caterina and her children walked out in full mourning. She held the hand of Bernardino, her son by Feo, then three years old. Feo would be laid temporarily in the chapel of the Manfredi, while a splendid tomb was created for him. Caterina was not finished with Feo's murderers. The Marcobelli and Orcioli families, accomplices to the plot, had their houses destroyed. The della Selle family had relatives thrown into dungeons and possessions sacked. The priest Domenico da Bagnacavallo was betrayed into her hands and tortured with fire until he gave her the list of names of all those involved. Caterina would be devastated to read that those names included Cardinal Raffaelo Riario and her own son Ottaviano![51]

In her fury, Caterina had the priest stripped and tied by his feet to the back of a mule, which was driven outside the city to the place where Feo had been killed. The priest was then dragged around the area, but surprisingly survived. Then his face was slashed open as punishment for the defacement of Feo's face, and he was then beaten and stabbed to death, before his corpse was dismembered.

Caterina then turned to deal with her family. Ottaviano had taken refuge with the Paolo Denti family. Denti was the man who had refused to hand over the Riario children after their father's murder seven years before. Ottaviano was taken to Ravaldino and what happened there, between him and his mother, is known only to the very few witnesses present, who were never to speak of it. He was then put under house arrest.

The violence carried out even against people on the very fringes of the plot against Feo continued. The mistress of Antonio Pavagliotta and her three children were murdered. The priest was scorched over a fire of hot coals and then beheaded. Heads remained outside Ravaldino for over a year and body parts were hung as a warning.

Unfortunately, Caterina's extreme vengeance disgraced her. Even though she had disclosed that Feo had been her husband, not merely a lover, it did not excuse the excessive force used. Corbelli listed thirty-eight people killed, many others tortured, imprisoned or exiled.

Caterina was concerned only with a memorial to Feo, to be kept within the walls of Ravaldino. She commissioned *The Miracle of the Hanged Man* by Marco Palmezzano, which shows Feo as the central figure, while her first husband, Girolamo Riario kneels in front of Caterina. She was to spend the winter of 1496 in deep mourning, and in a letter to her uncle she confessed that she had thought of drowning herself.[52] She also destroyed the palace where she and Feo had lived to eradicate memories on which she intended to turn her back; from then on she would concentrate on being a Sforza. With the future in mind, she arranged a marriage for her heir Ottaviano with the daughter of Giovanni Bentivoglio of Bologna, but the girl rejected him and chose to enter a convent. Duke Ludovico of Milan offered a new marriage for him, with a daughter of Gonzaga of Mantua,[53] but Caterina refused that one, fearing Ludovico's interference. Ottaviano became a soldier though he was unable to maintain discipline, and her second son, Cesare, was destined for the church, as Caterina's relationship with Cardinal Raffaelo Riario soured after Feo's death.

Giovanni and Lorenzo di Pierfrancesco, of a cadet branch of the Medici, had changed their name to 'Popolani' meaning 'of the people' to take advantage of the reform fervour preached by Girolamo Savonarola.[54] Giovanni began to visit Forli in 1496 and the attraction for him was Caterina herself. She was then thirty-three years old (Giovanni was then thirty) and still beautiful. She initially preferred only a business partnership with him, but she had in fact found her ideal partner. He was well born and clever, shared her interests in books and botany and was already a member of a ruling family, so posed no threat to her sons through his own ambition. Her growing affection for him seemed far more sensible than the blind passion she had shown for Feo.

Her relationship with Giovanni resulted in a pregnancy and in August 1497 she married him secretly in the Fortress of Castrocaro, to avoid her uncle's spies. Their child was born at Ravaldino the following April and was named Ludovico Sforza de' Medici.

Venice was also incensed at the idea of a Riario/Medici alliance, and began to launch full-scale assaults on her castles. Warnings from her uncle prompted her to declare 'When Venice attacks I will have enough spirit to defend myself... If I must lose because I am a woman, I want to lose like a man!'[55]

Unfortunately for her new happiness with Giovanni, he suffered badly from gout, a condition shared by many of the Medici family. It caused him to visit Bagno during August, hoping that the mineral waters there would cure him, but he was to die there of a fever the following month, with Caterina in attendance on him. Her soul mate was gone, and her town was then in danger of attack.

She would fight off Venice again, but the Serene Republic was still determined to beat her.

Florence still expected her to send her best troops, commanded by Ottaviano, but this was something Caterina had already refused, given that she had not been paid for the previous services rendered, and she was also under threat and needed them herself. Niccolo Machiavelli had been sent to persuade her, and the Borgia Pope also had alliance in mind, this time for a marriage between Ottaviano and his daughter Lucrezia. On the face of it, it would have been a brilliant match, but one which would require Caterina's retirement, to allow the Pope's son-in-law to rule. This was also refused, and the refusal brought with it the enmity of Alexander VI. The following May a Bull was issued calling Caterina 'A daughter of iniquity'. The Pope obviously intended to depose the Riarios in favour of his own son Cesare Borgia. Caterina sent 3,600 ducats to the Pope, which was the sum of unpaid tribute he claimed from her, but he remained unappeased and she knew that military action would follow. She needed the support of Florence against the Borgias, so was obliged to welcome Machiavelli again, though while Florence seemed keen to use her troops, it was very much less keen on supporting her against the resentful Pope.

By October she had heard that she had been granted an audience by King Louis XII of France to hear her case, after she claimed the protection of Florence as an ally. The Pope was still adamant that he intended to besiege Forli and Caterina was beset on all sides. She heard from Florence that 'everyone is waiting for your undoing and ruin, most of all in Rome, from whence comes all this evil.'[56] If Caterina had believed she could gain support from King Louis she had been mistaken. He said, 'We are not the judges of the Pope, nor can we forbid that he acts as he wishes in his own jurisdiction.' The King spoke to others of the problems Caterina was facing: 'Her captains have the right to defend her against any other powers, but against the Pope, who is our overlord, it is not lawful!'[57] The following day, with a note written in his own hand, the Pope formally deposed the Riario family and they were instructed to surrender Forli and Imola immediately.

Caterina immediately went on a war footing, with the inhabitants told to harvest all wheat and other crops, leaving the land bare, and to move further away. Every citizen must have four months rations and those who could not afford such outlay would be assisted. Her best horses were to be sent to the Marquis of Mantua, along with a letter in which she said 'We will not abandon our home, but will defend our possessions as long as we can, and perhaps they will not find the conquest as easy as they think.'[58]

Pope Alexander was well aware of the legends surrounding the Countess, and he did his utmost to deflect sympathy away from her. He wrote to Florence in November, claiming that she had tried to poison him, a pretence that he then spread elsewhere. Whether anyone believed it or not, it became obvious that any help for Caterina would anger the Pope, and although Florence remained friendly, even going so far as to refuse the sale of ammunition and gunpowder to Cesare Borgia, not everyone was so loyal.

Giovanni della Selle, hoping to negotiate terms under a Borgia rule, offered the submission of Forli to Cesare Borgia, who accepted, making the Forlivesi the shame of Italy, after they celebrated what they imagined would be their future safety at Caterina's expense. Cesare Borgia entered Forli in December, and Caterina was at bay.

On St Stephen's Day he rode to Ravaldino and spoke to the Countess personally, slyly assuring her that if she surrendered the fortress to him, the Pope would give her another. He offered her land in compensation, even a house in Rome, but said that if she resisted, there would be bloodshed.

She reminded Cesare that, unlike him, she had an honourable name and she would not disgrace it.[59] She told him that if she died there, her name would live on forever. A few hours later, Cesare tried again, this time with Caterina playing him at his own game. She allowed him onto the castle drawbridge, and as she turned to retreat, with Cesare behind her, the drawbridge began to rise, and Cesare was forced to jump back. Infuriated at his own near-capture, he threatened her and shouted at the troops that a thousand-ducat reward would go to the man who brought him her dead body. She replied by shouting back that she offered to give five thousand ducats for Cesare's!

Time was then on her side, as Duke Ludovico was about to march to take Milan back from the French. Many experts believed that Ravaldino was strong enough to withstand a siege of four months, but Caterina knew Cesare had more men and was determined. If her walls did not hold, the siege would be over.

News of this one woman's defence against the Borgias soon spread, and the diarist Antonio Grumello of Pavia wrote 'There has never been seen a woman with so much spirit!' Even Venice, always her opponent, said of her 'She has shown herself to be a female of great governance.'[60]

Cesare was having difficulty in controlling his mercenary troops, and the Forlivesi who had capitulated to him were regretting that decision, being turned out of their homes by soldiers and having their businesses ruined. Borgia then made everyone in Forlì wear the white cross of the penitent, to show their subservience. He raised the bounty on Caterina to ten thousand ducats, without any result, as public opinion was then in her favour.

Cesare concentrated on the weakest section of the wall of Ravaldino, while the defenders continually repaired it. Eventually, however, its frailty began to show, and the soldiers at the breach began to desert. Caterina strode out of the keep with her brother Alessandro Sforza when the Riario and Sforza flags came down, and fought alongside her brother and her stepson Scipione Riario. She refused to yield even when her officers called the retreat. For two hours she showed that she knew how to use a sword and 'she wounded many men.'[61] She had no intention of being captured alive, even when her captains, her Castellan and her brother were taken prisoner. She backed away towards the keep again, while Cesare called to her to prevent a pointless waste of life. Suddenly, she was apprehended by a Frenchman, and realised that she had been betrayed from inside her own castle.

Many people, considering the fall of Ravaldino, surmised that there had been treachery. Cesare, in a letter to his father the Pope, admitted that he 'would never have taken the castle if all the men had had the Countess's spirit.' The Ambassador to the Duke of Ferrara said that the castle had been lost 'pathetically' and could have held out at least fifteen more days. Caterina commented that her death in battle was preferable and far more honourable than any survival through surrender. As several prisoners were being killed, she was led from her home. Some of the nobles were granted ransoms, but not her. The chronicler Bernardi said that 'from that time, Paradise was governed by the devils.'[62]

Cesare had imagined that all her children would be handed over to him, and was dismayed to be informed that they had already been sent to Florence before the siege began. They were Florentine citizens through her marriage to Giovanni de' Medici and would be well protected. Cesare took out his anger on Caterina by raping her. He then boasted to his men, 'She defended her fortress better than she defended her honour!' and he liked to give the impression that she was with him of her own free will, as his willing mistress. The Duke of Milan received a letter about the fall of Forli, informing him that 'It is believed that Borgia has treated her badly.' Even at the Vatican, when the news spread that her children were safe from the Borgias, it was well known that he had punished her by 'taking her and subjecting her to cruel torments'. Bernardi wrote of the 'injustices to the body of our poor unfortunate Countess'. Even though such behaviour towards a noblewoman was frowned upon, both in France and Italy, Cesare delighted in the situation, and those who had seen Caterina in Cesare's rooms reported that she hardly spoke and looked always as if she had been crying, although she still held her head high.

Isabella d'Este, the Marchioness of Mantua, said 'If the French criticise the cowardice of our men, they should certainly praise the daring and valour of our women!'[63]

Shortly after the fall of Ravaldino, Cesare went to Pesaro on Giovanni Sforza's territory to begin a siege there, taking Caterina with him. He was stopped by a French force led by Yves d'Allegre, who was angry at the idea of Caterina being held by Cesare when she should have been under the protection of Louis XII. He claimed custody of her in the King's name, intending to take her to France. Cesare had no choice but to hand her over, but he was not finished with her. Shortly after, he met the French captains and demanded her return, using his authority as captain of the victorious army. Though the French protested, they eventually accepted the full reward of 10,000 ducats for her, in effect selling her back into Cesare's hands. She then began the journey to Rome, where she would be at the mercy of the Borgia Pope.

She was initially kept at the Belvedere there, one of the villas belonging to the Vatican at that time, with pleasant views over Rome. The Mantuan Ambassador, who saw her at that time, said that she was 'still furious and strong-willed'.[64] Although Caterina had several ladies with her, she also had guards, and could receive no letters not first vetted by papal agents. She was continually pressured to sign over her children's rights to Forli, which she continued to refuse, but unfortunately her children were less than loyal to her. They were pinning their hopes on the Borgias, looking for church appointments and other rewards, and putting very little value on the territories their mother had fought so hard and long to defend. Her youngest child was in the care of her heir Ottaviano, who made it clear in his letters to her that he wanted to be relieved of the responsibility; he also wanted to turn his back on Forli and receive a cardinal's hat from the pope.

Caterina was determined to escape from her imprisonment, and found an ally in Abbot Lauro Bossi of Milan, who was an old friend. Unfortunately, any plans they had made came to nothing when the Abbot was seized in the night. The Borgias knew that killing Caterina would be counter-productive, but she was also proving to be a liability and her attempted escape gave them the excuse they needed to transfer her to the prison of the Castel Sant'Angelo in June 1500. There she was to suffer again from Cesare's sadistic sense of humour, at one point being marched out as if to her execution, to find others executed in her stead. She became ill with stress but managed to recover without help.

Yves d'Allegre reappeared, demanding to see the Pope and showing that he was again disgusted that Caterina was living in far worse conditions than before. He stated that if she were not immediately liberated, he would enforce the matter. The Pope eventually had to give in, but only on condition that she renounce all claims to her lands at Forli and Imola. When d'Allegre saw Caterina's actual condition, he was horrified. In order to end her eighteen months of imprisonment she finally agreed to sign over her territories in exchange for her freedom. The Pope still prevented her from leaving Rome, though she was at least out of the Sant'Angelo prison, and he actually demanded payment of 2,000 ducats to cover the expense of having kept her a prisoner. Abbot Lauro Bossi was also released, and Caterina was to appoint him as her Chaplain.[65]

Once away from the Vatican and the Borgias' demands, Caterina stayed at the house of Cardinal Raffaelo Riario, though he and his brother, Cardinal Giuliano Riario, were carefully keeping away from Rome and out of the Borgias' clutches. Caterina received d'Allegre there, and took his advice on her future. Though the cruelty and rapaciousness of Pope Alexander and Cesare Borgia were already well known, she said to d'Allegre that if she told all that she knew about them, she would 'shock the world'.

In July she took a boat to Ostia, then met a ship heading for Livorno, under French control. She knew she needed at all costs to avoid all papal territory, and from Pisa she rode to Florence. There she finally met her children, and there she hoped to be able to make her home.

As soon as Caterina's return was known, her brother-in-law Lorenzo di Pierfrancesco de' Medici arranged a home for her. Unfortunately, she had no money, and no revenues to bring in any, and found it difficult to survive. Her son was still sole heir to the fortune of her late husband Giovanni de' Medici, but his brother Lorenzo had no intention of handing over any money either. She was requested to leave the villa they had provided for her, but she had already been pushed far enough and resisted stoutly. Lorenzo was to claim custody of her son, stating that due to her imprisonment she was unfit to care for him, but she resisted again, fighting in court for the right to keep her son. She did find some solace, in those troubled times, at the Convent of the Murate, where laywomen were permitted to live.

On 18 August 1503 Pope Alexander VI died, and at the same time Cesare Borgia lay seriously ill. Pius III, Francesco Piccolomini, became Pope, but he also died less than a month later, and was succeeded by Giuliano della Rovere who took the name of Pope Julius II. This man was a cousin of the Riarios, and it seemed finally to be a good time to get the inheritance back.

Antonio Maria Ordelaffi was in Forli, having taken advantage of the confusion to reclaim it, actually with the help of Florence. Caterina was encouraged to claim it back, with complaints to Florence and '...to cry for vengeance until the people were amazed by such ingratitude'.[66] Despite Caterina's marriage to a de' Medici and her alliances with Florence, it was considered that Ordelaffi could hold Forli more peaceably than she had, but the new Pope, Julius II, was undecided, and withheld the confirmation of Ordelaffi's rule.

Giovanni Maria Ridolfi, a Florentine captain, wrote '...if the countess were dead, part of the countryside and the people of Forli would not be displeased to have Ottaviano in her place, whom they consider to be a good man.' But Caterina still had some supporters in Rome, and both Cardinal Raffaelo Riario and Cardinal Ascanio Sforza were pressing firmly for her restitution. However, by the end of 1504, it had become clear that the Pope had no intention of putting Forli or Imola back into Riario hands.

Caterina did regain her youngest and most dear son, as in June 1505 the lawsuit was resolved in favour of him, and what remained of her husband's wealth was returned to her. She immediately changed the child's name to Giovanni Di Giovanni Di Medici, to emphasise his paternity by her third husband.

She then concentrated on making a life for herself. She took an interest in herbs and such remedies as she could grow in her garden at Castello. She made unguents to aid health and beauty, but in May 1509 her own health began to fail. She complained of pains in her chest, described as *mal di costa,* or a rib sickness, and several times suffered from malarial fevers, then developing pleurisy. The medicines available at the time could not reduce the inflammation, merely easing the pain, so she decided it was time to write her will.

Her family, her friends and the nuns at the Murate were all taken care of, her servants were rewarded, and she faced her end as bravely as she had faced her difficult and dangerous life. Shortly after her will was signed, Caterina Riario Sforza de' Medici died, at the age of only forty-six.

Condolences and tributes poured in from all over Italy, and she was buried in the chapel at the Murate. She had lived a life of glory and loss, of supreme courage and determination, and had succumbed when she at last found peace. She was to be remembered as one of the most extraordinary women that the Renaissance ever produced.

'For Love of Family': The Borgias

Despite their legendary association with Rome, the Borgia clan hailed originally from Spain, where King Jaime I of Aragon ennobled Esteban de Borgia in 1240 for his part in the expulsion of the Moors from Valencia. The family seat of Jativa, about 40 miles from Valencia, dated back to the Roman Empire.

Alfonso de Borgia was made a Cardinal by Pope Eugenius IV in 1444. He subsequently moved to Rome, and immediately began touting for favours for his family. In 1445 he appointed his fourteen-year-old nephew, Rodrigo Borgia, as Sacristan at the Cathedral of Valencia. During 1448, Rodrigo Borgia became Canon of the Cathedral chapters of Valencia, Barcelona and Segorbe and in 1449 he was granted the right to receive his income from these benefices in absentia 'whether living in Rome, or studying at the University', to allow him to leave Spain and join his uncle in Italy. He proved to be competent, suave, good-natured and eloquent, as well as being considered handsome and having an amazing attraction for the ladies. His tutor said of him 'It is quite remarkable how beautiful women are attracted to him, more powerfully even than a magnet attracts iron.'[1]

During his years in Rome Cardinal Borgia had established a good reputation, as a religious and kindly man, as well as one who was honest and to be relied upon. He was known to 'live an honourable and virtuous life' and had also done his best to advance his family, as all Cardinals did, though he kept his personal life modest.

At the beginning of 1454, the health of the Pope, Nicholas V, began to decline and by March he was dead. Naturally, Cardinal Borgia would have to attend the Conclave to elect a successor, but he had no personal expectations. He was not considered to be *papabile*, a front-runner in the elections, the ones from whom the next pope was likely to be chosen.[2]

On Good Friday 1455 Alonso Borgia and fourteen other cardinals went into the Vatican and the doors were sealed behind them. They would vote daily, sometimes twice daily, putting the paper with the names of their preferred candidates into an urn, from where they would be taken to be counted. Most of the cardinals available (five were too far away to reach Rome in time), were allied to either the Colonna or Orsini factions, the two families who then dominated politics in Rome.

For several days the votes were stuck, until it became obvious that a compromise candidate would need to be elected. On 8 April Alfonso Borgia found himself elected Pope, choosing the name Callixtus III. He was already seventy-seven years old, and the oldest cardinal then present. One ambassador wrote, 'They have agreed on the Cardinal of Valencia, because he is old, and they all hope to have their own candidate elected at the next Conclave.'[3]

He immediately ordered an audit of the accounts of the last Pope, and subsequently made cuts to expenditure, even selling off Nicholas V's expensive furniture. He also stopped the late Pope's programme of urban renewal, considering it to be too ambitious. An inventory was drawn up listing the valuable manuscripts that Nicholas V had bought for the library, but this economy drive turned people against the new Pope, and the Pope's bookseller remarked sarcastically that the Borgia was a philistine who had no idea of the value of the church's treasures. However, Callixtus was not quite as stupid as he appeared. He removed the gold and silver from the covers of the books, using the money raised from it for the Crusades, but he kept the texts intact, and in the library.

In May he proclaimed his intention to crusade against the Turks. He did, however, find time to remember family loyalties, and promote the careers of two of his young nephews, with the result that Rodrigo Borgia was made the Dean of Santa Maria in Jativa and the son of another of his sisters, Luis Juan de Mila, became Governor of Bologna.

The Pope then turned to promoting his other nephews. Pedro Luis Borgia, the elder brother of Rodrigo, became Captain-General of the Church, and Governor of Castel Sant'Angelo. Callixtus held a Consistory when he persuaded twelve cardinals to sign documents creating three new cardinals, Luis Juan de Mila, Rodrigo Borgia, and Prince Jaime of Portugal. He intended the names of the appointees to be kept secret for a while, but that if he were to die unexpectedly then Rodrigo's name would be disclosed, so that he could take part in the next election. The Pope's preference for Rodrigo Borgia was obvious to all, and he soon became Vice-chancellor of the Curia.[4] Callixtus was working as quickly as he could, being aware that his years were against him. He was to canonise two saints at this time, Osmund Bishop of Salisbury, and St Vincent Ferrer, who forty years earlier had predicted his election as Pope. He also overturned the sentence passed against the Maid of Orleans, Jeanne d'Arc, proclaiming her innocence.[5] He would also leave to the world a son, Francisco de Borgia, who would eventually be appointed a cardinal by Alexander VI.

The Pope was delighted to hear that the crusade he had instigated at great cost had begun to go well, and the Milanese Ambassador reported 'He said God had granted us this triumph in order to shame all those who had denounced the crusade.' He also said that he had been accused by King Alfonso of wasting on it the money that other popes had saved.[6]

In September of 1456 he finally made public the creation of his nephews as cardinals, and in mid-November they were given their titular churches, Luis Juan receiving Santi Quattro Coronati, Rodrigo receiving San Nicola in Carcere. A month later the Pope further persuaded the College of Cardinals to allow him to create six more cardinals, though complaints began that there were too many already.

In 1457 Callixtus was still concerned with his crusade, but was finding it difficult to raise money and the relationship between him and Alfonso of Naples began to deteriorate, despite his having entertained Alfonso's mistress in Rome the previous year, at great expense. Cardinal Piccolomini observed:

> She had visited Rome with all her retinue which was as grand as if she were a queen. The Pope received her in Consistory with all the cardinals and treated her with honour... The cardinals

considered it inappropriate that a royal mistress should be so acclaimed by His Holiness.[7]

Piccolomini's sarcasm missed the point that Callixtus was trying to maintain his alliance with King Alfonso, though it was even then doomed to failure.

Pedro Luis and Rodrigo Borgia took charge of more work for their ageing uncle, but their popularity plummeted further. It was said 'the Pope is blinded by his love of his family.'[8] His other obsession was still the crusade and when, in June 1458, gravediggers found an ancient marble sarcophagus holding two wooden coffins, the Pope had the silver linings removed and also took the rich gold-embroidered fabric in which the two bodies had been wrapped. He sold the precious metal to raise another thousand ducats.

By the following month he was suffering badly from gout, and shortly after the Mantuan Ambassador reported that the Pope had been ill for eight days, 'weak with fever, he cannot digest anything, the food goes in and comes out unchanged.' Rumours of the Pope's imminent death spread and rioting began, but he lingered on until August, when the Milanese Ambassador reported 'His Holiness is gravely ill, yesterday evening he received the Last Rites and there is now no hope of his life, indeed it is only the medicine that is keeping him alive.'[9] His nephews, bearing in mind the resentment against them, made themselves scarce, and the Milanese Ambassador observed, 'The Pope died today at nightfall and the Catalans have all fled. Those who are harbouring them are so detested that it will go hard with them if they are found out before the election of a new pope.'[10]

Callixtus had done his best, had established his family in Rome, and had lived to nearly eighty years old, after a papal reign of just over three years and three months. Unfortunately, his cardinal-nephews were too young to have any chance of being elected.[11] After Callixtus' death the voting was frenzied and Rodrigo Borgia, already showing the pragmatism that would mark him out, threw in his lot with Cardinal Piccolomini who was elected as Pius II in August 1458.

Rodrigo Borgia would be a career cardinal, and was aware that he would need both money and influence in the future. He did, however, have another side to his character, one that would come to the fore as is own status grew. He liked not only money, but women, and had already started to establish a reputation for licentiousness, even though he had been confirmed as Vice-chancellor by Pope Pius II. Surprisingly, he would hold that office for thirty-five years and it was said of him that in all that time he never missed a Consistory, except when ill. This showed the hard work and determination that ran alongside his love of pleasure. It was that love of pleasure, however, shared with many of the other cardinals, which was criticised by Pius II in 1460 when he took them to task for their behaviour: 'You refuse to give up hunting and gambling or the company of women. You host unsuitably grand banquets and wear vestments far too rich, you amass expensive gold plate and keep an excess of horses and servants.'[12]

This rebuke had no obvious effect, and daily life for the majority of the cardinals continued exactly as before. The Pope wrote a little later to Cardinal Borgia and Cardinal d'Estouteville about their conduct during the celebrations as godparents to the daughter of a Sienese nobleman: 'From what has been said, there was much dancing and flirting and you behaved as the worldly boys. Decency forbids a full account of what took place, things of which the very names are unsuitable to your positions.'[13]

Cardinal Borgia was obliged to apologise and promise to amend his ways, and the Pope counselled him to 'behave more discreetly', though this fell on deaf ears, as Rodrigo's first child, Pedro Luis, was born in that year. The mother's name is unrecorded, as is the name, or names, of the mother, or mothers, of his daughters Isabella (born in 1467) and Girolama (born in 1471). We cannot know if these three children were actually the offspring of the same woman. Interestingly, Isabella's great-great-grandson, Gianbattista Pamphilj, would become Pope Innocent X (1644–1655). Girolama was to die shortly after her marriage to Gianandrea Cesarini.

Rodrigo Borgia would always show deep affection for his children, but children were more than merely evidence of his virility. They would be helpful in creating a solid powerbase for the Borgias. The prevalence and preferment of bastards surprised nobody in fifteenth-century Italy, as they were considered to be just as useful as their legitimate counterparts. Children were always counted a blessing, to be placed in key positions, or to be married into advantageous alliances. Rodrigo Borgia could let his lustful nature and his dynastic interests work together for the greater advancement of the family.

His personal family would soon grow to include its most famous members, when Rodrigo began his relationship with Vanozza (Giovanna) dei Catenei in about 1468–1470. She had been born in around 1442 in Mantua, later moving to Rome. There she invested in the ownership of several Inns, first in the Borgo area, then later in the Campo di Fiori. She would bear Rodrigo four children, all acknowledged by him and grandly provided for. Cesare was born in 1475; Giovanni (Juan) was born in 1476; Lucrezia was born in 1480 and Gioffre in 1481.

Vanozza had a husband, Domenico d'Arignano, but he died just before Giovanni was born and Rodrigo arranged another marriage for her with Giorgio di Croce, an Apostolic Secretary. During that marriage Vanozza also had a son, Ottavio, by her husband. In 1486 Giorgio himself died, and Rodrigo arranged a third marriage for his mistress, with Carlo Canale. Rodrigo Borgia's relationship with Vanozza certainly lasted a long time, though it had faded by the time he became Pope. However, a firm bond remained between them and he respected her as the mother of his children. His love for these four in particular was to be strong and durable, determining the whole framework of his future career. He would lavish vast sums of money on Vanozza's children, and even when her position as his favourite mistress was ended, she would always retain her position as the matriarch of the family, and would remain his close friend and influence him throughout his life.[14]

His appreciation of her loyalty was shown in the respect with which she was treated, not only by him, but also by others. However, despite his domestic felicity with Vanozza and her children, Rodrigo also enjoyed to the full his undoubted attraction for other women. Pius II, himself a great lover of women all his life, was to ask frequently if it was consistent with a cardinal's position 'to court young women, and give those you love presents of fruit and wine and give no thought to anything other than your sensual pleasures'.

Bartomeo Bonatti, the Mantuan envoy to Siena, commented disapprovingly on the general atmosphere at the papal court: 'If all the children born within the past year could appear dressed like their fathers, they would appear as priests or cardinals!' Bonatti reported to his own mistress, the Marchesa of Mantua, that Rodrigo Borgia 'was seen in the company of the most beautiful woman that ever was.' She was a courtesan named Nachine, and was very wealthy. Her relationship with Cardinal Borgia was well known. One early letter shows his affection for Vanozza (he refers to her as Rosa), as well as his ambitions:

> Rosa, my dear love, follow my example and stay chaste until the day I am able to see you, and blend our affection into endless voluptuousness. Until then, let no lips profane your charms, let no hand lift those veils which cover my sovereign blessings. A little more patience and I shall then have what my uncle left me for an inheritance, the See of St Peter. Meanwhile, take particular care of our children, because they are destined to govern nations and kings.[15]

Any man with worldly ambitions needs a suitably magnificent background, and this he had. His office of Vice-chancellor brought him the sum of 8,000 gold florins and he also held numerous Abbeys in Italy and Spain, plus three bishoprics. He built a palace in Rome that some would compare to Nero's Golden House, both for to its magnificence and for what took place there. Cardinal Ascanio Sforza wrote:

> The palace is splendidly decorated, the walls of the entrance hall are hung with fine tapestries, the carpets on the floor harmonise with the furnishings, which include a sumptuous daybed upholstered in red satin and with a canopy over it. There is a chest, on which is laid out a vast and beautiful collection of gold and silver plate. Beyond this there are two more rooms, one hung with fine satin and carpeted, and with another canopied bed covered with Alexandrine velvet. The other is even more ornate, with a couch covered in cloth of gold. In this room, the central table is covered with a cloth of Alexandrine velvet and is surrounded by finely carved chairs.

When Pope Pius II died Rodrigo was still considered to be too young to be elected as pope, and Paul II (Pietro Barbo) succeeded. But Rodrigo already had influence and when Paul in turn died, in 1471, Rodrigo was able to secure the election of Francesco della Rovere as Pope Sixtus IV. He naturally received power in return for this support, but by that time Rodrigo had been Vice-chancellor for fifteen years, and was already a force to be reckoned with. He was the man chosen to crown the new Pope, though the Romans themselves proved less than enthusiastic, as della Rovere was from a modest background and they expected him to bring in a period of austerity, so they pelted the papal litter with stones all the way to the Lateran Palace.[16]

Cardinal Borgia then left Rome to spend sixteen months in Spain. This was ostensibly a legation on behalf of the new Pope, but it also served for him to visit his Episcopal see. The Pope had intended it to help raise money for a war with the Turks, and it was also an embassy from the Vatican on the occasion of the marriage of Isabella of Castile and Ferdinand of Aragon. Rodrigo took with him the Papal Dispensation for that marriage, due to their consanguinity.

When he returned to Rome, it was to find that the Pope's crusading fervour had dissipated, and he then busied himself in simony, nepotism, and the gathering of power. His own nephews, Pietro Riario and Giuliano della Rovere, were very much to the fore, and were being heaped with honours. Sixtus IV made a favourite of Girolamo Riario and was implicated in the Pazzi conspiracy against the Florentine house of de' Medici, while Girolamo became Lord of Forli and Imola due to his marriage to Caterina Sforza.

During these years Rodrigo concentrated on consolidating his own power. He amassed benefices, not only adding to his already considerable wealth, but gaining areas of strategic control.

When Sixtus IV died in 1484, Rodrigo Borgia was fifty-three years old and had become one of the most senior and experienced of the cardinals. He must by then have entertained hopes of the papacy, but he would again be disappointed. He was opposed by della Rovere who pushed through the election of the perfectly ordinary (apart from having fathered a large family) Cardinal

Giovanni Battista Cibo, who became Pope Innocent VIII. He would prove to be a weak pope, entirely in the hands of della Rovere, and Rome again became a city in turmoil with murders and robberies happening so regularly that the cardinals lived in fortified palaces guarded by armed servants.

Innocent VIII ruled for eight years, while Rodrigo waited. He was aware that the next papal election would be his final chance. He was getting older, but fortunately for him, Innocent's incompetence had badly undermined della Rovere's own chances. Borgia carefully cultivated his allies, using his cousin Adriana de Mila as a helpmeet. She had acted as governess for Rodrigo's children once they left Vanozza to be educated, and was a widow. Rodrigo extended family influence by finding another husband for her, and arranged a marriage with Ludovico Orsini, while Adriana's new stepson, Orso Orsini, was betrothed to Giulia Farnese. Orso and Giulia were married in 1489, when the bride was fourteen years old, but already so lovely that she was known as 'Giulia la Bella'.

Her marriage to Orsini would prove unhappy, but her future lay elsewhere, as Rodrigo Borgia quickly became her lover.

Innocent VIII had become very unpopular due to his flaunting of his family and the general corruption of his reign. He became ill in 1490. Rodrigo meanwhile had gained great prestige and had acted with diplomacy. His vices were certainly known, but he had learned to show some discretion. He was then sixty years old, and described as being 'tall, with a medium complexion, neither dark nor fair, with dark eyes and a full mouth. His health is excellent and he has enormous energy. He is eloquent and has innate good manners, which never leave him.'[17] The College of Cardinals had gradually changed, with a large number of members already affiliated to one party or another. At the end of Innocent's reign there were twenty-seven cardinals, and of these no fewer than ten were the nephews of previous popes, eight were Crown nominees, four were Roman nobles, and one had been made a cardinal due to family service to the Holy See. Just four of the possible candidates were capable 'career' churchmen, and only three of these were considered to be *papabile*. Ascanio Sforza was connected to Milan, Giuliano della Rovere was for France, and Rodrigo Borgia was seen as an 'independent'. Della Rovere was in fact being bankrolled by France to the tune of 200,000 gold ducats, plus another 100,000 from the Republic of Genoa.

Borgia had the disadvantage of being of Spanish descent, which was rather looked down on, but he had worked hard and gained popularity. His son Cesare was to study at the University of Perugia with the church as his intended career, and his daughter Lucrezia, then aged eleven, was earmarked for a marriage with the Spanish nobleman Juan de Centelles. In July of 1492 Rodrigo received the news that King Ferdinand of Spain had received a favour from the Pope, the elevation of Valencia to the status of an Arch-Diocese, which made Rodrigo the Cardinal-Archbishop of Valencia. Even more exciting, Innocent's life was fading fast, and on the evening of 25 July, he died.[18]

Surprisingly, the usual disorder and rioting did not take place, and for once the Pope's death seemed to improve the situation. The College of Cardinals was split between the supporters of Ascanio Sforza and those of Giuliano della Rovere. It was considered by the Ferrarese Ambassador and others that Rodrigo Borgia might prove to be a reasonable outside bet, due to his long-standing position as Vice-chancellor. However, the voting, once started, proved to be very slow. No candidate had anything like the sixteen votes required to win the election. So slow was the election that the cardinals were eventually restricted to one meal a day, in an effort to persuade them to make a decision. The Florentine Ambassador, tired of waiting, reported, 'From Monday, if there has been no election by then, they will get only bread, wine and water!'

It was later said that during the night of 10 August Cardinal Sforza decided that he and his party should back Cardinal Borgia, to break the deadlock. To be fair, Sforza had been voting for Borgia since the election began. On 11 August, it was then announced that Rodrigo Borgia was the newly elected Pope, and he would take the name of Alexander VI. He had won on an almost unanimous vote.

The Milanese Ambassador was triumphant, claiming that 'Cardinal Ascanio Sforza was entirely responsible for the election of Cardinal Borgia, and has gained so much credit thereby, that he is not only the first of those next to the Pope, but practically the Pope himself!' But they would all find that Cardinal Borgia had been planning for his election for far too long to want to be anyone's puppet, and that he had worked so hard entirely for the advancement of Borgia, not Milan.

There were many glowing recommendations. Sigismondo de' Conti described the new Pope: 'Few men understand the rules of proper behaviour as he did. He knew how to appear at his best, to converse elegantly, and behave impeccably, and he had the advantage of majestic height. He was physically strong with a lively intellect, he was indeed wonderfully suited to his new position.'

Others proved to be rather less enthusiastic. The Florentine Ambassador, Francesco Guicciardini, said that the new Pope was '...extremely shrewd and wise. A good judge of character, immensely persuasive, and a skilled master at the political game. But those good traits are utterly surpassed by his vices, his obscene behaviour, his lack of sincerity, audacity, mendacity, disloyalty, impiety, greed, ambition, barbarous cruelty, and a deep desire to glorify his children.'

After the election, Giuliano della Rovere complained that Rodrigo Borgia had 'bought' his pontificate. He said that Borgia had given his main supporter four mule-loads of silver. It is quite likely that he had, but della Rovere's complaint was less indignation at such corruption than chagrin that he had offered his supporters less, and had therefore failed.

Alexander VI was crowned on 26 August 1492 and spent 12,000 ducats on materials for his officials' outfits alone. Every possible luxury – flowers, greenery, tapestries, garlands, statuary – was organised. There were fountains dispensing wine and water. The heat was intense and the new Pope was overcome by it at St Giovanni in Laterano and needed to be revived with cold water. He was not the only victim of the temperature, as the Mantuan Ambassador, after describing a long list of the glories of the coronation, added, '...but I also wanted to tell your Excellency that the whole court was almost dead with exhaustion, having had to spend the whole day on the dusty streets, under the sun.'

By that time, Lucrezia, the Pope's favourite daughter, was twelve years old. Within days of her father's election as Pontiff, Cardinal Ascanio Sforza was eagerly suggesting a marriage between her and a member of the Sforza family. The previous negotiations with the Spanish nobleman were already broken off, as Alexander's new position had increased Lucrezia's marriage value enormously. She was described as 'attractive, of average height, and gracefully built, with rather a long face but with a fine nose and blonde hair. She has rather pale eyes and a full mouth with dazzling white teeth. Her neck is elegant and her bosom well-proportioned. She also has a cheerful and happy manner.' Her father's doting fondness for her was also remarked upon.[19]

As soon as Alexander was crowned pope, he started to build his power base. He had five living children – his daughter Isabella and his four children by Vanozza dei Catenei. His eldest son Pedro Luis and his daughter Girolama had died before his election, but the other Borgia relatives could profit by it. Several cousins and nephews moved to Rome, including Juan Borgia and his son Francisco Loritz, and another Rodrigo Borgia, who became captain of the papal guard. Risking criticism, he also appointed his head of household, five valets, two financiers, his secretary, several doctors, and even his fool, from Catalans, thereby creating an entirely non-Italian household. His pride in his illegitimate children also caused comment: 'Alexander VI could be moved to anger and other passions, but principally by his excessive desire to magnify his children, whom he loved to distraction.'[20]

In February of 1493 the announcement was made of the betrothal of Lucrezia Borgia to Giovanni Sforza, Lord of Pesaro. The groom was then twenty-six years old and a widower, and was cousin to Milan's ruler Ludovico Sforza. Also in February, the Pope legitimised his youngest son Joffre and made his nephew into Cardinal Juan Borgia, Bishop of Olomouc. He also gave his son Cesare three lucrative abbeys with which to finance his future church career. The marriage of Lucrezia, then aged thirteen, was celebrated in June, the bride being given away by her brother Juan, Duke of Gandia. The details of the elaborate wedding were given by Johannes Burchard in his diary:

Don Juan of Gandia, son of the Pope and brother of the bride, escorted his sister. They processed through the rooms … his sister's train was carried by a young negro girl. She was followed by Battistina, daughter of Pope Innocent VIII, whose train was also carried by a negro girl. After her came Giulia Farnese, the mistress of Pope Alexander. She was followed by one hundred and fifty Roman ladies, who, despite my scolding them, did not genuflect when they passed the Pope on his throne, except for his daughter and one or two of the others ... when all the ladies had kissed the Pope's foot, the Lord of Pesaro [the bridegroom] and the bride knelt on two cushions.[21]

The marriage contract was then signed and the banquet began.

Four of Cardinal Colonna's squires entered, dressed in animal skins as savages, and they recited verses about love. The banquet was served by the valets and squires ... around two hundred dishes of sweets, marzipan, candied fruits, and various sorts of wines... At the end the guests threw large quantities of sweets to the people outside. [Later that evening] the Pope was in the premier seat ... the bridegroom and some other guests, among whom were ladies, including the Pope's daughter and his mistress Giulia Farnese. At the third rank were Battistina [then wife of Niccolo Orsini]. All the guests were at the same table and each cardinal with a young lady next to him. The meal went on until after midnight with bawdy comedies which made everyone laugh. When it was over the Pope accompanied his daughter to the palace of Cardinal Zen by the steps of St Peter's, where the marriage was consummated.[22]

The same week, a Milanese agent reported to Ludovico Sforza that he was impressed with the new Pope's political skills. 'He has managed to marry his daughter to a Sforza, a man with an income of 12,000 ducats a year, in addition to the allowance paid to him by the Duke of Milan. He has managed to draw 35,000 ducats out of Virginio Orsini and make him an ally, and has managed to connect himself to the King of Naples, obtaining a wife and state for his son... I do not think that these are the achievements of a man with no brains.'[23]

On 20 September of the same year, Alexander VI gave out twelve cardinal's hats. Before that time no other pope had ever given out more than eight. One of those was given to his son Cesare Borgia, then aged only eighteen, and another went to the twenty-five year old brother of his mistress, Alessandro Farnese. (Cardinal Farnese was to be known as 'the petticoat cardinal' due to his sister's Giulia's influence having provided him with his promotion. He would later become Pope Paul III.)

According to Ludovico Sforza's Ambassador the news of these appointments so infuriated Cardinal Giuliano della Rovere that he could not continue with the game of cards he had been playing when he heard. He had to retire to his rooms, where he could be heard 'ranting and roaring' and was so upset that he made himself ill with a fever. Cardinal Carafa was also furious, but was able to hide his feelings more effectively.

Lucrezia was present in Rome for the marriage of her brother Joffre to Sancia of Aragon. She was the illegitimate daughter of Alfonso of Calabria (who would briefly become King of Naples). Alexander invested the bridegroom with the title of Prince of Squillace with an income of 40,000 ducats per year. The wedding took place in May when the bride was sixteen years old and the groom fourteen. Alexander was forging important alliances, particularly as Juan, his eldest son by Vanozza, also had his marriage arranged, to Maria Enriquez de Luna, a member of the royal house of Spain, who had originally been betrothed to his deceased half-brother Pedro Luis, whose title of Duke of Gandia had also been given to Juan.

After those celebrations Lucrezia left Rome to travel to her husband's home at Pesaro and Alexander's attention was again centred on politics and on Giulia Farnese. The lovely Giulia was the daughter of Pierluigi Farnese and Giovanna Caetani and she had four siblings, as well as a husband. She had been married to Orsino Orsini with a dowry of 3,000 gold florins. Orsini was reported as being squint-eyed and lacking in self-confidence and must have seemed an odd choice for the fascinating girl. Adriana de Mila had suggested the match to her second husband as a way of gaining higher status for her stepson with the Vatican. Giulia would bear one daughter, Laura, and the paternity of the child was never certain, though she was claimed as the Pope's child so that she could reap the great advantages of being so.

Charles VIII had invaded Italy intending to seize the throne of Naples with the support of Ludovico of Milan, and by October he had reached Piacenza, where he refused to meet with Alexander's peace envoy. He had sent back the insulting reply that he would 'see the Pope when he entered Rome'. In November, troops in the vanguard of the French army, led by Yves d'Allegue, captured Giulia Farnese and Adriana di Mila while they were on the road between Viterbo and Capodimonte. The ladies and their attendants were taken to Montefiascore and, on being assured by Cardinal Ascanio Sforza that 'all are well and have not in any way been molested,' Alexander paid a ransom of 3,000 ducats to have them returned safely.[25]

The Milanese ambassador had earlier reported, 'If we can persuade Cardinal Giuliano della Rovere to change sides and support France, we will have created a powerful weapon against Pope Alexander.' However, della Rovere was ahead of them, as he had already left his castle at Ostia and set sail for France under cover of darkness. He took the precaution of leaving the fortress well guarded and stocked with every provision, in quantity enough to last two years.[26]

The Pope was now obliged to consider the defence of Rome itself, as French troops could be seen outside. By Christmas the situation was hopeless, and by 31 December Alexander sent his secretary and four leading citizens, along with his master of ceremonies, Johannes Burchard, to discuss French entry into the city. Despite a 'peaceful' entry, the French still brought chaos. They pillaged the palaces, requisitioned houses, and on returning home even Burchard found a French nobleman had taken over his rooms. The house of Vanozza dei Catenei was also broken into.

By January Pope Alexander had taken refuge in the Castel Sant'Angelo along with most of his cardinals, but there would shortly be agreement between the Pope and Charles VIII in exchange for cardinal's hats being given to two French bishops. Alexander named his son Cardinal Cesare Borgia as Legate to the French court for the following four months, but Cesare was more of a hostage than a willing visitor. He would not be captive for long, escaping from the French disguised as a royal groom. Burchard also reported a trick that Cesare Borgia had played on the French. He had left Rome with nineteen mules, supposedly laden with items of value. After his escape, it was found that the chests that seventeen of them had carried were empty![27]

The Tiber flooded that winter, causing great devastation and loss of life, with damage estimated at 300,000 ducats. Alexander had to spend another 80,000 ducats on repairs to Castel Sant'Angelo after the previous year's depradations.

Lucrezia, then fifteen years old, returned to Rome in the spring with her husband, but he soon left again with a contract for raising troops and joined his men. Joffre then arrived in Rome with his wife Sancia, being met by Lucrezia and all the cardinals. Alexander waited at the Vatican to greet them. At the feast of Pentecost in May, there were complaints about the seating arrangements. Burchard noted:

> Sancia and Lucrezia, the daughter of the Pope, sat on the marble bench where the canons of the Basilica usually sat to chant the epistle and the gospel. Many other ladies were seated around the pulpit. This indignity was disgraceful and scandalised all.[28]

There was, unfortunately, further trouble brewing. In March Cardinal Ascanio Sforza wrote to his brother, Ludovico Duke of Milan, that the Pope intended to dissolve Lucrezia's marriage to Giovanni Sforza. When the news reached Giovanni, he went to Milan to discuss the matter with his cousin. Lucrezia was sent to stay with the Dominican nuns at San Sisto, but she was heard to complain that she had never felt welcome in Pesaro with Giovanni's family.

In June of 1497 the Pope created a new Duchy of Benevento, intended for Juan, while Cesare was appointed Legate to Naples, where he was to crown their new King, Frederico. Though this was looked on as an honour for the young and inexperienced cardinal, Cesare was not particularly impressed. He was becoming increasingly impatient with the religious life, especially after seeing the honours heaped upon Juan.

On Wednesday 14 June Cesare and Juan dined with their mother Vanozza at her villa near San Pietro in Vincola. After the dinner, quite late in the evening, the two brothers left to return to the Vatican, but Juan separated from Cesare. He said he 'had a private visit to make' and left accompanied only by his groom. The following morning he had not returned, and throughout the day the Pope became increasingly uneasy. He apparently hoped that Juan had merely been held up at some party, or that he was with some woman, but there was no word and nobody had seen him. The Pope, saying he was 'troubled to his guts', desired to have information at any cost, and ordered men who were used to carrying out orders discreetly to find out whatever they could, by any means possible.[29]

By Friday there was still no word, Alexander was extremely distressed. During that day the Civil Guard found Juan's groom, badly wounded and unable to explain clearly what had happened. The morning of Saturday brought the answer, as a timber merchant reported seeing a body thrown into the Tiber late on Wednesday night. The body of the Duke of Gandia was found not far from Santa Maria del Popolo – he had been stabbed nine times and had his throat cut. Burchard reported the evidence of the wood merchant,

> They interrogated a certain Giorgio Schiavo who ... in order to protect his merchandise from theft, regularly spent the night on his barge on the Tiber. He had seen two men on foot come down an alleyway, looking carefully to right and left ... a rider on a white horse then appeared with a corpse slung over the horse behind him. The head and arms were on one side, and the legs on the other. The two men then lifted the body and threw it into the Tiber, with as much force as they were able. The man on the horse then asked them what the black thing was, that was floating on the water, and they replied that it was the coat, so one of them threw stones at it, to make it sink.[30]

At a consistory held on 17 June, the Spanish Ambassador apologised for the absence of Cardinal Sforza, saying it was due to his fears of the Spaniards in the wake of the Duke of Gandia's death. The Pope announced at this time that he intended to dissolve the marriage of Giovanni Sforza and Lucrezia Borgia, on the grounds of non-consummation.

Who the perpetrators of Juan's death were was never made clear. Juan's widow blamed Cesare, but at the time of the death he was not suspected. Juan had always been very unpopular in Rome, and he had many enemies. He was described as having been 'an avaricious youth, self-important, proud, vicious, and irrational.'[31] He had also had many mistresses, which caused a good deal of ill-feeling, one of whom was reputed to be his sister-in-law, Sancia of Aragon. He was a selfish, boastful and rather obnoxious young man, but of course his father the Pope saw him differently. Many people suspected that the Sforzas, owing to their difficulties with the Borgias and the impending separation of Giovanni from Lucrezia. Giovanni deeply resented the idea of having to admit to being impotent in order for the dispensation to go through. He refused to comply by giving evidence, claiming that he was certainly not impotent, and would not say that he was! He cited as evidence of his potency that his first wife had died in childbed.

In early September, Cardinal Cesare Borgia returned to Rome from Naples. He immediately had a long talk with his father, and next day it was noticed that the talking had stopped. Rumours then spread rapidly that Cesare had told Alexander that he intended to resign his cardinalate. This would certainly have vexed Alexander, who had cherished hopes that Cesare would follow in his footsteps and become the third Borgia pope. Cesare had other ideas, and much preferred the idea of being captain of the papal army, the Pope's enforcer, rather than being just another cleric.

About the other pressing matter, Alexander did get his own way. Giovanni Sforza had finally been persuaded by his pragmatic family to declare in writing that the marriage between him and Lucrezia had never been consummated. On 20 December the marriage was declared invalid, and the resentful ex-husband was obliged to return the dowry of 31,000 ducats that he had received. Pope Alexander and Cesare had other plans for Lucrezia, and the humiliation of her discarded husband did not matter.

Cardinal Ascanio Sforza had had a very hard time trying to persuade Giovanni to relinquish either the wife or the dowry, and was exhausted by the negotiations. All that he had managed to salvage was the return of some jewels and other items given by the family to Lucrezia, worth only a thousand ducats. Lucrezia seemed to take very little part in the arrangements for her future. She had married Giovanni at the behest of her family, and she also separated from him without demur. Few people believed the claim that they had not slept together, which had technically allowed the four-year marriage to be dissolved without hindrance. For many the idea that she was still a virgin was ludicrous, and the Perugian chronicler Matarazzo (admittedly hostile towards the Borgias) was scandalously delighted – 'it was a conclusion that set all of Italy laughing' – and he quoted Sforza's allegation that Lucrezia had slept not only with him, but also with her father and her brother Cesare.[32] The family's noted closeness was fuel to the fire for accusations of incest. Lucrezia was very likely the only woman Cesare ever really cared for, but that does not imply that they had any sexual connection.

There was a suggestion for a real lover for Lucrezia at this time, and the man most likely to have proved attractive to her was one Pedro Calderon, known as Perotto. He was Spanish and served in the Pope's chamber. His body was found in the Tiber on 14 February 1498, along with the body of a lady of Lucrezia's household. It was suggested that they had both been killed to prevent Lucrezia's affair with Perotto becoming known, just when her marriage to Giovanni Sforza was being dissolved. An agent of the Bentivoglio family of Bologna, Cristoforo Poggio, claimed that Perotto had vanished for 'having got His Holiness's daughter Lucrezia with child'. By March there were reports that she had actually given birth to a child, just at the time when her second marriage was being arranged following claims that she was still a virgin.

There was a child born around this time. Giovanni Borgia, known as the Infans Romanus, was later legitimized by Alexander VI in 1501. Alexander would eventually claim paternity of this child himself, but without naming the mother. Some said it may have been Giulia Farnese, but the Pope had never been secretive before about his mistresses and when Giulia Farnese had given birth to her daughter Laura there was no secrecy. The child would be brought up as Lucrezia's half-brother, though it could just as easily have been her own son, as the timing fits this possibility.

In June 1498 Lucrezia's new bridegroom was announced. He was Alfonso of Aragon, Duke of Bisceglie, the illegitimate son of the late Alfonso of Naples and brother of Joffre's wife Sancia. The dowry this time was set at 41,000 ducats.[33] The couple married in July and their entertainment included a theatrical piece in which the bride's brother Cesare appeared dressed in the costume of a unicorn, a symbol of chastity. It was a good joke, in view of his reputation for debauchery, but it was equally likely to refer to the supposed chastity of the bride.

The fun-loving Cesare finally renounced his cardinal's hat on 17 August and Louis XII immediately invested him with the title of Duke of Valentinois. He travelled to the French court, where he was hoping for a French royal marriage, but that certainly would not please Isabella and Ferdinand of Spain. Their envoys arrived in Rome in December and promptly accused the Pope of having bought his election, but Alexander was not the sort of man to be browbeaten and he retorted that at least he had been elected unanimously – the Spanish sovereigns had usurped their thrones.[34]

By January 1499 the sovereigns of Spain were demanding that Cesare be recalled from France and made to take up his cardinalate again, and their envoys were six cardinals from Spain, who presumably could not understand why he would want to give up the honour. 'After a long speech from the ambassadors, a violent and furious argument developed between them and the Pope.'[35] There was no possibility of Cesare complying as he was already in negotiation for the marriage he had hoped for, with Carlotta of Naples, then residing at the French court. As prospective bridegroom, his immediate worry was that he had contracted syphilis and the unsightly rash of the second stage of the disease was visible on his face. He did his best to disguise it by drawing attention to his magnificent and extravagant dress and jewels. Even his horse was wearing red silk and gold brocade, with harness and shoes of silver. His pages, squires and grooms were wearing crimson velvet halved with yellow silk, and all his attendants were equally well dressed. He had twelve baggage carts, fifty baggage mules, riding horses and chargers. Burchard, well accustomed to the lavish Italian lifestyle, referred to the splendid show as being 'without pomp' but his opinion was not shared by the French, where such display created disgust.[36]

Cesare went to Avignon where the papal legate Giuliano della Rovere resided, who had made his peace with the Pope over a year previously. Despite this show of amity, he would never really be a friend of the Borgias. The King of France met Cesare with honour, but his friendship was more to do with his need for a dispensation from the Pope, as he wanted to dissolve his own marriage to his cousin Jeanne and marry his predecessor's widow Anne of Brittany, which would bring France and Brittany together.

Cesare faced his own problems, as the bride-to-be, Carlotta, proved to be not only extremely plain of face, but also very outspoken. She was not impressed with the idea of marrying the Pope's bastard son, who had so recently been a cardinal. Despite this setback, Cesare did his best to get on well with the rest of the court, and della Rovere wrote to the Pope saying 'The most illustrious Duke Valentino is endowed with modesty, prudence, ability and every virtue of mind and body, so that he had conquered everyone. He had found much favour with the king, and all the princes of this court, and everyone holds him in esteem and honour, of which fact I willingly give testimony.'[37]

Louis XII was enabled to change queens as he had wished, but Cesare's marriage was delayed as Carlotta could not be persuaded to go ahead with it. The Pope remarked that if the marriage failed to take place, they would be the laughing stock of Italy. King Louis was curt with the envoys from Naples, but they did not dress up their message. The King of Naples' opinion was that '... to a bastard son of the pope, the King would not even give a bastard daughter, let alone a legitimate child.'

Ascanio Sforza told the Pope bluntly that in sending Cesare to France, he was bringing ruin on Italy, while the Spanish spoke of convening a council to attempt to dethrone Alexander on the grounds of simony, and also reproached him for his blatant nepotism. Alexander retorted that the Spanish monarchs were more severely punished, as they were at that time without direct heirs. But the danger was real and Alexander even feared that Louis XII might hold Cesare as a hostage.

Carlotta remained obdurate and her father supported her in her refusal, so the King of France was obliged to save face all round by finding an alternative bride. He settled on Charlotte d'Albret, whose mother was a kinswoman of the queen, and whose brother Jean had inherited the crown of Navarre. She was then described as being 'unbelievably beautiful' and Cesare accepted her for that, and for her connection to the French royal house. The contract was finally signed on 10 May 1499 and the wedding took place two days later.

Meanwhile, Lucrezia had miscarried her first child with Alfonso Bisceglie and was pregnant again by August. She had been made Governor of Spoleto and travelled there with her brother Joffre. Burchard recorded that she left on horseback, but with a litter with damask cushions and a magnificent canopy provided for when she became tired. There were men available to carry it to ensure her a restful journey.

Giulia Farnese was re-installed as the Pope's mistress after a short interval apart. By October they were all in Rome, where Lucrezia gave birth to a son named Rodrigo, in honour of his grandfather. Burchard again reported that the christening of the child was extremely grand. It took place in the chapel of Sixtus IV in St Peter's on St Martin's Day (11 November). The child was carried in to the sound of trumpets and was baptised in a silver-gilt shell by Cardinal Caraffa, who became his godfather. The following day Lucrezia was given a gift by the College of Cardinals, consisting of two sweetmeat dishes of silver filled with two hundred ducats disguised as bonbons.[38]

While Lucrezia experienced the joys of motherhood, Cesare was busy trying to subdue Caterina Sforza, the ruler of Forli. Her castles and cities fell to him 'like whores' but the indomitable Caterina held out bravely in her Castella at Ravaldino. Cesare caused horrified comments by abducting a young noblewoman, Dorotea Malatesta Caracciolo, who had been travelling in the Romagna in the north, on her way to Venice. Several of her retinue had been severely wounded and a storm of indignation met the news that a respectable noblewoman, under the protection of Venice, had been attacked. The Pope's reaction was that the kidnapping was 'a brutal and detestable thing' and he added plaintively, 'if the Duke has done this, then he has lost his mind.' The action certainly showed the recklessness that lay beneath Cesare's abilities. Machiavelli described it as 'rash self-confidence, which made him do unnecessary and even foolish things, on a whim, just for the devilry of it.' The action fuelled Venice's mistrust of him, and Cesare seemed unable to comprehend the depth of enmity that such actions caused. He eventually returned to Rome, carrying with him a far more important hostage, Caterina Sforza herself.[39]

Lucrezia at that time lived retired, possibly believing that her life was secure from further troubles, but the Pope's plans for her future, let alone Cesare's, were far from over.

Lucrezia enjoyed the excitement and display of the Holy Year far more than the Pope's master of ceremonies Johannes Burchard did. He was driven crazy with trying to organise everything, particularly when Cesare returned bringing 1,000 infantry with him, as well as his personal household and the illustrious prisoner Caterina. Having been repeatedly raped by Cesare, she was first housed within the Vatican, but after her firm refusals to sign away her rights and those of her children she was transferred to the Castel Sant'Angelo as a prisoner. With Sforza opposition dealt with, Cesare's hopes then rested on France, and King Louis XII looked to assert his 'rights' to Naples. That would mean that the Aragonese, including Lucrezia's husband, would be surplus to requirements. However, Lucrezia was very fond of her husband, and sided with him and his sister, for once in opposition to Cesare. It was to be their undoing.

First, though, a great storm was to take the roof off the *Sala dei Papi* in the Vatican, which collapsed onto the Pope who was sitting underneath. The banker Lorenzo Chigi, who was with the Pope, was killed and Alexander was only saved by the strong canopy over his chair. Even then he was knocked unconscious. It was a reminder that all the power of the Borgias depended on that one man's life and that without him they had many dangerous enemies.[40]

Two weeks later, Lucrezia's husband, Alfonso Duke of Bisceglie, was attacked on the steps of St Peter's by 'persons unknown'. Burchard reported that four men attacked him and dealt him three strong blows, 'one on the head, very deep, one across the shoulder, either one of which could easily have killed him, and another smaller one on his arm... They say he is very ill ... it is said that the wounded Duke was taken back into the palace, the Pope went to see him and Madama Lucrezia was in a dead faint.'

The attackers fled to where about forty other horsemen waited for them, who accompanied them through the Porta Pertusa. A witness said that they had been dragging Alfonso away, as if to throw him into the river, but were surprised by the guards. Sanudo reported three days later 'It is not known who wounded the Duke, but it is said that it is whoever had killed the Duke of Gandia and threw him into the Tiber.'[41] Suspicion began to fall upon Cesare who then had good reason to wish his now useless brother-in-law out of the way. Cesare said 'I did not wound the Duke, but if I had, it would be no more than he deserved.'

While Alfonso was recovering, only the doctor of the King of Naples was allowed to attend to him, while Lucrezia dealt with all his food herself, fearing poison. However, on 18 August, a month after the attack, more violence took place. Alfonso, his sister Sancia, Lucrezia and two others were together in his apartment in the Borgia Tower when 'Michelotto' burst in. He was Miguel de Corella, Cesare's sinister henchman. He forced the envoy of Naples and Alfonso's uncle out of the room, and they were led away by armed men. Lucrezia and Sancia screamed for help and tried to protect Alfonso. Michelotto told them to run to the Pope for the release of the captured men. This they did, while in their absence Michelotto suffocated the helpless Alfonso.

When the women returned they were prevented from entering the apartment, and were simply told that Alfonso was dead. 'The women, beside themselves with grief, filled the palace with their shrieking, lamenting and wailing, one calling for her husband, the other for her brother, and their tears were without end.'[42] This time there was no doubt who the perpetrator was, as Michelotto was known to be Cesare's 'enforcer'.

It is suggested that while Cesare was away from Rome, Alfonso and Sancia of Aragon had tried to persuade the Pope to return to his old allegiance with Spain. Lucrezia was also being drawn in and even Joffre, largely a nonentity, was being influenced by Sancia. Cesare was not the sort of man to allow his family to pull away, especially when threatened his own interests. His deep affection for Lucrezia was well known, and it would have angered him that she had fallen under Alfonso's spell. The excuse for the murder was that Alfonso had attempted to kill Cesare with a crossbow. Brandolinus gave the opinion of many when he said that it was actually 'motivated by the supreme lust for domination of Cesare Valentino Borgia'.

The atmosphere of Rome was conducive to crime and Cesare merely took advantage of the power of the papacy to live and act as others did, albeit on a greater scale. He had married Charlotte d'Albret, then left her pregnant in France, and he would not see her again. Meanwhile, he was the father of several bastards, including Gerolama and Camilla Lucrezia Borgia, whom he openly acknowledged. A document of 8 August 1509 legitimising Camilla Lucrezia refers to her having 'been born of Cesare' and an unnamed married woman. Speculation at the time was rife that the woman was Dorotea Caracciolo but it was never confirmed. His only legitimate offspring was Luisa, daughter of Charlotte d'Albret. There were several other claimants to his bloodline, but he probably never knew how many children he had sired.

One famous incident shows his habits. On 31 October 1501 there was a dinner at his apartment in the Vatican. Fifty prostitutes were present, and they danced after supper, first fully dressed, then naked. Lighted candelabra were placed on the floor and hot chestnuts were thrown among them, to be picked up by the women as they crawled between the lights. Cesare, Lucrezia and the Pope watched the entertainment, and the men present were offered prizes of rich clothing, for competing in who could have sex with the women the greatest number of times.[43] If this orgy sounded too difficult to believe, it was recounted by Johannes Burchard, an eye-witness and reliable source.

It would not be the only incident of its kind. Agostino Vespucci wrote to Machiavelli in the same year:

The Pope, who is surrounded there by his illicit flock, had brought in from outside every evening, to the palace, twenty-five women or more, from the Ave Maria to one o'clock, so that the palace is made manifestly into the brothel of all filth.

Though Lucrezia took no personal part in the sexual shenanigans in the Vatican, it is clear that she at times witnessed them. On one occasion, Matarazzo's *Chronicle of Perugia* claims 'The Pope, returning to the hall, had all the lights put out, and all the women who were there, and many men as well, took of all their clothes, and there was festivity and play.'[44]

Burchard recorded another incident of, shall we say, horseplay. A peasant had brought in wood to Rome and the guards threw the harness off the mares carrying it, leading them into the courtyard. They then freed four stallions from the stables, who proceeded to fight over the mares. 'The Pope and Donna Lucrezia laughing with evident satisfaction, watched all that was happening from a window above the palace gate.'[45]

Despite these actions, particularly distasteful in the presence of his daughter, the Pope was still a man who took his religious duties seriously. It seems that he saw no connection at all between his position as Pontiff and his personal life. He insisted on all taking part in religious rituals, which even some of the cardinals would avoid if they could, but Alexander ensured that they all attended. He appeared to enjoy these just as much as he did the debauchery which took place in his apartments.

Cesare paid no lip service to God or the church, simply using his father's position to support his power as Generalissimo of the papal army. The Pope was able to deflect, or shrug off, criticism and Cesare hardly noticed it; but one of the most potentially damaging of criticisms was circulated by the Roman nobleman Silvio Savelli in the form of a letter. It listed all the charges against the Borgias, specifically the murder of Alfonso Bisceglie, plus the sexual scandals, Cesare's Romagna conquests having been won by using the money intended for a crusade, and every other crime that the author could imagine:

His father favours him because of his own perversity and cruelty... the cardinals see all but keep quiet, flatter and appear to admire the Pope. But all fear him and above all fear his son, who from a cardinal has made himself into an assassin. He lives like the Turks, surrounded by a flock of prostitutes, guarded by armed soldiers. At his order men are wounded, killed, poisoned, thrown into the Tiber, despoiled of all their possessions.

This was a dangerous document as the Pope was in negotiation for Lucrezia's next husband and the Savelli letter was widely circulated. It was to also be repeated by historians over the centuries.

Lucrezia's prospective father-in-law was Ercole d'Este, Duke of Ferrara. Due to the scandalous rumours his envoy thought it necessary to reassure him of Lucrezia's good character. 'Lucrezia is a most intelligent, lovely, and exceedingly gracious lady. She is modest and lovable and decorous. Moreover, she is a devout and God-fearing Christian. She is beautiful but her charm of manner is still more striking. In short, her character is such that it is impossible to suspect anything "sinister" of her.'

Ercole d'Este had been trying to delay the marriage and it was only finally agreed when the Pope declared in anger to the Ferrarese envoys that their master was 'behaving like a tradesman'.

At the end of November, Cesare ceded his castles of Rossi, Solarolo and Granorolo in exchange for Cento and Pieve, to guarantee payment of the dowry, which was set at 100,000 ducats. The bridal procession left Ferrara and extravagant preparations were made in Rome for its reception. This was no illegitimate son Lucrezia was marrying, but the young Duke, Alfonso d'Este, and his family had driven a very hard bargain. Guicciardini recorded the rumours about Lucrezia's reputation: 'It was said that she had slept with both her father and her brothers, and that her father had dissolved her first marriage as he could not bear having her husband as a rival.'

The celebrations were designed to turn attention away from such stories, and Alexander also announced the concession of a cut in the census due from Ferrara, from 40,000 ducats to only 100. Lucrezia's son, Rodrigo of Aragon, then nearly two years old, was made the Duke of Sermoneta, but would remain in Rome after his mother's new marriage. It was not the custom for a woman to take with her the children of a previous union when she married again.

Lucrezia left her palace by St Peter's wearing a gown of gold brocade. She was escorted by the brothers of her new husband Ferrante and Sigismondo, and fifty Roman ladies came next, also magnificently dressed. The procession went to the Vatican where the Pope waited with thirteen cardinals and Cesare.[46] Again, Burchard was a witness, and to him fell the responsibility of ensuring that all went smoothly. Lucrezia was presented with jewels on behalf of her new husband.

After giving the order for the casket to be opened, Cardinal Ippolito d'Este took out a tiara set with fifteen diamonds, with rubies, and about forty pearls. Eight brooches of various designs ornamented with precious stones to be used on the clothes or on a hat, then more brooches of divers sorts and four more of great value. There were four large pearl collars, and four superb crosses, one in the form of a St Andrew's cross and the other three like the cross of Christ. All covered with diamonds and precious gems. Finally was brought out another tiara, almost as valuable as the first one, and all the jewellery was estimated to be worth 8,000 ducats.[47]

On 5 January 1502 the Pope granted an audience to the brothers of Alfonso d'Este and handed over his daughter's dowry. The new Duchess of Ferrara left Rome the following day with her household and an escort provided by her father-in-law. She arrived at her new home on 30 January to be greeted by the seventy-year-old Duke Ercole. She would make her formal entry on the following day. Ferrara was prosperous, dealing in silks, velvets, and other luxury goods, but also in fish, salamis, candied sweets, and 'the best cakes in the world'.[48]

The formal entry was marred only by the firing of a cannon, which caused Lucrezia's horse to shy and she fell off. She was unhurt and immediately provided with a 'very beautiful' mule to ride, so she continued her journey accompanied by her new husband, his household and courtiers. Zambotti was impressed by the bride, saying 'She is about twenty-four years old and most beautiful with smiling eyes. She is upright in form and personality, prudent, wise, happy, vivacious and kind. The Ferrarese like her very much and are thankful, expecting great things from her for the city, and from the Pope who is said to love his daughter dearly, as he has shown by the dowry and castles given to Don Alfonso.'[49]

Unfortunately, the private relationship between Lucrezia and Alfonso was not to be so warm. He had not chosen his bride and did not wish to marry her. He would not be either tender or romantic with her, which must have made her regret the loss of her previous husband, of whom she had been very fond. However, the proprieties would be observed and Alfonso would perform his marital duty satisfactorily. Another problem for the bride was her new sister-in-law Isabella, who was married to Francesco Gonzaga, the Marquess of Mantua. Though Lucrezia tried to be friendly with this woman, they would never become friends, and Isabella was always quick to criticise. Adriana de Mila and Lucrezia's cousin Angela, who attended her, advised her to take her time, but Isabella was clever and took every opportunity to show Lucrezia disrespect.

Isabella's malice and Alfonso's indifference must have made Lucrezia's first months in Ferrara very uncomfortable. She clung to Adriana de Mila for company and comfort, but her father-in-law declared her household excessive and said 'the Pope should therefore direct the ladies to return.' Lucrezia was given a list of the people who would comprise her future household, and anyone not on the list would be expected to return to Rome.

There was also a difference of opinion about her allowance. Ercole offered her only 8,000 ducats, but Lucrezia said she could not maintain her household on less than 12,000 ducats annually. Ercole finally gave her 10,000 ducats. Lucrezia vented her resentments on the Ferrarese members of her household and kept her own small circle of friends. She was soon expecting her first child. She would miscarry after suffering a series of fevers during which she became delirious and did not know she had lost her daughter. She was slow in recovering and Alfonso showed some concern, but he still found emotional closeness very difficult.

At this low point in her life, Lucrezia met the poet Pietro Bembo. It was to become an important relationship and, much later, Lord Byron would read some of the letters they had sent each other, and call them 'the prettiest love letters in the world'. This unfaithfulness on her part was the mirror image of Alfonso's own, as he continued to have mistresses throughout their seventeen-year marriage, though he and Lucrezia would produce another two daughters and five sons together.

During her first years in Ferrara, Lucrezia wrote to the Pope every week and he had intended to visit her. He was unable to do so, but assured her that in 1503 he would certainly see her. He was by then seventy-two years old and in good health, but overweight. His closeness to Cesare at that time is explained by the need to hand over a strong papacy at his death, and he had begun to pack the College of Cardinals with people likely to be favourable towards Cesare in the future.[50] Of nine cardinals appointed, five would be Spaniards, but his dream had always been to form a league of Italian states, to work together to expel both France and Spain from Italy. 'Although Spaniards by birth, and temporarily allied with France, we are Italians, and it is in Italy that our future lies.'

That summer was unbearably hot in Rome, and the political situation prevented the Pope from retiring from the city into the country. He was heard to remark, 'This month is a bad one for fat people.'

On Saturday 5 August Alexander and Cesare went to Monte Mario to dine with Cardinal Adriano. The following week Alexander was running a fever and soon Cesare was also affected. It was important to keep news of the Pope's illness from becoming common knowledge. At one point Cesare seemed to be the more ill, having convulsions and being bathed with ice-cold water. Cesare would later tell Machiavelli that he had planned for every contingency, except that he would be lying helpless on his sickbed at the time of his father's death. Burchard in his diary stated:

> The Pope fell ill on 12 August and a fever appeared between six and seven o'clock and remained permanently. On the 15th thirteen ounces of blood were drawn from him. On Friday the 18th he confessed to Bishop Gamboa of Carignola who read Mass to him. After he received Communion, he gave the Eucharist to the Pope, who was then sitting up in bed. The Pope then told him that he felt very bad. At the hour of Vespers, after Gamboa had given him Extreme Unction, the Pope died.

Michelotto had been sent to claim the keys to the Pope's treasury, and took away silver goods and around 100,000 ducats in two coffers. While the valuables were being secured, the Pope's valets were stealing everything, including his clothes. When Michelotto had to announce the Pope's death there was nothing left except the chairs and some tapestries on the walls. Burchard arrived to take charge, dressing the body in red brocade and exhibiting it in the Sistine Chapel as was traditional. But it had already begun to decompose in the heat and had to be covered with an antique tapestry.

While many were to criticise Alexander VI, particularly Guicciardini, his vices were actually no worse than those of many others, and he had done his best for the papacy and for his family. Though he had had mistresses, he was closely attached to Vanozza dei Catenei and took good care of their children.[51]

Cardinal Ippolito had the unpleasant task of breaking the news of the Pope's death to Lucrezia. All conflicts would be forgotten and she was devastated. She refused to eat, had her rooms draped in black, and even refused candles to relieve the gloom. Her in-laws made no pretence of grief, and Ercole d'Este wrote to his envoy in Milan, 'You ask how we are affected by the Pope's death, this is to tell you that it was in no way displeasing to us.' Pietro Bembo tried to help ease Lucrezia's grief by visiting her. He found her dressed in black, lying on the floor in her dark and airless room, weeping. He could think of nothing suitable to say to her, but next day wrote her a letter: 'Perhaps this happened to me because you had no need either of my sympathy or my condolences, for, knowing my fidelity, you would be aware of the pain I felt on account of your sorrow.'[52] His devotion to her at that time was to transform their flirtation into something far more serious and important to them both.

Meanwhile, Cesare was convalescent and desperately trying to salvage whatever he could from the disaster. The Papal Conclave proved to be the usual free-for-all with Cardinal Giuliano della Rovere again trying his luck. Cardinal Francesco Todeschini da Piccolomini had already fathered twelve children, but nobody seemed to mind that, and he became a compromise pope, reigning as Pius III, but for only one month. The following Conclave would give Giuliano della Rovere his chance and he was finally elected as Pope Julius II in November 1503. On the very day of his election he declared:

I will not live in the same rooms as the Borgias lived. He [Alexander VI] desecrated the Holy Church as none before. He usurped the papal power by the Devil's aid and I forbid, under pain of excommunication, that anyone speak or even think of the Borgias again. His name and memory must be forgotten. It must be crossed out of every document and memorial. His reign must be obliterated! All paintings made of the Borgias, or for them, must be covered over with black crepe. All the tombs of the Borgias must be opened, and their bodies sent back to where they belong – Spain!

It was obvious that in the face of such hatred, Cesare could expect nothing. He would later be betrayed by a man he considered his ally, Gonzalo Fernandez de Cordoba, while facing the hostility of Ferdinand of Aragon. He was taken to Spain and imprisoned in the Castle of La Mancha but managed to escape and reached Pamplona in December 1506, where he was welcomed by King John III of Navarre, his wife's brother, who needed an experienced military commander. Cesare would work for John of Navarre until March 1507, when he was besieging Ferdinand's ally the Count of Lerin. He was irritated by the slow capture of the Castle of Viana, which he considered an easy target, and in foul weather, with his usual consideration for his troops, had withdrawn his sentinels into the town. His adversary, de Beaumonte, had waited for an opportunity and then led a convoy of supply mules within reach of Viana. Beaumonte's name was called and the alarm sounded, and Cesare, dressed hastily in light armour, leaped onto his horse, followed by seventy horsemen. He outdistanced his followers, seeing Beaumonte's rearguard retreating, and rode furiously forward, possibly not realising that he was alone. De Beaumonte sent three of his knights and some foot soldiers to intercept him, and Cesare was ambushed in a narrow ravine. He was run through the body with a lance. Unhorsed and mortally wounded he fought desperately, but fell, overwhelmed by men stabbing from all sides. There were at least twenty-five wounds on his body when it was found. De Beaumonte's men stripped him, and he was left lying naked and still bleeding. One of them had the decency to cover his genitals with a stone. It was 12 March 1507 and Cesare was only thirty-two years old.[53]

King Louis XII promptly suggested that Alfonso d'Este should find a way to divorce Lucrezia, telling the Ferrarese envoy at his court, 'I know you were never satisfied with this marriage, and this Madonna Lucrezia is not Don Alfonso's real wife.' Ercole decided to ignore the suggestion and from then on her father-in-law began to show Lucrezia slightly more consideration.

In April 1504, Francesco Gonzaga had arrived in Ferrara. He had promised to try to help Cesare, though it may have been a way of insinuating himself into Lucrezia's confidence. Relations between Mantua and Ferrara had been poor for some time, and he may also have thought that he could use her to gain information. Ercole had died that spring, and Alfonso treated her with a little more affection, but it was not to last, and he continued to visit brothels regularly. Lucrezia was then six months pregnant, and the plague arrived in July, so she was sent to the family castle at Reggio. Alfonso had already had two stillborn children, one by his first wife and one by Lucrezia. Perhaps his concern was more for the unborn child than for her.[54] Though she lived in physical comfort, her emotional life was arid and she sought the affection and friendship that people such as Pietro Bembo and Ercole Strozzi could give her. Alfonso had never liked her relationship with the poets and had made communication with them difficult. Francesco Gonzaga was already a part of the family circle, though closeness with him meant that her relationship with her sister-in-law Isabella, his wife, became even more strained. Francesco had a romantic nature, and his courtship of Lucrezia was just what she then needed, after losing the support of her family. Isabella's affection for her husband had never been great, and had hardened into great resentment of his mistresses, but she was a cold and spiteful woman and his wooing of her had ended shortly after their marriage. Though they did their duty and had produced six children together, Francesco found outlet for his emotional life elsewhere.[55]

When Lucrezia had first heard of Cesare's escape from his imprisonment, she was elated, and when news finally came that he was apparently safe at the court of his brother-in-law, his popularity had soared. Guicciardini believed 'The people had very good cause to love their Duke, for he gave them the best government they had ever known.' The rejoicing at that time had not been shared by the new Pope, who showed great anxiety at the freedom of his enemy. The Duke 'was greatly beloved not only by men of war but also by many people in Ferrara and the states of the church, something that seldom falls to the lot of a tyrant!'[56]

When Cesare had first reached Navarre, he had sent Gonzaga a letter telling him all that had happened, and Lucrezia celebrated by spending most evenings dancing with her household. She shortly after miscarried, and Alfonso blamed her for it.

In the spring Alfonso left for Genoa to confer with Louis XII, leaving Lucrezia as Regent, and it was during this period, when she was without her husband's support, that she heard of Cesare's death. It was said that she heard the news in silence, then when it was all said, she remarked 'The more I try to do God's will, the more He visits me with misfortune.' But her apparent calm was shock, and later she could be heard endlessly repeating her brother's name. Ercole Strozzi addressed a lament to her:

> Give way to tears, a just cause, Borgia, thou hast for grief. The chief pride of thy race has fallen. Thy brother, mighty in peace, mightier in war, whose arduous glory is equal both in name and in deed to the Caesars!'[57]

Cesare's death was appalling for her, and this time her husband proved sympathetic. He allowed her to have her son Rodrigo from her second marriage visit her in Ferrara. The boy was then eight years old and had not seen his mother for five years, but he was to spend the summer with her. She also realised at this time that she was pregnant again, and to protect the pregnancy she rested as much as possible, while making lavish preparations for the coming child. The following April, her son Ercole was born, the future Duke of Ferrara, and the child was healthy.

Alfonso appeared delighted to finally have the heir he needed, but shortly after the birth he left for France. He and Francesco Gonzaga were to join the League of Cambrai together. It was a union that Pope Julius II had been eager to advance, and was intended to bring together France and Spain to nullify the formidable power of Venice, but it would eventually crush Italy's independence. At the last moment, Julius seemed to fully comprehend the immensity of the monster he was creating, as it was three months before he reluctantly joined the League himself. He would find, as all Italy did, that as the powers of France and Spain grew, those of Italy would diminish. Alfonso and Francesco had only joined because the Pope had initiated the League, to avoid coming under suspicion of being enemies of the Holy See; but the two superpowers would eventually exercise such a stranglehold that they repressed not only independence, but also the will to maintain it. So much so that even in 2004 an author could quote a common expression: 'O Francia, O Spagna, basta che a mangiare!' suggesting indifference to whatever rulers were in power, as they were all alike, French or Spanish, so long as the average Italian had enough to eat.[58]

The following spring France declared war on Venice, and Pope Julius II named Alfonso the standard-bearer of the church. The actual standard was received with solemn religious ceremonial, but King Louis of France still did not trust the Pope and was not pleased at Alfonso's honour. He reasoned that he must be fully assured that Alfonso's first loyalty would be to France, before he could receive the king's 'protection' – and the sum of 30,000 ducats had also to be paid to ensure it.

While Alfonso was away, Lucrezia was entrusted with the government of Ferrara. Though lacking power to make any changes, she used what influence she had for the benefit of the people, who were trapped between the *grandi* (nobles) and the *grassi* (wealthy merchants).[59] The Venetians had not taken the League of Cambrai seriously, and were left without allies to help them combat the united forces of France and Spain.[60] The battle of Agnadello demoralised them further and they attempted to make peace with the Pope. However, Julius was not impressed by their apparent capitulation until he had extracted all that he could from his victory. Though he agreed to negotiate with Venice, he put every possible obstacle in the way of settlement and the fighting continued.

The Battle of Legnano had barely begun when Gonzaga and some of his men were surprised while resting. Gonzaga escaped through a window, where a peasant found him. Offered money to hide him, the peasant first agreed, then led the Venetians to where he was hiding. When the Pope heard of his capture, he threw his hat on the floor and cursed St Peter loudly *in orrende bestemmie* (with horrendous blasphemies). Gonzaga's capture did not upset his wife Isabella at all, and she immediately paraded their son Federico around the countryside to show him as the heir.

Lucrezia heard of his imprisonment when she was almost due to give birth and ordered prayers for his release. Gonzaga was infuriated by his wife's immediate replacement of him by his son, and however politically astute the action may have been, it showed clearly that she had no personal affection for him. 'We are ashamed to have her for a wife ... a woman who is always ruled by her head.'

He never forgave her for the blow to his pride, turning instead to Lucrezia for consolation during his eleven months imprisonment.[61]

They were to find that although Pope Julius may have been warlike, he was certainly not reliable. He was shortly to come to terms with the Venetians and would then order Alfonso 'as standard bearer of the church' to cease from 'molesting' Venice and to break with France.[62] He even began to draw up a Bull of Excommunication against Alfonso.

For Lucrezia, to whose father and brother Julius had always been such an enemy, Alfonso's decision to continue the war raised misgivings, which she shared with Gonzaga rather than with her husband. Gonzaga had lost faith in his wife's ability to arrange a settlement that would release him from prison, or even her commitment to do so. He asked Isabella to send their son to Venice, as a sign of good faith, and was incensed when she refused. He threatened to strangle her with his bare hands, crying 'I have lost my state to that bitch!'[63] Desperate for freedom, he then suggested that his son Federico be put into the care of his sister and brother-in-law the Duke of Urbino, which seemed a reasonable compromise, but again Isabella refused. Pope Julius then made it clear that he would make no further excuses for 'that whore of a Merchesa' and said that her husband had every right to be furious with her, for he was 'no longer a prisoner of the Signoria of Venice, but of his wretched whore of a wife!'[64] Many assumed that her intransigence was due to her blind support of her brother Alfonso d'Este and her willingness to sacrifice her husband in his favour, but it also seems that there was an element of resentment concerning Francesco Gonzaga's attachment to Lucrezia.

Only when the Pope persuaded the Venetians to send Francesco to Rome without any commitments did Isabella go there. Gonzaga found that his wife was still doing all in her power to aid Alfonso, and deeply resented her for doing nothing at all to help him. At that time Lucrezia had written to him, begging him not to abandon her, 'I have more faith in you than in anybody in the world.'

The Pope sent for Gonzaga and gave him the post of Captain-general of the Venetian army and agreed to replace Alfonso as the church's standard-bearer. Gonzaga made excuses, saying he had a recurrence of the French disease (syphilis) and he could not travel. The Pope was immediately sympathetic, as he had often had the disease himself, and warned Gonzaga against using unguent of mercury, as he had found it to be worthless and that it might even do harm. However, when Gonzaga seemed to show no sign of recovery the Pope, himself familiar with the progress of the disease, grew suspicious and sent his own doctor to examine him. He was then obliged to appoint himself to command the papal troops.

The Pope was making preparations to besiege Ferrara and when Gonzaga heard the news he appealed for clemency for 'the Lady Duchess'. He even asked the Pope to turn her over to him, 'and this because of the loving and loyal terms that she alone, among all our relatives, used to us at the time of our imprisonment, which oblige us in these days to show her gratitude, for had the providence of Your Holiness not helped, there was nobody else who showed that they held compassion as much as this poor girl.'[65]

He had even prepared an apartment for her and described it to her with enthusiasm, saying 'Let us hope that we shall enjoy it together after so much tribulation.'[66] Gonzaga was obviously viewing Lucrezia as a romantic ideal, a woman who had loved and supported him when nobody else did. Lucrezia also needed affection, keeping the correspondence between them going and thanking him effusively for small gifts. She also greatly praised him to others, but tried to keep his feelings in check when he wanted to express them too freely.

The Pope, meanwhile, was suffering a reverse in popularity. The French drove his troops out of Bologna and the citizens pulled down Michelangelo's statue of him, dragged it around the city and finally broke it into pieces. (When the artist had asked Julius II whether he wanted a book placed in the figure's left hand, signifying scholarship and intellect, the Pope had responded, 'Give me a sword; I am not a man of letters.') The pieces were then sent to Alfonso to make a cannon. When it was made, to taunt the Pope, it was named *La Giulia*, the feminine of his name.

The war finally ended with the Battle of Ravenna on Easter Sunday 1512. Julius, who had invited the French in in the first place, was then hailed as a liberator for driving them out, but it left Alfonso and Ferrara exposed. Alfonso had no choice but to ask for the Pope's mercy. Knowing how Julius had betrayed Cesare, Lucrezia can have had no confidence in him, and offered daily prayers for Alfonso's safety. He was safe, but he was still excommunicated and Julius demanded Ferrara's return to the Holy See, offering Bari in its place.

During this anxious time, Lucrezia heard that her son Rodrigo Bisceglie had died of malaria, so she had effectively lost the boy twice. He had been the son of the husband she had loved, and she grieved deeply, 'so bowed in grief that there was no way to console her,' as the Mantuan envoy reported.[67] She knew that her present husband, Alfonso, would not wish to see her grieving for another man's child. She also realised that Alfonso and the children she had had with him were all she had left, and that the past was completely over for her.

The Pope, ever belligerent, ordered the Duke of Urbino to lead troops against Ferrara the following spring, but Isabella, though she would have liked to see Lucrezia imprisoned, asked her son-in-law to spare the city for her brother's sake.

The Pope who had been the Borgias' greatest enemy would see no more springs. The Venetian ambassador said 'The Pope is not exactly ill, but he has no appetite. He eats but two eggs in the day. He had no fever but his age makes his condition serious.' Pope Julius II died on 20 February 1513 aged seventy. The new Pope, elected three weeks later, was thirty-eight and took the name of Leo X. He was Giovanni de' Medici and was happy to begin his reign 'more like a gentle lamb than a lion'. He lifted the ban of excommunication from Alfonso and Ferrara.[68]

When Julius died and Leo became Pope, Alfonso was thirty-five and Lucrezia thirty-three. They were hopefully entering years of peace and could concentrate on domestic things. Lucrezia dressed elegantly, and a list of the jewels she owned in 1516 has 399 separate items, including 2,000 large and beautiful pearls, innumerable rosaries fashioned from silver, rubies and mother of pearl, flat diamonds to be worn on the head, and a hundred buckles of gold and enamel.[69]

Many still considered her beautiful, though she had never had classical beauty, though it must have been a sadness for her that despite all the years together, her husband did not consider her desirable. However, as he grew older he gave up his preference for visiting whores, and Lucrezia was to have three more children with him.

Francesco Gonzaga had always shown his love for Lucrezia but illness was overtaking him. His wife Isabella had long since proved that she cared far more for ruling than she did for him personally, and his resentment towards her continued. They spent more time apart and Francesco's close friendship with Lucrezia continued to fill an emotional void for them both.

Lucrezia's mother Vanozza died in November 1518 aged seventy-six. She was buried with honour in Santa Maria del Popolo and left a large collection of jewels, many of them given to her by Alexander VI. To commemorate Cesare, her favourite child, she had had a silver bust of him made and placed in the *Ospedale della Consolazione*.[70] A further great grief for Lucrezia was the death of Francesco Gonzaga on 19 March 1519. Isabella could only complain how little authority he had allowed her during his latter years, but for Lucrezia it was another huge void that would never be filled.[71]

By May of that year she was also ill. She was pregnant again but this time was filled with feelings of foreboding. She asked the Bishop of Adria to appeal to the Pope for a special blessing for her pregnancy, which he gladly gave. On 14 June she gave birth to a daughter who was immediately baptised as Isabella Maria. Lucrezia then developed a fever and Alfonso stayed by her side, displaying anxiety at her condition.

On 22 June she lost both sight and hearing temporarily, then rallied and wrote a letter to the Pope, asking for his blessing 'in extremis'. She became ill again the following day and Alfonso ordered a religious procession. Those who saw him on that day were in no doubt that he cared deeply for his wife, but there was to be no recovery, and on 24 June 1519 she let go of life. She was buried in Corpus Domini and Alfonso fainted away at her funeral. Giovanni Gonzaga, Francesco's brother, who attended the funeral on behalf of his nephew, said 'her death has caused the greatest grief, throughout this city, and his Ducal Majesty displays the most profound sorrow.'[72]

Despite her notorious family name, the love of the Borgias for each other transcended any emotion they felt for anyone else. Lucrezia had always tried to live a respectable life and was certainly not the siren depicted in later stories. The love between her and her brother Cesare was probably the deepest and most genuine that either of them experienced during their lives.

Many people are now proud to trace their ancestry back to the Borgias. From Cesare's daughter Luisa (with his wife Charlotte d'Albret) descend the Bourbon counts of Bussett and Charlus. What would have most pleased the always status-conscious Rodrigo Borgia is that the Stuart line descends from Lucrezia's Ferrara marriage. The late Diana, Princess of Wales, could claim descent from Lucrezia Borgia, along with many of the royal houses of Europe. Lucrezia's descendants are her greatest achievement, apart from the affection she created in the hearts of the people who knew her best.

6

The Strong Woman and the Weaker Men: Felice Della Rovere

Felice is believed to have been born in Rome in 1483. Her mother was Lucrezia Normanni, a member of one of the oldest Roman families, tracing their lineage back to the eleventh century, and her father was Cardinal Giuliano della Rovere, then aged around thirty years old. In about 1480, when he first met Lucrezia, Cardinal della Rovere was a tall, handsome, commanding presence, he was dark-haired, with a strong profile, and the sense of authority that comes from having powerful family connections.

His uncle was Pope Sixtus IV (Francesco della Rovere) and in the famous portrait painted with his nephews, Giuliano stands proudly in the centre of the canvas, robed in scarlet, drawing all eyes, appearing to dominate even the Pope, while his cousins Girolamo and Raffaelo Riario stand behind him.[1] The portrait was painted in 1480 giving us a clear picture of the attractive young prelate who would become Felice's father.

Pietro Riario, another nephew, was then the favourite of the Pope, adept at staging the court entertainments and useful for impressing visitors. Giuliano, on the other hand, chose to concentrate his talents in more practical ways. He was fond of military matters, a good manager and tactician, and he had a taste for action which would later earn him the nickname of 'the warrior pope.'[2] He had been awarded the titular church of San Pietro in Vincoli and in 1476 had been made Archbishop of Avignon. Because of the ongoing tension between France and Rome, Giuliano would go there to show a papal presence, but he also succeeded in forging good relations with the French court.

Pietro died in 1477 and, rather than Giuliano, the new favourite of the Pope became Raffaelo Riario, the Pope's sixteen-year-old great-nephew. Raffaelo was one of the batch of seven new cardinals recently created. Giuliano, possibly feeling unappreciated, returned to Avignon, where he occupied his time in improving the Bishop's Palace. The church was certainly a potentially rewarding career for the upwardly mobile young men who thronged it. That is not to say that piety could not exist among them, but it was very often subsumed under the necessity of everyday living and ambition became the paramount concern. It was, in fact, necessary to keep an eye on the main chance, as the tenure of any pope might be short, so relatives of the prelate at all levels would expect to be given a helping hand, while the going was good. At the pope's death they may well find themselves surplus to requirements, trying to find some way to mark themselves out.

This career struggle, absorbing though it could be, did not prohibit them from normal social contacts, including with women. If they fathered children with their mistresses, then they invariably acknowledged them freely, and resumed the career struggle on behalf of their offspring.

The *Julius exclusus ei coelis* was published in 1517, four years after Giuliano's death, attributed to Erasmus. In it he imagines the exclusion of Pope Julius II from Paradise (he was never a friend of Giuliano's). A supposed conversation between the Pope that Giuliano became and St Peter ends with a shocked exclamation from Giuliano, saying 'What is so strange about them having children? They are men, not eunuchs!'[3] This was then a common opinion, and although Giuliano would have fewer offspring than many of his colleagues to find places for when he became pope, he was certainly not celibate. However, would not indulge in the intense family dramas that characterised Rodrigo Borgia. He preferred to work on his career and became not only Archbishop of Avignon and Cardinal-Bishop of Sabina, but also Cardinal-Bishop of Ostia. He would eventually hold eight bishoprics, serving as Camerlengo to the Sacred College in 1479, and became Papal Legate to France in 1476 and 1480.

The Roman lawyer Stefano Infessura considered that 'The life of a Roman cleric has been debased to such an extent that there is almost not one who does not keep a mistress, or at least a common prostitute.'[4] Lucrezia Normanni could not be described as a common prostitute, with her noble if not wealthy family; and her relationship with Cardinal della Rovere was not fleeting, as she did not give birth to their daughter until 1483. Respectable arrangements would then be made for her, which would include the provision of a husband of suitable standing to provide a cloak of decency for the mother and a family protector for the child. This usual arrangement also covered the relationship between the mother and the Cardinal, should della Rovere wish to continue the association with Lucrezia. Once these proprieties had been observed, then the fact that she had borne the child of a cardinal was not shameful, in fact, the child would benefit from its father's position. For any family with noble blood but little money, great benefits could be expected.

The general disgust regarding sexual matters shown by the early church fathers such as St Augustine, Arnobius, Methodius, and St Jerome (who called sex of any kind 'disgusting, shameful, filthy, degrading, unclean and a defilement of both parties') makes one wonder how the human race was expected to propagate at all. Even when sexual relationships took place only within legal marriage, they were expected to be conducted with due gravity, fulfilling only the requirements of reproduction.[5] Fortunately, despite the censure of the church, some common sense had prevailed, and sexual relations between consenting adults (even clerical ones) were later accepted, if not always fully condoned.

The child born to Lucrezia Normanni, though technically illegitimate, would be raised, educated and nurtured properly in line with her father's position. In the meantime, the stepfather chosen for her was Bernardino de Cupis. He was a major-domo who ran the household of Giuliano's cousin, Cardinal Girolamo Basso della Rovere. Giuliano was closer to him than to his Riario cousins, and the family connection would form a link between Lucrezia and her child, and the family of the child's father.[6] Lucrezia had more children with the husband chosen for her, as Francesca and Gian Domenico are known to have been born later. When Cardinal della Rovere's child made her appearance, she was named Felice. Meaning 'happy' or 'lucky' this was an unusual name for a girl, it tended to be given to boys. The infant Felice was brought up by her mother, and this was also a break from tradition, as the child of a notable father was usually handed over to his family to be reared and educated.[7]

Lucrezia seems to have settled happily enough with Bernardino de Cupis, and he later made her one of the beneficiaries of his estate in his will of 1508, an unusual move for a man with a male heir. We may assume that Felice's childhood was a normal one, and though she was acknowledged as being the Cardinal's child, many attitudes of her stepfather helped to shape her. He was fiercely loyal to the della Rovere family, and when at the turn of the sixteenth century he commissioned Baldessare Peruzzi to paint a fresco of the Virgin and Child in the church of San Oratorio, he used the acorn as a decoration. The name della Rovere means 'of the oak' and the oak tree and its fruit were often used by the family as personal symbols. Felice and her family lived comfortably in the Palazzo de Cupis on the Piazza Navona, then called the Platea in Agone, after the church of Sant'Agnese in Agone on one of its long sides.[8]

Sixtus IV had encouraged rebuilding and had passed a Bull allowing any properties in disrepair to be bought up and restored. Bernardino had bought several small properties alongside the Navona on the same side as the church, and rebuilt them as one, creating a substantial palazzo. It was described by Albertini in his guide to Rome's architecture as the 'house of Bernardino de Montefalco (where Bernardino originally came from) in the Square of Agonis, which has a most beautiful well.'[9] This was not only a water feature but a great luxury, in a city where fresh water was difficult to acquire and most people had recourse to the public fountains.

Late fifteenth-century Rome was a city of great changes. The streets were narrow and sometimes oppressive, with the relics of the ancient world largely destroyed, not only by invaders but also by random building projects which took no notice of the beauty or value of what had come before. The chronic lack of water in the city at that time, caused by the destruction of the hydraulic system by the Goths, had caused a shift in population, with housing tending to move towards the river, leaving other areas under-populated.[10]

At the beginning of the fourteenth century the city had been so full of internal conflict that many noble families lived in a state of siege. The Colonna and the Orsini had long been bitter enemies, and they had controlled the Quirinal and the Sant'Angelo district respectively. The Frangipani ruled the Palatine (where the ancient Imperial palaces used to stand) and the Savelli ruled the Aventine. The Trastavere district was occupied by the Pierleone, the Paparaschi and the Normanni, in a state of uneasy truce. These families were in contention for the power of the papacy and their mutual hostility cannot be over-emphasised. Popes had died due to their feuds and the fortunes of many people, including the Normanni, had been destroyed, leaving them nothing but their pride.[11] These people would never fully recover from their losses, and the Colonna and the Orsini had become the first families in Rome by the fifteenth century.

The city underwent a clearance of unauthorised buildings and an effort was then made to regulate the water supply. Diplomacy and force of arms re-established papal control and ended most of the brigandage of previous years.[12] By the time of Pope Sixtus IV the face of Rome was transformed, with the beautification of the city continuing throughout his pontificate, but he was to die in 1484, just after Felice's birth, to be followed by another della Rovere-approved Pope, Innocent VIII (Giovanni Battista Cibo).

Felice's father, Giuliano della Rovere, who had managed to keep a low profile during the reign of his uncle Pope Sixtus, would also be transformed, becoming the new Pope's chief advisor. Lorenzo de' Medici was counselled by his Ambassador in Rome to 'send a good letter to the Cardinal of St Peter (della Rovere) for he is Pope, and more than the Pope!' Such advice proves his great influence. He was then in a position to award promotions and give rewards for loyalty, and this was reflected in the way Felice was regarded. She was always known as a della Rovere and the other della Roveres in Rome treated her as a member of their family. Her illegitimacy did not make her inferior, in fact quite the reverse, as a child of a cardinal. However, in 1492 Pope Innocent VIII died and things changed dramatically for the della Roveres when Rodrigo Borgia became Alexander VI.[13]

The Borgia Pope would prove to be an excellent administrator, but was determined to advance his own family, particularly his four children by Vanozza dei Catenei. As we have seen, his very special love for his daughter Lucrezia Borgia both intrigued and scandalised Rome, and she was treated as a queen. There would be no place at his court for most of the della Rovere connections, though one or two did have his confidence, notably Raffaelo Riario and Domenico della Rovere. The new Pope intended to promote Spanish interests and the King of France and the Duke of Milan were uneasy with his choices. A Milanese envoy wrote: 'If Cardinal Giuliano della Rovere can be persuaded to ally himself with France, a tremendous weapon would be forged against the Borgia pope.'[14] He was happy to comply as he had enjoyed political influence and had no wish to be consigned to the sidelines, but to take a stand against a pope such as Alexander was to make a very dangerous choice. This led to Giuliano's decision to travel to France in April 1494. He would not return to Rome for many years, but would enjoy a new position as advisor to King Charles VIII.

Unfortunately, his move would leave Felice exposed. Children were not only of value for the future, they could also be a weak point, whereby control of a parent could be enforced.[15] Giuliano was aware that Felice's existence could be used against him and her life could be forfeit. She had to be moved to a place of safety. She was then around eleven years old, still too young for the protection of a husband and his family, so she was taken to Savona, the della Rovere home town. By 1504 records describe her as 'Donna Felice da Savona', implying that she spent several years there. The enforced flight from her home in Rome would stay with her as a very unpleasant memory. During her exile in Savona and her father's exile in France, she developed hostilities and resentments towards her father's enemies who had overturned their lives.[16]

She would find the town very different from Rome, where the church was at the centre of life and a cardinal's daughter was someone special. Savona was a small town, with the harbour at its heart, and its princes were the merchants. To the relatives she then lived with, she was merely a bastard and though she would be cared for and protected, she had lost her importance. She did not even speak the Savanese/Ligurian dialect, which increased her sense of isolation. Her provincial relatives thought nothing of her pretensions and she felt herself disregarded and trusted them less than she had the clerics in Rome.[17]

Meanwhile, Giuliano della Rovere had hopes of making the area into a principality for himself, with the help of the French. He wanted them to take over Genoa and Savona and started to build a residence there fit for his future position. The Palazzo della Rovere would be the largest in Savona, overlooking the harbour.[18] He had not, however, forgotten his daughter. Some time after 1497, when she was fourteen years old, he was looking for a husband for her. It would later be said that she turned down several suggestions, but that is open to question. It is to be assumed that whoever Felice's first husband was, he would have been a man to serve her father's purposes and Felice would have been expected to obey her father in his choice. In any event, it would not be a marriage of long standing, as she was widowed early in 1504. Her later attitude showed that, for her, the marriage had not been happy and she had no desire to repeat the experience. She must, however, have been fully aware that as she was still a teenager, she would certainly be required to marry again.

In the meantime, as a young widow, she had gained a measure of independence. She had the dowry given at her marriage, which was returned to her as a widow, and with her father's continued absence there was nobody in direct control over her. As a widow, her status was very different. It accorded her respect and living in her father's new palace gave her power. He was still frequently absent, but supplicants made their way there, and people were anxious to befriend him by leaving gifts for his daughter. This proved to be a good training for her future life.

Felice's feeling of being an outsider led her to champion other people on the margins, and she may have taken comfort in being able to show them the sympathy she felt she had not been given. It also took her mind off the fact that her father would soon insist on a new marriage for her. Both their lives, however, would change dramatically again in the coming years, starting with the death of Pope Alexander VI in 1503. He had initially been laid to rest in the chapel of Santa Maria della Febbre (Our Lady of the Fever) which suggests the possible reason for his death. This rotunda had been built in the second century, and after 1506 was converted into the sacristy of the new St Peter's Basilica.[19]

Cardinal della Rovere cannot have been unhappy at the death of the Borgia Pope; he certainly wasted no time in returning to

Rome to take part in the Conclave to select a new Pontiff. He was to say 'I have come here on my own account, not other people's,'[20] suggesting that he had personal hopes of success, but there were opposing factions including a desire on the part of the French king to see a French cardinal on the throne. Such factions only ensured that an 'outsider' candidate was elected, a usual ploy when the papacy needed someone who could do little damage during a short pontificate. Pius II had been sixty-four at his election, while della Rovere was still only fifty, but the new Pope, Francesco Todeschini, a nephew of the Piccolomini pope Pius, seemed to be a man of integrity, and the ideal compromise candidate. His health was also not good, which suggested that the reign would not be lengthy. It was, in fact, to be shorter than anyone might have expected, as he died after being pope for only twenty-seven days.[21]

Another Conclave would have to be held, and Giuliano della Rovere had another chance. He did not intend to fail again, as the man elected might last for too many years, robbing him of a further attempt. He had been rather young at the election of Alexander VI, being then only thirty-nine. Cardinals were not usually considered *papabile* until they reached more mature years, and this time, at the age of fifty, he might just slip through. He intended to take no chances of failure, and though he had criticised Rodrigo Borgia for bribery when he was elected, he was to use the same methods himself. Having done all he could, he entered the Conclave with every hope of success. After the shortest Conclave then recorded – only a few hours – Giuliano della Rovere's efforts paid off. He was elected Pope, taking the name of Julius II.

His was a difficult legacy as Italy was still full of dissension regarding the rightful heir to the throne of Naples, and Cesare Borgia's position as general of the papal army would need to be rescinded. Cesare had to leave Italy and his cities would be brought back under papal control, as Julius intended to be known as a great statesman, as well as being a warrior for the church. His years of exile had focused his mind, and he knew exactly how he intended to rule. He was still only in vigorous middle age and could hope for the strength to carry on long enough to achieve all he wanted to do.

He very quickly began to display a fearsome temper when crossed and became known as *Il Papa Terribile*, the leader who would brook no opposition.[22] While he began to establish his position, his daughter Felice, then twenty years old, was still in Savona. She knew that her own years of exile would soon be over – after all, this Pope had only one acknowledged child, making her unique; but things would also change in other ways, and her father would soon insist on her remarriage, for if her position was unique, so was her value.

Julius spent upwards of 60,000 ducats on his coronation, but as it took place in November of 1503 it was spoiled by bad weather. Felice did not appear, which may have disappointed her, but Julius was eager to show that he was not like the Borgia Pope. He would not begin his career by filling the Vatican with his children and other family hangers-on. He wanted to avoid any suggestion that he was over-fond of his daughter.

Despite this apparent coolness towards Felice, Julius had her on his mind. The first reference to her is dated January 1504 and reads 'The Pope is arranging a wedding for his only daughter Felice, who is in Savona, and is awaited in Rome, she is to be married to the Signor of Piombino, Lord Appiano.'[23]

By the end of February, her travel plans were complete and Sanuto reported 'Madama Felice, the daughter of the Pope, is coming from Savona. The Pope has sent some of the galleons that are at Ostia, to honour her. Also this week the prefects of the Cardinal of San Pietro in Vincoli will come, and he will do them great honour.'[24]

Felice returned to her childhood home at the Palazzo de Cupis. Her family was aware that her new position changed everything. They would also profit from the connection with the new Pope, as Julius would make Bernardino the Treasurer of Perugia and Umbria. When Girolamo Basso della Rovere died in 1507, Bernardino's brother Teseo would receive the Bishoprics of Recanati and Macerata.[25]

Julius and Felice met while she was still at sea – an impressive honour, not just for her benefit, but also for the prospective husband, the Lord of Piombino, who could see from the expensive welcome how much the Pope valued his daughter. This man, Jacopo Appiano, had only recently had his lands returned to him after having fallen foul of the Borgia Pope. He was on good terms with Florence, Pisa and Siena and his family had an alliance with the King of Naples. His connections alone made him attractive to Julius; but for Felice there were problems, as he already had a son from a previous marriage, and that child would take precedence over any children she might have. To counter this, the terms of the proposed marriage were very much like the ones that Rodrigo Borgia had arranged for the marriage of his daughter Lucrezia. The Medici secretary, Bernardo Dovizi da Babbiena, reported the details:

> The daughter of the Pope, Madonna Felice, is to be married to the Lord Piombino with those conditions that Pope Alexander VI placed upon the marriage of Madonna Lucrezia Borgia. That is to say, that the said Lord will make a priest of the son he already has, and if Madonna Felice should bear a male child, he will inherit the estate. If the Lord should die without children, then the estate will go to the said Lady, who can dispose of it as she pleases.[26]

It was certainly not usual to expect a man to disinherit his eldest son, and, in particular, the proviso that Felice could dispose of the estate as she wished gave her a level of autonomy very rare for her time.

However, only a month later, the proposed marriage was off. The Pope was then said to be negotiating a marriage for Felice with the son of the Duke of Lorraine, but gossip was also rife and Felice may have heard that Jacopo Appiano had once hoped for a match with Lucrezia Borgia, who had refused him. Nothing came of the Lorraine proposals either, and Felice went back to Savona. This time her father commissioned her to act as an agent between himself and the mercantile community, which was his first sign of trust in and appreciation of her. Had Felice made it clear that she did not intend to marry the man who had been refused by Lucrezia Borgia?

Shortly afterwards, she was summoned back to Rome, with her Aunt Luchina in tow, her arrival being reported by the Venetian Ambassador in Rome, Antonio Gustiniani, on 31 May 1504. He said that Julius' sister Luchina was expected in Rome 'in the company of Madonna Felice, the daughter of the Pope, for whom the galleys set sail several days ago to fetch from Savona.'[27] He also reported the festivities of a few days later, saying 'These ladies, the daughter and sister of the Pope, in the company of the Prefectress, have gone publicly to the Pope's castle attended by many courtiers and cardinals, they enjoyed themselves until late in the evening with His Holiness.'[28] The fact that Julius had entertained his female relatives within the Castel Sant'Angelo again showed his preference for decorum. Though attached to the Vatican by the 800-metre brick wall and passageway of the Pasetto di Borgo since the late thirteenth century, the Castel Sant'Angelo was always considered to be a separate building. It fulfilled many functions – prison, armoury, barracks and offices – but there was also a series of beautifully appointed rooms suitable for the entertainment of the Pope's female relatives, without causing scandal by having them in the Vatican itself.

The Villa Belvedere, built in the 1480s by Innocent VIII, was another useful venue. It was described as 'a most exquisite and delightful place' by the ambassadors who went there and it became a favourite for family meetings. Julius II spent money on improving it, commissioning Bramante to connect the two buildings and also construct a garden and courtyard for his collection of antique sculptures.[29]

During one of the lavish events at the Belvedere, Felice gave proof of her resentment against her della Rovere relatives – she stayed away. These entertainments were special and everyone who was anyone wanted to attend. The one which took place in July 1504 was described by Emilia Pia, lady in waiting to the Duchess of Urbino, Elizabeth Gonzaga. She described the clothes worn by the ladies and the jewels of the Pope's nieces, particularly a headdress of diamonds worn by Madonna Constanza 'believed to have been given to her by the Pope'. She ended with 'Madonna Felice did not appear at all, as she said she was feeling ill.'[30]

Felice's absence was remarked upon, as she probably intended. As the only daughter of the Pope she may have felt that she deserved better than to be preceded and outshone by her cousin Constanza. Felice, as a widow, could not wear the 'yellow dress covered in slashed white pendant trimmings' that she wore, let alone a headdress of diamonds. Yet, as an attractive young woman, still only in her early twenties, she must have longed for a chance to shine at such a gathering. Being on the sidelines, in widow's weeds, would have been humiliating.

Three days after the Belvedere party, Julius was actively planning another marriage for her. He wished to consolidate relations with the Colonna family and Marcantonio Colonna was suggested as her husband.[31] There were other possibilities, as in the autumn of that year the sons of Ercole d'Este, Duke of Ferrara (Ferrante and Ippolito) were briefly considered. Their extreme youth was against them, as they were the sons of the Duke's second marriage to Lucrezia Borgia and a whole decade younger than Felice.

Felice seems to have always nursed a great jealousy of Lucrezia. The Duchess of Ferrara's life may have been exotic, sometimes dangerous and with its share of unhappiness, but she had always been able to bask in the openly expressed love of her father and her brother Cesare. Felice's own father's intention to show himself to be quite different to the Borgias made her feel that he loved her less, and she deeply resented his coolness towards her. She felt it made her look less wanted and less honoured. This was to have an unfortunate effect on her personality, as after her alienation from her della Rovere relatives, she became distant and critically outspoken.

She vigorously opposed the next proposed marriage, to Roberto di Sanseverino, Prince of Salerno. The negotiations for this were well documented, stretching from December 1504 to February 1505. Roberto's father, Antonelo di Sanseverino, was an ally of Pope Julius who was prepared to restore the family's estates after they had been lost to the King of Naples. The Duke of Urbino felt that Roberto might usurp his own position with the Pope, and he did not welcome the marriage – but its fiercest opponent was Felice.

The Venetian ambassador reported the difficulties: 'The Lady has contested it, simply saying "No!" and in that she has not shown respect towards her father who wished for the union.'[32] Two weeks later:

The marriage of Madonna Felice and the Prince is in difficulties and the cause is the Lady, who does not want it to take place. She cites his poverty and also because he has another woman.

This woman has let her words be heard, and now it has reached the ears of the Prince ... the Lady would not wish to enter into his hands, for fear she would have an unhappy life with him ... she has always found reasons to be opposed to the men proposed for her, saying she prefers to be left to depend on her own resources. However, the Pope is disposed to give her away to anyone, and to send her away from Rome, so as not to have to behold this shameful creature in front of his own eyes.[33]

Poor Felice! Did none of these all-powerful men understand the reasons for her opposition? Could they not see that she felt disregarded and unloved? The marriages proposed for her were not rich or important enough for a Pope's daughter, and did not make her feel that her father had her best interests at heart. She had no wish to be sent away, to live with a stranger in poverty in a run-down palazzo, miles from home. It was also awful for her to know that her father wanted to be rid of her. So she stood up to him. Other people were frightened of his tempers, but Felice had a temper of her own and must have felt that she had little to lose. She did not want to let go of her small share of freedom and independence, and find herself the prisoner of some marriage that brought her nothing. Had her father shown her any affection, she may have trusted him, knowing that he would make proper provision for her. Felice knew that she was merely a pawn, and she had nobody to rely on but herself. Her fierce intransigence caused Guidobaldo da Montefeltro to describe her as 'unstable', a typical male attitude towards recalcitrant women. Beneath her show of defiance, she must have been frightened and humiliated, wondering what her future would hold.[34]

Felice could not retreat into the sweet modesty expected of a young woman. She had to make her presence felt. She would later come to prominence in cultural matters, and the scholar Angelo Firenzuiola (a defender of the intellectual powers of women) would describe the 'prudentissima (wisdom and intelligence) of Felice della Rovere... of whom with no small amount of praise do many men speak, with a resounding voice.'[35]

Though she was attractive, Felice knew that she had to rely on brains rather than beauty to cultivate the style then and now known as *sprezzatura*, elegance and grace achieved without obvious effort, which was the goal of all courtiers. For this, she needed the friendship of Baldassare Castiglione, who had grown up in the Duke of Mantua's court, become a diplomat, and transferred to Urbino. He was a friend of Raphael, who painted him, and he wrote the *Book of the Courtier*, which was a guide to etiquette.[36]

She also wanted the friendship of another strong woman, Isabella d'Este, sister of the Duke of Ferrara, and sister-in-law of the hated Lucrezia Borgia. Isabella was extremely antagonistic towards Lucrezia, her brother's wife, as well. Felice knew that Isabella could be of value to her, opening up contacts for her that should have come from her relationship with the Pope. Their friendship, at first based merely on mutual spite against Lucrezia, was to become a genuine relationship. Her close friendships provided her with a shield against her father's indifference.

However, the prospect of another marriage could not be ignored. Julius could not allow his daughter to defy him, though for a time she had been pushed to the back of his mind as he was concerned with employing Michelangelo Buonarotti to make him the finest possible tomb, and several months had been spent in discussions. He also wanted to re-create St Peter's, as the fourth-century Basilica was a conglomeration of buildings squeezed against each other. Julius wanted a place of greatness, and again having employing the architect Bramante, on 18 April 1506 the first stone of the new Basilica was laid. Only then could the Pope turn his attention back to Felice.

She was twenty-three years old in 1506, quite old to be a bride. The older she became the less chance there would be of any nobleman wanting her for a wife, as her chances of producing children would diminish. She was aware that she could not continue her present existence, and that if she remained unmarried, sooner or later she would be pressured to enter the religious life. Only a widow of mature years, with children to vouch for her respectability, could remain at large in the world.

This time, her father produced a rather more acceptable candidate. Gian Giordano Orsini was the leader of one of Rome's most powerful families. As his wife, there would be no need for her to leave Rome, and she would be free of the strictures governing a woman alone, though even then her freedom would largely depend on her husband's goodwill. Orsini had already been married, to the illegitimate daughter of King Ferdinand of Naples, Maria of Aragon. He had fathered three children, Napoleone, Carlotta and Francesca. His first wife had died in 1504. For Julius, the marriage had the benefit of ending the Orsini/Colonna feuds, as he intended to marry Felice to Orsini and his niece Lucrezia to his rival Marcantonio Colonna, keeping a hold over both, yet seeming to honour both.[37]

The Orsini were not poor, having vast tracts of land which supplied food to Rome, and several properties including the Palazzo del' Orologio, part of the ancient theatre of Gnaeus Pompeius Magnus close to the Campo di Fiori. They had also provided the papacy with an Orsini Pope, Nicholas III. Gian Giordano was born in the 1460s making him older than Felice by about twenty years, and he was also a condotierre, a contracted soldier of fortune and loyal to France.[38] Francesco Sansaverino wrote of '… this hero, who for his incomparable fortune and valour, and the stable reputation of his paternal state, was a prince of the house of Orsini.'

Julius gave Felice's cousin Lucrezia a dowry of 10,000 ducats, his palace at the church of Dodici Apostoli and the town of Frascati. Felice was to receive from her father only her dowry of 15,000 ducats and the restoration of some estates that the Orsini had lost during the Borgia administration. There was a further humiliation in store for her when the Pope arranged the marriage of his nephew Niccolo to Laura Orsini, the daughter of Giulia Farnese and Alexander VI. Julius attended that wedding personally and blessed the nuptials. He also gave the bride the gift of a gold necklace, set with a diamond, two emeralds and a ruby. A book of poems was commissioned in celebration and Felice was expected to attend.

Her own wedding took place at the end of May 1506 and was referred to in a public ordinance issued by Julius. Sanuto reported: 'The Pope does not wish there to be any public demonstrations, as Pope Alexander would have done, merely because she is his daughter.'[39] Felice's ceremony did not take place within the Vatican but in a property belonging to her cousin, Galeaotto Franciotto della Rovere, who was Cardinal of San Pietro in Vincola at that time.[40] As a final snub, Julius, who had attended and blessed the

ST PETRONILLA. She was the presumed daughter of St Peter and a first-century virgin martyr. (Metropolitan Museum of Art)

Above: ST PETER'S BASILICA.
The present basilica was built between 1506 and 1626. The original was on the same site since the fourth century. It had incorporated many original Roman remains, now lost. Pictured here at the inauguration of Pope Francis in 2013. (Fczarnowski)

Left: MAROZIA.
The Mistress of Pope Sergius III (860–911). Her family ruled Rome during its 'Dark Age'.

EMPRESS THEODORA. Wife of the Eastern Emperor Justinian I (482–565). She was a former prostitute who became one of the most powerful women of the early medieval period.

Above: JOANNA OF NAPLES (1326–1382). A queen who was twice tried for the murder of her first husband, and was eventually also murdered. Depicted here resigning her kingdom to Pope Clement VI. (British Library)

Left: CATERINA SFORZA (1463–1509). A woman of determination who fought even the Borgias to keep her lands free.

PALAZZO RIARIO, ROME. Was known as the Cancelleria, or Chancellory. It was the home of Caterina Sforza's husband Girolamo Riario. (Francesco Gasparetti)

FORTRESS OF RAVALDINO, FORLI. The Sforza stronghold, and scene of the great siege. (AC2BR3L)

Left: PINO ORDELAFFI III (1436–1480). The builder of Ravaldino and Lord of Forli before Girolamo Riario was given it by the Pope (taken from a bust in Castel Sant'Angelo).

Below: POPE SIXTUS IV (1414–1484). (Metropolitan Museum of Modern Art)

DEVICE OF POPE CLEMENT VII. Carved and painted ceiling in the Papal Apartments within Castel Sant'Angelo, where Clement VII was effectively imprisoned during the Sack of Rome. (Author's collection)

MASS AT BOLSENA. Felice Della Rovere (1483–1536), daughter of Pope Julius II, can be seen just above the left corner of the door frame.

CAMPO DI FIORI, ROME. Still a busy business and market area, where Vanozza dei Catenei, mother of Alexander VI's most famous children, invested her money in four taverns. (Myrabella)

CASTEL SANT'ANGELO. ROME. Originally the tomb of the Roman Emperor Hadrian, it became a fortress, a prison, an armoury and a place of refuge for the popes. (Dennis Jarvis)

Above: BELIEVED TO BE LUCREZIA BORGIA (1480–1519). Daughter of Pope Alexander VI and Vanozza dei Catenei. She eventually became Duchess of Ferrara. (National Gallery of Victoria)

Left: GIULIA FARNESE (1474–1524). Mistress of Alexander VI and sister of Alessandro Farnese, the future Pope Paul III. The image is taken from a statue of Giulia on the monument to Pope Paul III in St Peter's Basilica. (Author's collection)

lexander sextus

Right: POPE
ALEXANDER VI
(1431-1503).
(Rijksmuseum)

Below: ARMS OF
ALEXANDER VI,
OUTSIDE CASTEL
SANT'ANGELO.
(Author's collection)

CATHERINE DE' MEDICI
(1519-1589). Niece of Pope
Clement VII, married King
Henri II of France, and became
regent for her sons.

OLIMPIA MAIDALCHINI
PAMPHILIJ (1591-1657).
Sister-in-law, supporter,
advisor and probable mistress
of Pope Innocent X. Bust by
Alessandro Algardi.

Above: PALAZZO PAMPHILIJ, PIAZZA NAVONA, ROME (left). Extended by Olimpia Pamphilij to make a suitable background for her brother-in-law Gian-Battista Pahmphilij. (Lalupa)

Left: POPE INNOCENT X (1574–1655). (Metropolitan Museum of Art)

ST AGNESE IN AGONE, PIAZZA NAVONA, ROME. Showing the Bernini Fountain of the Four Rivers planned by Olimpia, and the Egyptian obelisk topped by the Pamphilij dove. (Lcrame)

QUEEN CHRISTINA OF SWEDEN (1626–1689). Whose abdication and conversion to Catholicism took her to Rome, but her scandalous life caused her to be dubbed 'The Barbarian'. (National Museum of Sweden)

Above: PALAZZO FARNESE, ROME. Now the French Embassy, where Christina of Sweden became the tenant from Hell. (Myrabella)

Left: POPE PIUS XII (1876–1958). The Second World War Pope, whose policies caused controversy and whose relationship with Pascalina Lehnert created scandal.

PASCALINA LEHNERT (1894–1983).
Housekeeper, secretary and confidante
of Pope Pius XII, who became very
powerful at the Vatican.

MOTHER PASCALINA. Shown at the
funeral of Pius XII in October 1958.
She was obliged to leave the Vatican on
the same day.

Above: POPE
JOHN PAUL II
(1920-2005).
His relationship
with Anna-Teresa
Tymieniecka lasted
for over thirty years.

Left: POPE
FRANCIS (b. 1936).

festivities for his niece, took no part in his daughter's wedding at all, he did not even attend it. Gian Giordano also dragged out the proceedings by wanting them set back three hours, claiming it was due to some astrological consultation, but he turned up in hunting clothes and Felice had to wait while he got ready. She must have hated every minute. Her delicate ego was already badly bruised by her father's indifference, displayed to everyone, and her husband was also treating her with no consideration or respect.

There is no record of what she wore on that day, nor any record of gifts of jewellery. Paris de Grassis, then the Vatican's master of ceremonies, described what took place and who attended: 'Cardinals, the ambassadors of France, Spain and the Emperor, Giovanni della Rovere (Prefect of Rome and Felice's uncle) was there, along with many of the extended Orsini family.' He also remarked, rather coyly, that Gian Giordano gave Felice an 'osculo gallico' or French kiss, when the vows had been exchanged. They then retreated to a nearby bedchamber where the marriage was consummated immediately to ensure its legality. Emilia Pia reported, 'They lay together fifteen minutes and many believed that they were performing other "secret acts" in that time,' possibly referring to the French kiss.[41] After the rapid consummation, with the guests standing outside the room, the wedding party went to the palace of Monte Giordano. Paris de Grassis was offended by the state of the property, with dismantled walls, boarded-up doors and piles of wood lying around. He remarked that the only new furniture was the bride's bed, and that was only just being carried in. Emilia Pia had more to say, complaining that the bridal party had had to go on foot, past 'women of ill repute' and that if the bridegroom was a gentleman he would have chosen another route. The rooms were badly decorated and the food was terrible with little cutlery available, so that many left early being unable to eat. Emilia Pia also said that the groom 'spoke in French and Spanish at the dinner, which appeared to be his only virtue'.[42]

Felice's opinions were not recorded but it must have been clear to her that it was an inauspicious start to her new life. Two days later, she and her new husband left for Bracciano, north of Rome, riding through land owned by one branch or another of the Orsinis. The journey on horseback, though through attractive countryside, was probably not what the city-bred girl had expected, but she was a quick learner and determined to add to her knowledge. Felice would soon become not only accustomed to horses, but knowledgeable about them.

The Palazzo at Bracciano was an improvement on the half-restored Monte Giordano and within a month of their arrival Gian Giordano arranged for the celebrations necessary for the bride's position if her status as chatelaine was to be accorded respect. After her father's neglect of her pride, courtiers would be quick to notice if her new family did not appear to value her. As it was, some of the Orsini held themselves a little aloof and she had to work to show them that she was their equal. The same could be said of the staff who ran her husband's properties, as they had the ability to make her life comfortable or otherwise, depending on their acceptance of her authority.

She had always got on well with the clergy, as she considered them men who had risen by their own abilities, not merely accident of birth. She particularly liked Cardinal Giovanni de' Medici, a relative of the Orsini, and they developed a strong bond.

Gian Giordano left for Spain shortly after the marriage, and wrote a letter to Felice describing the black velvet he had been able to acquire. It was an expensive fabric as the black dye made it difficult to maintain in pristine condition. Black may have been the colour of widowhood, but when combined with silk velvets it was an opulent and noble material and Felice would wear black regularly. The relationship between her and her husband appears to have been civil and respectful and he was prepared to allow her to concentrate her energies on management and developing her diplomatic skills, while in turn she had brought him the useful papal alliance. There is no evidence of a romantic attachment or even any sexual attraction between them, but that was not necessary. Even the immediate consummation of their marriage prompted by legal rather than lustful requirement.[43]

The main aim was to create a family. If the man was so inclined he could satisfy himself with other women, preferably discreetly. The woman, if unfulfilled with her husband, usually had to put up with it, or perhaps turn to prayer.[44] Felice and Gian Giordano would grow to understand each other, and treat each other with honour and the formal courtesies. In private they largely went their separate ways, except for the one thing required of Felice, the production of children, preferably sons. As stipulated in the marriage contract, if Felice did produce a male heir, then her husband's son by his first marriage, Napoleone, would give up his place in the succession to her child, and the title would eventually pass to Felice's son. This gave her a strong stake in the family and in her position of Regent if her husband died.

She bore her first child in 1507, a girl named Giulia. A year later Marino Sanuto was able to report that 'a son has been born to the daughter of the Pope.'[45] Unfortunately, this child did not live long. Once her marriage had become a fact, her father relented a little towards her. He invited her and her husband to the Vatican, where 'he had a great banquet for them, which they attended, along with several Roman lords, the Prefect of Rome and four cardinals.' There was singing and dancing and Felice was sent a cross of diamonds which the Pope had just received as a gift from Venice.[46] Other similar occasions were enjoyed, and the Ambassador of Ferrara reported later than year, 'Madonna Felice and Gian Giordano entered Rome surrounded by ladies and gentlemen. This evening His Holiness went on horseback, and took dinner in the gardens with Monsignor Ascanio Sforza, where the Lady Felice and the other gentlemen were to be found.' Although it was customary for a woman to take her husband's rank, ambassadors were already realising that she was more significant than her husband. She even began to attend parties as the female guest of honour, sometimes being the only woman present.

Julius had given her a meagre dowry, which was already spent by her husband on buying back Orsini land confiscated during the Borgia era. Late in 1508 Julius then gave Felice 9,000 ducats to spend as she wished. It would be her safety net in case of her husband's death and she dealt with it sensibly, not wasting it on frivolous spending, or even letting it sit idle, Felice bought herself a castle. It was at Palo, a few miles north-west of Rome and bought from Giulio Orsini, her husband's cousin. Giulio, like all the Orsini, had suffered under the Borgias and Cesare had for a time occupied Palo himself. For Giulio, not only was he in need of money, but the castle could technically stay with the family. Felice, though, would always feel differently, and to her Palo was hers alone. It would enable her to become 'a woman dedicated to letters and antiquities' as well as a businesswoman.

It had been built in 1367 on a site of great antiquity, founded by the Pelargi.[47] Julius maintained a large fleet of galleys at Ostia and was in the process of building another harbour at Civitavecchia. Felice's property was between the two and would make another connection with him. She wanted more than the prestige of owning her own castle on the coast, she wanted it to earn money. Palo was in an extremely fertile area and Rome always had a great need of wheat; many of the city's workers still received a part of their wages in bread. The revenues from the sale of grain grown on the estate at Palo would make Felice wealthy in her own right. She established a business partnership with the Vatican through Giuliano Leno, who was the most powerful secular person there and had marriage ties with the della Roveres. Before long, Felice was selling her grain direct to the Vatican, providing every day the pope's daily bread. These business dealings caused no friction with her husband, though most men would not have wanted their wives to become independent, but Felice's husband was already realising that he had married a capable and ambitious woman and was man enough not to feel threatened by it.

Felice also began to dip into diplomatic matters. The Orsini and Savelli families had for some time been wary of each other, and the Savelli had a tendency to side with the Colonnas, so had to be watched. Felice was able to establish a bridge between them by befriending Portia Savelli who was married to her brother-in-law Carlo Orsini. The Mantuan ambassador reported that representatives of the two families had appeared before the pope, 'vowing to quarrel no more'.[48]

Felice also worked to prevent the Orsini from forming an alliance with Venice. The Venetian Republic had been a thorn in Julius's side ever since he became Pope, as they challenged papal authority. They asserted themselves militarily owing to the ever-present Turkish threat, but Julius did not want them armed and dangerous and disliked their pretensions. He wanted any military action to be undertaken on his own terms.[49]

The anti-Venetian League of Cambrai was intended to curb them but they were happy to fight back and had asked Gian Giordano and Giulio Orsini to be their commanders. This caused embarrassment to Felice, and angered the Pope. He arranged a meeting at the Vatican on 1 July 1509 with the bankers da Doto and Bonvixi who were responsible for the salaries of the condottieri. He then left 'Madonna Felice' to ensure that the rest of the money promised did not reach the Orsini. The negotiations were volatile and Felice stayed the night in the palace, 'with an armed guard'. Once starved of funds the Orsini had to meet with Felice. 'They have reached an agreement with the Pope, and the cause of this is Madama Felice, the daughter of the Pope, wife of Gian Giordano Orsini. She went to find these Orsinis and reconciled them with the Pope and they have returned the 16,000 ducats they had from our orators.'[50]

Both sides were able to use Felice to negotiate as it solved the problem, yet absolved them of full responsibility. The Venetians would then hold her personally responsible for the cancelling of the Orsini contract. For Felice, there was no material benefit, but a vast political one, showing her to be a skilled negotiator and political mediator. This gave her the recognition she had always wanted and her good reputation spread. Ludovico di Fabriano, stressing her involvement, sent a message to the Mantuan court: 'Those Orsini have reached agreement with our lord the Pope, and came yesterday to kiss His Holiness' feet... Through the mediation of Madama Felice they have undertaken not to fight without a papal mandate.'[51]

Julius could then focus on France, wanting to have their presence in northern Italy ended. The League of Cambrai was dissolved and the Holy League formed instead, to include Henry VIII of England. Felice was used to inform the Orsini to prepare against France.[52] However, Gian Giordano was a long-standing ally of France, so he needed to work slowly and arbitrate between France and the Pope, visiting the Vatican to discuss proposals, taking Felice with him. 'Madama Felice came from Bracciano in order to strengthen the agreement,' Sanuto reported.[53] Felice was providing her husband with moral support in the negotiations with her father, and even though the Orsini were unlikely to be able to convince him, Julius was astute enough to realise he could use Felice's talents elsewhere.

This time he wanted her to enter into dialogue with the Queen of France, Anne of Britanny.

Queen Anne was a woman Felice admired, one who had successfully governed the country during her husband's absences. She knew her husband desired glory and that prevented him from withdrawing troops from Italy. When she met Gian Giordano and Felice at Blois the most they could manage was a public relations exercise. In a letter to Isabella d'Este, the Mantuan envoy reported that 'Madama Felice has been begged by the Queen of France that she begin talks with Louis XII on the subject of peace.'[54] Stazio Gaddi wrote to Isabella from Rome, 'It is hoped to be a good end for peace, being managed by two such sage women as the Queen of France and Madonna Felice.'[55]

The 'two sage women' persevered for two years and Stazio reported that the Queen of France had sent 'letter after letter' in her own hand to the Pope seeking peace and that 'Madonna Felice, along with the Cardinal of Nantes, had been managing the affairs.'

Felice at that time was Rome's most powerful woman, and being seen as the leading player was important to her. More important than whether peace was actually achieved. To be treated as an equal by the Queen was an achievement in itself, plus the fact that her father now recognised her abilities, which was the accolade she really sought. Cardinal Bernardo Dovizi da Babbiena said 'It appears that His Holiness wishes … according to the wishes of Madonna Felice.'[56]

Julius finally began to show his daughter affection openly and an emissary from Mantua reported that 'at court Madonna Felice is everything.'[57] It had taken many years but at last the Pope appeared to be fully aware of his daughter's value. Eleanora Gonzaga, Duchess of Urbino and daughter of Isabella d'Este, wrote to her mother about a visit to the Vatican where the Pope showed her and Felice the wonderful jewels he was collecting. Later that year he became ill and the Venetian ambassador said that nobody was allowed to see him, except for his sister-in-law Eleanora Bartolomeo della Rovere, the Duke of Urbino, and his daughter Felice.[58]

One person the Pope could not renoncile with was Alfonso d'Este, Duke of Ferrara, the husband of Lucrezia Borgia. He was always hostile towards the Pope and also refused to halt his hostilities towards Venice. In August 1510 Pope Julius excommunicated him. He looked on Alfonso's relatives with equal distrust. This meant that Isabella d'Este's family lost lucrative church benefices and the revenue from certain taxes. Felice tried to help her friend and wanted the Pope to consent to her daughter Giulia being married to one of the sons of the Duke of Ferrara, but Julius became angry at what he saw as interference, and told Felice roughly to 'go away and attend to her sewing.'[59] Felice tried again the following year, as well as asking for support for Isabella's brother Cardinal Ippolito.

Stazio Gaddi sent regular reports of proceedings at the Vatican, using the code name of 'Sappho' for Felice. He wrote to Isabella on 17 June 1512: 'She is well disposed to do good work... she will be going to Rome for four days, and desires nothing more in the world than to see her daughter in the house of d'Este... Signor Gian Giordano is happy that she comes to Rome.'[60]

Isabella also wrote enthusiastically to Felice, showing how far the Pope's daughter had grown in that lady's estimation. 'I want you to know how much I esteem your efforts and authority which I know His Holiness prizes greatly... I hope you will continue in favouring my brother and particularly the Cardinal ... you will acquire a friend and a house that will perpetually serve you.'[61]

Alfonso d'Este continued to annoy the Pope, refusing to visit the Vatican to swear fealty to him. Felice tried without success to calm her father and he turned on her in other matters, refusing to allow her to become Governor of the city of Pesaro. This was a major port and Felice had plans for it, but her cousin Francesco Maria della Rovere also wanted it. He was then Duke of Urbino at only twenty-two years old, and was feckless and unreliable. Stazio Gaddi wrote that Felice had been rebuffed over Pesaro, as the Pope wanted the Duke of Urbino to have it, and obviously the Pope saw the future of the della Rovere dynasty lay with Francesco Maria, despite his faults, not with his daughter. Still the refusal angered Felice and Stazio Gaddi said 'he spoke to her in such a way that she has left Rome weeping.'[62]

Felice had been humiliated again and it was probably all the more painful as she believed she was then on good terms with her father. However, when it came to dynastic needs the man would always be preferred. The Pope's rebuff caused her to abandon her hopes of marrying her daughter Giulia to the Duke of Ferrara's son, and she stayed away from the Vatican. Some considerable time would pass without contact, and during that time Julius was in poor health. In late 1512 news reached Venice that 'the Pope has shivering fits and the negotiations are already beginning for the choice of his successor.'[63]

Felice was not indifferent to Julius, and paid for the Pope's doctor, Archangelo, to visit her with news of her father's condition. During the final phase of Julius's life she was to ask him a final favour. She wanted him to make her nineteen-year-old half-brother Domenico de Cupis into a cardinal. She not only wanted to reward the de Cupis family but also to have one member of the Sacred College loyal to herself. Unfortunately, Julius also refused this request, though he made Felice a gift of 12,000 ducats, making a total of 21,000 ducats he had given to her, plus her dowry.

Pope Julius took to his bed early in January 1513 and died on the 21 February. For many people his warlike nature had created resentments due to his insatiable demands for money for military projects. He had also spent a good deal on art, including the painting of the ceiling of the Sistine Chapel, but in that way he had improved Rome forever.

Felice had had another child in 1512, it was the son she needed, named Francesco. She would give birth again in 1513, producing another son, Girolamo, and in 1514 her final child would be born, a daughter named Clarice. It is debatable how much time she spent with any of these children.

Julius would be succeeded by a man Felice already knew, a man who had attended her wedding. This was Cardinal Giovanni de' Medici, who became Pope Leo X.[64] Leo would be very different to Julius. He was a corpulent man, a great partron of the arts who spent money freely and then borrowed from others. He was a cheerful man who enjoyed music and the theatre and was a maker of Latin verses. His remark 'God has given us the Papacy – so let us enjoy it!' defines his attitude and his pleasure-loving character. Also unlike Julius, he was a peace-loving man and would undertake no war unless personal interest was involved. He loved masquerades, jests and buffoonery, enjoyed hunting and kept a menagerie, including an elephant named Hanno. He did not fill the Vatican with mistresses and their bastards, but only because he preferred boys, though he did issue a Bull requiring the cardinals to 'keep fewer boys and live soberly and chastely'.

Felice began well with him, but he already had several women in his family who vied for his attentions, demanding incomes and benefices for their children almost from the first. Felice did not make unreasonable demands of him as she could support herself, and she even lent money to his family when required, advancing 2,000 ducats to his brother Giuliano, Duke of Nemours.[65]

Pope Leo started with good intentions, but his extravagant lifestyle soon made him unpopular. Not only for his passion for hunting, which dominated his life, but also for his greed for money. He created a grain monopoly which badly affected the price of bread in Rome, and showed indifference to the struggles of the poor. He borrowed the Castle of Palo from Felice, because the estate possessed extensive forests where he could hunt, but found the castle itself neglected as Felice had never lived in it. She used the estate only as a farm. The luxury-loving Pope came to an arrangement with her whereby he would renovate and improve the property in exchange for using it rent-free. As this arrangement did not affect the attached farmland and Felice's grain markets were still in her hands, this suited both. She was seeing her property improved at no cost to herself. For Leo, it was a double bargain, as he was able to use the same building supplies that were being delivered into Rome to rebuild St Peter's. Felice received a greater reward for her acceptance than merely having the Pope as a tenant. He actually gave her a licence absolving her from any serious crime that she might commit, a very unusual gift, but very useful.[66]

Leo's unpopularity at the Curia became a problem. While he was a cardinal he had tried to engineer the downfall of Pope Alexander VI. Now that he was Pope, the Spanish cardinals tried to arrange for his downfall, and one, Cardinal Alfonso Petrucci, tried to poison him. When the plot was discovered, Petrucci was imprisoned and then strangled. Leo's response to the general antipathy was to dilute the College of Cardinals by appointing his own supporters. These new cardinals included his own nephews, but he also gave the honour to Felice's half-brother Gian Domenico, which her father had refused. Like all the de Cupis family, he was a talented bureaucrat and useful to the Pope, so his rise created no difficulties, except that the women of the Pope's own family resented that he had given the reward to please Felice, believing that only their relatives should benefit.[67] It was very satisfying for Felice, knowing that she had the Pope's close friendship as well as her husband's trust, particularly as she had given her husband sons and was therefore invested in the Orsini fortunes and future.

Being a full part of the Orsini family was important to her, despite her pride in her ancestry. It made her the great lady to whom requests were brought and gave her status and authority. She improved the Orsini castle at Bracciano and built a public fountain there to bring fresh water to the town. She used the Orsini rose extensively as decoration, leaving a permanent family legacy. She was also always aware of the power of money, as later on, when her husband died, she would relinquish the Orsini castle at Blois to the King of France, knowing that it would not be used and any upkeep would have been wasted. However, she did make it clear that she wanted her tapestries back, as they were not only valuable in themselves, but Bracciano was on a hill and was cold in winter.[68]

Her husband was equally conscious of the security of his family after his death and needed to leave everything in order. By the early autumn of 1517 his health had begun to fail and he wanted to make sure that Felice had the authority to serve as his son's Regent when he died. One of the Orsini chiefs of staff, Giovanni Roberto della Colle, was present when he made a will. During the recounting of Gian Giordano's wishes, Felice and her five-year-old son began to cry. She wanted to leave the room, but her husband said 'Donna Felice, sit down and please listen to me, there are things I want to say. I shall leave my children everything and you, their good mother, as the new Lady and Guardian when I die.' Felice replied 'My Lord, I would rather die as a slave in this house, than as a queen anywhere else.'[69]

Whatever was lacking in the their emotional bonds, they had managed to work well together as partners. They both knew that some of the Orsini family would object to Felice being given full authority, so her husband needed to make his statement before witnesses, and while still well enough to do so, to prevent any future suggestion of coercion or duplicity. Gian Giordano died about a month after he had dictated his wishes, on 11 October 1517. He left his children by Felice and their half-brother Napoleone all his worldly goods and overnight Felice became one of the most powerful people in Rome. Her governance had to be ratified by Pope Leo X. He issued a Bull stating he 'recognised Donna Felice della Rovere, the second wife and widow of Gian Giordano Orsini, as Guardian and Caretaker of his children of minor age, on the condition that she remains a widow.'[70] She would, of course, require a lawyer to act for her, being only a woman. She appointed Galeotto Ferreola da Casena, who testified to the Senate on the Capitoline Hill that 'as Guardian and Caretaker of her children Francesco, Girolamo, Giulia and Clarice, she promises faithfully to administer the interests of her charges, and to compile an Inventory of goods and provide an account of her management of the estate.'[71]

Felice would begin to avoid her Orsini in-laws, aware that they were resentful of her position. With her two sons still very young (aged only five and four), she would have a long period of authority and to some people this seemed almost too convenient. Felice, usefully, had her indulgence of absolution for all crimes, whether needed or not, but her stepson Napoleone, then seventeen years old, had his own supporters who felt that he should be the ruler of the Orsini, not his still-young stepmother.

Over the previous decade, she had gained respect, but her position still remained unusual. Felice had no time to retire, nor could she take up the usual widow's pursuits as she still had a large estate to run properly for the sake of her children. She did make time to write her own will, again unusual in a woman of only thirty-five, but she could not afford to die intestate should any accident – or deliberate move against her – take place. She set aside 1,000 ducats for a tomb in the Church of Trinita dei Monte and gave legacies to other churches as memorials. She also made an inventory of her late husband's estate as she had promised. This document was not finished until 25 April 1518 and detailed 'every single movable and immovable good'.[72] It also included a box of Orsini documents which had to be kept safe, as well as ones made by her, along with family expenses and account books.[73]

She was to rely heavily on Statio del Fara, who was described as her *cancellerio* or secretary. He was well educated and loyal, and kept a keen eye on expenses. He had developed a comfortable relationship with her which, though respectful, was expressed in a casual style. 'I am sending you ten palmi of velvet. The merchant told me that it was the best and one should not dress in anything else. I have faith in him at the moment, but if it does not satisfy you, I will quarrel with him so terribly that I will almost wring his neck.'[74]

Though he spoke and wrote to her familiarly, he was not reproved, for Felice knew he was trustworthy. He sent her gossip, shopped for the family, and sometimes had to remind her to send him money to deal with household expenses. Another man she began to rely on was her young half-brother Cardinal Gian Domenico de Cupis, who was also eager to serve her.

The famous 'Pasquino talking statue' at the Piazza Pasquino was the place where messages were left, including notes, criticisms and satires. (It still is.) Gian Domenico was sometimes mocked there for being 'dear to his mother' and for 'the love he bears to his relatives' because he still lived at home. His sister Francesca was also useful, acting as Felice's agent in buying textiles and other things, though she was married to Angelo del Bufalo. Felice's main concern was for the properties, not only because of their financial value, but their social and political importance for the family. She needed to keep up the Trinita Palace on the Pincian Hill and the church and convent of Trinita dei Monte where she intended to be buried.[75] The palace now forms part of the Villa Malta and is surrounded by gardens.

Felice's daughters were growing and dowries would have to be supplied for them. Her stepson Napoleone had to be consulted regarding the marriage of his sister Carlotta to the Count of Mirandola, but Felice had the entire responsibility of her own daughters. Giulia married the Prince of Bisignano but the Prince wanted to have a cardinal in the family rather more than he wanted a wife, and Felice had to negotiate with Leo X. The Pope agreed that if the betrothal took place, he would make a cardinal of Antonio Sanseverino; but the Prince would have to pay a high price. He had to not only break a previous betrothal to the sister-in-law of the

Viceroy of Naples, but give the Pope 25,000 ducats 'eight thousand of which he will receive now, in cash, and he had promised to give another sixteen thousand to Madama Felice'.[76]

The marriage, unfortunately, opened up further resentment from the Orsini males, who were unhappy that the dowry for Giulia was more than that given for her stepsister Carlotta. Napoleone, in particular, was furious that Felice had arranged a cardinal's hat also, believing that he should have been offered one instead.

The agreement that if Felice had a son, then that boy would be the heir, might appear unfair, but it was intended to give legitimacy to her line, and through her the descendants of her father the Pope. It could not be expected to please anyone who was disinherited by it, but Napoleone had been exceedingly well provided for in return for what he had lost. He had the Abbey of Farfa, and this was a huge estate, almost as large as the entire Orsini holdings, and Pope Leo had also granted him 1,000 ducats a month as Abbot, though Napoleone was not required to take any form of Holy Orders. Despite the provisions for his security, the relationship between him and Felice was always strained.

She knew that conciliatory gestures on her part would be taken as a sign of weakness, but was unable to ignore his attitude completely. She ran his estates for him, while he was young, only to be later accused of interference. As a teenager, he began to be very wild, and his dislike hardened into something like hatred over the matter of the cardinal's hat for Sanseverino. Felice knew that if she arranged one for Napoleone also, it would merely give him power to work against her. The affection and support she received from Leo X meant that Napoleone could do nothing against her, but on the 1 December 1521, the Pope, Felice's close ally, died. Charles V's candidate Adrian VI became Pope and was a very different sort of man and no friend to Felice. He saw her only as an exemplar of papal corruption, and she was left without Vatican support. Napoleone was given the opportunity to attack her without censure and he did so, by reclaiming the estate and castle at Palo. He occupied Bracciano when Felice was absent and her friend Gian Maria della Porta, the ambassador from Urbino, reported 'the lady Felice is very unhappy because one of her dearest servants at Bracciano has been imprisoned ... he has taken the castle and she is worried because all the most important family accounts and documents are kept there... The 'Abbot' has made threats in the cruellest manner possible, saying he will bring death to all who are her servants.'[77]

After a couple of months Napoleone found his support disintegrating and he had to abandon Bracciano and return Palo to Felice, but this did not improve things between them. In the summer of 1522 he was still making trouble, even towards Bartolomea Varana, the niece of Francesco Maria della Rovere, her cousin, who was then in her care. A letter from della Porta to Francesco Maria early in September 1522 said 'Madonna Felice has sent word that Madonna Bartolomea must leave, as she is afraid that "the Abbot" will attempt to come and ravish her.'[78]

Though the rape of young females was far from unusual, it showed that Napoleone would threaten anything to disturb her. He wrote claiming that he intended to study in Padua for a few years, but Felice was sure he was merely up to his tricks again, and her reply to him was cool.

Pope Adrian died in October 1523 after a reign of only twenty months. Many of the cardinals had deeply resented him, as his reign was gloomy, and Leo's cousin Giulio de' Medici was then elected as Clement VII. It was a relief for Felice, as the Medici had always been her friends.

As Felice's sons grew older, Napoleone agitated for them to be declared adults earlier than agreed, in order to end Felice's Regency and because he knew that he could influence and dominate them. Felice was obliged to turn to the new Pope for help, and in October 1525 he agreed to 'an Ordinance between Felice della Rovere and her children, signed in the presence of Pope Clement VII'.[79] This document gave her another four years as 'sole and unique administrator of the estate' until her sons were aged eighteen and seventeen years respectively. It would give her time to get Clarice safely married and away from Napoleone and it also confirmed that he must in future 'live at his own expense and not at that of the Orsini estate'. He must also agree to 'take no armed men' to Bracciano. If Felice were to fall ill, then 'a qualified person, not of the House of Orsini, would govern' in her place, and if Napoleone refused to agree to the terms then Pope Clement would arbitrate personally.

Clement also decreed that as Felice had spent two thousand ducats on the palazzo at Trinita dei Monte, it should be considered hers alone, and not form part of the Orsini estate.

In 1527 the troops of the Emperor Charles V began the Sack of Rome. The antagonism between Charles of Spain and Francis of France was bound to drag in the Pope, whose allegiance was expected by both sides. As a Medici his sympathies lay with France, and although Charles later pretended that he had not given any such order, 30,000 troops invaded Italy. By May of that year the city was surrounded, and the troops, eager for loot, began to invade the city and appalling destruction began. Felice and her children were just a few of the terrified people caught there when hell broke loose. Monte Giordano was one of the first places to be attacked, but Felice was fortunately at the Palazzo de Cupis with her family. All the cardinals' palaces were sacked, valuables stolen and things that couldn't be carried away were wantonly destroyed. The people suffered rapes, tortures and murders, while inside the Vatican the Pope was helpless. At length, he escaped down the Pasetto di Borgo tunnel, into the Castel Sant'Angelo, where he was just as imprisoned and helpless, though personally safer. In early June he was obliged to pay a ransom of 400,000 ducats in exchange for his life, and by the time he escaped from Rome for Orvieto he had determined never to fall out with the Emperor again. This would have far-reaching effects even in England, where King Henry VIII wanted to divorce his first wife, Katherine of Aragon, the Emperor's aunt.[80] The Sack left 45,000 people dead or exiled from Rome and immense financial losses.

When the Sack was about a week old, Felice and her family, along with the Nuncio for the court of Urbino, Ferrante Gonzaga, had to pay the Spanish Imperial forces large amounts of money, plus all Felice's jewels, including the precious diamond cross she had been given by her father Pope Julius, in order to get out of the city. They eventually made it to Mantua, and Felice was fleeing not only the Imperial troops, but also Napoleone, knowing that in such times of general outrage, personal hatreds could be expressed in violence thatcould go unpunished. They stayed with her cousin Francesco Maria della Rovere and his wife Eleanora Gonzaga, and though she worried about her properties, she and her family were at least safe, which could not be said of the victims left in Rome.

Many other Roman nobles had the idea of retreating to Urbino, so she arranged that she would occupy a palazzo in the small town of Fossombrone. There she tried to keep to as normal a routine as possible for the sake of the children, arranging saddlery for her sons, and clothing for Clarice. Cardinal Gian Domenico was in Venice and sent fabrics to them, '... and also some pink silk, because you asked for something for Madonna Clarice, and I thought it best to send her a piece of pink.'[81]

Her relationship with Isabella d'Este would suffer from Isabella's selfishness about her property, along with Ferrante Gonzaga's greed. He was taking 'sureties' (ransoms) from other nobles, which Isabella sanctioned. Felice was disgusted that they should profit from the terrible times, and though ties were not completely severed, the relationship certainly cooled.

The Imperial troops did not leave Rome until the autumn of 1528 and their departure was followed by plague. Felice waited, aware that her main danger still came from Napoleone. He had taken control of the Orsini estates in her absence, using Bracciano as his base, and even took up piracy, holding up the Spanish ships on the Tiber until the Imperial army drove him away.

Pope Clement, Felice, and the other nobles gradually returned to Rome, to find it was almost destroyed. The population was decimated by violence and disease and beautiful buildings, some created by Felice's father, were gone. The Orsini properties had been totally sacked as the family's pro-French feelings were well known. Felice would tackle the Monte Giordano property first, and when renovations were complete would spend more time there than previously. It was important for family esteem, but the Palazzo on the Campo di Fiori was necessary economically, and would have to be let out once it was repaired. It had always been rented out, usually to cardinals who did not have their own palaces. As such, it had always generated a good income. Accommodation in Rome would be at a premium, though Felice did not spend as much on it as she did on her own apartments at Monte Giordano.[82]

The friars at Trinita dei Monte had suffered, and Felice had left valuables and documents with them for safekeeping. Many had died from violence or from plague and the buildings had been set alight, with all the documents being removed by the Spanish. Felice was grieved by the loss of gifts from her father, particularly the diamond cross, and tried to trace it. In 1532 she would finally hear of it, and that it was damaged. Giovanni Poggio in Madrid wrote that the Viceroy of Navarre knew his late brother had had it: 'He held a diamond cross belonging to you, valued at 570 ducats, and the cross has lost two diamonds. If you wish the cross restored you can pay the 570 ducats, less the value of the missing diamonds.'[83] Once the gift of the City of Venice to Pope Julius, who had given it to his daughter as a symbol of their reconciliation, the cross was of great sentimental value to her, but she did not have the cash to redeem it, so had to let it go.

St Peter's and the Vatican had been targets during the Sack, with Raphael's frescoes defaced and the tombs of the popes plundered. Even the rings had been taken from the fingers of Julius II. He had intended to have a tomb created by Michelangelo but it had never been completed, and Julius's heirs had signed a contract with him in 1513 to have the project finished. It would not be completed until 1545 and stands now in St Pietro in Vincoli, not in the Vatican where the body of Julius lies.[84]

In her later years, Felice concentrated on her children. She kept them on a tight budget, refusing to spoil them, and wanted her sons properly trained to take over the estate. For her daughter Clarice, things were put on hold owing to the effects of the Sack of Rome and the resulting financial problems. Felice had heard that Napoleone was still full of hatred and feared for Clarice's safety, knowing the girl was her weakness. She was her uncle Gian Domenico's favourite, an attractive and serious child, who knew of the problems caused by her half-brother. In 1532 she was eighteen years old, and Guidobaldo, the son of Francesco Maria della Rovere, wanted to marry her. His father wanted him to marry Giula Varano, heiress of the Duke of Camerino, who would bring the title into the family. He reminded his son of Napoleone's hatred, which might be turned towards them. He also told his son that Clarice's mother '...was only a bastard, and we do not take in marriage the bastards of our house. If you do not seek to honour and exalt your house, then at least do not debase it!'[85]

Felice must have been very hurt by the remarks, her cousin had always been close to her and it was particularly galling to have him refuse her daughter in such terms. Although she may have favoured the match with Guidobaldo, she now put it aside. She arranged a marriage for Clarice with Don Luigi Carafa, Prince of Stigliano. The family was on decent terms with Spain, and earlier problems may have been on Felice's mind. Also, Cardinal Gianpietro Carafa was important, and would become Pope Paul IV in 1555.

Felice's sons, born to wealth and position, had never had to struggle to establish themselves. Her eldest son, Francesco, aged eighteen in 1530, received the Abbey of Farfa that had belonged to Napoleone. This was an enormous property, requiring steady administration. Francesco would never marry, but had several illegitimate children, and had neither the capacity nor the patience for work, putting the place in the hands of staff who exploited it. Pope Clement was displeased as Farfa was church property, and Francesco's lack of application would always be a problem.

Girolamo grew up even wilder. Though Felice had intended him to become Lord of Bracciano. he wanted to be a condottiere like his father and would eventually serve the Emperor against the Turks. Felice was aware of his hot-headedness and sent him to stay with his sister Giulia and her husband, but he remained restless and the Prince of Bisignano wrote 'Girolamo wants to return to Rome, and all the entreaties that I and the Princess have placed on him, will not dissuade him.'[86]

Girolamo passionately hated his half-brother Napoleone and saw him as an enemy and a constant threat. Clement VII was obliged to give Napoleone a one-year safe conduct on the understanding that he would make peace with his half-brothers, but it would not last.

Felice had sent Girolamo to serve under Ferrante Gonzaga and he had sent on 200 men ahead of the main body of troops, leaving only a minimal escort. Napoleone heard of this and marched on the family's property at Vicovaro with 300 men, taking Girolamo prisoner and demanding a substantial ransom for him. Felice did not trust Napoleone to keep any agreement, and was proved right when he further demanded the towns of Castelvecchio and San Gregorio. She wrote to Francesco 'I am very much afraid that Girolamo is in danger of death.'[87] Clement VII authorized military action to rescue Girolamo, considering Felice's children under his protection.

Felice knew how unstable Napoleone was, and genuinely feared for her son's life, especially on hearing that Vicovaro had turned into a siege, knowing that this feud between the half-brothers could have no good end. She continued to refuse Napoleone's demands, and the matter dragged on, with papal troops camped outside the town. Attempts to penetrate the castle were hampered by bad weather and Luigi Gonzaga received an arrow wound in the shoulder, which turned gangrenous and caused his death two months later.

Seeing that the matter was not going his way, Napoleone attempted to break out of the town, taking Girolamo with him, but their escape route was blocked and they were forced to retreat. The castle was then abandoned by Napoleone shortly afterwards and he escaped from it alone, followed by its capitulation. Girolamo was found guarded by only three men. The Pope, who had been put to great expense, then demanded that the Orsini brothers negotiated a truce.

Felice had been humiliated by the war between them, but struggled on, completing the restoration of Monte Giordano, buying furniture and entertaining guests, though Girolamo was full of resentment. He must have believed that Felice cared little for him, or she could have arranged for his earlier release. He was embittered regarding Napoleone and determined to get his revenge. Napoleone actually appeared in Rome at Monte Giordano itself and pretended he wanted to pay a social call on his sister Clarice – he had always been aware of her potential hostage value. Clarice and her husband left as soon as possible, accompanied by Felice, Francesco and Girolamo, but Napoleone followed them. Girolamo, enraged at his persistence, finally drew a sword and killed him. The Prince of Bisignano remarked, not unreasonably, that 'the reason for this act was due to the enmity he had, from the time when Napoleone had captured him.'[88]

Girolamo would be condemned to death for the killing of his half-brother, but in May 1534 the sentence was commuted to a short imprisonment and a fine. In April 1534 a letter to Felice from Girolamo mentions *disgratia* but there is very little regarding the killing in the family records.

Pope Clement cannot have been entirely sorry that Napoleone was gone, as he had for a long time been a serious problem, though his death could not go unpunished. Clement had wasted further money on the siege of Vicovaro, so he confiscated it, along with Bracciano. Without Bracciano the Orsini could not function, so Felice had to employ all her diplomatic talents to get it back. No terms had been made by the Pope and this gave Cardinal Ippolito de' Medici the opportunity to broker terms for its restitution, though Felice would have to humble herself before the Pope and Ippolito. Clement expected a considerable sum of money in return for the estates, and Felice was still short of cash. She had had to repair three palaces, and pay for Clarice's wedding and dowry. The mercenaries sent to rescue Girolamo wanted to be paid and the grain crop had been damaged in floods the previous year. Worse still, Clement was ailing, so time was running out, as any new pope who took over in the middle of negotiations could declare any agreements void.

Felice was under enormous stress and desperately needed money. The papacy had quoted 10,000 ducats as the sum for opening the bargaining, and that would have to be borrowed. She wrote to Francesco in July 1534 that the Archbishop of Benevento would advance them 8,000 ducats paying 10% interest on the loan, with Vicovaro and Bracciano as security. The Prince of Stigliano, Don Luigi Carafa, provided the rest. She then began to negotiate with Cardinal Ippolito de' Medici. She was forced to reassure him repeatedly that her sons would never again cause trouble in Rome. The Pope's health continued to cause concern and Felice was desperate for the matter to be settled before his death, but he was too ill to confirm his intentions. Then his condition improved for a while, and the release of Vicovaro was arranged.

With joy and relief she wrote to Girolamo: 'Today I went to kiss the feet of His Holiness, you can rest now with a quiet soul, for His Holiness is more loving than I can say. God be praised for everything.'[89] On 25 September 1534, just two months after the agreement to return Bracciano was finalised, Pope Clement VII died. He was interred in the Dominican Church of Santa Maria sopra Minerva.[90]

Felice, now 52 years old, had then to arrange a marriage for Girolamo, who had taken possession of Bracciano. He and his brother had already begun their adult lives and Felice's position had changed, though she still had many responsibilities. She was still competent and assured as the Orsini matriarch, but neither of her sons had the capability to be the careful Lord she had hoped for. She had to sell the castle of Palo to raise money, and it must have been a wrench for her. She had always treasured it, not merely as her own property, but as a symbol of her first step into independence.

She hoped that Girolamo would attend to all the necessary problems at Bracciano before she stepped down officially as head of the family, but she had to remind him that there were poor people on the estate who needed his attention. It was clear that she doubted his concern would stretch so far. He did not find his obligations interesting, and was self-centred, wishing for a military career and considering responsibility a tie. Felice's children had always been able to leave things to her, and disliked the coming changes.

She was always careful to ensure that Francesco did not feel left out, or nurse resentment against Girolamo for becoming Lord of Bracciano. She told him of the proposed marriage between his brother and the daughter of Count Bosio, but that she also wanted a bishopric for Francesco, worth around 4,000 scudi annually, until he could attain a cardinalship. The wife of the Count of Bosio, Constanza, was the daughter of Alessandro Farnese, who had just been elected Pope as Paul III. This meant that Girolamo and his future bride, Francesca Sforza, were both the grandchildren of popes. Felice had expected Farnese to be elected, which had made her keen to acquire a Farnese bride for her son. However, Felice was obliged to keep writing to Francesco with recommendations and reminders regarding his responsibilities.

For herself, she hoped that Trinita dei Monte might fill the space left by the sale of Palo and wanted to improve the place. She asked Francesco to help her but he was slow to respond and again reminders had to be sent. The stresses and frustrations of dealing with her sons may have affected her health, which began to fail when she was 53 years old. She had ordered a litter to be made, such as her dear friend Leo X had used while suffering from gout, and was frustrated when its construction was delayed. She had to ask Francesco to request that the Brothers of San Cosimato at Vicovaro let her have the sedan chair that 'Papa Giulio' had once used. The final letter from Felice in the Orsini Archive was to Francesco, dated 15 September 1536, and two weeks later she wrote her will.[91]

In it she asked to be buried at Santa Maria del Popolo, the della Rovere family church. She died shortly afterwards, worn out by a life of struggle and duty. Though the estates were depleted at her death and money was short, it was the fault of war, not lack of good governance on her part. She had made a success of life, despite her father's early indifference, even achieving some personal independence and gaining the friendship of two popes, Leo X and Clement VII after the death of her father, in a time when she might easily have been forgotten. She was an example to all, proving what a determined and intelligent woman could achieve, in a time that had expected nothing of her.

The Weaker Men

ROME in 1527 had up to 1,000 known prostitutes (excluding part-timers). This is a comparatively high figure for a city with a total population of approximately 55,000 at that time. These women made themselves visible in a way that 'respectable' females did not. Any respectable woman, married or not, was largely confined to the home, concerned with family matters and when married, with her regular pregnancies and the rearing of her children. The more disreputable women were out in the open, walking about the streets attracting attention and showing themselves off to men. It was said that they often wore men's clothing, that they were shameless, shouting loudly and rudely at passers-by, making nuisances of themselves. They even touted for business openly in the churches.

It may seem incredible that, in the heartland of the Catholic church, such behaviour could be tolerated, but it must be remembered that Rome was essentially a city of single males, who outnumbered women six to four. Not only was it the home of hordes of clerics, many of whom took their vow of celibacy very lightly, but there were also many workers from outside the city coming into Rome to work, leaving their own women at home. The local prostitutes found a ready and eager clientele at all levels.

On the higher level, there were the courtesans, and these women, like Japanese geisha, were valued just as much for their wit and intelligence as for their sexual skills. These were not qualities expected, or even wanted, in a respectable wife. They offered a different and exciting kind of companionship for the men who could afford them. It was said of them that they often had large, circular beds, with hangings enclosing a private space. They were certainly patronised only by high-ranking men, keeping them beyond the level of the ordinary cleric or immigrant worker. They would have no experience of life on the streets as it was lived by the ordinary prostitute who served the poorer men.

One of those successful and often rich women was named Imperia. She was famous for her 'celebrity' clients as much for her personal charms and was known to have been patronised by the painter Raphael and the wealthy banker Agostino Chigi, as well as by Cardinal Giulio de' Medici, the future Pope Clement VII.[92]

Clement VII – Giulio de Giuliano de' Medici (1478–1534)

He began his papacy in November 1523, though technically he should have been barred from it owing to his illegitimate birth. Although this carried little stigma in social terms, it still created a legal barrier to any career in the church. His father Giuliano de' Medici, the brother of Lorenzo the Magnificent, was killed one month before he was born. They had both been attacked in the Cathedral of Florence by enemies of their family who were trying to end Medici rule in the city. The mother of the child soon to be born was probably Fioretta Gorini, the daughter of a University Professor. Giulio spent the first years of his life with his godfather, the architect Antonio da Sangallo.

He was then taken in by Lorenzo de' Medici, who raised him as one of his own sons. He grew up physically handsome and shy in temperament, becoming an excellent musician. When Lorenzo died, he was passed into the care of Giovanni de' Medici, who would later become Pope Leo X. This connection was to turn the young man from a somewhat surprising career in the military to a rather more suitable one in the church. This Pope greatly favoured his nephew, he also legitimised him and gave him his start in the church, and eventually, a cardinal's hat.[93]

Giulio took as a mistress a 'Moorish or mulatto slave' who was actually the wife of a mule-driver employed by his aunt. The woman was named Simonetta de Collevecchio and a boy child was born to them in 1510 and was named Alessandro. That this child was brought up as the child of Lorenzo II de' Medici (grandson of Lorenzo the Magnificent), was surprising, as there was little or no stigma in any man, even a cardinal, having fathered a child, and there seems to have been no reason for the apparent secrecy at the time. However, the child's appearance made him stand out as his African ancestry was obvious. The portrait of him as an adult by Agnolo Bronzino clearly shows him to have African facial characteristics, so perhaps that was the reason why the child was 'protected' within the family, as the son of Lorenzo rather than Giulio de' Medici, though he was given the nickname 'Il Moro'.

The *Encyclopaedia Italiana* says of him 'his skin colour, his lips and his hair all bear this out, and reveal his African ancestry.' Benvenuto Cellini, who worked for him, said 'It was common knowledge that he was the son of the Pope.'[94] In 1530 the de' Medici were restored to power in Florence, after the city had been a Republic for a brief time. Pope Clement VII appointed Alessandro Hereditary Duke, in preference over Ippolito de' Medici, who became a cardinal. He married Charles V's bastard daughter Margaret of Austria in 1536 but his only children were with his mistress, Taddea Malaspina, who bore his son and daughter, Giulio and Giulia de' Medici. His rule of Florence was not popular and in 1537 he was assassinated by a cousin, Lorenzino de' Medici.

For his father, Clement VII, life would also be difficult. It was to be his tragedy that he was elected Pope at a time of great political turmoil throughout Europe. The Venetian Ambassador Marco Foscari said of him in 1523 'The Pope is forty-eight years old, a sensible man, but slow in decision, which explains his irresolution in action. He talks well and sees everything, but he is very timid.'[95] Clement's sobriety and frugality would be seen as coldness, but he had inherited a bankrupt papal treasury, plundered by Leo X's cheerful extravagance. He would be obliged to endure the Sack of Rome, and his subsequent subservience to Charles V as a result of it, which would lead to further problems with King Henry VIII of England, who could not see the wider picture and understand that

Clement could not afford to offend Charles, and therefore could not give Henry permission to cast off his first wife Katherine of Aragon, who was Charles' aunt.

Pope Clement would have better success with his niece Catherine de' Medici, who had been married to the second son of the King of France. Due to the death of the heir, her husband became Henri II and though she suffered an unhappy married life because of his devotion to his mistress, Diane de Poitiers, she emerged from it as a widow to become Regent for her sons, and to rule as Queen Dowager, becoming all-powerful.[96] She would survive the wars of religion, treading a careful path with a combination of political acumen and brilliant diplomacy that the male members of her family might have envied. Unfortunately, none of her sons had her capacity and France was left to suffer for it.

For Pope Clement himself, the most important lesson in his life was patience. In knowing that he could not please everyone, he developed his dilatoriness into an art form, letting time sort problems for him and nature take its course. It was a pity that he lived and ruled in a time when a strong and determined pope was needed, for had he lived in a more peaceful era, he might have been remembered fondly as a good pastoral pope, and a patron of the arts, instead of being torn between France, Spain and England. After his death the considered opinion of him was that 'although he had not been a good pope, he was always a good Medici.'[97]

He died aged fifty-six in September 1534, so fortunately did not have to suffer knowing of the assassination of his son Alessandro. His biographer Emmanuel Pierre Rodocanachi said 'according to the custom of his times, his death was attributed to poison.'[98] However, his health had been poor for some time, so that assumption is not borne out by the facts.

Alessandro Farnese – Pope Paul III (1468–1549)
The Farnese family had played their part in Rome's history since the twelfth century. The man who would become the future Paul III begun his education in Rome and then completed it in Florence in the household of the de' Medici family. He would become a personal friend of Giovanni de' Medici, who was the future Pope Leo X.

Alessandro Farnese was a cardinal by 1493, appointed at the same time as Cesare Borgia and by the same Pope, Cesare's father Rodrigo Borgia, Pope Alexander VI. He suffered a little under the nickname of 'the pettitcoat cardinal' as his elevation was popularly believed to have been entirely due to the influence of his sister, Giulia Farnese, who was then the favourite mistress of the Borgia Pope.

Unfortunately, as a cardinal, his morals were no better than those of many others and he was to father five illegitimate children, two of whom were later legitimised by Julius II. Their mother was Silvia Ruffini, his long-term mistress, who gave him three sons and two daughters, Pierluigi, Paolo, Ranuccio, Constanza and Lucrezia Farnese.

Alessandro was particularly fond of Pierluigi, who became Duke of Parma and Piacenza. He intended this favourite son to become the true head of the Farnese family, and spoiled him terribly, refusing to listen to the stories of his vices, but Pierluigi deeply resented his situation as 'the bastard son of the Pope' and made a name for himself for decadence, ruthlessness and sheer cruelty. He was to marry Girolama Orsini and was murdered in 1547. Though his father, then Pope Paul III, grieved over him, nobody else did, as it was said of him

> This Pier (Peter), being the darling of the Pope, insofar as when told of his vile doings, the Pope would merely smile and say 'he did not learn these things from me' but everyone knew of the detestable abominations he committed, particularly on the body of the Bishop of Fano, which I abhor to relate [he had allegedly raped the young Bishop Cosimo Gheri, who subsequently died], or that at length the man's own domestics, no longer able to endure his tyrannies, or his filthy abominations, got him out of the way in 1547.[99]

Pope Paul met in consistory after his son had been stabbed to death, accusing Ferrante Gonzaga of the murder, but it had probably been instigated by Charles V of Spain, for whom Ferrante had been spying on Pierluigi Farnese, and a conspiracy of distant relatives had enacted the assassination.

Alessandro Farnese's daughter Constanza married Boso II of the house of Sforza, and, shortly after Alessandro's election as Pope Paul III he raised two of his grandsons, Alessandro Farnese and Ascanio Sforza, to the rank of cardinal, despite their being only fourteen and sixteen years old respectively. He was undaunted by the criticism this caused, and went on to raise Pierluigi's son to cardinal's rank when he was only fifteen years old.

Paul III had fully expected to be made pope at the death of Leo X and then again at the Conclave following the death of Pope Adrian IV. He was particularly incensed to be ousted by Clement VII and would often say that Clement had 'robbed him' of ten years of his papacy.[100] When he did finally achieve the papacy, he at first attempted to behave discreetly with regard to women, breaking off his relationship with his relatively respectable mistress, who was the mother of his children. Instead he indulged himself in passing relationships with other women, some of them far from respectable, appearing with them at masked balls and feasts. He also celebrated the fact that his sister had been responsible for his rise in the church, by having a gold medal struck showing a naked woman watering a lily, which was taken to be Giulia Farnese, and was considered to be highly irregular in the circumstances.

He also failed miserably to avoid the pitfall of family advancement, into which every Renaissance pope fell, and when his favourite son the dissolute Pierluigi was finally murdered, he made his son-in-law Ottavio the Duke of Parma and Piacenza in his place. The Emperor Charles V despised the Pope, being offended by the neutral role he attempted to play, and the fact that he wished to further advance his family by giving Milan to his grandson Ottavio Farnese, though that hope was doomed to failure.

When the Pope gave Parma and Piacenza to his son Pierluigi, followed by his son-in-law, the Emperor was furious, as he considered he had a claim to the city. Due to this he failed to win the Emperor's support and had allowed his personal ambitions for his family to stand in the way of the interests of the church he was supposed to serve.

The Council of Trent would eventually be summoned to attempt to deal with the problems of Lutheranism, but was convened too late to bring about any possible reconciliation with Protestant views.

Paul III would go on to persecute the Protestants viciously, and it was said that his son-in-law the Duke of Parma, along with his grandson Cardinal Farnese, shed so much blood in the religious wars against them, 'that their hordes should have been able to swim in it'. Another account claimed that 'after he became infuriated against the Lutherans, his nephews became the executors of cruelty on his behalf, and were not afraid to boast in public of having caused rivers of blood to flow, deep enough for them to swim their horses.'

Paul had more success with cultural and architectural aims, resuming work on St Peter's Basilica with Michelangelo in charge, and commissioning frescoes for the papal apartments inside Castel Sant'Angelo, although their pagan themes were criticised. Copernicus dedicated to him his book 'On the Revolution of the Heavenly Bodies' but, ironically, fifty years later, there would be a clampdown on astrology, so the work would be placed on the Index of Forbidden Books.[101]

The famous painting of Pope Paul III with his grandsons, by Titian, shows him as a cowed figure, dominated by Cardinal Alessandro Farnese standing above him, while Ottavio the Duke of Parma is about to kneel. Paul had used the papacy as a means of consolidating family power, and in return his family ruled him. By the time he reached old age, he was aware that his reputation as a pope would have been far greater, had his devotion to his greedy relatives been less.

The Time of the Termagant: Olimpia Pamphilj

On 26 May 1591, Sforza Maidalchini was disappointed at the birth of a daughter to his second wife, Vittoria Gualtieri. He already had a son, by his deceased first wife, and wanted another.

The child was baptised Olimpia and would grow up not only knowing herself to be unwanted, but aware that, as a female, she was inferior. Pope Innocent III (1198–1216) had declared that women's menstrual blood was 'so impure and detestable that, from contact therewith, fruits and grains are blighted, bushes dry up, grasses die, trees lose their fruits, and if dogs chance to eat of it, they will go mad.'[1]

Though extreme, these sentiments are ones that women have been faced with since earliest times. Even the ability to actually produce children, which was a woman's married duty, meant that she was merely a convenient vessel, and Aristotle described the female as 'a kind of soil, dirt actually, in which the man planted his seed.'[2] St Thomas Aquinas declared that women were 'misbegotten men', inferior by nature, incapable of leadership, in every way defective. Even for a woman to enter the Vatican could contaminate and pollute its purity and nuns were forbidden to approach the altar to receive the Sacrament, if menstruating.[3]

For an intelligent and determined girl-child, life was not going to be easy. The little Olimpia was recorded as being 'dominating by nature, she decided what games to play, and always wanted to win.'[4] It was also considered that the all-important wifely virtues (such as obedience) would be damaged by too much female education. It might make the woman question her husband, or other men in authority over her. An educated female was also believed to be less satisfied with the secondary role assigned to her. Young Olimpia had a mind capable of grasping mathematics, and of understanding the work her father did, although it was 'not for her' unless she was to spend her life in a convent, where some administrative skill might be useful.

Olimpia's parents lived at Viterbo, a picturesque town where Pope Clement IV had died in 1268. The Conclave, gathered to choose his successor, could not make a decision, and the matter dragged on through 1269 and even into 1270.[5] To finally push the cardinals into making a decision, they could be made more uncomfortable, so instead of allowing them to retire to palaces for food and rest, they were all locked into one building. When that failed to inspire them, the Viterban authorities removed the roof! Baskets of bread and water were then lowered down and, after the longest election in church history, they elected Teobaldo Visconti of Piacenza, who became Pope Gregory X. (1271–1276).[6]

It showed the Viterban spirit, its determination and forcefulness, which Olimpia would inherit in full measure.

Another important lesson would be learned when Olimpia was eight years old. News from Rome, fifty miles to the south, reached the town that on 11 September 1599 a twenty-two year old noblewoman, Beatrice Cenci, had been beheaded for playing a part in her father's murder. He had been a violent man who had sexually abused her. He had been found the previous year at the foot of a castle cliff, with his head smashed. Not only was Beatrice executed, but also her mother and her two brothers. The authorities had known of Francesco Cenci's violent and abusive nature but had done nothing to help the family who had suffered from his tyranny. Under torture, the brothers admitted having thrown him off the cliff. Beatrice's involvement in the plot, and her subsequent execution, caught the popular imagination, though her abuse had won her no mercy. The reaction to killing of the head of the family made it clear that opposition to parental authority – indeed any authority – was unacceptable.

By that time, Olimpia had two sisters, Vittoria and Ortensia. Their father decided that he was not prepared to waste the family inheritance on providing dowries for daughters, and that his only son, the product of his first marriage, should be sole heir. Therefore the girls would go into convents. For any girl to enter a convent, a dowry would be required, but it would be far less than that expected by a son-in-law. Friendships between nuns were frowned upon, as no nun should have any 'singular' relationship. In strict orders, not even pets were allowed, and there was little outside contact, except with occasional family visitors, speaking through a grille. For everyone except the deeply devout, it was a death in life.

The story of the Nun of Monza, the heiress Marianna de Leyva, who was put into a convent by her father, becoming notorious as Sister Virginia de Leyva, was enough of a cautionary tale for any girl. She formed an attachment with a local young man, became the mother of two children, and their illicit liaison resulted in murders, the destruction of his family, and Sister Virginia being condemned to spend the rest of her life walled up. She survived almost fourteen years of that living death.[7]

Though the convent was a fate the two younger sisters were to experience, Olimpia did the unimaginable thing – she refused! In 1606, Ortensia, then thirteen or fourteen years old, along with twelve-year old Vittoria, entered the convent of St Dominic, where their sacrifice would do honour to their family. Sforza Maidalchini, still determined that no daughter would share the inheritance he intended for his son, Andrea, at first tried to persuade her gently to join her sisters.

A girl would, in theory, have to convince the Bishop that she took the veil willingly, but they knew themselves to be unwanted, and that it was required of them, so they would acquiesce reluctantly. Olimpia, then aged fifteen, watching her younger sisters being locked away, without ever tasting life, refused again.[8] The family was ranged against her, she was faced with pleas to consider their position, their future shame at her refusal, the danger to her brother's prospects (he was already married with a family of his own, enjoying a life his sisters would never see).

The Abbess of St Dominic, who was Olimpia's own aunt, was enlisted to speak to her. She was told that she might one day be an Abbess herself, when she could have an interesting and full life, but Olimpia replied 'Lady Aunt, it is better that I should lose my family, than that my body should burn.' She was referring to St Paul's letter declaring, 'It is better to marry than to burn.'[9]

Her refusal was becoming common knowledge and her father, humiliated, lost his temper with her. He engaged a highly regarded Augustinian confessor to remain with Olimpia all her waking hours to convince her. His arguments went on endlessly, until Olimpia finally wrote a letter to the Bishop of Viterbo, Girolamo Matteucci, who was a strict man. She pleaded with him to enforce the rule of the Council of Trent, requiring a girl's willingness to comply. She emphasised her reluctance, and then – just to shock him further – she accused the confessor of attempting to sexually molest her.

The priest was arrested, found guilty, and sentenced to six months on bread and water; his promising career wrecked. Whether or not he did molest Olimpia, the Bishop was furious and forbade her father to force her into a convent.[10] Olimpia had won, but at what cost? Her family was shamed, her sisters still locked away, even though both were under the legal age of sixteen.[11] Olimpia had also gained herself a reputation as a troublemaker. Many people felt that her accusation had been invented, and she had ruined the young priest's career in the process. Olimpia was reported as having said at that time, 'I am like a beaten horse, the beatings just make my coat glossier.'[12] an insight into the treatment of both women and horses.

Her family life became very unhappy after the incident, and the bishop was furious; even worse, the Holy Inquisition was displeased. Sforza Maidalchini was ridiculed and his business suffered, For a couple of years there was an uncomfortable truce at home, until Olimpia's godmother, Fiordalisa Nini, suggested that her nephew, Paolo Nini, needed a wife. He had a fortune, church contacts, and seemed interested in Olimpia. He was then eagerly encouraged, and Paolo finally agreed to take her for a dowry of only 5,000 scudi, quite a low figure given the status of the groom. Olimpia found herself married to the richest young man in Viterbo in 1608, and went to the family's two palaces, which faced each other across the Via Annio. Paolo's father lived in one, and the newlyweds would have the other. Olimpia established herself in her new household with a large staff. She could indulge herself with jewels, gowns and other luxuries, though for her the pleasure would always be in their financial value, rather than the admiration of other women. Shortly after her marriage, her sisters were professed as nuns and their 'marriage to God' must have contrasted pitifully with her own.

She became pregnant quickly and bore a daughter, named Constanza, but the child died after only a few months. She gave birth to the wanted heir in 1611 and Nino Nini was named for his grandfather. It was the child's father, Paolo, who became ill, dying on 6 June 1611. Olimpia was twenty years old, the mother of a child only a few months old, and already a widow.

Unfortunately, the following March, the infant Nino also died leaving Olimpia bereft of her husband and two children in only three years. But she was rich, having inherited her husband's palace, farms, gardens, pastures, vineyards, and money. The only problem was that it was not considered 'proper' for a young woman, even a respectable widow, to live alone. It was considered that any widow, having known the 'joys' of marriage, was likely to be lustful. If any woman suppressed these natural inclinations, it could lead to her having 'vapours' rising from her private parts to her head, resulting in all kinds of strange behaviour, usually termed 'greensickness'. The only alternatives were the convent, or re-marriage. Olimpia started to look about for another husband.[13]

This time, she could offer youth, health, proven fertility, and plenty of money. She was looking for somebody noble, as she wanted to be in the centre of things, and had her eyes set on Rome. She could find a nobleman there who wanted a wealthy wife, but perhaps she could also find political power, and her nature craved it.

Olimpia's uncle, Paolo Gualtieri, had married a Roman lady named Antonia Pamphilj, from a family of minor nobility accustomed to government and church appointments. One of them had married a great-granddaughter of Alexander VI. In 1604 uncle Girolamo Pamphilj had been made a cardinal. This gentleman had lived at the Palazzo Pamphilj, dying there in 1610. It was then occupied only by his two nephews, who needed funds.[14]

Gianbattista Pamphilj, aged thirty-eight, was closer in age to the twenty-one-year-old Olimpia, but was a priest. His elder brother, Pamphilio Pamphilj, was unmarried. They were living quite poorly for noblemen, and an inventory of 1611 showed they only owned five horses between them, with Gianbattista paying for their upkeep from his salary. Pamphilio rented out shops at ground level on three sides of their home, in the old Roman tradition.[15] Pamphilio was then almost fifty years old, but considered still to be strikingly handsome, and known for his exquisite courtesy, learned at the ducal court of Tuscany. He had returned to Rome aged about twenty-five and was appointed to the government in the Campidoglio.

All he could do was marry money, and Olimpia needed to buy her way into a noble family. Love was never a pre-requisite for marriage, but if the couple could tolerate each other, all could be arranged. Pamphilio may have been pleased with Olimpia's looks, while she could see that he would not be a dominating husband. The marriage contract was signed on 1 November 1612 and Pamphilio agreed to make her his legal wife, while she could endow him with all her worldly goods, which were considerable. Her father promised her 3,000 scudi at her wedding, along with a pearl necklace and some other jewellery and silver. He agreed to pay a further 2,000 scudi in instalments. Gregorio Leti recorded that the wedding was celebrated 'with all possible pomp and with the entire satisfaction of both parties'.[16] Olimpia was not only safely married, but a noblewoman.

The Pamphilj family home was in the very centre of Rome on the Piazza Navona. This Piazza, built over the ruins of the 15,000-seat stadium of Domitian, had been erected for the athletic games known as *agoni*. The stadium was disused by AD 330 and became a convenient quarry from which the local houses and churches had been built. After the Viterbo palaces, Olimpia was likely to have been disappointed in the Pamphilj home, as it was four stories tall, but narrow, with an irregular façade. The majority of the rooms were on the 'wrong' side, overlooking not the Navona, but the narrow Via Pasquino, with one apartment in the rear, on the cobbled Via dell' Anima. If the Navona was busy, the Pasquino was busier and noisier. The fragment of the statue of Hercules which had once decorated the stadium had been put on the corner and was used as a place to leave verses, messages, and political statements. Another statue at the foot of the Capitoline Hill used to 'answer' it, talking by means of the messages and remarks left attached to them.[17]

This could be annoying for the neighbours, and Olimpia may have disliked the cramped rooms and the small courtyards, so unlike the spacious gardens she had once had. The place had only about 10,000 inhabitants. Gang violence between rival families was common and floods were regular, as the Tiber was level with the streets.[18] When the water rose, the prisoners in the Tor di Nona prison sometimes drowned, and most of the local buildings were patched up, so falling masonry was another hazard.[19]

If Olimpia imagined that her husband would discuss his work with her, she was mistaken. He was horrified at female interference, and she had to confine herself to household and charity work. The great families also resisted the attempts of social climbers to break into their ranks, though they were often far poorer than Olimpia. The nuances of etiquette would mask outright rudeness, but the newcomer could still be put firmly in her place. The entourage that a nobleman or woman trailed around with them showed their dignity, and once Pamphilio was in possession of Olimpia's money, he hired more servants and bought more horses, even though they had to be stabled elsewhere.[20]

Rome was always busy, always noisy, and before the Lenten period would be carnival, including races run by naked prostitutes, Jews, or even old men. By Ash Wednesday everything changed, becoming serious for the Easter Duty of confession and communion.[21] Much of the excitement centred around the Piazza Navona. Spain's ambassador lived there, and every June on the 28th he would present the Pope with a white horse, the *chinea*, as nominal rent paid by the King of Spain for the Kingdom of Naples.[22]

While enjoying the social life, Olimpia got off on the wrong foot with Gianbattista. He remarked that he had known nothing of his brother's intention to marry, though he referred to her as a 'most noble wife'[23] On her arrival Olimpia considered all in the house to be hers, including Gianbattista's personal items. He was to write to his brother, protesting about this:

I placed them in the last room of the Piazza Navona house before Signora Olimpia came to Rome, along with my other things, to empty the rooms for the occasion. If Signora Olimpia says I gave them to her, I imagine I only said it out of fear or persuasion of Signor Pamphlilio, but I insist that they be returned to me at all costs.[24]

Gianbattista had led a wild life, taking Holy Orders lightly, and often refusing to wear church robes. He kept his hair long and it took persuasion from his uncle to make him conform. When the transformation occurred, his uncle's friend Pope Clement VIII made him a consistorial lawyer and by the time he met Olimpia he was courteous and sober, but unfortunately also indecisive and mistrustful. Olimpia was intelligent and very interested in the lawsuits he dealt with and he gradually realised that her opinions were sound. Her sharp mind made difficult points seem clearer, and he began to rely on her, discussing business with her each day.

Gianbattista had finally found someone he could trust, and Olimpia had found someone who needed her and did not look down on her for being a female. Their friendship was naturally noticed, especially when they took the air together in a carriage, laughing and enjoying each other's company. They also spent time in Gianbattista's private rooms away from Pamphilio. In his biography Gregorio Leti remarked:

> This woman went more often in the carriage around town with her brother-in-law than with her husband. They were locked up for hours on end in his cabinet, longer than propriety could approve, longer than her husband could tolerate. Sometimes, he sought his brother and his wife without finding them, which is proof that he found it necessary to look for them, and that she didn't take a step without her brother-in-law.[25]

He went further in his analysis:

> One thing obliged many people to have a better sentiment of her conduct, that they could not understand how a woman with an agreeable body and face could resolve to fall in love with the ugliest and most deformed man ever born, for such was her brother-in-law ... from this one can judge the grand ambition that rules women, and she, who wanted only to command, loved him all the more because he allowed her to govern.[26]

Olimpia was working to get Gianbattista made a cardinal, as when Uncle Girolamo had died the family had not only lost its link to the pope, it had lost its prestige too. The first step was to have Gianbattista made Nuncio (papal ambassador) to some foreign court. Spain was the most important, or France, or even Venice. He had qualifications for the post and years of legal experience, his only handicap was that he was awkward in social situations; but that would be dealt with if Olimpia acted as his hostess. She had already met all the cardinals in Rome – especially the ones considered *papabile* – and Alessandro Ludovisi was the front-runner. Then, surprisingly, after seven years of marriage, Olimpia had a child, a healthy girl named Maria. Gianbattista hired the Teofili house next door to make room for the nursery.

On 28 January 1621 Pope Paul V died after a sixteen-year reign. The Conclave to replace him began on 8 February and on the following day their friend Alessandro Ludovisi became Pope Gregory XV. By the end of March Gianbattista Pamphilj was Papal Nuncio to the Kingdom of Naples and his family would go there with him, with Olimpia as his official hostess. Pamphilio and the two-year old child Maria would go to make the whole thing look respectable.[27]

They arrived in Naples in April 1621 and were to live for the duration in the Nuncio's Palace bought by Pope Sixtus V in the 1580s. Gianbattista disliked it and wrote to the new Pope. 'It is too small for the family of a prelate, who will be situated in an indecent place.'[28] Gianbattista had to write a weekly dispatch to Rome, reporting in code on all business conducted. The courier system was efficient, with a fast horse making the journey in three days. The Nuncio was also expected to spend a good deal of his own money, and he was lucky that Olimpia was willing to help promote his career. He was an indolent man, and she needed to keep him interested. For Olimpia it was the ideal situation, being needed and being busy. The Venetian ambassador to Rome, Alvise Contarini, summed up the situation: '...to the same Signora Donna Olimpia he (Gianbattista) declared himself very much obliged for the rich dowry carried into the Pamphilj family and for having provided for his needs.'[29]

Cardinal Sforza Pallavacino, who would later know Olimpia well, wrote

She carried into the Pamphilj family much patrimony that was used most instrumentally to honourably sustain the house.

From this came the greatness which successively followed Gianbattista. Let me add that she possessed an intellect of great value in economic government and she had always administered with care the possessions of the family, with great advantage to the purse, to relieve the cares of her brother-in-law.[30]

Olimpia's own brother, Andrea, was living outside of Naples and in September 1621 she wrote to her mother that he was four days into his governorship of the town of Averso. He was then forty years old and busy siring the ten sons and many daughters he would have with two wives. Olimpia was on good terms with him. Though close to brother and brother-in-law, she seemed to distance herself from her husband, and a document in the Vatican Archives makes it plain that Olimpia would allow no opposition: 'Married to Pamphilio Pamphilj in the second marriage, she showed such a stubborn mind that many times he was forced to tolerate her many importunities and many insolent rebukes.'[31]

Despite such marital difficulties, Olimpia gave birth to a son, Camillo, in February 1622. The family then not only had her money, and her determined and capable assistance, but she had provided them with an heir. However, some people in Naples wondered if the brother-in-law she favoured had not fathered the child, rather than the discounted husband.

Pope Gregory XV was another indolent man, though he had the excuse of ill-health. He was to say 'Just give me something to eat and you can take care of the rest.' He did canonise Teresa of Avila, Ignatius of Loyola, Francis Xavier and Philip Neri, as well as revising the papal elections, but he largely left other work to his nephew Cardinal Ludovico Ludovisi.[32] The Pope died in 1623 and the Roman diarist Giacinto Gigli said of him, 'After the death of Gregory the treasury was empty and aggravated by large debts, without anyone knowing how this had occurred. The Pope gave everything to his relatives, who in just twenty-nine months had accumulated the greatest riches.'

The next pope was Maffeo Barberini, who became Urban VIII. When the Pamphilj family returned to Rome from Naples, after being away for four years, Gianbattista was chosen for a special mission. Cardinal Francesco Barberini wanted to go to France, as a dispute had arisen between France and Spain over the area of Valtellina in Lombardy. The Pope was aware that his nephew was too inexperienced for such a delicate mission, and wanted Gianbattista to direct it. It was destined to fail, but due to French stubbornness rather than any failing on Gianbattista's part.

During his absence, Olimpia was busy networking with the embassy wives and an eighteenth-century pamphlet adjudged that 'She insinuated herself into the graces of the Barberini brothers ... and with Cardinal Antonio, procuring with her gentle manners the exaltation of ... Monsignor Pamphilj to the Nunciature.'[33]

Gregorio Leti refers to a letter written by Gianbattista at this time, addressed to Olimpia:

> My dear sister, my business does not succeed as well in Spain as in Rome, because I am deprived of your advice. Far from you I am like a ship without a rudder, abandoned to the inconstancy of the sea, with no hope of its own happiness. I feel obliged to let you know this because I would not know how better to show you my affection.[34]

In September 1627 Gianbattista heard that the Pope had named him Cardinal 'in pectore' which means, 'in the chest' or secretly for now. Gianbattista would receive his cardinal's hat when the next batch of cardinals was appointed. It was to be in the future, but it was definite. Olimpia's work, and the careful use of her money, had paid off.

The Barberini Pope indulged in neptotism to excess (the term has its roots in 'nipote', meaning nephew), and this tendency was a direct result of the papacy not being hereditary. A pope's relatives lost all power once he died, so it made sense for them to make as much as possible out of his position while they could. Jealousy was rife in the Vatican, and the nephews protected the pope's person and interests. They supported him and if one of them became pope, he could hopefully continue his uncle's policies.

Once Gianbattista was to be a cardinal, it was decided that Casa Pamphilj was by no means grand enough to be his residence. The Pope's nephew Taddeo Barberini lived in a palace and was made a prince, taking precedence over all the ambassadors.

This resulted in the ambassadors of France and Spain boycotting functions attended by him. Two other Barberini relatives were cardinals, and Cardinal Antonio Barberini, who received his advancement when only twenty years old, ruined his chances by chasing lovers, both male and female. Olimpia knew about him as one of her own cousins, Gualterio Gualtieri, who was also a nephew to Gianbattista, worked for him, having entered his service as a page.

One day, when called away by the Cardinal from a game of cards with his friends, he cried angrily 'I have him in the ass all night, he should at least leave me in peace during the day!'[35] The remark was quickly passed around and the Cardinal was furious.

He sent the teenager to the battlefield to fight the Protestants, where he was killed. Olimpia and Gianbattista were angry as well as grieved by his death.

Gianbattista Pamphilj officially became a cardinal in November 1629 along with eight others. In June 1630 the Pope also decreed that cardinals should no longer be referred to as Excellency, but should take the title of Eminence.[36] Gianbattista was then appointed to one of the most important of the 'congregations', that of the Council of Trent, which showed that he was considered to be reliable.[37] He was also to be appointed to the Holy Office of the Inquisition, to discuss the problems of heresy.[38]

Only Gianbattista's brusque manner let him down, his excellent qualities sometimes hidden by his surly exterior, which is why he relied on Olimpia so often; she softened and supported him. Gregorio Leti stated:

> The good Cardinal was an excellent master in the art of dissimulating everything perfectly, except for the love he had for his sister-in-law. In the congregations he appeared gentle, in conversation he was humble, in church he was admirably devout ... but with all his skill it was impossible for him to hide his affection for Donna Olimpia... He loved her, he adored her, in public and in private all the world was truly astonished that a Cardinal, who had pretensions to the Pontificate, worked so openly to win the good graces of a woman, and his sister-in-law at that.[39]

Olimpia bought the two neighbouring houses, including the one Gianbattista had rented, and they were added to the original property, creating a home of better dimensions. For two years the house was being remodelled to allow him the space that his new dignity required and to provide room for entertaining. He was still not considered one of the 'rich' cardinals, but life had improved.[40] Gianbattista now outranked his elder brother and was given the best rooms in the house, overlooking the Piazza Navona. Pamphilio's rooms were at the back, overlooking the narrow Via del'Anima. Olimpia's suite had connecting doors to the rooms of both her husband and her brother-in-law.

Olimpia's husband lived a secluded life in the 1630s, suffering from kidney stones. During his illnesses, Olimpia gave him her attention, and arranged for doctors to attend him, though their ministrations often made his pain worse. In August 1639 he suffered a particularly bad attack, with nothing able to ease his searing pain. The priests were sent for, Olimpia and Gianbattista attended him, and he was given the Last Rites. He died on 29 August after twenty-seven years of marriage. Olimpia was to wear widow's weeds for the rest of her life, which then included a large black hood, peaked over the forehead.

Malicious people said that she had always shown more affection towards her brother-in-law than her husband, and some even went so far as to claim that Pamphilio had been poisoned, though that was a usual accusation at the time. An autopsy proved that he had died from a blockage caused by an unusually large stone. The house went into mourning. Gianbattista wrote to a friend in Spain:

To the Duke of Gandia in Madrid,

I am obliged to inform Your Excellency of the news of my family... having lost the illustrious Pamphilio, my only brother, and the head of this family aged seventy-six, to my infinite grief, after a very painful illness of the stone, which turned out to have weighed six ounces and was without remedy.[41]

Olimpia, as a widow, was entitled to administer her own money, but Gianbattista wanted her to take charge of the Pamphilj money also, including dealing with the comforts of his sisters,

Agatha and Prudenzia, in their convents. To be the official administrator of a noble family's finances was a great honour for any woman, but the Ambassador of Mantua said that she deserved it 'for her great intelligence and economy'.[42] He added that in his opinion, Gianbattista was afraid of her remarrying and leaving him without her help, and also without her money! There is no evidence that she ever intended to remarry. She was already forty-eight years old, the mother of three children, and enjoyed being in control of Gianbattista's household. By that time, she was also doing a good deal of his work for him, and it was known that if anyone needed him they would be obliged to go through Olimpia, who would then tell him how to respond.

Olimpia's son Camillo was seventeen years old and officially head of the family, but his mother would always wield the real power. His two sisters, Maria and Constanza, were also very much in the shadow of their mother, though Gianbattista made a favourite of Maria, who was pious. In 1649, aged twenty-one, she was to marry the Marquess Andrea Guistiniani, who was well-connected, though Gianbattista thought him uncouth as he had casual manners and very little money. Within a year there was a child, a girl named Olimpia, but usually called by the diminutive Olimpiuccia. This child would resemble her grandmother and would grow up equally headstrong. Olimpia wanted to bring the child up herself, and the parents did not object. The granddaughter would prove to be the love of Olimpia's life. She made a will in the girl's favour leaving her the Maidalchini-Nini wealth, excluding her son Camillo. He would then inherit only his father's, which was much less. Camillo and his mother disliked each other and being disinherited by her increased his resentment. Leti said of him, 'He was so ignorant that he barely knew how to read at the age of twenty.'[43] Whether this was due to any neglect of his education, or merely a lack of learning ability, is not clear. The French ambassador remarked 'Fortune supplied him with what nature had declined to give.' So he may have been a low achiever, distancing him from his capable mother. He appeared to be good looking and charming, an excellent horseman, good dancer, and something of an artist. So long as he married the woman his mother chose for him and produced children, he would have to do.

Olimpia lived life well, hunting, attending the theatre, spending time with her brother-in-law, and though she always wore the funereal weeds of the widow she also often wore diamonds. The ambassador of Mantua said, 'She was haughty and entered into conversations more than was seemly for a widow, and also spent many hours gambling.' Olimpia obviously saw no reason why she should live in retirement and did not care how others believed she should behave. Her main aim was to support Gianbattista and to help to make him pope. He was sixty in 1634 so was of the right age, and his positions of responsibility had enhanced his reputation. In 1637 Pope Urban VIII suffered a serious illness, though papal power was taken over by his nephews.

One of Olimpia's problems regarding making Gianbattista into a pope was Cardinal Antonio Barberini, who was responsible for the death of the Gualtieri cousin. He intensely disliked Gianbattista and his malice could easily work against him. They could not know how much time they would have to prepare, and needed to win favour, particularly from France and Spain – always delicate, as they were always at odds, and offered generous pensions to tempt supporters. Cardinal Virginio Orsini found out the difficulty of pleasing one side without falling out with the other, as he had been a Spanish ally, but later 'became a Frenchman, then turned back towards Spain. At present he is "French" again, though for how long nobody knows.'[44]

Cardinal Mario Teodoli complained that he never received anything and met with the influential Spanish Cardinal Gil Alvarez Carillo de Alburnoz to ask if anything could be done for him, but was informed that – regretfully – Spain could not afford to outbid France! He remarked sadly, 'Since the Spaniards don't want to help me, I have gone with the camp of the French, though reluctantly.'[45] The situation became so ridiculous that a man could change his allegiance to France or Spain by showing the colour of his stockings (red or white respectively). Likewise a woman could wear coloured ribbons on the left or right side of her head. Olimpia did not involve herself in such play-acting, she was pro-Gianbattista and pro-Olimpia only.

In July Urban's health took a turn for the worse. He was then seventy-six years old. His nephew Cardinal Francesco reminded him that there were still vacancies in the Sacred College and suggested they fill them with supporters, but Urban was past such concerns. He died on 29 July and was buried four days later in St Peter's.

The city immediately erupted into violence, rioting against the Pope's greedy family. They called Urban *Papa Gabella*, or Pope Tax, as he had placed sixty-three new taxes on the people, to provide for his nephews. The Treasury at his death was 19 million scudi in the red. Mobs went around Rome with hammers, defacing the Barberini bees while Pasquinades appeared making fun of the defects of the cardinals hoping to be the next pope.

The heat was intense that August and it was suggested that the Conclave be moved to the Quirinal, where the air was cooler. The Vatican doctor agreed that the Vatican was likely to be lethal due to 'miasmas and infections' but Cardinal Antonio Barberini, using his authority as Camerlengo, refused to move in the interests of tradition. Many cardinals made their wills before attending.[46]

Leti was to write about the final, frantic preparations and Olimpia's participation in them:

> Donna Olimpia threw herself into keeping watch over all things, making the most extreme effort to discover the intrigues, plots and intentions of the cardinals, with regard to the election. Even though she had a natural stinginess, she spent a great deal on spies to be well aware of all things. She staged a campaign to be informed of the least intrigue ... and made every possible effort to learn what was happening.[47] ... The evening they entered the Conclave, Cardinal Pamphilj spoke a long time with his sister-in-law but I have never been able to discover what passed between them.

Despite the cardinals being locked in, messages were passed back and forth. Olimpia received reports of Gianbattista and other friendly cardinals and was able to send back instructions.[48] Each cardinal was allowed two servants (old and sick ones were allowed three), and they listened at the dividing walls and carried tales. The French ambassador visited, favouring those candidates of Cardinal Mazarin, Prime Minister of France.[49] Mazarin's first choice was

Guido Bentivoglio and his second was Giulio Saccetti, both very friendly towards France. Pamphilj was considered 'Spain's man', although he actually had no preference for either party. Mazarin sent sacks of gold to distribute among electors to help them make up their minds, while the Spanish ambassador offered Spanish bishoprics, princesses for nephews to marry, and estates in the Kingdom of Naples for those who would vote for Spain's preferred candidate – Gianbattista Pamphilj.

At the age of seventy, Pamphilj was considered likely to rule for six or seven years, yet was old enough not to hang on forever. His two sisters were nuns sworn to poverty and he had only two nieces (one already married) and one nephew, who wasn't too bright but also did not appear too greedy. Some thought Pamphilj 'rigid and bitter' while others disliked his uninspiring looks. Leti said of him, 'Many took the occasion to say it would not be good to make … a pope who had a face so horrible … that it scared the children.'[50] This emphasis on Gianbattista's looks seems strange to modern eyes. His famous portrait by Valasquez does not show him to be any more bizarre than the other popes. Perhaps it was his severe and serious appearance which put people off. What did put some people off was the fear that he might live a long time, with his sister-in-law at his side. This, too, was only due to her sex, and if his closest advisor had been a man it would have caused no problem; a woman being in a position of influence behind the pope could not be tolerated.

When the voting began the Barberini did all they could to elect Cardinal Saccetti. Cardinal Alburnoz rose repeatedly to declare that Philip IV discounted him due to his affinity with France, and enquiries were made whether such blatant exclusion was legal, and the questioners were informed that it was indeed interference, but nobody had the courage to ignore Spain's wishes.

While Olimpia was waiting for news, she heard her granddaughter cry out. The child was in Gianbattista's bedchamber where she had followed a white dove. The bird settled on the canopy over Gianbattista's bed. It was the Pamphilj symbol and with such a sign from Heaven Olimpia acted quickly. She contacted Antonio Barberini, aware that he feared a Pamphilj pope would persecute his family. All the money he had acquired from his uncle was on his mind. Olimpia not only reassured him, but offered her son Camillo as husband for Antonio's fourteen-year-old niece, Lucrezia Barberini, if he would swing his block of votes towards Gianbattista. Antonio was tempted, but the French ambassador was unwilling, so the Conclave continued.

Malaria was added to the discomforts of the cardinals and it was remembered that back in 1623 eight of them had died while in Conclave. Cardinal Bentivoglio was already ill and Francesco Barberini was feverish. Gianbattista's greatest ally, Giovanni Panciroli, began to work on Antonio Barberini: 'On you alone the Sacred College depends, you alone can create the Pontiff,'[51] Barberini decided not to wait for Mazarin's decision, he suddenly wanted to be the pope-maker. He met the Spanish cardinals and their supporters and agreed to switch his block of votes to Pamphilj. That evening so many cardinals (over fifty) were trying to get into Gianbattista's small room, offering him congratulations, that very many could only shout to him through the door. One reported, 'There was such a multitude of people in that cell, that they stole all his silverware!'[52]

He sent a message from the Conclave at 3am to wake Olimpia with the news of his imminent election. She and Camillo received the message in their nightclothes, holding candles. Leti described the '... transports of joy of Donna Olimpia, who was so beside herself with happiness that she seemed to be only twenty-five years old, although she was closer to fifty!'[53] It was reported that Gianbattista hardly slept at all, partly from happiness and partly from fear. Next morning he asked Cardinal Albornoz whether all the supporting cardinals were present. Alburnoz replied 'Yes, they are here. Your Eminence must have good courage.' The votes were cast, then tallied, to reveal the expected overwhelming majority for Pamphilj, who accepted election, taking the name of Innocent X. (He had originally wanted Eugenio, but was reminded that the last Pope Eugenio had been chased out of Rome in 1434 by an angry mob, which threw rocks at his boat as he sailed down the Tiber; to avoid the stones he had to hide under a shield in the bottom of the boat.) Cardinal Bichi, appalled at the election of the 'Spanish' candidate, raced back to his cell and sent a message to France, 'Gentlemen, we have just elected a female pope!'[54]

Initially the citizens didn't agree, and were pleased at having a Roman pope. It was the custom that the new Pope's apartments were looted, but Olimpia, pre-warned, had removed all valuables and had replaced them with mediocre items from the markets. The mob complained but she remained gracious, triumphant at outwitting a crowd of thieves.

That evening she and Camillo saw Gianbattista and she started to laugh as, according to tradition, she knelt to kiss his feet. Overcome with emotion, he raised her as tears rolled down his cheeks. 'He received her with an extraordinary demonstration of love and affection.'[55] She was then visited by many people and after a few days began to take on a 'proud and haughty' air.

The biggest shock came when she announced that she intended to take up residence in the Vatican, in the apartments reserved for the Pope's nephew, adjoining the Pope's own. For them such proximity was nothing new, but to the cardinals it was horrifying. Cardinal Panciroli was almost apoplectic at the idea, though Gianbattista had favoured it, knowing that he would need Olimpia's help more than ever. He finally gave in, and confirmed that she would live at the Piazza Navona house, but would be able to come and go as she pleased. This settled down to a regular evening visit, from sunset to midnight, as Gianbattista did his best work after dinner. He was crowned as Pope Innocent on 4 October 1644 with 'the most excellent Signora Donna Olimpia Maidalchini' in a place of honour near the main altar. Next to her was the Marquesa Guistiniani, her daughter, and a number of titled ladies. Diplomatic dispatches posted that day refer to the 'prudence and valour' of Olimpia, and the fact that she would be an asset to the Pope.[56]

In September he made a new will, leaving all his worldly goods to her – as sole heir – stating that she could do as she wished with his money. The new Pope gave his niece's husband the title of Prince of Bassano, so Maria became a princess and was provided for. Constanza was unmarried but the handsome Prince of Caserta was showing interest and may have been her preferred suitor, but her hand was given to the fat, twice-married Prince of Piombino, because he was the owner of a string of titles and a Grandee of Spain. Camillo was very reluctant to marry his mother's choice, Lucrezia Barberini, though Olimpia needed the Barberini family's support. She was aware that Gianbattista (now Innocent) was already seventy, and when he died they would be in a position to do her harm. She wanted them tied to the family. Camillo declared his intention of going into the church, becoming a cardinal-nephew and gaining power on his own. It was a blow, but it was possible to give the family name to a daughter's second son, to extend the family line. Maria already had one son and if she had another it might be possible for him to become a Pamphilj.[57]

Camillo became a cardinal in November 1644 after Innocent created his friend Cardinal Panciroli Secretary of State. He would instruct Camillo on foreign affairs, and he hoped to gain huge wealth from people needing his uncle's support. He continued to live at the Navona house but his relationship with his mother did not improve and he would not let her help him with business matters.

Though Olimpia was banned from living at the Vatican, she made the Navona house beautiful. She bought two more small houses alongside and incorporated them, tripling the size of the Casa Pamphilj by 1634. In 1644 she was to double it again, with her private apartments taking up seven rooms across the front, which had doorways of red marble splashed with white, and parquet floors. The gilded ceilings were painted with mythological scenes and frescoes decorated the walls. The most important room, the Galleria, was used for receptions, measuring one hundred feet long and twenty-four feet wide, with a thirty-foot high ceiling painted by Pietro da Cortona with the story of Aeneas. This room is still used, and lit at night so that the ceiling can be viewed from the Piazza outside.

Olimpia was given a title in October 1645, becoming Princess of San Martino, which was a church-owned territory near Viterbo. It included a fourteenth-century abbey and she planned to have a fine apartment there. She was suffering from arthritis in her knees, so Francesco Borromini, her architect, designed a double spiral staircase. The inside spiral had low and gentle stairs, the outside one was larger, to allow for her sedan chair or even her carriage. Bernini decorated her seven-roomed suite there, with a papal audience chamber at one end of the building for when Innocent visited. As usual, her bedroom was connected by a small inner door to the one intended for the Pope, so that, unseen by anyone in the house, they could meet at night.

She even sent for the priest, whose career she had ruined in Viterbo nearly forty years earlier. She asked him where she would be if she had taken his advice to become a nun. He sighed and said 'Most excellent Signora, my goal was not to advise you to do evil.' Olimpia said 'No, but if I had done it, I would not have done well, I would not have become what I now am.'[58] She then arranged with Innocent that he should be made a bishop, before turning her attention to helping oppressed women, particularly prostitutes.

There had always been a thriving sex trade in Rome, and the fact that most of the clients were in holy orders was irrelevant. Rome was the centre for the 'career' priests, who far outnumbered the truly devout. The Renaissance sex worker was often far more than a street prostitute. She could become very rich, owning her own Palazzo and riding the streets in a carriage. There were prostitutes at all levels, catering for all levels of wealth in men, from the expensive courtesans to the lowly 'candle tart' who lit a little candle when a customer arrived, and stopped whatever she was doing the moment it burned down. Pope Pius V (1566–1572) had attempted to ban 'loose females' but had to reconsider as the Senate was concerned that amorous priests needed them, or they might seduce honest women. There was also the disease aspect to consider, and the hospital of St James specialised in treating sexual disorders. They used mercury treatment, then the standard, useless and dangerous medication.

When Olimpia took the prostitutes under her protection, they put her coat of arms over their doors, which protected them from the police and church officials. They could also use carriages if they painted her coat of arms on the doors, '...allowing them to ride in carriages, without any regard, just as if they were honourable people'.[59] Olimpia created more scandal by attending the Pope at the Vatican for political consultations, taking with her piles of petitions and requests. What was even worse, was that she had often already written out the replies, requiring only that Innocent sign them, which he invariably did.

The Venetian ambassador remarked on this, saying '...she goes from time to time, with masterly haughtiness... into the Palace with a pile of petitions, most of them her own decrees, and spends hours with His Holiness to discuss the matters ... the jokes then going about the court were hidden from the Pope.'[60] Even Panciroli, the Secretary of State, and the only man the Pope trusted, had to pay court to Olimpia, though later events would show that he was irritated by it. Most people flattered her, gave her gifts and asked for her advice. Even those who disliked her had to admit her abilities, and that few people could have managed as well as she did. Whether she and Innocent had been lovers or not, by the time she was in her fifties they were busy setting the Vatican finances in order. Giacento Gigli wrote of her strict control: 'In everything, one sees a discreet slenderness.' The first anniversary celebrations of Innocent's election were without a peal of bells, as she had saved money by sacking the bellringers.

The problem of course with Olimpia's power was that it was held by a woman, working in one of the most misogynistic of institutions. It was not mistresses, or male lovers, or bastard children, who threatened the church, as they had no claims of inheritance. The word 'celibacy' tended to mean lack of a marriage, not lack of sex, and the church accepted women serving men in one capacity or another. It was not liked for any woman to 'rule' over men or take ecclesiastical property. Women such as Lucrezia Borgia had managed by hiding intelligence under a sweetly demure exterior, but Olimpia, making her own way in the world, had to develop a harder shell, with male resentment as the result.

Cardinal Mazarin of France had to defer to a pope he had expressly excluded from the papacy, and wanted to ease his humiliation. Cardinal Ascanio Barberini had also backed the wrong horse, and Innocent was being pressed to investigate the Barberini family for corruption. Olimpia supported this, as the Barberini then opposed her too, believing that her offer of the marriage with her son had been false, as he was then a cardinal. They could have little idea how difficult Camillo then was.

For the two decades that their uncle had been pope, the Barberini had used the papal treasury as their personal bank, keeping no accounts. Mazarin, by supporting them, could provide a thorn in Innocent's flesh. Innocent knew that the Barberini had helped themselves to vast amounts of money, and needed detailed accounts which did not exist, but he also knew that without their votes he would not have been elected pope. Eventually, the money problem came first, and all Barberini accounts were frozen and the family put under surveillance. Despite this, Prince Taddeo and Cardinal Francesco sailed for France where Mazarin welcomed them and Innocent lost face, saying 'The Catholics are scandalised to see a pope so scorned as I am.'[61]

Camillo remained a problem, being lazy and useless and regularly at odds with the Pope. Olimpia tried to help him, but he complained to the Pope that she should be put into a convent to stop her meddling. It was something she would never forgive him for. Her son-in-law Niccolo Ludovisi hoped to take Camillo's place, but the Pope 'had little tenderness' for him. He responded to the rebuff by telling everyone that he would not have married the 'daughter of a nobody like Olimpia, if he hadn't expected to receive power in return.' He was eventually made commander of a fleet intended to help Venice against the Turks, to get him out of the way.

Innocent felt that good money was being wasted on St Peter's much-needed repairs. He employed Gian Lorenzo Bernini to work on the Baldachino, which angered Borromini who claimed the bell towers were too heavy; he was right and they had to be dismantled.

Camillo, meanwhile, was flirting with Olimpia Aldobrandini, Princess of Rossano, who was wife to Prince Paolo Borghese. The husband conveniently died in 1646 leaving the Princess with one son and one daughter. The son would inherit the Borghese fortune, but another son was needed to inherit the Aldobrandini fortune, if he took that name.[62] She needed to remarry and bear another son to secure this inheritance. Camillo Pamphilj was interested, and had only taken minor orders (until 1917 it was not necessary for any cardinal to also be a priest, the title was a dignity, not a sacrament, and could be removed). The Aldobrandini widow also wanted to rule, in place of Olimpia Maidalchini! Giving up the cardinalate was not exactly usual, but it was certainly possible (Cesare Borgia had done it to become Duke de Valentinois) and what surprised people the most was that the widow would 'throw herself away on a man who was known to be a very simple person'.[63] For her, it was not Camillo who mattered, but the prospect of power. Olimpia Pamphilj, in her turn, was horrified at the idea of a power-hungry and manipulative daughter-in-law.

The Pope was not opposed to it, as he was glad to be rid of a useless cardinal, but could not openly oppose Olimpia, so Agatha, the Pope's sister, was enlisted to persuade. It was agreed, but on condition that the pair lived in the country, though the Princess disliked the idea, wanting to live in Rome. The battle lines were quickly drawn. Olimpia ignored the bride's resentment and decided she needed to build her tomb, intending to be buried at the church of San Martino, but first the ancient building needed repairs.

Mazarin had thawed a little towards Pope Innocent, as he wanted a cardinal's hat for his brother, sending the Marquis de Fontenay to Rome, though realising he would need to negotiate through Olimpia. Fontenay was pleasantly surprised to find her so cultivated and Mazarin responded 'We must do favours for the Donna Olimpia and it must go beyond everything that His Holiness could desire for her.'[64]

Innocent knew that with Camillo gone he needed a new cardinal, but Olimpia had her alternative candidate ready, her half-brother Andrea's son, Francesco Maidalchini. He was only seventeen years old (the minimum age was then twenty-two but that was usually an avoidable impediment). He wasn't bright, and would need tutoring, though Gregorio Leti said of the effort, 'This was no more than to sow corn on a rock.' The cardinals were disgusted, particularly as Innocent had for four years refused to give Mazarin's brother the red hat precisely because of his stupidity. Innocent was left with no further excuse – if Maidalchini got one, Michael Mazarin had to also have one, even though neither of them would be of the slightest use to him.

In November 1647 the Princess of Rossano (Olimpia Jnr) announced she was pregnant, and complained that her home was cold, and she was being punished for nothing. Camillo also claimed he had left much valuable furniture at the Casa Pamphilj and Olimpia was reluctant to give him anything until Innocent ordered it. She was then displeased as he had not supported her.

Camillo and his wife returned to Rome, moving into the Palazzo Farnese, owned by her cousin the Duke of Parma. The exile had not actually been lifted, but the Princess was determined to have her child born in Rome. She gave birth to a son, naming him Gianbattista after the Pope. Olimpia left the birth chamber in disgust at the news, though Innocent was pleased. Olimpia feared that his pleasure would mean he would lift the exile ban, and allow the couple access to him at the Vatican, fearing for her own position. She had a long talk with him, and it was said that when she left him, his pleasure was all gone, and although he did lift the ban, Olimpia would not allow them any involvement in important matters. Cardinal Pallotta informed the Pope of the current bread shortages in the city, of which he had been unaware.

The Cardinal was furious: 'I would rather be in a monastery, obedient to a monk, than in Rome under the domination of a woman!' Olimpia was told what he had said and left for home, but her carriage met the Cardinal's on the way, and she shouted out of the window at him that he and his family were spies! The Cardinal yelled back that he was no spy, but it was a shame that Rome's government was in the hands of 'a whore'. Gigli reported the argument, adding 'It was publicly known that Donna Olimpia had slept with her brother-in-law before he became Pope, and people were always talking about this.'[65]

Innocent began to be concerned for his dignity and chastised Olimpia for her display of bad temper. As towns were rising up against their governors, he decided to requisition grain. Giancinto Gigli reported on the bread the poor were eating,

> ... of a very bad colour and odour ... beans and other vegetables had been thrown in, even the dogs and cats in my house wouldn't eat it, but if I gave them decent bread, they would eat it willingly. Even the dumb animals know that the bread is not good.[66]

By July the strangely coloured bread had certainly become whiter, but also oddly crunchy, as it then had small pieces of plaster in it. The people demanded help from the Pope, and the 'talking' Pasquino statue criticised Olimpia freely. She was accused of taking bribes, and her relationship with the Pope was aired again, calling her 'the Pimpaccia of the Piazza Navona' (Pimpa being a greedy power-hungry woman in a popular play). Another verse punned on her name, 'Olim pia, nunc impia' (once pious, now impious.) The *avvisi* sent to foreign governments were also damaging, and an agent of the Duke of Modena was arrested for referring to 'the Popessa' or female pope. The Pope was insulted at the idea that he took orders from her, but everyone knew it was true.

Innocent retreated to the Quirinal Palace for the sea breezes, and then liked it so much he refused to return. He wanted only to visit the Vatican when business was urgent. Olimpia didn't help by putting on a comic play about a young fool who would not obey his mother and made an unfortunate marriage, and own his life a misery. Innocent was obliged to ban it, as everyone knew it referred to Camillo, for the shine had already rubbed off his marriage to Olimpia Aldobrandini in less than two years, as she had quickly realised that she had indeed married a fool.

As we have seen, Olimpia was now in the habit of writing her own petitions for the Pope to sign without his bothering to read them; one of Innocent's lawyers, Francesco Mascambruno, spotted an opportunity. Mascambruno had slipped in a few of his own, and found himself in the position of being able to sell signed indulgences, making a healthy profit. The collecting of holy relics was also fashionable, and Olimpia wanted one for her church at San Martino, especially something from St Francesca's coffin, whose relics had reportedly performed miracles. The coffin was due to be moved in March 1649, which was the ideal time to obtain something. Olimpia wanted the shoulder bone, and removed it before the tomb was sealed, but the nuns complained to the Pope, who did nothing. To be fair, Olimpia wasn't the only person collecting, the cardinals had done their share, but of smaller items. It was considered sacrilege, and the Pasquino statue criticised the Pope for allowing her to steal holy bones.

Olimpia's greatest achievement would not be the Palazzo Pamphlij itself, but the Piazza Navona onto which it faced. The Palazzo had no gardens, but the Navona marketplace was large, and she wanted to recreate the ambience of Domitian's stadium that had once filled the area. Olimpia commissioned Gian Lorenzo Bernini to design the Fountain of the Four Rivers, which is still the Piazza's centerpiece. The water was diverted from the *Acqua Vergine*, the nearest source, and the immense obelisk above it had been taken to Rome by Caligula. It was found, badly damaged by the Goths, half buried in the ground by the San Sebastian gate, and was dragged by teams of oxen to the Navona to dominate the space. It was generally a time of great archaeological finds, as in 1649 the Baths of Trajan had given up a lapis-lazuli floor and fifty-four intact statues. On the Via Latina ancient tombs were opened to reveal urns, sarcophagi, frescoes and even jewels. Some of these treasures found their way into Olimpia's possession, but others were equally keen, Cardinal Scipione Borghese had done the same thirty years previously, though it was another black mark against Olimpa's name.[67]

Holy Jubilee year was held from December 1649 to the end of 1650. Not merely a religious celebration, it was a festival, with showmanship, extravagance, and pilgrims visiting to see Rome. Churches were refurbished, trees planted, streets re-paved. Donations were of course expected, and pilgrims wanted to take something home, particularly the gold medals distributed by the four Basilicas.[68] Olimpia also wanted gold medals, but not just one or two. Each Jubilee church had a chest of them, and by 24 December Olimpia was already in possession of three out of the four of them. It would be the biggest Holy Year ever, with 700,000 visitors from all over Europe. Even the Emperor of China sent a delegation, which took two years to arrive. Holy fervour often led to riots and Gigli described 2,000 pilgrims marching in opposite directions, trying to push in front of each other. 'Many were wounded with cudgels, among them the Marchese Santa Croce, who was beaten on the head ... these tumults happen on the streets nearly every day... if they come upon one another in a group they fight with fists, because each wants precedence.'[69]

On 16 May a large crowd thronged the Quirinal Palace where the Pope bestowed blessings. People were trampled, crushed and suffocated by the masses, many wanting to see the Pope, but others hoping to see Olimpia. Hearing of her close relationship with him, they may have imagined a glamorous creature, but Olimpia was then plump, plain and middle-aged. That surely meant that she held the Pope in thrall by witchcraft? They watched her house and saw the Pope visit her there, they rushed her carriage as it passed in the streets, and were fascinated by her being at the heart of affairs. One morning the church of St John Lateran sported a sign, obliterating the Pope's own inscription, saying 'Olimpia I, Pontifex Maximus'.[70] The Pope felt it had all gone too far, and made a new will. In it he revoked Olimpia's right to dispose of his possessions. All would eventually go to Camillo.

Swamped with work, Innocent needed reliable help from a cardinal-nephew. Francesco Maidalchini was useless, though whoever replaced him would not please Olimpia. Cardinal Camillo Astalli was recommended and when Olimpia was looking for a wife for Astalli's brother, the Pope suggested one of her nieces, making Cardinal Astalli into a relative. He would then become known as Cardinal Astalli-Pamphilj and would eventually be Camerlengo of the Sacred College, as an adopted member of the Pamphilj family. He was allowed to live in the Palazzo Pamphilj on the Navona, and had free use of all the silver and furnishings. He suddenly became the second most important person in Rome, a move that made Olimpia anxious. Gigli said, 'She knew she was losing her dominion, and control. She scorned him and entered into a frenzy … she sent him a message saying she had no other nephew than Cardinal Maidalchini and did not recognise Astalli as being of the house of Pamphilj.'[71]

She had an angry meeting with Innocent, and threatened to leave, but the Pope – perhaps for the first time – shouted back at her. She pretended to be ill. Cardinal Panzirolo remarked, 'She is too ill-tempered and wants to have everything her own way.' However, the Pope's anger towards her and the elevation of Astalli did not please everyone. It alienated Prince Ludovisi and Giustiniani, who both left Rome. Astalli's inexperience also caused comment and the diplomatic community was no longer sure about protocol with the Pamphlij. Some said the Pope was senile, and feared Olimpia's retribution. Innocent was then seventy-six years old and his new protégé could not expect a long tenure. Olimpia, who had used Cardinal Maidalchini, dropped him, earning his enmity too. She still believed she could bully Innocent and her jovial manner towards him became more hard-edged. It was an error, as it forced the Pope to consider her removal. Though she had placed him where he was, and always supported and advised him, owing to her greed and lack of sensitivity she was making him a laughing-stock.

He had for years ignored the vulgar talk about their relationship, and had Olimpia behaved discreetly he would probably have continued to do so, but her rages could no longer be ignored.

He needed to regain his dignity, to 'put a stop to the tongues, not only in Rome, but in northern parts, where the Protestants were taking this female liberty as a great joke … mocking him licentiously'.[72] He was painfully aware that he owed everything to her, but also that he was not much respected and her constant presence had badly affected his reign. He had allowed her far too much leeway, but the idea of betraying her still caused him anguish. The day after their public altercation Olimpia found herself ostracised. People who had rushed to do her bidding suddenly ignored her, or worse, felt free to gloat about her fall from favour.

Holy Year ended in December 1650 and the future looked very bleak for Olimpia. The Pope began trying to re-connect with his family who were happy to rejoin him, while Olimpia stayed at San Martino where she was still honoured. The Venetian Ambassador Giustiniani actually praised her for facing her disgrace 'with matronly decorum, refusing to appear in public and showing not the least shadow of authority'. Another contemporary remarked, 'After Donna Olimpia finally fell into the hole she had been digging for herself for a long time, she learned, in her great need, to use prudence.'[73]

The Princess of Rossano, Camillo's wife, was delighted to take Olimpia's place in Rome, openly making her mother-in-law's enemies into her friends. She gave lavish parties, and excluded all those who had got on well with Olimpia. She, meanwhile, found plenty to occupy her at San Martino, and still had her spies in Rome. She heard that the Fountain of the Four Rivers was finally completed and was the talk of Europe, even the fountains at Versailles would be based on it, but she was not then to see the glory of the fountain she had inspired.

Cardinal Panciroli had expected to become the Pope's advisor with Astalli-Pamphilj as his assistant, but Astalli-Pamphilj made it clear he did not intend to be second. His elevation had gone to his head and the Pope seemed happy to have him close by, though he would quickly realise that he was almost as vain, shallow and lazy as the last one, enjoying the pomp of the position but not the responsibility.

Innocent was also finding life without Olimpia very difficult. The family felt free to make constant demands on him, but Olimpia had always kept them in check. They gave him no peace, agreeing only on hating Cardinal Astalli-Pamphilj. Cardinal Pallavacino remarked, 'The Pope, full of years, was leaning on an inexperienced and unknown crutch.'[74] Innocent could see he needed someone else with diplomatic experience and Monsignor Fabio Chigi, the Papal Nuncio to Milan, was chosen. He would become the new Secretary of State. He showed himself to be incorruptible, refusing bribes and gifts and the Pope had to insist that he accepted benefices suitable to his office. Astalli-Pamphilj, fearing for his own position, had persuaded the Pope not to make Chigi into a cardinal, but even without that title he quickly became the Pope's favourite. Olimpia was aware of it and made sure she was able to correspond with Chigi on courteous terms. Her daughter-in-law had the advantage of being in Rome and tried to impress him, but he was not fooled by her, treating her politely but exactly the same as everyone else.

One of the problems Chigi faced when he assumed his position was that the Portuguese Count of Villafranca had recently been married by his village priest. Unfortunately, he was married already, and his second 'bride' was a teenaged boy dressed as a woman, with whom he consummated his nuptials immediately. The Spanish Inquisition had thrown the Count, the 'bride' and the priest in jail, and the penalty for sodomy was burning at the stake, but the Count paid 40,000 gold pieces to be released into the hands of a bishop who was a family friend. Chigi was disgusted by the story, and the Pope denied ever having signed a Bull in the matter, but agreed on investigation. There was no Bull, but a forged one, and Francesco Mascambruno, the lawyer, was implicated. His rooms were searched and 14,000 gold pieces were found, plus gold and silver plate and a bank record showing large deposits. Also found were a further seventy Papal Bulls, already signed and available for sale! The Pope had, of course, signed them unthinkingly, as he used to do when Olimpia was in power.

The culprit tried to throw blame onto Olimpia but it was soon shown that they had been signed after she left Rome. After her exile Mascambruno's greed had got the better of him, and he'd tried to pass documents through the Pope. Innocent was grateful at the attempt to save his good name, and decided to make Chigi a cardinal, though he preferred to remain as he was. Innocent was impressed by his humility: 'We have not seen such a man ... nothing moves him.'[75] Chigi finally became a cardinal in 1652, also becoming Cardinal-priest of Santa Maria del Popolo and Archbishop of Imola.[76]

Mascambruno was sentenced to be hanged and beheaded, with his remains put on display at Castel Sant'Angelo, but Astalli-Pamphilj pleaded with the Pope and the sentence was reduced to beheading, then burying at a church after a period of exposure. First he had to be defrocked, as a priest could not be executed. This took place at the church of San Salvatore in Lauro. Many other offenders were in prison and harshly dealt with. Innocent had tried to cleanse the papacy of scandal by exiling Olimpia, but without her he had lost control and things were worse. The family had begun to irritate the Pope, who had been comfortable with Olimpia after forty years together. As her daughter-in-law having the same name had caused confusion, the younger woman was known as the Princess of Rossano, but that meant that Camillo became known as Prince of Rossano and was humiliated at taking his wife's name.

Olimpia was getting back at enemies without doing anything. Camillo humiliated, her daughter-in-law had lost influence, and the Pope wanted her back. Cardinal Panciroli was dead, and Cardinal Astalli-Pamphilj was proved to be useless. Innocent had also been involved in a resounding scandal which had damaged his reputation.

Innocent decided to build his tomb, turning to the church of St Agnese in Agone where the original chapel was in one of the arches of Domitian's stadiuim, fifteen feet below ground level, with a house above it. He decided to buy the house and make it into his grand new family church, as it was alongside the Palazzo Pamphilj. His health was failing and he lashed out in anger at friends, family, staff and the cardinals, listening only to Chigi. People began to think Olimpia should be sent for, as she was the only one able to relieve his burdens and make him laugh. Cardinal Pallavacino said, 'The most highly regarded prelates of this court, who knew of the monstrous greed and power of this woman, and how she had abused it ... desired her back to help them as an angel of intercession.'[77]

Nothing had gone right for Innocent since she left, he missed her clever mind, her ability to keep things running smoothly and he also missed her company, and being able to gossip and laugh with her. He was afraid he would be laughed at again, first sending her away and criticising her in public then being unable to cope without her, but many cardinals believed that she would have learned her lesson and would behave better. Chigi did not agree but realised that the Pope did need her. The Pope's sister was called in and a compromise was reached, with Olimpia making a polite formal call on her daughter-in-law and the Pope's sister, the nun Sister Agatha, welcoming her home. She met Cardinal Astalli-Pamphlij and then saw the Pope privately, remaining with him at the Quirinal until after midnight. She had been separated from him for over two years.

Olimpia needed to impress Cardinal Chigi, who failed to be impressed. Expensive gifts she sent him were politely returned, while his gifts to her were paltry. He disliked seeing cardinals bowing to her and told them to keep their dignity. People wishing for the Pope's favour were expected to go through Astalli-Pamphilj who was still officially Cardinal-nephew, but everyone knew he had no influence so they quickly returned to Olimpia, as in the past.

She was enjoying life again, but was more aware of her security and also of her revenge. The hated Princess of Rossano was again banned from all but the most formal occasions, and the Cardinal Astalli-Pamphilj, who had taken many of her possessions, was obliged to return or replace them. The Pope himself, who had sent her away, could no longer be completely trusted by her. He had betrayed and humiliated her beyond belief, and she was not likely to forget that the man she had loved and supported and had actually made into a Pope through her hard work could embrace her enemies. She was aware that he was old and would be replaced before long, probably by one of her enemies, and she preferred Cardinal Antonio Barberini, still in Paris, needing him on her side as he could control a large block of votes in the coming Conclave. The idea of a Pamphilj-Barberini marriage appealed, and she decided that her granddaughter Olimpiuccia Giustiniani, then twelve years old, could join the two houses together by marrying Prince Maffeo Barberini. He was then twenty-two years old and better looking than his elder brother Carlo, who could be made into a cardinal and give up his place to Maffeo.

The Barberini, aware of Olimpia's need, demanded a huge dowry plus all their confiscated property returned, but it was a price she was willing to pay. Olimpiuccia preferred to be a nun, and she and the prospective bridegroom did not like each other, but would have to resign themselves. They were married by Pope Innocent in the Sistine Chapel; the bride cried all the way through the ceremony. The bridegroom's mother, Anna Calonna, was equally unhappy, considering the marriage beneath her son. Afterwards Olimpiuccia locked her bedroom door and shouted out of the window, telling the revellers in the Piazza Navona that she was married against her will.

Marriage without consummation could be declared invalid, so this performance caused further family humiliation and the groom had to go home without the bride. This impasse continued for several months, affecting the Pope's health, so Olimpia took him to Viterbo for a visit. His health improved there so dramatically that on his return to Rome some people reported gloomily that he might yet reign another ten years![78]

In Rome, however, the old stresses returned and the Barberini marriage remained unconsummated. One evening, Olimpia decided that enough was enough, having Olimpiuccia put into her carriage and taken to the Palazzo Barberini where she personally threw the girl into the arms of her bridegroom, as reported by the Mantuan Ambassador: 'The grandmother took her there, almost violently, one evening.'[79] The marriage was finally consummated and the Pope ordered the Treasury to wipe off the records all the Barberini debts, allowing the family gladly to return to power.

Olimpia then embarked on her most important mission, which was to gather together as much money as possible before the Pope died. She knew her income would cease the moment he took his last breath, and the relatives of a new pope would hold out greedy hands for papal wealth. Giustiniani reported:

When offices fell vacant at court, nothing was decided without her good pleasure. When church livings were distributed the ministers of the Dataria had orders to defer all appointments until notice had been given to her, of the nature of those benefices, so that she might select such as she pleased for her own disposal. If Episcopal

Sees were conferred, it was to her than candidates applied and that
which most effectively revolted every upright mind was to see that
those were preferred for them who were the most liberal in giving.

Cardinal Chigi still visited her, as the Pope had made it clear that
he wanted them to be friendly, but they did not like each other.
She was stealing from the Pope while accusing Astalli-Pamphilj
of selling benefices. Innocent wanted rid of him, knowing how
efficient the Barberini cardinals had been in comparison, but Chigi
claimed that removing him would result in further scandalous talk.

Olimpia and the Barberini were also in secret talks with the Pope –
the Barberini wanted a principality before it was too late, hoping for
Naples, as the Spanish hold on it was tenuous and it was the Pope's
ancient feudal territory. They wanted to raise an army to march on
Naples and oust the Spanish and Innocent gave in to them, ignoring
the fact that Spain had far more resources than he did. Word of the
plot leaked out. Olimpia believed that Astalli-Pamphilj had betrayed
it and had his rooms searched, and dispatches were found. Cardinal
Chigi wrote, 'The Pope reprimanded him, calling him ungrateful...
Cardinal Astalli, seeing danger all around, tried to put things right
but could not.'[80] Olimpia wanted him defrocked but Innocent was,
as always, hesitant to act, fearing further dishonour. He decided to
leave Astalli nothing but his cardinalate, stripping him of all other
honours and telling him to leave Rome, taking nothing with him,
and also ordered him to cease to use the Pamphilj name and arms.
Chigi, afraid of scandal, pleaded with Innocent without success.
Innocent wrote the brief removing Astalli from his offices, saying
'The Cardinal knows well the reasons for his disgrace,' then ordered
the questioning of Astalli's servants. One carpenter admitted that he
had made Astalli a ladder, and that 'The cardinal intended to use it
... to go out to visit, with greatest secrecy, the pretty ladies.'[81] The
Pope was furious, not only about the 'pretty ladies' but because
Astalli had probably used it to visit the Spanish Ambassador.

In spring of 1654 Innocent's health was worse and Olimpia was
deciding who to rely on. Several *papabile* already disliked her. Two
of her friends, Azzolini and Gualterio, were to be given cardinal's
hats in an attempt to dilute Chigi's influence.[82] She did her best
to secure wealth, though failed to remove Chigi. She was buying

property in Umbria when news arrived that Queen Christina of Sweden wished to abdicate, become a Catholic and move to Rome. This cheered the Pope, but other news was less good. Locusts ruined harvests that year, and part of the Colosseum had collapsed, losing three of its arches. There was a fire near the Barberini Palace and strange lights were seen in the sky, causing rumours of the death of the Pope. There was a solar eclipse on 12 August and a lunar one on the 27th, many people spending those days in church.

On enquiring about the progress of the church of St Agnese in Agone the Pope was told that all work had stopped as the builders had not been paid. This distressed him as he still hoped to be buried there. By the end of the year it was clear that Innocent was dying, and riots began, making Olimpia an easy target. She could not leave the city as she intended to be inside the papal palace at the end, in order to remove all the valuables from the Pope's apartments, knowing that once he was dead she would be denied access and others would steal them.

Mainly, though, she wanted to get her hands on the Papal Treasury. This was usually kept at the Castel Sant'Angelo, but she had managed to convince Innocent to have the gold reserves taken to his apartment. During his last illness, she was busy taking the gold from his room, a little at a time. She was with him all day, putting the gold into small sacks, which went into her sedan chair. Her porters actually joked that she was always a lot heavier to carry at night, than she had been in the morning! This, to Olimpia, was not theft. It was a matter of taking back, for the benefit of her family, all the money she considered she had wasted over the years, in promoting the career of an ungrateful man.

Cardinal Decio Azzolino would often see Olimpia at the Pope's apartments and he always spoke to her with courtesy. One man not usually available was Chigi, who, as Secretary of State, should have been present but was avoiding Olimpia. She sent him a message, asking why he never greeted her as the others did, and his reply was that he was busy dealing with state matters, and praying for the Pope. If she needed him he would call on her at the Palazzo Pamphilj. It was his way of making it clear that no woman should have free access to the papal palace. Olimpia retorted, 'Thank God I don't need anything from him!'[83]

Pope Innocent wanted to see his family in order to say goodbye to them and, in the presence of his cardinals, ask forgiveness for any wrongs done to them during his reign, which was customary. He would give recommendations regarding his successor and ask them all to pray for him.[84] He then made it clear that he wanted to make Gianbattista Pamphilj into a cardinal while he still could. Such an honour for a six-year old boy was not unheard of, but aware of public opinion, the cardinals talked him out of it. On the evening of 27 December Innocent was given the Last Rites. Cardinal Chigi was pleased that Olimpia was not in attendance, but furious to hear later that she was trying to enter the Pope's bedroom. The cardinals were scandalised again that the woman, reputed to have been his mistress, was still attempting to get close to him, even when his thoughts should have been only on Paradise.

What they did not realise was that Olimpia's desire to get into Innocent's room was not driven by sexual desire, or even misplaced affection, but that she was concerned only for the remaining gold, which was still underneath his bed. The following morning, when Olimpia again appeared and asked for access, she found the Pope's confessor blocking the door. People often tried to see a dying Pontiff, to beg for last-minute favours, but Cardinal Chigi forbade everyone entrance.

By 30 December Innocent was unable to eat anything and his legs had swollen. Chigi stayed with him, kneeling in prayer. As usual, all the Pope's possessions were being stolen while he lay helpless, and Chigi reported with disgust, 'There wasn't even a bowl or a spoon, with which to give the Pope his soup ... he had only the shirt on his back, all others were gone. There was only one candlestick, made of brass, which also soon disappeared and was replaced by one made of wood.'[85] Such widespread thieving was usual in times of change, but did not concern Innocent. He made only one request – that his family would stop fighting among themselves – and recommended Cardinal Chigi as his successor. Early on the morning of 7 January 1655, Pope Innocent X died.

His Pontificate was summed up by Gregorio Leti: 'This was truly a pope worthy of the best memory, if his sister-in-law had not lost him his reputation. Instead, one was constrained to bury him in eternal oblivion so as not to mention her.'[86] The Pope's body was removed to be washed and dressed for his burial, and once the bedroom was empty, Olimpia burst in, accompanied by two servants, and with their help she removed the remaining gold and had it put into her carriage. She needed to be back at her palace before news of the Pope's death became common knowledge, and once back in the courtyard of the Piazza Navona house she ordered all the doors and gates were to be barred. When the Pope's body had been prepared and was ready to be returned to his bed before the funeral, it was found that his sheets had been stolen!

There was a funeral mass for him on 10 January, but Olimpia was not mentioned and was not present. A pope's family traditionally paid for his funeral, sending the coffin to St Peter's Basilica after the body had been on public display for the faithful to pay their respects. Unfortunately, no coffin had been sent from the Pamphilj family, and it soon became clear that none would be. The Burial Committee asked Olimpia, but she told them she could not afford to pay for Innocent's funeral, 'being only a poor widow'. She referred them to Camillo, who was then nominally head of the family, and after going up the Corso to his magnificent palace, they were told that he too refused to pay anything. Other family members were then also approached, but, seeing no reason why they should pay for the funeral when Olimpia would not, they also refused.

By that time, Innocent's body was beginning to decompose, and the Committee, in despair, suggested taking it to the Piazza Navona and leaving it there, forcing Olimpia to take action to give him a decent burial. But common sense prevailed; they feared that she would still refuse to accept her responsibility and leave the Pope's body lying outside her house, where it might be open to abuse from the mob. Even the vestments might be stolen from the Pope's body, and the idea of the late Pontiff, lying naked in the Piazza Navona, was too appalling to contemplate. All they could then do was move it out of the main part of the Basilica where his funeral mass had taken place, carrying it on a plank to be hidden in a janitor's cupboard, out of sight, for decency's sake. On 13 January, Riccard, the Ambassador of the Grand Duke of Tuscany, reported, 'The Pope is not yet buried … no-one can be found who will pay for it … and so his Beatitude remains there in a corner.'[87] This, then, was Olimpia's final revenge on Gianbattista Pamphilj, whom she had made into Pope Innocent X, for those years in exile. This was the retribution she had decided on for him, to leave his body unwanted and unburied, being attacked by rats, while hidden disgracefully away.

Finally, with the situation acute, the late Pope's major-domo had to take action. He paid for a cheap wooden coffin himself, and a former major-domo also came forward, out of pity, paying five scudi to have an unmarked grave dug in the basement of the Basilica.[88] Innocent could never have envisaged when Olimpia returned to him that her affection for him had turned into such hatred and resentment, or that she could be so unfeeling as to leave him the laughing stock of Europe. However, with the papacy vacant, others would also behave unfeelingly towards her. Power devolved temporarily onto Cardinal Antonio Barberini, who returned to Cardinal Astalli all the benefices which Innocent had taken from him. Cardinal Maidalchini also disrespected his aunt, and moved into one of her properties near where the Trevi Fountain would later be built. She had him thrown out, and also made it clear that she would ask the new pope, when one was chosen, to punish him.

The Conclave opened on 18 January 1655 and Olimpia and Cardinal Azzolino hoped for the election of Cardinal Giulio Sachetti, who could do them no harm. An epidemic had broken out by the end of the month, unusual in winter, and tensions were high. Several cardinals became ill and Cardinal Carafa died, while not only strong words but even slaps were exchanged between Astalli and Azzolino. It almost became a fight over Olimpia, with candidates who favoured her opposed to those eager for her ruin. 'Everything centred on the protection of Donna Olimpia, to see her ruined the cardinals who were her enemies would give their vote – not only to an unworthy candidate – but to the very devil... so long as he was her enemy.'[89] After a long and tedious Conclave, Cardinal Fabio Chigi was elected unanimously, taking the title of Pope Alexander VII. Olimpia sent congratulations, but was wary and did not visit in person. He returned thanks, but coolly. Olimpia tried again, sending a gift of two large gold vases, but they were returned with a message that she should keep away from the Vatican, as it was not a place for women.

Alexander started off charitably, selling silver plate and giving the money to the poor. He was crowned in April 1655 and Olimpia stayed at San Martino. She heard that her granddaughter had given birth to her first child just a month before her own fourteenth birthday, and the child was to be named Constanza. The new Pope did not have a large family and was determined to avoid the charge of nepotism. His brother, Mario, had already set off for Rome but was intercepted and told to go home to Siena. If the Pope did not want his family to benefit, others still hopefully sent valuable gifts and the Venetian Senate made him a Nobleman of the Serene Republic. He was to say, 'Fabio Chigi had relatives, but Pope Alexander VII has no family but the church.' Not a popular attitude, giving rise to the impression that if he could not take care of his own, how then could he care for millions of Christians? Other rulers considered that a frugal papacy was an insult, preventing them gaining the Pope's goodwill by giving pensions and brides with large dowries. It also made the families of previous popes feel like thieves, as they had done so well out of nepotism.

There were requests that Olimpia be punished in some way. Chigi disliked her but was reluctant to act against her, until the audits of the last reign came in and he began to see how much had flowed through her hands. He did not wish for further scandals, but the sheer scale of her embezzlement was an embarrassment. He ordered investigation, and there were soon thousands of documents, as well as witnesses giving evidence against her.

Olimpia was virtually a prisoner in the Navona house, and asked Cardinal Francesco Barberini to speak on her behalf. He did so, but the result was not encouraging. Alexander sent a list of the main charges and demanded an accounting of the money she had taken from the Treasury, as well as the names of the people to whom she had sold offices.[90] She replied firmly, saying that Innocent had been monarch of the Papal States, and had been entitled to do as he pleased with its resource, during his life, as other popes had done. The Pope told her to leave Rome within three days and refused to see Camillo until she had left. She returned to San Martino and the Pope arranged for witnesses against her to give testimony.

Alexander VII had his own problems with the College of Cardinals, who made it clear they thought it 'unseemly' for him to leave his family living in poverty.[91] He was to find that the nepotism he feared was closing in on him. The Jesuit Father Oliva said, 'The Pope would have committed sin, if he had not called his nephews to him.'[92] Alexander would soon find out what it would cost to keep a greedy family happy.

Plague hit Europe again in 1656 and 1657 and was in Rome, despite the ports being closed. Hospitals were set up to help the poor and try to keep infection from the rest of the population. A quarantine period of twenty-two days was declared in the hope of containing the spread of infection, and during the worst weeks of summer Romans were ordered to stay indoors. One thirteen-year-old girl, chasing an escaped chicken, was hanged as an example to others.[93] People soon became bored with their enforced imprisonment and surgeons visiting the sick began to relax their hygiene precautions. The city's prostitutes still did good business. The plague spread northwards and Viterbo was endangered. Olimpiuccia, pregnant again, begged her grandmother to leave the area, but Olimpia only moved three miles further away, intending to wait it out in her palace.

Towards the end of September she began to be ill, and it quickly became obvious that she was another plague victim. She had a doctor in attendance but no friends or family close by. The doctor found he could not drain the buboes, which might give her a chance of life, as they never came to a head, and some of her servants abandoned her in her extremity. On the 26 September 1657 she died, aged sixty-six. Camillo travelled to Rome to arrange her funeral and found that all the decent coffins had already been used, a final irony. One had to be made hastily from wooden cases used for packing furniture. It seemed almost to be retribution for her abandonment of Pope Innocent's body. She was interred at San Martino, close to her palace there, in her packing case coffin.

She was to be disturbed in 1762 as one of her grandsons, Prince Girolamo Pamphilj, expressed a wish for the honour of being buried alongside the founder of the family's fortunes. The coffin she was in was considered unsuitable and an elaborate one was prepared, and when she was examined it was reported that she had not been buried in the widow's weeds she had always worn, but in 'a gown of ribbed silk, the colour of crimson ... under the body was a cushion but none could tell what material it was made of ... the hair was still on the skull, part of it being a wiglet. You could recognize the well-done braids by their gold colour and they are as pretty as can be.'[94]

Olimpia had not been without admirers, and Cardinal Gualterio wrote to his friend Niccolo Cafferi: '...the kindest affection I have for that most illustrious woman of happy memory. Oh my dear Signora, whom I can no longer serve... God have compassion for that soul and give me the light of understanding from this lesson.'

Many rejoiced at her death, but it was a form of release for her family. Pope Alexander could not prosecute them once she was dead, and the matter also had to be laid to rest. In fact, it was later realised that the Barberini family, when in a similar position, had acquired a far greater fortune than Olimpia ever had, so it was far better to let sleeping dogs lie. The Pamphilj family was left to enjoy the wealth that she had created for them, and they in their turn created the wonderful art collection which now graces the Galleria Doria Pamphilj.

She had certainly paid the price of unpopularity, but it was her determination to be free to do as she wished, and to make Gianbattista Pamphilj into a pope, which drove her to break through the restrictions placed on women's lives. It was probably her greatest legacy. There is still a superstition in Rome that Olimpia can sometimes be seen on the Piazza Navona, galloping home to the Palazzo Pamphilj in her carriage stuffed with gold from the Papal Treasury.

The Barbarian: Christina of Sweden

If Pope Alexander had imagined that his female problems were over once Olimpia Pamphilj was buried, he had not reckoned with the woman who descended on Rome as Olimpia left it.

When Christina Vasa was born, she was completely covered with a caul, and the birth of a son was joyfully announced. The news had to be changed when the child was examined more carefully and revealed to be a girl. Statistics tell us that about one child in a hundred is born with malformed genitals, and this makes it difficult to determine its sex. Most common is congenital adrenal hyperplasia, which is a result of a biochemical defect. This can create a pseudo-hermaphrodite, a person organically female but rather masculine in appearance.[1]

When Christina's remains were examined in Rome in 1965,[2] the skeleton was certainly female, and as the soft tissues had disintegrated no examination of the external genitals could be made. The result of the examination was therefore inconclusive. She would later say of herself: 'As a young girl, I had an overwhelming aversion to everything that women do and say. I hated their tight-fitting and fussy clothes... I only wanted to wear short skirts... I despised everything belonging to my sex.'[3] As the only surviving legitimate child of King Gustavus Adolphus of Sweden and his wife Queen Maria Eleanora of Brandenburg, she succeeded her father as Queen of Sweden at the age of six, after his death at the battle of Lutzen. She became ruler in her own right at the age of eighteen, in 1644.

By the age of twenty-three, when she had reigned for over five years, she prepared for her coronation, but at the same time the French Ambassador was sending word home that she had no intention of reigning for long. The Queen had already hinted to him that she was dissatisfied with Lutheranism and also with the difficulties of governing, and was seriously considering an abdication. First, she would need to have her cousin, Karl Gustav, made Hereditary Prince in order to succeed her. However, the Riksdag, already pressing Christina to marry and produce heirs, was not happy as the change of name would effectively end the Vasa dynasty. Christina did not back down from her intentions, and gathered support by promising the commoners a resumption of relief from their burden of obligations, while at the same time promising the nobles protection from the commoners' most extreme demands. She in turn received what she needed, being their support for the advancement of Karl Gustav, and the Riksdag had to capitulate.

She was then crowned in a magnificent ceremony, with festivities lasting for weeks. This was done to increase her personal prestige and authority, which she would need for the struggle ahead of her. Within a year, her family and the Riksdag were fully aware of her desire to abdicate, though the Riksdag discounted her claim of finding the burden of rule too heavy, reminding her again of her duty to remain as Queen. Christina told them that she required 'not advice, but assent' from them. Although Karl Gustav had been accepted, nobody had intended his accession to be immediate, and the country could certainly not afford another coronation so soon. In October 1651 she summoned them again, determined to obtain their agreement, and the senators seemed to win, leaving the Queen apparently reconsidering. But to her it was only a postponement, and the stress made her ill. By the end of the year Karl Gustav received a letter exhorting him to depose the Queen, calling her a spendthrift and saying that her ministers were irresponsible. It was a warning for Christina, and she was deeply shocked to find herself so disliked.[4]

By the autumn of 1653, discontent with her rule was widespread, not only due to her continued refusal to marry, but to her wasteful habits. Her constant talk of abdication was unsettling for the country, and she had been in talks with Jesuit priests regarding her conversion to Catholicism. This was greatly feared and suspected in Sweden, and its practice was actually illegal there, with severe penalties. Even the masses held in the private chapels of foreign diplomats were often interrupted by Lutheran officials. It was a very dangerous road for her to take. So why would she wish to do it?

It was partly the Lutheran idea of womanhood that offended her. Luther had said regarding the ideal Protestant woman, 'Let her bear children unto death.' This was, to her, a horrifying idea. Also drawing her was that the celibate life was valued within Catholicism, and there would be no pressure on her to marry and produce children. As she had already sensibly said, 'I could just as easily bear a Nero as an Augustus!'

There was also an increasing boredom on her part with life in Sweden generally. She felt isolated there and away from the centre of things. Lastly, there was her character, very independent and determined, and also with a desire to shock. In this matter, she intended to do the most unbelievable thing, not only in leaving her homeland, but in accepting the religion and lifestyle that her homeland forbade. She intended to leave behind the cold and distant land of her birth and become part of Rome. There is no doubt that this was a definite draw for her, she wanted the culture, the beauty, the history and the warmth of the sun – Stockholm could not, and never would, compare with Rome for her. But while abdication was achievable, Catholicism was a step too far, and this is where her desire to shock came into play. She would not only leave her country behind, she would leave it dramatically.[5]

Being in Rome could put her at the centre of things, and she would be a celebrity there, where her conversion would gain her friends among people who might otherwise ignore the arrival of an ex-queen who had merely retired. Retiring was never her intention. She was still young and she wanted light, warmth, freedom and excitement, while knowing it would not be an easy transition, and would take time. She also wanted an annual pension from Sweden, to the sum of 200,000 Riksdaler, but negotiations for this were slow and she was eventually obliged to take the amount in land rather than hard cash.

She had first contacted the Jesuits in 1651 with questions about the church's attitudes. Then she mentioned her intention to Antonio

Macedo, a Jesuit priest and the Portuguese Ambassador's secretary. He went to see the Jesuit General in Rome in *'tutto giubilante'* as he recorded, and once in Rome the secret became a rumour. Her first letter asked only for 'friendship and your correspondence' but it was quickly passed onto Pope Innocent's Secretary of State Cardinal Fabio Chigi. Encouraging replies were sent back marked *altissimo segreto* (top secret). Two Jesuits, Malines and Casati, were then sent to Stockholm disguised as travellers, instructed to avoid all political discussions and reminded that, despite their secular attire, they must not succumb to 'worldly temptations'. By the spring of 1652 they were in Stockholm and already instructing the Queen in the Catholic faith. In three months she appeared to be convinced: 'We must submit blindly to the Roman Church, it is God's only oracle. To believe in more is superstition and to believe in less is infidelity.'[6] The arrangements for her reception in Rome were then begun.

On 6 June the ceremony of her abdication took place at Uppsala. Christina attended dressed as a queen, and the crown and robes were removed during the proceedings. This left her wearing a plain white dress and it was reported that 'she was without the least show of reluctance for what she had done.'[7]

She would only later, after leaving her homeland behind, be received into the Catholic Church, when the Jesuit Pallavacino would call the conversion, 'One of the most memorable and glorious for our Faith ever recorded.'[8] After travelling through Europe, she would be received in Rome with a magnificent formal procession, with cannon booming from Castel Sant'Angelo as she moved towards St Peter's. On Christmas Day she received the sacrament from the hands of Pope Alexander VII (previously Cardinal Fabio Chigi) before retiring to her apartment. She had taken the confirmation name of Alexandra, as a compliment to the Pope, adding Maria at his request. At that time he was pleased with her, and she was well pleased with what Rome had done for her, in giving her a new home at the Palazzo Farnese, near the Campo di Fiori, which was intended to be her permanent residence.[9] It was then owned by Duke Eduardo Farnese, but had been uninhabited for some time.

'Her Majesty was enraptured with the tapestries, statues and paintings' that filled the rooms, but not all of the Palazzo was habitable and in some rooms the plaster was crumbling. One room, the painted gallery, was beautiful and Christina added her own choice of paintings to it – some of them rather shocking to the Duke's representative, the Marchese Giandemaria. Her reply to his criticism was that she 'would not be bound by rules made by priests'. She succeeded in making close friends among the cardinals, who tended to be men of culture. Prominent among these was Cardinal Decio Azzolino, then thirty-two years old, very clever and a survivor of the Pamphilj years. He was already known to 'have had certain amorous liaisons, less than decent'.[10] He had been propelled forward by the patronage of the Pamphilj family, though he also possessed natural talents, yet was still considered something of a 'poor' cardinal, and was in receipt of a certain amount of financial assistance from the papal coffers to enable him to maintain a suitable position.

Christina would have heard of his love affairs, but was not put off by them, particularly as she was attracted to him herself. In fact, Azzolino was to become very much attached to Christina, and his visits became so frequent and lengthy that he was obliged to reassure the Vatican. Despite an enforced stay in the country, he returned in the same mind, and Christina blossomed under his attentions, becoming more feminine and taking more care with her appearance. The gossip soon paired them as lovers, and their close affection lasted for many years. Christina was of a bawdy turn of mind, far from prudish, but for her the sex act was one of submission for the woman, and the 'other' side of her nature could not allow her to submit, so whether their association actually included sex cannot be proved, but they were certainly important to each other, politically as well as emotionally.

Unfortunately, Christina was already regretting the loss of her crown, and was turning her eyes towards Naples, long the bone of contention between France and Spain. The Barberini had also long intended to try to incorporate it within the Papal States, and Christina imagined herself as its ruler. In Rome she could never rule, where there were several families of wealth and prestige, but as a queen in Naples she could have an independent life, yet still have power. She began to associate with Neopolitan patriots such as Pompeo Colonna, the Prince of Gallicano, the Marchese of Palombra, and the Marchese Gian-Rinaldo Monaldeschi, who was just the sort of adventurer Christina liked.

Her next move was to visit Cardinal Mazarin in France, to discuss plans personally. The timing was fortuitous as she was in great need of money and there was a plague in town. The Pope lent her (or rather gave, as she never repaid), 10,000 scudi and Santinelli and Monaldeschi were in charge of her finances. Cardinal Barberini also lent her money but he demanded security, and the Pope provided all else for her journey, from the ships to the food. He was still pleased to have his celebrity convert but had begun to find her wearing on a personal level. An English spy recorded, 'They begin to grow weary at Rome, with their new guest the Queen of Sweden.'[11] Within the Palazzo Farnese – which had already suffered a great deal from the carelessness of her entourage – the Marchese Giandemaria wrote 'I can hardly believe that she's gone ... every moment I am afraid of seeing her still in the place.'[12]

Christina travelled to Paris, arriving at Fontainebleu in early September. She was comfortably installed there and for a week entertained with music and ballets. The Duchesse de Montpensier (la Grande Mademoiselle) met her there and they found they had a good deal in common. The Duchesse had distinguished herself by fighting against her cousin the king (much to his disgust) at the Battle of the Fronde. Both women had cultivated tastes and loved riding and hunting. Christina quite envied the Duchesse, though her actions against the king had earned her his permanent distrust.

The two women watched a ballet together, followed by a play, where Christina surprised everyone by her behaviour, lounging in her chair, swinging her legs over the arms of it, 'now to the right, now to the left' repeating aloud the parts she liked, swearing, and adopting a posture, according to the Duchesse, more suitable to one of the clowns at the *Commedia dell'Arte*. Christina said she 'more than anything' wanted to be present at a battle, as the Duchesse had been. She also made the mistake of saying that she would recommend the Duchesse to Cardinal Mazarin, not realising that it was to oust Mazarin that the Duchesse had fought in the civil war, and had been exiled from court.

Mme de Motteville, in her *Mémoires*, remembered Christina:

...the Queen of Sweden, of whom we had heard so many extraordinary things ... her bodice had slipped off her shoulder, she was wearing a short skirt showing her ankles, and a man's shirt fastened at the neck. She had mannish footwear and on her head was perched a dark wig, ill-fitting and left uncurled. Her face was covered in dust and her hands were filthy, but once I had looked at her and got used to her clothes and hairstyle, I saw she had beautiful, lively, eyes and a sweet expression, and was proud. I realised I liked her.[13]

It was remarked upon that 'she had no ladies in waiting, no officers, no retinue, and no money', so servants had to be provided by the King. She only had 'two or three poor looking fellows with her' (these were the Santinelli brothers and the Marchese Monaldeschi) with two women, who were obviously not ladies of quality. She proved to be well informed but also that she was a mischief maker, certainly with regard to Cardinal Mazarin, who still had enemies at court (and had twice had to flee into exile during the Fronde). His niece Marie Mancini was then the King's sweetheart, although Mazarin was aware that a marriage between them would be disastrous for him.

Christina praised the girl fervently, saying she was 'fit to be a queen' and told the King, 'In your place I would certainly marry for love,' but to Azzolino she wrote that Mazarin would never be such a fool as to allow his niece to marry Louis. The mischievous remarks did not endear her to the court, or the Cardinal, and Mademoiselle scolded, 'At court, people don't like it that you meddle in things that don't concern you.'[14]

Christina and her group moved on to Pesaro and Azzolino's friend, Monsignor Luigi Gasparo Lascaris, met with Christina, and wrote to Azzolino of his concerns at her continued extravagance and the 'band of ruffians' she was with. He also teased his friend regarding his relationship with the bawdy Christina. She had told the Queen Mother of France, who was very devout, that 'fucking is what pretty girls are for!' Lascaris described Christina as wearing black velvet and blue ribbons, reading a part from a French play so well that he said to her, 'Madame, they say I'm a wily old bird, but this evening you have made me feel like a young cock!'[15]

Amusing and flattering for Christina, but otherwise she was bored in Pesaro and had no money to move on to Rome. There was no intellectual stimulation in the little town and very little of anything else. She was to languish there for seven months. Francesco Santinelli had been sent on to the Farnese Palace in the hope of raising some money and this he did, but he collected far more for himself. The Marchese Monaldeschi hated Francesco Santinelli and hoped to turn Christina against him, knowing that he was selling everything he could lay his hands on.

Monaldeschi was aware of the lying letters that Santinelli sent to Christina, and also about the money he had kept for himself. Unfortunately, instead of speaking to her directly about it, he foolishly forged several letters supposedly from Santinelli, which were very prejudicial to Christina, and contained details of her private life, intended to bring disaster on him when they were found out. They came into the hands of the priest, Pere le Bel, who was told that the Queen wished to see him on 6 November. The Queen then asked him to keep her business confidential and gave him a packet of letters to keep on her behalf. On the 10th she asked to see him again, and he went to her lodgings taking the letters with him.

He recorded 'Her Swedish Majesty was with a man she addressed as Marchese, with three others present.' (One was Santinelli's brother Ludovico). In a loud voice she asked the priest to return her letters to her, which he did. She opened them and gave the papers to the Marchese, asking if he recognised them.' He denied it, but his voice 'trembled' and the Queen then denounced him, saying she knew that the handwriting and signature was his own. Monaldeschi claimed that he had meant no harm, saying that Santinelli's letters and the revelations in them had been shocking and he had decided to circulate only the most inoffensive parts. He claimed that if he had suppressed them completely, Santinelli would know that the Queen's mail was intercepted.[16] When questioned again he declared his innocence, then threw himself at the Queen's feet begging her pardon. The Marchese then got to his feet and for almost two hours walked in the gallery with the Queen, insisting on his loyalty. She listened 'with no sign of emotion or anger' while the other three men waited with drawn swords.

Eventually, she turned to the priest and said, 'Reverend Father, you are my witness that I am not acting in haste or without good reason. I have allowed this faithless man more opportunity than he had a right to expect, to justify his actions towards me.' She spoke again to the Marchese and he took from his pocket some papers and some keys, which he gave to her. Some silver coins fell from his pocket and the priest later said, 'I do not remember which one of us picked them up.'

The Queen spoke again, a sentence destined to chill the priest, though she spoke quietly. 'Reverend Father, I shall now withdraw, I leave this man to you, prepare him for death and take his soul under your protection.' The Marchese and the priest fell to their knees before the Queen, and the priest reported, 'Had I been condemned myself I could not have been more terrified!' He went on to claim that he begged her to have mercy on the man, but she said she could not allow mercy to prevail. She had given the Marchese her trust and had showed him favours, all of which he had abused with ingratitude. Then she withdrew into her room.

The Marchese then clung onto the priest, begging him to go after the Queen and speak for him. Ludovico Santinelli went in, and came back out, to say that the Queen insisted that the execution be carried out without delay. He was in tears when he told the Marchese to make his confession.[17] The Marchese begged the priest again, who went in to see the Queen, and fell at her feet weeping. He begged for the man's life, but she remained 'perfectly calm, as though nothing was happening'. She expressed sorrow, but said she could not spare the Marchese and that after the cruelty he had inflicted on her, he could expect neither pardon nor pity. 'For lesser crimes,' she said, she 'had had men broken on the wheel.'

Pere le Bel tried to explain that she was a guest there, and that a summary execution would cause great offence. Christina replied that she was a refugee, and owed allegiance to nobody. She maintained her right to judge her own people when she chose, and claimed to be acting not against the Marchese but against his treachery and disloyalty. The priest pleaded yet again, asking for the Marchese to be turned over to the law, but the Queen indignantly dismissed this, no doubt fearing that the accusations in the letters would become public knowledge. She said she would inform King Louis and Cardinal Mazarin personally, then she instructed the priest to prepare the victim's soul saying, 'On my honour, I cannot grant what you ask!'

He returned to the gallery in tears and embraced Monaldeschi, who shrieked and fell to the floor, then he began his confession. He was distraught and twice rose to his feet 'crying out in Latin, French and in Italian'. The Queen's chaplain then arrived and he and Monaldeschi retired to a corner where they spoke at some length. The chaplain then left, taking Santinelli with him, but Santinelli immediately returned crying out 'Pray for forgiveness, Marchese, you are about to die!'[18]

He pushed the Marchese towards the end of the gallery and the priest turned away, but not before seeing Santinelli push his sword into Monaldeschi's stomach. Monaldeschi tried to grab the sword, but Santinelli pulled it back, cutting off three of the Marchese's fingers. Santinelli realised that his sword had bent and called out to the other men that Monaldeschi must be wearing chain mail! He struck him in the face and Monaldeschi cried out, prompting the priest to go to him. The Marchese was then on his knees, begging for absolution, which was given. Pere le Bel (he claimed as a penance) then told him to 'bear his death patiently, and forgive those who caused it'. Monaldeschi threw himself onto his stomach and the second man stepped forward and struck him on the head, knocking out a piece of his skull. Monaldeschi pointed to his neck, inviting the final blow to end his suffering, but the man struck him 'two or three times without doing much damage, as his coat of mail was covering his neck.' Pere le Bel claimed that he was at that time still exhorting the victim to 'bear it all patiently'.

Santinelli then turned to the priest and asked whether he should continue with the execution and the priest said he could not advise him. The door opened and the wounded Marchese turned to see the Queen's chaplain standing at the end of the gallery. Monaldeschi dragged himself towards the chaplain, taking his hands and trying to make another confession. The chaplain told him to beg God's forgiveness, and asked Pere le Bel if he could give him another absolution. When this was done he asked the priest to stay with the victim, while he spoke again with the Queen. The second man stepped forward and with his long narrow sword ran Monaldeschi through the throat. He fell towards the priest, but was unfortunately still not dead. The poor man lay in agony for a further fifteen minutes, while Pere le Bel prayed by his side until he died.

The three men then went in to the Queen to announce Monaldeschi's death and Christina expressed some slight regret and said she would pay for masses for the repose of his soul. Pere le Bel was told to dispose of the body and he sent for a bier to carry the Marchese's body away, which was buried within two hours. Two days later, Christina sent the monastery £100 to pay for thirty masses for him and received a receipt.[19]

The story of the brutal murder spread quickly and even in that violent age everyone was shocked and horrified by the callous performance of it and the Queen's indifference. Mazarin tried to cover up the details, suggesting Christina was an innocent bystander, but she didn't accept that role. She replied boldly to the Cardinal, freely admitting her part in it, and justifying it to her own satisfaction. The Cardinal tried to make her see reason, and realise how damaging the incident could be, but she replied defiantly, 'As to what I did with Monaldeschi, I can tell you that had I not already done it, I would not go to bed tonight without doing it, I have no reason to repent of it, but a hundred thousand reasons to feel satisfied. These are my feelings on the subject, if you accept them I shall be pleased, but if not, I shall continue to hold them anyway.'[20]

Christina was back in Rome in May, to find that the Pope refused to receive her, old friends were strangely unavailable and the Pasquinade messages were busy, describing her as 'A queen without a realm, a Christian without a faith, and a woman without shame!' She claimed she was waiting for the call to be queen of Naples, but when the Pope, who was trying to broker a Franco/Spanish peace after twenty-five years of war, asked her to leave the city, she had nowhere to go. Only Cardinal Azzolino was loyal. Despite the scandals, the money troubles, the talk of the crown of Naples, and even a murder, he was always there and ready to help. The Pope wanted Christina to move out of her then residence the Palazzo Mazarini, as it faced his own, and Azzolino found her somewhere else to live, in the Palazzo Riario.[21]

The new French Ambassador, the Duc de Crequy, was then living in the Palazzo Farnese, Christina's former home, which had been repaired. He was not diplomatically astute enough to douse the resentment between France and the Pope and demanded precedence over all the cardinals. Each day the Corsican Guard paraded across the Piazza in front of his residence on their way back to their barracks, and the Ambassador demanded that they stop disturbing him in that way. His complaint was not really about the guards themselves, but an excuse to antagonise their commander, Don Mario Chigi, the Pope's brother.

One evening, while crossing the Piazza, the Duc's men abused them, throwing one of the guards to the ground. The Palazzo Farnese was quickly surrounded and when the Duc appeared on the balcony a shot narrowly missed him. His wife, returning from church, had her carriage attacked and its windows smashed, her page was killed, and in the resulting fight two other French soldiers died.[22]

Christina had been in her garden with Azzolino when she heard the commotion. She offered assistance to the Duchesse de Crequy, which was declined, so then she decided to act as mediator, pushing herself again into matters which did not concern her. She told the Pope that his nephew should apologise for the incident, but her own men had a reputation for brawling and may well have been involved. Her interference was coldly dismissed by the Ambassador, so she wrote to the King. His reply was even more cool, and remembering the disgraceful Monaldeschi affair he basically told her to mind her own business. It was a direct reference to the Monaldeschi killing as well as a rebuff:

> It is all very well to counsel moderation oneself, and if Your Majesty had been ill-treated by even the least of your servants ... I am sure Your Majesty would have had sufficient spirit and care for her reputation that she would by no means follow her own counsel.[23]

By that time everyone was looking beyond Pope Alexander into the future, but Christina's concern was then with Stockholm. The Regent had made it clear that, though she had money problems and wanted to check on her lands, she was not welcome, but she went anyway. She took with her a large entourage, including one Clairot Poissonet, supposedly a cook but actually one of her spies. She may have achieved her financial aims in her homeland had she proceeded carefully, but caution was not in her nature.

She immediately caused great offence by flaunting her daily masses and was reprimanded by the Regent. She lost her temper and left in a huff, heading for Hamburg, which she described as 'dirty, stinking, and barbaric', while writing angrily to Azzolino blaming everyone but herself.[24]

Azzolino had been busy for Pope Alexander had finally died, largely unmourned, having been described as a miser and a hypocrite. The new Pontiff was Giulio Rospigliosi, who would reign as Pope Clement IX. This Pope was a friend, a theatre lover, and appeared to want to put an end to nepotism. He appointed Azzolino as his Secretary of State, along with his own nephew Giacobo Rospigliosi, which was an inconsistency he preferred to ignore.

However, Christina's long relationship with Azzolino had effectively come to an end, and even before leaving Rome to head for Stockholm she had been aware that he intended to end it. Friendship might certainly continue, but due to his new elevation, any sign of closer association must cease. Christina was distressed and very bitter, knowing that Azzolino did not want her in Rome. She had written 'Do you want me to stay away forever? Can you think I would ever do so?... I would rather live on bread and water in Rome than have all the treasures and kingdoms in the world and live anywhere else!'[25] His relationship with her had become a political liability for him. Her unconventional behaviour and total inability to realise her faults caused many problems. They were widely believed to be lovers, and when he became Secretary of State he could be regarded as *papabile* and it was time to jettison her, or give up all hope of ever becoming pope.

Unfortunately, the friendly Pope Clement did not live long, having a stroke just over two years into his pontificate. The new Conclave was to last more than four months, with Cardinal Azzolino locked away with the others. Christina was determined to keep in touch with him, so rented the Palazzo Ingilterra within the Vatican boundary, from where she could pass messages to him. Christina saw herself as a go-between for France and Spain and loved to feel involved, but Azzolino's chances of becoming a pope were fading fast. A pro-Spanish pope was finally elected, Emilio Altieri, becoming Pope Clement X in April 1670. He was to prove different to his easy-going predecessor and Azzolino's glory days were over.

One benefit to Christina was that once his hopes of the papacy were dashed, Azzolino no longer had to hide his attachment to her. As the years passed and they grew older, their love became platonic (if it had not always been) but it was still strong and became the focal point of both their lives. They often spent their evenings together and still wrote regularly to each other, while Azzolino's letters were more affectionate than formerly. 'Your dear little letter arrived just as I was thinking of you. Dearest, I did not enjoy the play so much yesterday evening, because it prevented me from being with you. Dearest, I thank you for all the comfort you have given me and I embrace you with all my soul.'[26]

Christina was beginning to feel her age, not merely the loss of face and figure and a lessening of interest in appearance, but the loss of old friends and the focal points of life. She had fainting fits in February 1689 and made her will, becoming gravely ill and confirming that Azzolino was her principal heir. She rallied in the spring, but a nasty incident set her back when a girl in her household, Angelica Quadrelli, was sold by her own mother to the Abbé Vanini, who was a notorious seducer, for 1,000 crowns. The girl was abused by him, and through his connections he evaded punishment. The girl was wounded and ashamed, and kept to her room. Christina, who had liked her, asked for her repeatedly and demanded the Abbé's head when she heard the truth. He escaped to Naples and Christina was so furious about the assault that she developed a fever and became very weak. The Pope sent her a letter of absolution and she received communion. Azzolino stayed by her side and she died in his presence on 19 April 1689, after contracting pneumonia. She was sixty-two years old.[27]

She had asked for a simple funeral, but Azzolino, who was so upset at losing her that he was unable to remember the date for his letter, said '...but the Glory of God and his Church and the honour of His Holiness demanded otherwise. A simple funeral would be a triumph for the heretics and a scandal and disgrace for Rome.'[28]

Azzolino made all the arrangements and was determined that so public a figure should not be laid to rest quietly. Consequently, Christina was embalmed and exhibited publicly for four days at her home, dressed in a white satin gown embroidered with gold crowns and trimmed with ermine. There was a silver mask covering her face and a silver crown and sceptre. She was then taken to the Church of Santa Maria in Vallicella where her Requiem Mass was said the following day, with the 'whole college of cardinals in attendance' except for Azzolino, who could not bear to watch. That night she was taken to St Peter's Basilica with a great train of mourning, and laid to rest in a triple coffin in the crypt, where she lies surrounded by popes.

The grieving Azzolino did not long survive her. He was sometimes seen wandering through the streets, 'in deepest mourning and in lowliness and dejection' and went through her papers burning private correspondence after reading everything carefully. He would describe his sometimes fraught association with her as 'my greatest glory'.[29]

Azzolino said that the loss of Christina was 'appalling... I am inconsolable and will always be inconsolable.'[30] Once she was gone he faded and died on 8 June 1689, just fifty days after she had died. He was buried in the Church of Santa Maria in Vallicella, where Christina's funeral mass had been held.

The Time of the Religious: Mother Pascalina

The woman who would be known to the Vatican as Mother Pascalina was born in August 1894 and named Josefine. She was one of seven children born to George and Maria Lehnert, who lived on their small farm twenty-five miles south-east of Munich. Josefine was religious even as a child, as well as willing, able to work, and keen to always find a 'better' and more efficient way of doing things. She was full of confidence and determination, enjoyed her studies, but was also adventurous. An early memory was of her brother John, then twenty years old, giving her rides on his motorcycle, for she enjoyed speed and later in life would encourage the driver of any vehicle she was in to 'go faster!'[1]

She became an attractive teenager, blonde and blue-eyed with plenty of admirers, but began to be irritated by the privations of life on a small farm. In 1910 she attended the Passion Plays at Oberammergau and always believed that seeing them formulated her plan to become a nun. Her parents did not approve, and would not discuss the matter with her, though she remained determined and, sponsored by her pastor, she left home at sixteen to join the Teaching Sisters of the Holy Cross at Altotting near Munich.[2]

She took her final vows when she was nineteen, assuming the name of Pascalina, from Paschal the Easter Festival, and was immediately assigned to the Stella Maris retreat house at Rorschach in the Swiss Alps, where she could help to nurse priests back to health.

It was there, in 1917, that she met an Italian Prelate named Eugenio Pacelli, who was a close friend of the Pope and already an Archbishop at only forty-one, being in charge of the Vatican's foreign office. Pope Benedict XV had chosen him for the difficult work of international negotiations during the First World War, and his health had suffered. He was an aristocrat, from a family who had long served the papacy.[3] A man of great dignity, he was also aloof and sometimes impatient. He had been on a diplomatic assignment to Munich to help broker a peace plan when his father died. The blow had damaged his health and he had been sent to Stella Maris to recuperate. Sister Pascalina was assigned to look after him. When he recovered, she had never expected to hear from him again, but three months later her Prioress had a request from Pacelli to supply a nun as housekeeper for him at the Nuncio's office in Munich. Pascalina was assigned, not then realising that the Prioress and the Archbishop had already known of the proposed transfer, which had been authorised by the Pope a few days earlier. Pacelli had asked for her specially, having been struck by her beauty and manner as well as her care and consideration.[4] The transfer went through immediately and Pascalina was on her way to Munich.

Her first responsibility was taking care of the Nuncio's household, which was large. Pascalina tried to make changes but the staff ignored her, to the point where she found herself with a strike on her hands. 'Your Excellency, she leaves or we do!' Pacelli tried to placate them, but Pascalina would not, preferring to do all the work herself rather than give in. Pacelli was then struggling with the problem of exchanging prisoners of war, but when he had time to consider his domestic situation he realised that all was in perfect order.[5] He never actually thanked her, but his coldness towards the rest of the staff showed he knew of her efforts and appreciated them. He was worn out with his negotiations, treating with the neutral Swiss, the Vatican, and the Red Cross. Through all that difficult time, Pascalina was his support. She attended to the house and to the beggars who came regularly to the door for help, but her main concern was always for him.

The Kaiser fled to Holland in 1918 leaving behind a huge bitterness at the defeat and what was seen as his betrayal. The Bolsheviks appeared in early 1919, breaking windows at the Nunciature and demanding to see Pacelli. Most of the other diplomats had already left so he had become the focus of their hatred.[6] They were told to leave, but demanded food and money, to be told that everything had already been given away. The Communist shouted 'That's a lie!' but before Pacelli could speak, Pascalina defiantly cried 'It is true!' The leader of the mob hit Pacelli with his gun and Pascalina lost her temper, shouting at them to get out. After a short while they left, but the Nunciature was attacked again a few nights later. On one occasion, when they were together in the car, they were stopped after delivering medical supplies to a children's hospital. This time it was Pacelli who outfaced them, telling the mob that he had no weapon but the cross, and intended harm to nobody. After some hesitation, they were allowed to proceed.

A few days later the Communists were gone, driven out by the Free Corps Rebels who were to help General Erich Ludendorff to form an interim government. Pacelli refused to comply with the demand that he hand over any Communist sympathisers, but insisted on his neutrality, which infuriated Ludendorff.[7] Hitler would see the Free Corps and other Bavarians as instruments to be exploited in his own cause. In 1919 Munich Nationalism was born and it would become the centre of Hitler's dreams. He visited the Nuncio's residence one night and Pacelli spoke with him, also giving him money to aid his work against Communism, which was considered a great threat to the church.[8]

After the war, Pacelli and Pascalina went for a month to Stella Maris to learn to ski and to relax. Pacelli was troubled at the idea of being seen on holiday with his housekeeper, aware of the scandal it could create, although he had begun to require her presence for her practicality, her attention to his comforts, and for her sense of humour. She ignored any criticism she heard, and her attitude took him out of his shell. 'Father Pacelli's mother was too inclined to baby him,' she would later remark. 'As a result he became introverted, overly concerned with his health. There were times, when we were both young, when I was tempted to say to him he was not made of glass!' She also said, 'If Father Pacelli had left his home as a young man, instead of remaining with his family to be pampered by his mother, he would have adjusted more easily to the ways of the world.'[9]

He would sink back into melancholia when his mother died, though he was then middle-aged and Pascalina had again to persuade him to take up the threads of life. During the 1920s she worked to transform the quiet and introspective man into an influential religious leader and prospective pope. They moved to Berlin in 1925 to a larger property, of which the then thirty-one-year-old nun took full charge. She organised everything, not only making sure the household ran smoothly but acting as his steward and choosing the musicians and wines for diplomatic guests; though dealing with Pacelli was sometimes more difficult. He could be filled with life and humour as the perfect host, but could just as easily retreat into his shell, needing solitude. She said of him, 'If he had his way, he would have withdrawn into a world of asceticism, largely away from people.'[10]

They had then been together for eight years and Pascalina lived simply within the splendour of the Nuncio's residence. As visiting was forbidden by her order, she was obliged to make her work the centre of her world, but she and Pacelli suited each other, understanding each other's needs and giving one another space. They agreed on the running of the residence, preferring to live frugally when not entertaining officially.

In the 1920s Rome was threatened by Benito Mussolini, who was feared and despised by the then Pope, Pius XI (Ambrogio Ratti). Once Mussolini assumed real power, his anti-religious propaganda was altered, as he realised that he would do better with the Church on his side, and the Vatican was prepared to make its own demands of the Dictator, who wanted to have the Pope's ostensible public imprimatur.[11] Pacelli had said 'Mussolini has begged God's forgiveness and mercy.' Pascalina's reply was less abstract and more pragmatic: 'A man like Mussolini can never be trusted.'

It was inevitable that their close friendship should pose a threat to Pacelli's career, as even in Berlin it was considered very 'modern' for a young nun to be in charge of the Nuncio's residence. Her very attractiveness posed a problem, and Pacelli was headed for Rome. He had been thrilled to be told that he was needed there, and Pascalina had expected that his full household would go with him, but was told no, not at the present. He told her he would live with his family, and be cared for by his sister. An argument followed, with Pascalina insisting that he still needed her, and Pacelli withdrew into his habitual coldness, telling her 'The Vatican is not Munich, or even Berlin! It cannot be at this time, so say no more!'[12]

Pacelli departed, full of eagerness and pleasure at the new opening for him, and Pascalina was left behind in Berlin waiting for his letters. At the end of that year, he again invited her to go with him to the Stella Maris house to ski, and she delightedly accepted, only to find him recalled to Rome shortly after they arrived. The Pope was intent on making him a cardinal, so better things beckoned for him. He hosted a dinner at the residence in Berlin, knowing that it would be his last time there, as a place had been found for him at the Papal Palace, and Pascalina could not join him there. He received his cardinal's hat in December 1929 and became Secretary of State in February 1930.[13]

Pascalina had certainly supported him in his rise, and had always encouraged him, but with him gone and no prospect of her being able to join him, her own position had greatly deteriorated. After a further four months she wrote desperately to him 'I miss you, and I truly hope that you need me.' She begged for a transfer to the Vatican, saying 'I'll even be content in the basement, I don't mind, just so long as I can be by your side and care for you. May I please be of help again with your decisions and ease your burdens?'

He replied with a cool, official letter turning her down, though he added a postscript saying that he missed her, her companionship and her brilliance – but that any suggestion of impropriety would scandalise the church. In 1930 Pascalina was so much 'outside' of Pacelli's life, that she did not realise that she had a new 'rival' in Monsignor Francis Spellman, an American priest. He had been in Rome for five years and became close to the Pope and also to Pacelli. When Pacelli and Pascalina arranged their holiday in the Alps as usual, she was annoyed to find that Spellman was going with them. She took an instant dislike to him and unfortunately let it show. She pointedly argued that Spellman should go to enjoy the Passion Plays at Oberammergau and persuaded Pacelli to arrange for him to travel to Bavaria to see them. Spellman was aware that her antagonism was the reason for the trip, but could hardly refuse. In a letter home, he recounted with some amusement 'I could hardly say no!'[14]

Sister Pascalina questioned Pacelli on the wisdom of allowing Bernardino Nogara to have a free hand in organising the Vatican Treasury. He was a close friend of Mussolini and therefore untrustworthy. During their discussions on the subject she was dismayed to find that Pacelli's attitude was changing, he was being seduced by the need to fill the Treasury, and money-making had taken over from principles for him. This would become the contradiction for all high-ranking Vatican insiders in the twentieth century.[15] Only one pope would try to reverse the worrying trend and that would have tragic consequences for him.[16]

Pascalina was aware that she was in danger of losing her hold on Pacelli altogether, and she later said, 'If I hadn't had my faith in Jesus, there would have been nothing to keep me going.' After Spellman's return, Pascalina was surprised to find that she was growing to like him. He was able to lighten the atmosphere when Pacelli was in a bad mood and when he suggested that they should do some European travelling together, Pacelli told him, 'You are exactly like our dear Sister Pascalina, when it comes to daring ideas!' Then his own enthusiasm grew and he said 'Tell you what ... in the weeks ahead let us do all the foolish things we would do, if we were children again.'[17] Seeing Spellman's astonishment, he added 'Wipe that silly look of amazement off your face Monsignor Spellman! Don't act as if we were back in the Vatican, with the Holy Father watching every move!' They were to spend several weeks driving through Switzerland, Austria and Germany, staying overnight at convents, monasteries and church rectories. The three of them spoke French, Latin and Italian, but usually conversed in German, though Pacelli asked Spellman to start to teach them English too.

Sister Pascalina enjoyed the fuss and ceremony wherever they went, after all Pacelli was Cardinal Secretary of State, and the 'vice-pope', but she could also see that he was beginning to accept the pomp and ceremony as his due. Despite Pacelli's rather insular temperament, that holiday forged a bond between them, deeper than before. Pacelli said privately to Pascalina, 'All along I have wanted you at my side, but my hands have been tied.' Spellman impressed Pascalina with his sympathy and consideration, and he would become a regular correspondent. He told her later that he was working to persuade Pacelli that a place at the Vatican should be made for her.

Eventually, the eagerly awaited call came, but Pascalina found herself not at Pacelli's side, but in the kitchens, cooking and cleaning. It was Spellman's friendship that kept her going and he eventually found – or made – a place for her in his office in the Curia, though her domestic work had also to be done officially.

She was to meet with disapproval from another assistant, Monsignor Giovanni Montini, whose dislike she simply ignored, but her indifference to his opinion was to be regretted when, three decades into the future, he became Pope Paul VI. He should, however, have been more sympathetic to her situation, in view of the scandals he would later face with accusations of his homosexuality becoming widespread.[18]

In the early 1930s Pacelli resumed his habit of asking Pascalina for advice. He then disagreed with the Pope's attitude towards Mussolini, as despite Mussolini having pressured the government to provide over ninety-two million dollars to save the Vatican from bankruptcy, the Pope was unwilling to meet him as a gesture of goodwill. Pascalina was then thirty-six years old and committed to defending her principles. Pacelli was fifty-four and equally determined to act diplomatically.

In 1932 Spellman was appointed as Auxiliary Bishop of Boston, while Pascalina's own administrative talents were idle, though the situation was about to change. Pius XI became aware of corrections she had made on a document and sent for her. He told her that 'better use could be made of her mind' than continuing to work below stairs, and she was sent to the Secretary of State's suite in the Secretariat.[19] Many people, even her own confessor, considered the appointment scandalous but for once she let her heart rule her head and accepted it gladly. She told her confessor 'It is a good relationship, ours is a respectable love and Jesus himself would bless it.'

They moved into a routine of hard work and private moments, when they could sit in the gardens and share opinions. Many prelates had been used to popping into the Secretary of State's office at will, and were appalled to be told that they would have to make an appointment to see Pacelli. He was once accosted by a group of cardinals, furious at the 'effrontery of an ordinary nun', but it got them nowhere. By 1936 Pacelli had been named

Camerlengo and with the Pope nearing eighty, and with only three more years to live, it was obvious that he would have to organise a Conclave in the near future.[20] Pascalina believed that she had behaved pleasantly when she first became protectoress of Pacelli's office, but she soon realised that any unbending on her part was taken as a weakness, and she subsequently became very authoritarian. Pacelli was at one point forced to tell her that the cardinals had met with the Pope to demand her removal from the Vatican. She was being referred to as 'Pacelli's female valet', which implied impropriety in his private quarters. He reassured her that 'His Holiness sent them from his presence, and I also will not allow you to leave.'

On 10 February 1939 the Pope suffered a heart attack and Pacelli was with him when he died. Not only would he have the responsibility of organising the coming Conclave, but everyone believed that he stood a very good chance of becoming the next pope. The late Pope had already told the cardinals that in his opinion Pacelli had the necessary qualifications to be Pontiff. Nineteen days after the death of Pius XI the Conclave began and Pascalina immediately sparked further controversy by going in with him to look after him. The voting was to be very short, with a decision being made on the second ballot. When the voting was in his favour, Pacelli said, 'I ask that each Eminence search his heart and vote for someone other than me.' He then left the chapel. Pascalina persuaded him to pray for guidance, before they returned to the Sistine Chapel. At the next vote the result was unanimous and, after hesitation, Pacelli accepted it, asking to be named Pius XII in memory of his friend.[21]

Church historian Corrado Pallenberg wrote of Pascalina:

She rigorously supervised everything, from major decisions to minor details... She kept all the Pope's papers in order, his desk supplied with writing paper ... and she changed his cuffs, which he so often soiled with ink. He took to dictating to Pascalina not only the official papers but the daily entries for his private diary... His trust in her was complete... She never once betrayed his confidence in her.[22]

Within six months of Pacelli's election the Second World War broke out. His many years in Germany had given him a true love of the German people and though Pascalina favoured the last Pope's hard-line stance against Hitler, Pacelli favoured appeasement.

From the day Pacelli became Pope Pius XII, Pascalina's control of the papal palace was absolute. She reorganised the kitchens, making it clear that what had been good enough for Pius XI was certainly not good enough for Pius XII! Not everyone was afraid of her, and in her drives to the markets for food she was sometimes abused by other shoppers, who hated the idea that a nun, who actually arrived in a limousine, should be competing for cheap food. She tried to counter this antagonism by telling them that the Pope would pay for the food they bought that day, working as she always did to put a good light on Pius XII, even with those who traditionally had no love for the papacy.

Spellman had ties with the White House and it was considered wise to make him Archbishop. He had been in America for seven years, and was needed to clear up the New York diocese's financial situation, but his elevation as Archbishop of New York was put down to his friendship with Pascalina and her influence on Pius XII. He was to revitalise the Archdiocese and accrue an immense cash surplus in only a few years, but not everyone was impressed. Cardinal Tisserant referred to him as 'Cardinal Moneybags', as Spellman gave a one million dollar donation to the papacy for every year that he was Archbishop.[23]

During the war, Tisserant would upbraid Pascalina for not doing more to persuade Pius to help the Jews as well as their own clergy who were being persecuted. He thought she should use her undoubted influence on the Pope to work for good, and often tangled with her and infuriated her by his 'arrogance'. Pius firmly believed that the church should remain neutral but knew that many others considered his stance pro-German and even anti-Semitic. Tisserant became a particularly harsh critic on the matter, though Pius had very little actual scope for action at that time.[24]

Archbishop Spellman warned Pius he had information from President Roosevelt that the Nazi war crimes accusations were true, and that Jews were being gassed in their thousands. He was deeply upset and sent for the German Ambassador, Diego von Bergen, to have it out with him. After a bitter denunciation, Bergen remained polite, but warned the Pope, 'Do not be surprised if relations between the Third Reich and the Papacy are broken off!' The standoff continued for some time, but the Pope remained officially silent regarding the atrocities. Pascalina's first concern was, as always, for Pius himself. She was anxious about his health, fearing that the strain might prove too much for him. To help ease it, she suggested that they could provide sanctuary for thousands of Jews, and the Pontifical Relief Committee was born. It would require not only tact on Pius' part, but also duplicity. He agreed with the Nazis that papal property, including churches, convents, monasteries, and even Castel Gandolfo, which was fifteen miles from Rome and actually in the war zone, should be kept sacrosanct. Kesselring sanctioned this, and it allowed thousands of Jews to be housed and protected, with 15,000 at Castel Gandolfo alone. On numerous occasions there were suspicions that Jews were being hidden in Vatican properties, but Pius was able to charm the ambassador (Ernst von Weizsäcker, who Pascalina knew was a secret anti-Nazi), and her confidence in him was justified.

In September 1943 Hitler heard that Pascalina was falsifying identity cards for the hidden Jews (even the Vatican was not immune to informers), but fortunately a proclamation on 14 August by the Italian Government declared that Rome was an 'open' city, so they were assured that the autonomy of the Vatican would be respected. Mussolini, briefly imprisoned by the Allies then daringly rescued, wanted revenge and Pascalina had to urge the dazed Pius to barricade St Peter's. She had despaired of him, as he seemed to be shattered by the war, but he defiantly refused to leave the Vatican, finding his courage in action.[25] With attacks from both sides, the Pope was under extreme pressure to re-establish the papacy in a neutral country, which he refused to do, though he did absolve the cardinals from their oaths of fealty, giving them permission to leave, which they in turn refused.

On 15 February the Americans dropped bombs on Monte Cassino and on 1 March Nazi aircraft struck the Vatican. Shortly afterwards, Pius spoke to 300,000 people in St Peter's Square, blasting with fury the devastation created by both sides.[26] Mussolini sent his mistress, Clara (Claretta) Petacci, to plead with the Pope on his behalf. She told him that Mussolini had split from the Fuhrer and had a workable plan for peace. She could not be received by the Pope, and was instead sent to the Archbishop of Milan. Pascalina was authorised to read the proposal, which sought sanctuary for Mussolini, his family and for Clara Petacci. If granted, he would surrender unconditionally. Pius was inclined to accept it, and sent the proposal to Eisenhower with that recommendation, but it was refused, with a very curt reply.

Mussolini and Clara Petacci fled Milan on 25 April 1945 heading for the Swiss border, but they were captured and shot the following day, their bodies being taken back to Milan and left in a public square to be insulted and abused, before being hung upside down above the local service station. Two days later Hitler and his mistress Eva Braun killed themselves. The Allied nations celebrated, but Pascalina saw only the toll on Pius's mental and physical health. 'Almost every day throughout the war... he was the recipient of confidential information... I will never forget when His Holiness was told that in Poland alone 2,647 priests ... were either gassed or shot... There were times when the revelations were exceedingly more terrifying.'[27]

Once the war was over the church faced the problem of the Sicilian Mafia, with accusations that many priests were agents for the organisation. Some priests confessed to having committed all sorts of crimes, claiming, 'we had to come to terms with them, to prevent worse things happening to the villages.' Pascalina felt that Pius made the same mistake with this problem, in that he had refused to take a stand. She visited Sicily to attend the funeral of a brave man, Angelo Cannada, who had been murdered, and reported back to Pius that she found many of the Franciscans there were living like bandits. Pascalina gathered all the evidence that she could, on extortions and even murders, to effect a prosecution. Ultimately though, the Pope preferred again to keep the lid on church scandals, to Pascalina's despair.

Archbishop Cushing wrote, 'Her hands were tied in many ways. Even though she was close to the Pope for most of her life, she was still looked upon as a mere nun at times, even by Pius himself... Church clergy maintain an inbred prejudiced mentality which is entirely convinced that the male mind is right... Pius was certainly a pope with that kind of intellect.'[28] It was this prejudice that Pascalina had struggled with all her life.

The investigation of the Franciscans over the Cannada affair was derailed and Cushing blamed Spellman for it. Every member of the monastery was arrested. It would be only after Pius's death that they were brought to trial, even though the charges were very serious including extortion, attempted murder, and murder itself. But they would all be exonerated. As author Joe Pieri wrote, 'After months of the organised verbal chaos and histrionics which masquerade as a trial in parts of Italy, the friars were acquitted on all charges.' They would not be retried until 1963, when they were all found guilty and sentenced to various terms of imprisonment.

Pascalina said:

> At times, His Holiness would be fully dedicated to a cause... He would then procrastinate and dwell upon the harm that might result from some bold stand on his part... He would then alter his whole course of action... Pius was a holy man, but unfortunately like so many of us, he was misguided on occasion.[29]

Unfortunately, her own influence could also be counter-productive. She encouraged the Pope to exclude the cardinals from close contact with him, in effect 'freezing them out' of their traditional advisory position. In their place, his nephews Carlo and Giulio Pacelli became his advisors. Pascalina had her own reasons for preventing power being given to the cardinals, Cardinal Tisserant in particular. Pius also became known for his outbursts of temper and displays of contempt towards the cardinals. He had no patience for any personal mistakes, and Pascalina also took the blame for his regular explosions of fury against them. He was well known for his bias in favour of German clerics, which caused resentment to build up with the Italian ones, who considered his open preference an insult.

The greatest shock to the cardinals came with the announcement that Pius was setting up a Vatican Bank. He looked upon the Second World War as a financial opportunity and intended to profit by seeking new ways to increase the Vatican's influence. From the Bank's opening in 1942, it became a cover for smuggling vast sums of money across foreign frontiers, and this organisation would also become the centre of an appalling scandal in the decades ahead. Bernardino Nogara was the Vatican's first 'financial wizard', but there would be others, even more ruthless.[30]

By 1950 Pius's health was giving cause for concern. His mind would occasionally wander and Pascalina feared that others might use this weakness against her. He was then in his seventies, and had regular bouts of illness. Tisserant and Monsignor Tardini had been deputed to ask Pius for a full financial statement, an unprecedented move that infuriated Pascalina. Tisserant shouted at her, 'Give us the report woman, or we'll get it from the Pope himself!' Her response was to reach for the phone and demand the Swiss Guards remove the intruders. The two cardinals left, but Tisserant said, 'Woman, may God have mercy on you from now on!' Later he would say bitterly, 'It was bad enough when that woman took her orders from Pius, but now she wields such power that many of the hierarchy deride her as "La Popessa."'[31]

From then, only a few people were permitted regular contact with the Pope. Even his sister Elisabetta – his closest friend in the early years – had to defer to Pascalina. She used to take a bottle of wine when she saw her brother, and would pour it for him. Pascalina objected to it, reminding her 'His Holiness is not a well man!' Elisabetta answered her with 'Eugenio is no longer a baby – leave us alone and stop listening at the door!' As his beloved sister she could sometimes get away with standing up to Pascalina, but on other occasions she would find the door was closed to her.

Early in 1954 the Pope weighed only 105 lbs, and was very weak. His close relationship with Pascalina still held. On her sixtieth birthday she was called into his study, to find a birthday cake with sixteen candles. When she laughingly remarked on the number, Pius took her hands, kissed her on the forehead, and said to her, 'Mother Pascalina, you will always be sixteen to me!'[32] He later told her, 'I am not going to live much longer, and it would be better for you to be out of the way when the end comes.' He went on, 'You must let me find you a peaceful haven, where you can spend your remaining years.'

Pascalina persuaded him to stay on at Castel Gandolfo during the heat of summer, returning to the Vatican only in the autumn. His condition was deteriorating. He woke in the early hours of 2 December and began to pray, and then declared that he had seen a vision of Jesus standing by his bed. A few hours later, there was a definite improvement in his health and by Christmas he was well on the way to recovery.[33] It was the first time that a pope had claimed to actually see a vision, and by the New Year he was eager to tell everyone about it. Pascalina tried to dissuade him, reminding him that the public were very sceptical about such things, and might even ridicule him. She turned to Spellman for advice, and he promised to fly to Rome, but before he could, the Pope had broken his silence. The College of Cardinals felt it best to stay above the resulting controversy, but Tisserant confronted Pascalina about her knowledge of it. When she refused to be drawn, he threatened her with the words, 'Woman, your days are numbered!'

During the final months of Pius's life, he clung to his dignity, although his critics claimed that his reign had been a disaster for the church. They said that the papacy had 'lost any semblance of intellectual virility, any sense of pastoral mission, and any desire to come to grips with the problems of the real world'. Tisserant, typically, stated, 'The Church appears to be dying with him.'[34] Pius even considered stepping down from his position as he weakened, and Pascalina offered to take over his temporal responsibilities to leave him free to use what strength he had for his pastoral duties. It was an unbelievable move for a woman to even suggest taking over the duties of a pope. Pius did not actually give Pascalina permission to do it, but neither did he refuse it, so she decided to take his silence for consent.

She decided what papers the Pope should sign, and what business would receive priority. She ordered that nobody be admitted to his apartments without her consent, putting the palace guard on duty outside. She included the cardinals in the ban, and ordered that the guards be on duty for twenty-four hours a day to prevent him being disturbed.

Pius benefited from the regime, and began to feel better. He found he then had time for private prayer and meditation, and was distanced from all verbal attacks, seeing only those people who did not disturb him. Naturally though, the people who were kept outside of his private circle considered Pascalina's orders to be 'tyrannical and even humiliating'. She blamed Montini, who had not then been named as a cardinal, but was desperate for the papacy. He had worked hard with the Pope for sixteen years, but Pius told Pascalina,

'He is too progressive, in both his social and his political outlook, to ever be considered a reliable successor.' Both Pascalina and Spellman feared Montini, and spoke against him becoming a cardinal, with the result that he was exiled to Milan.[35]

Pascalina was also feeling her years. She had given up everything to serve Pius and the church, having no close friends at all and very little contact with her family. Her entire attention was given to Pius, even to instructing the gardeners to keep out of sight so that he could enjoy the gardens in privacy.

They were again at Castel Gandolfo in October 1958 when the Pope's gastritis became severe. She urged Spellman to get to the papal villa quickly, fearing that the Pope would not survive. She spoke with Spellman of his successor, saying 'They will pick someone opposite to him, so as to discredit him.' She clearly feared Tisserant, but was assured by Spellman that he had far too many enemies to have any chance of becoming pope.

Pope Pius XII finally died at Castel Gandolfo on 9 October 1958. Pascalina's carefully guarded relationship with him had forced her into a life of secrecy and her position had made her both feared and hated by the church hierarchy. Her enemies began to work against her as soon as Pius was dead and she told Spellman, 'Tisserant will have me out within the week, he had already denied me a place at the funeral and I need your help.' Unfortunately, Spellman's power, like her own, had died with Pope Pius.

Mother Pascalina did attend the funeral of Pope Pius, though she was not given a prominent position. Shortly after it was over, she met with Cardinal Tisserant in his office, and asked him for a few days in which to make proper arrangements for leaving, and also that she could take a small souvenir or two, in memory of Pius.

Tisserant replied roughly, 'You will leave the Vatican by nightfall, as the Sacred College has decreed. You may take only one thing of Pius's, his birds, and we will be well rid of them, and of you!'[36]

On the evening of 14 October 1958, the day of Pope Pius XII's funeral, Mother Pascalina left the Vatican, with only her two small bags of belongings, and a pair of cages containing Pius's pet birds. Nobody saw her off.

She went to the Stella Maris house where for several years she lived retired, until Cardinal Spellman persuaded her to build a home for women in their declining years. She was to found the 'Casa Pastor Angelicus' and served there as Mother Superior until her death in 1983, at the age of eighty-nine. She was buried in The Campasanto Teutonico at the Vatican, and her funeral was attended by several cardinals, including Cardinal Josef Ratzinger, the future Pope Benedict XVI.

As she had once said, 'Loneliness is not a matter of being alone – loneliness is the feeling that nobody else truly cares what happens to you.'

Pope John Paul I – 'When One Pope Dies, We Make Another One'

The year 1978 was to become known as 'the year of three popes' but the legacy that the first of these, Paul VI, left to his successor Pope John Paul I, actually began earlier, in April of 1966.[37]

Even earlier than that, in 1962, Pope Paul VI had set up a Pontifical Commission of sixty-eight members to investigate the problem of artificial birth control, due to the increasing availability of more reliable methods of controlling pregnancy and the demands of women worldwide to be allowed to have autonomy over their bodies and the number of children they produced. It also implied a right to have a sex life outside of any marital connection, if desired.

As with all Vatican investigations, it took time. For any liberalising of the Vatican's stance on the subject, it would also have to pass through a further, smaller, group of twenty cardinals and bishops. By April 1966 the Commission's opponents to change had been reduced to four, but these men were absolutely determined that all artificial forms of birth control should be forbidden.

Pope Pius XII had already softened the Vatican's opinion on the subject very slightly, by permitting the 'rhythm method' to be used as a contraceptive. This was often referred to as 'Vatican roulette', due to its unreliability. But what Pius's admission had actually allowed was the idea that sexual relations might no longer be viewed as being 'for procreation only,' which was the lingering medieval idea of sexuality.

Once that admission had been made, it opened the floodgates to the idea that married couples should be able to choose for themselves the size of their families, in accordance with their financial situation, which was an idea that the church had problems with and indeed still struggles with, even now preferring the rhythm method or abstinence to be the choices on offer, despite the worrying losses of church membership and the worldwide necessity of population control. This is even before considering the dismay of millions of Catholics who do not see artificial birth control as a sin, and continue to use various methods anyway, in defiance of the church's teaching.[38]

When the birth control pill became widely available in the 1960s, Catholic women had to ask for it in the knowledge that they were 'doing wrong' in the eyes of their religious leaders, and with a corresponding sense of guilt. When the Pontifical Commission finally made its report, it said that an overwhelming majority, (sixty-four to four), had decided that a change in the church's stance on birth control was both 'possible and advisable'.

Leading the still-opposing four cardinals was the Secretary of State, Alfredo Ottaviani, who was the most powerful man at the Vatican after the Pope. He initiated further reports, and pestered the Pope night and day from his position at his side and his knowledge that the other sixty-four members of the Commission had already returned to their homes. His persistence paid off, and eventually the minority of four manipulated Paul VI. On 25 July 1968 he published *Humanae Vitae*, which was intended to strengthen papal authority, but it had exactly the opposite effect when it informed millions of disappointed Catholics that '...in any use whatever of marriage, there must be NO impairment of its natural capacity to procreate human life.'[39] This disastrous decision was destined to split the church.

One of the men who had submitted reports and recommendations was Cardinal Albino Luciani. He had already been studying the problem for several years, asking the advice of doctors, sociologists, and particularly taking into account the opinions of married couples, living at the sharp end of the debate. The fifty-six-year-old Luciani had been born in the Veneto on 17 October 1912, in the town of Forno di Canale. He became a priest in 1935 and served as curate in his native area. He was made Bishop of Vittorio Veneto in 1958 and would, in December 1969, be made Patriarch of Venice. He was a genuinely good and kind man, who was very concerned about the poor, and particularly with the plight of Catholic women whose fate it was to bear child after child, sometimes in poverty and often to the detriment of their own health. His own brother Eduardo struggled to support his wife and family of ten children, and Cardinal Luciani fervently supported the use of the birth control pill for keeping families to a sensible and affordable level. His report had been submitted to Cardinal Urbani, who signed it and sent it directly to Pope Paul VI. Urbani praised the report fulsomely, and Paul VI also remarked how much pleasure it had given him to read it. The central matter covered in it was that the anovulant pill should become the Catholic birth control method. Many clerics expected it to be passed and were amazed to learn that the Pope, suddenly and in defiance of the reports and of public opinion, had backtracked and refused to allow it. The clergy, including Albino Luciani, had then no choice but to obey the Pope's decision, but it led to a ridiculous situation whereby some priests refused absolution to women who used it, while others turned a blind eye.

Throughout this period, the Vatican continued to benefit from the profits it accrued, derived from one of the many companies it owned – The *Farmacologico Sereno* – whose best-selling product was the oral contraceptive 'Luteolas'.[40]

Albino Luciani continued to live frugally and serve others. When he had become Cardinal and Patriarch of Venice he had taken with him only a small amount of linen, a few sticks of furniture, and his books. Before leaving his own diocese, he had been presented with one million lira, but declined it, saying it should be given to charity. He would later say, smilingly, that 'I came without five lira and I want to leave without five lira.' His frugality and basic common sense, together with his genuine love of the working people, especially in the industrial areas of what he would call 'the other Venice', meant that he tended to be looked down on by the aristocrats whose invitations to cocktail parties and receptions he usually declined, preferring to visit factories and prisons. He was disapproved of when he took a bicycle to the mainland to use during a petrol shortage, and again when he rode on the water bus, instead of travelling in the Patriarch's normal manner in a luxurious boat. Within a short time of taking office in Venice, he made it clear that 'The door of the Patriarch is always open and I will do whatever I can for you.' The result of this was that his office was always crowded with poor people begging for his help. His answer to his secretary's anguished response was 'Somebody will help us,' given with his usual friendly smile.

He was greatly dismayed to learn that the *Banca Cattolica del Veneto*, referred to as 'the priest's bank' and which had often helped him with his charity work, had been taken over by the I.O.R., the *Istituto per le Opere di Religione*, and was no longer prepared to give low interest loans to the clergy, who were told that they would in future have to pay the full interest rate. By mid-1972 the low-interest loans had completely stopped and enquiries showed that the I.O.R. had, since as early as 1946, had a majority share in the *Banca Cattolica del Veneto*. The bank that the clergy had believed was theirs, to use for their charity projects, had been sold over their heads without any reference to them, or to their Patriarch. The man responsible for this was the head of the Vatican Bank, Paul Marcinkus, who had subsequently sold it on to Roberto Calvi of the Banco Ambrosiano in Milan. Had the clergy who relied on the bank had any prior warning, they could perhaps have raised money and bought back their shares in the bank they considered 'theirs'; but Marcinkus had also kept the entire profits from the transaction, fuelling more anger. Knowing that Pope Paul VI had put Marcinkus in charge of the Vatican Bank meant that their hands were tied, although Albino Luciani and his friend the then Secretary of State, Giovanni Benelli, discussed the matter at length. Luciani could only tell his priests the facts, counselling patience. Despite his anger at the illegal movement of shares, along with tax evasion, there was nothing to be done in the face of the Pope's acceptance of the situation.

Pope Paul VI died on 6 August 1978 at his summer residence of Castel Gandolfo, after a reign of fifteen years. He had gone there the previous month to rest, and seemed comfortable and contented. He had many good qualities, but in the minds of his opponents he would always be the man responsible for the Vatican Bank fiasco, and in the minds of the people he would be remembered as the man who refused to allow them to use birth control. Such is the pragmatism of everyday life.

He had, in 1975, issued a set of new rules, which would come into operation at his death. The main one of these was that all the cardinals who were heads of departments would automatically relinquish their offices at the death of the pope who had appointed them. This was intended to give a successor a free hand to appoint advisors. The other main rule was that any cardinal over the age of eighty was banned from voting in a Conclave, or having any chance of becoming pope. This caused a great deal of angry comment. Unfortunately, as he had also reconfirmed his opinions on the anniversary of the publication of *Humanae Vitae* he left behind a poisoned chalice for his successor to deal with, not to mention the ongoing, and increasing, problem of the Vatican Bank.

On 26 August the Conclave began and on the fourth ballot it was already clear which way the vote was going. Cardinal Luciani of Venice was heard to say 'No, please, no!' He was asked 'Do you accept your canonical election as Supreme Pontiff?' After hesitation, he replied 'May God forgive you for what you have done in my regard. Accepto.' It appears that he was overwhelmed by the speed and size of the vote in his favour. He chose to be known as John Paul I.[41] The periodical *Il Mondo* wrote to the new Pope an open letter, asking whether it was morally correct for the Vatican Bank to act as a speculator.

It was not to be the only article of the kind, and Luciani was already well aware of the problem. Cardinal Benelli had explained to him the connection between the Bank, the American Mafia, one million dollars' worth of counterfeit securities and the linchpin of it all, American Archbishop Paul Marcinkus. The new Pope knew that he would have a terrible task ahead of him, attempting to re-establish transparency in the Vatican's tangled financial dealings and in replacing Paul VI's corrupt advisors with a few he hoped he could trust.

He also wanted to try to reverse the appalling injustice perpetrated on Catholic women everywhere by the archaic refusal to allow them control of their lives in limiting the size of their families. He retained his usual good humour and his delightfully open smile, but underneath he was steel. His opponents soon realised that despite his gentle appearance he was a better and far more decisive pope than any they had seen for years.

He immediately received reports of investigations into the Vatican finances and took further details and advice from Cardinals Benelli, Felici, and the deputy Secretary of State Giuseppe Caprio. He then made a number of very difficult decisions, and on 28 September informed his Secretary of State, Cardinal Villot, of his intentions to make a clean sweep,

The men he needed to dismiss had a lot to lose; within hours of that decision being made known, the new Pope was dead, and perhaps the cover-up began.[42] The world was told that he had died of a heart attack, an announcement which astounded his doctor, who knew that he had not only a perfectly healthy heart, but that he was on medication due to his low blood pressure. (Low pressure does not preclude heart attack, but it's certainly less common than for those with high blood pressure.) The various conspiracy theories remain just that – theories. Nevertheless, he was quickly embalmed, before the time allowed by Vatican rules, and his funeral was arranged immediately, to be followed by another Conclave to elect a more amenable pope.

The Amenable Pope: John Paul II and Anna-Teresa Tymieniecka

The man who would be chosen to replace Pope John-Paul I, who had reigned for thirty-three days, was of a far more careful disposition. Before leaving for Rome to attend the Conclave to elect a new pope, he took the sensible precaution of having an ECG examination of his heart done, and even took the print-out to Rome with him, showing that his heart was healthy, so dubious was he about the official heart attack diagnosis on his predecessor.[43]

He was the Cardinal-Archbishop of Krakow, Karol Wojtyla, and he would be elected Pope on 16 October 1978, taking the name of John-Paul II. He was born in May 1920 and would be the first non-Italian pope since Adrian VI in the sixteenth century.

Cardinal Wojtyla was brought up in Wadowice in Poland, where he had many friends, including from within the prospering Jewish community, and in his youth had a Jewish girlfriend named Ginka Beer. During the Second World War he had to leave his place at University when it was closed by the Communist takeover. He had been attending Jagiellonian University where he studied philosophy, literature and languages, an interest he kept up all his life, and by the time he became Pope he spoke nine languages fluently.

He was also interested in plays, both from the writing and acting perspective.

When his university closed, he took various jobs, including working for four years as a manual labourer in a limestone quarry. In 1942 he entered the underground seminary of Cardinal Adam Sapieha, the Archbishop of Krakow, where he helped Jews find refuge from the Nazis. In August 1944 the Warsaw uprising began and the Gestapo began to round up young men in Krakow to prevent similar actions. Wojtyla escaped to the Archbishop's residence where he then stayed. He became a priest at the end of 1946 and was sent to study at the Pontifical University of St Thomas Aquinas in Rome, becoming a Doctor of Sacred Theology in 1954. By 1958 he was Auxiliary Bishop of Krakow at the age of only thirty-five, making him the youngest bishop in Poland.

Meanwhile, Anna-Teresa Tymieniecka, who was to become so important in Wojtyla's life, was living in America. She had been born into an aristocratic Polish-French family, and at the end of the war studied philosophy at the Jagiellonian University in Krakow. After completing her course in two years, she moved to Switzerland to continue her studies and her doctoral study was later published as 'Essence and Existence' in 1957. She obtained her second PhD in French philosophy and literature at the Sorbonne in 1951, then between 1952 and 1953 she did post-doctoral research in Brugge. In 1956 she married Hendrik S. Houthakker, Professor of Economy at Stanford University (1954–60), who went on to teach at Harvard.

In 1973 she began a friendship with Karol Wojtyla while he was Archbishop of Krakow and served as his hostess when he went to New England in 1978; they enjoyed camping trips and skiing together. In 1979 she collaborated with him on the English translation of his book *Person and Act*. Their close friendship was to deepen, and they began a regular correspondence that was to last for over thirty years, as well as having regular meetings and sharing holidays. It was to become a closeness that brightened both their lives, even after the Archbishop became a Cardinal, and finally Pope John Paul II, elected after the untimely death of John Paul I.

There are many documents, now in the National Library of Poland, which reveal the deep affection they had for each other, and the problems this sometimes caused. There are photographs showing them on holiday together, enjoying being able to relax away from official cares. John Paul II was, in the eyes of the faithful, an accessible, decent and willing man, embracing all people. He did, however, return the Vatican to the ideas of the reign of Paul VI, certainly with regard to women, employing the usual double standard that they could not be good enough to be allowed ordination, that they were not moral enough to be allowed full control over their own fertility, and that they were not sensible enough to be other than second-class citizens in a male world. Yet, at the same time, he would bear deep affection for one special woman, who was clearly clever, moral, and sensible.

Their relationship began as a professional association, and her husband was then on friendly terms with Wojtyla. They certainly had to be very careful of the proprieties, as the Communist regime in Poland would have been quick to exploit any relationship with a Cardinal which overstepped the bounds of decency.[44] Their mutual letters were, in fact, often delivered undercover, another indication of how precious the relationship had become and how determined both parties were to keep it intact, despite the difficulties. The mail would be handled by nuns working for Cardinal Wojtyla.

By 1974 he was writing far more freely, from Rome, where he was attending a meeting of bishops. It was a far cry from the apartment he lived in, which he knew was bugged. He also knew that all mail, both private and official, was likely to be intercepted.[45] While in Rome he admitted to Anna-Teresa that he had taken several of her letters with him, so that he could have the pleasure of re-reading them at leisure, because they were so 'meaningful and deeply personal,' even if, he teased her, 'they are written in a philosophical code.' He added, '…there are issues which are too difficult for me to write about.'

Their letters at this time reveal the tensions in the relationship. Anna-Teresa had her family of three children, but although she had that outlet for her emotions, she admitted to him that she loved him. For him, the torture must have been even greater, for he had no other emotional outlet at all. In the summer of 1975, Anna-Teresa was to write 'what can only be described as a love letter'.[46] She 'desired to be in his arms, and to be able to remain there in happiness'. She apologised that she had 'not yet managed to be able to control her feelings'.

Soon after that, the Cardinal gave her his treasured scapular, writing 'It is an answer to the words "I belong to you,"' which Anna-Teresa had written to him. He followed this up with a letter of March 1976 in which he said 'God gave you to me, and made you my vocation.'

He holidayed with her family in Vermont in 1976, swimming, walking and enjoying the countryside. The editor of his letters, Ed Stourton, believes that during this trip she had repeated to Wojtyla that she loved him. He sent her a letter a little while later:

> You write about being torn apart, but I could find no answer to these words... Once, and I remember exactly when and where, I heard the words 'I belong to you' and the gift of the person resonated in them. I was afraid of this gift, but I knew from the beginning that I have to accept it as a gift from Heaven.

Their closeness intensified and he wrote in 1978, 'I think it's good that you sent the letter by hand, as it contains things too deep for the censor's eyes.' They had a camping trip together that year, and a photo of them together, with Wojtyla in a t-shirt and shorts, looking fit and relaxed, shows that they were comfortable and familiar with each other. He would later write, 'The telephone has the advantage that I can hear your voice, but it doesn't last long enough, so it cannot replace a letter, or a real conversation.'

He was elected Pope in 1978, but still wanted to receive from her 'the exchange of ideas which I have always thought to be so creative and fruitful'. There was a break in their correspondence when the Pope's book *Person and Act* was published. They had met many times while doing the translation, but critics said that she had altered the Pope's wording too much, and had adapted them. The Vatican was incensed that the Pope had collaborated with a woman at all on such a project, despite her evident qualifications for the task, and they launched a legal challenge to her work. Anna-Teresa was deeply hurt when Wojtyla did not defend her against her critics and their relationship suffered a break, becoming more distant for some years, characterised merely by the exchange of Christmas and birthday cards, without the intimacy of their earlier correspondence.

They were to be reunited dramatically in 1981, when the Pope was shot on 13 May in St Peter's Square, as he was about to address the pilgrims. He had been attacked by Mehmet Ali Agka, a Turkish gunman, and a member of the militant Fascist group, the Grey Wolves. The Pope was critically injured in the abdomen, with two bullets narrowly missing his mesenteric artery and abdominal aorta. He had to undergo five hours of surgery at the Gemelli Clinic.[47]

Anna-Teresa immediately sent a telegram to his secretary to give to him, saying 'I am overwhelmed by sadness and anxiety, and I want desperately to be close to you. I arrive on Saturday.' On Saturday 16 May Anna-Teresa duly arrived in Rome and went straight to the Gemelli Clinic, staying with him while he recovered from the surgery. She was one of the very few people allowed access to him at that time.

The Pope attributed his recovery to Our Lady of Fatima, for whom he had special reverence, and like many others attributed the attack on his life to the Third Secret of Fatima, which had predicted attacks on the pope and church. He was visiting Fatima to give thanks for his life being spared in the following year when another attempt was made on his life by a man who tried to stab him with a bayonet. The Pope was injured during that attempt, but tried to hide the non-life-threatening wound at the time. The assailant on that occasion was a Spanish traditionalist Catholic priest and lawyer, Juan María Fernández y Kron, who claimed to know that the Pope was an agent of Communist Moscow. This man was later treated for a mental illness.

There was a further Al-Queda-funded plot against the Pope's life during a visit to the Philippines for World Youth Day in January 1995, when a suicide bomber had planned to dress as a priest and detonate a bomb as the Pope passed by on his way to the San Carlos Seminary in Makati City. That particular plot was foiled in time, and all the parties involved in it were arrested.

During his Pontificate, John Paul II became a worldwide traveller, and also became famous for his 'Apologies' towards people who had suffered at the hands of the church, ranging from the burning of 'heretics' centuries before, to the slave trade, the silence of so many Catholics during the Holocaust against the Jews, and the sexual abuse cases which had darkened the church's reputation. Clerical sexual offenders had been routinely transferred to another area, with the likelihood of offending again, rather than being handed over to the secular authorities, in an effort to contain the problem and prevent public scandal.

The Pope would also write an open letter to 'every woman' to apologise for the injustices they had suffered at the hands of the Church, and the violation of women's rights regarding the lack of adequate contraception.[48] This offended those people who had been affected by the AIDS epidemic, when the Vatican had instituted a programme of 'Dying with Dignity' which seemed oblivious to the fact that, had condoms been allowed to be used and easily available, particularly in Third-World countries, many of the victims need not have died at all.

Throughout these years, John Paul II and Anna-Teresa continued to correspond and to see each other whenever it was possible. The Pope developed Parkinson's Disease when he was in his seventies, and Anna-Teresa often visited him in his private quarters at the Vatican. He regularly invited her to dinner there and, when apart from him, she sent him photographs and pressed flowers from her garden. He continued to write her affectionate letters: 'I am thinking of you, and in my thoughts I come to Pomfret (her home) every day.' In 2002 he made his final visit to Poland, and wrote to her of 'our mutual homeland, so many places where we have met, where we had conversations which were so important to us, and where we experienced the beauty of God's presence'.

His health grew worse over the following three years, and at the end of March 2005 he became ill with a urinary tract infection. Anna-Teresa paid him what would be her last visit. She sat with him at his bedside, and stayed beside him, giving him the final comfort of being with someone who had always cared deeply for him. He then developed septic shock, dying the day after her visit, on 2 April 2005.[49]

The pair had exchanged letters of deeply personal significance for over thirty years and visited each other, sharing many holidays together when younger. Anna-Teresa was interviewed by Carl Bernstein, the investigative journalist, and by the Vatican expert Marco Politi, who then dedicated twenty pages to her relationship with Pope John Paul II in their biography *His Holiness*, this being the first official acknowledgement of the importance of her presence in his life.[50]

Pope John Paul II had been a charismatic man, a man of great humour and temper, a man of great education and also naivety, of conviction and stubbornness. Like most other people, he was not all his public believed him to be. Despite visits to the US he never really understood Western democracy, considering that most of western society was entirely devoid of morality. He did not consider that Communism could be defeated, describing it in meetings with Anna-Teresa as 'impregnable'. He never fully realised the power of western opposition to Communism so in some ways he was, as Anna-Teresa described him, 'full of wisdom, yet entirely dismissive of the west, and ignorant of the benefits of either capitalism or democracy, considering them shallow'.

Despite his much-vaunted respect of women in general, and his obvious and long-lasting affection for one woman in particular, he stoutly refused to give them what John Paul I had wanted to give them, which was the freedom to enjoy their own sexuality without the threat of continual pregnancies. Thousands of good Catholics, still loyal to the church, cried out for reforms, for birth control to be allowed, for a church of the poor, and a sweeping reform of the Vatican Bank, so that the church they believed in could appear to the world to be open and honest, as John Paul I had wanted. But John Paul II gave them none of these things, allowing the old abuses to continue.

Anna-Teresa's relationship with him might have been an opportunity for him to see another kind of life, that of a woman of Polish birth and good education, who had thrived within western democracy, enjoying the privileges and freedoms it gave her. Unfortunately, despite all these advantages, she did not appear to have influenced him in favour of similar advantages for all women. Therefore his Pontificate which could, and perhaps should, have been a step forward, bringing to fruition the reforms that John Paul I had hoped for, had become instead merely a waiting time with no real advances or changes to ease the lives of ordinary Catholics.

It was a long reign, and in many ways a good one, but it could have been better and a beacon of light for future generations, who could have carried the church into the twenty-first century with strength and determination, but by 'playing it safe' John Paul II seems to have wasted the opportunity.

Anna-Teresa Tymieniecka survived Karol Wojtyla, Pope John Paul II, by eight years, dying on 7 June 2014.

10

Conclusion

Once the greatest of all Pagan cities, Rome became the centre of Christendom, and when the Aurelian walls were built in the third century AD they were Rome's final defence.

After Rome's collapse, the sacking of the city went on endlessly, but it was the Romans themselves who dismantled and destroyed the ancient city more than any invaders. They did it for the marble they found there, in the statues, the fountains and all the remaining buildings of irreplaceable beauty and history, which was to be burnt to produce lime.

Rome became a city of limekilns, even as it became a city of Christianity. The new religion was literally eating up the older ones, destroying the temples, the columns, the elegant market places and the official and administrative centres, ruining the aqueducts which fed the life-sustaining water, and reducing the glory of Rome to a rubbish heap.[1]

There had always been corruption, whether political, administrative, or military, from the earliest times, and that would continue, except that the new corruption would not be in the name of Empire, but in the name of God. Men would fight for the power as they had always done, and the bad popes would outnumber the good, vying not for love of God, but for the riches, influence, authority and all the amusements and treasures that the world offered, along with the illusory security and happiness they brought with them.

There are many histories of the popes, and some of them approach the holders of the Supreme Office with such awe and reverence that it would be easy to imagine that all the Holy Fathers were indeed holy; that they were all dedicated to prayer and the attempt to bring the lives of others in tune with the chorus of Heaven.

Other historians treat the papal biographies as largely fabrications, searching for sin, and only too often finding it, whether real or imaginary. The truth is somewhere in between, but to the reader or the researcher it often seems there is no *via media*. A man will be described in one biography as being practically a saint, another will describe him as a devil out of Hell, with the smell of brimstone still on him.

There is no doubt that many of the popes, from the earliest beginnings until beyond the Renaissance, treated the position they held as a free ticket to do exactly as they liked. Power corrupts in the Vatican, as everywhere else, and men use it to enforce their personal opinions and preferences on others. One pope hated cats (Innocent VIII), declaring them to be the idols of witches, resulting in the deaths of many innocent women whose sole companions the innocent creatures were.[2]

Several popes indulged in sex rather more than could be considered appropriate to their calling, such as Pius II (Enea Piccolomini 1458–1464) and Alexander VI (Rodrigo Borgia 1492–1503) who seduced women as a way of life. Others preferred the affections of men, including Boniface VI (Bonifacio 896–896), Paul II (Pietro Barbo 1464–1471), and, allegedly, Paul VI (Giovanni Montini 1963–1978). In the case of Boniface VI, scandal was his constant companion, as he had been defrocked twice for immorality even before becoming Pope![3]

Many popes used their power over other rulers in order to instigate wars, rather than promote peace, such as Innocent III (Lotario 1198–1216) who created a crusade against the Cathars, or encouraged others to bloodshed, such as John VIII (Giovanni 872–882) who prided himself on being known as a 'warrior' pope, and founded the Papal Navy. Clement V (Bertrand de Got 1305–114) went so far as to destroy the Knights Templar, culminating in the perfidy of Alexander II (Anselmo di Baggio 1061–1073) who encouraged the Norman Invasion of England, then denied his involvement. However, his active participation and interference helped to impose a feudal system on a free and viable country, reducing its people to virtual slavery.[4]

Many other popes, less enticed by the thrills of battle (at one remove), preferred the other basic excitement, that of amassing money. Pope Boniface VIII (Benedetto Caetani 1294–1303) instituted the idea of the Holy Year, which is still celebrated. But it was less for holiness than for the huge sums of money taken into the city by pilgrims. Dante was to place Boniface in the Eighth Circle of Hell in his 'Inferno' for the crime of simony, and a fifteenth-century manuscript in the British Library shows him, and other simoniac popes, buried head down, with their legs and feet in the air, and their souls on fire.[5]

For many men, the power itself was the draw and was worth not only bribery to achieve, but even murder. Common-or-garden fisticuffs could be the order of the day, if one man objected to seeing another elected to the position he coveted and considered his by right.

There was pandemonium in 1124, when Theobaldo Boccapecci was elected as Celestine II. Although he had been chosen unanimously, the decision displeased the powerful Frangipani family, who broke in at swordpoint, forcing the papal vestments onto their own candidate, Lamberto Scannabecchi, who was then declared to be Pope Honorius II. He started a six-year reign and the correctly elected Celestine was forced out.[6]

A similar situation occurred in 1159 when thirty cardinals elected Roland of Siena as Pope Alexander III. One of the few who had disagreed, Cardinal Ottavian, was of the influential Crescenti family, and declared that he was the new pope, calling himself Victor IV. He snatched the robe from Pope Alexander, attempting to put it on over his own head (apparently back to front), in a scuffle that was described at the time as 'scarcely believable confusion'. As described earlier, Victor claimed he had been 'elected by acclamation', a technicality which over rides the voting process. Both the warring popes then spent periods of time in exile, and one of these found Pope Victor living at Lucca, where he was successfully supporting himself as a brigand. They carried on their arguments for so long that the pragmatic Romans grew tired of them because of the detrimental effect on the pilgrim-tourist trade, and finally the original Pope Alexander continued his reign in relative peace.[7]

With all the problems, and so little holiness evident, it is not so surprising to find that between AD 64, when St Peter is reputed to have been executed, and AD 999 when Gregory V was murdered, there were no less than fourteen popes who were assassinated in one gruesome way or another. There were also eleven popes who were reputed to have been murdered. In general, assassination attempts have not been uncommon, with the most recent ones involving Pope John-Paul II taking place firstly in May 1981 (when he was shot in Rome), secondly when he was attacked in Portugal by a man wielding a bayonet in May 1982, and a terrorist attempt in 1995, which was foiled in time by the authorities.[8] There had previously been an attack on Pope Paul VI in the Philippines on 27 November 1970, when a Bolivian artist attempted to stab the Pope with a knife at the airport.

There has been schism in the church, with popes in the eleventh and twelfth centuries being elected and dethroned again with dizzying speed. One of these was Benedict VIII, (Theophylactus 1012–1024), a layman when he became Pope, and immediately famous for being tonsured, ordained, and enthroned all on the same day. So were two of his successors, who were his brother and nephew. Technically, any baptised male may be elected pope, but these days the Pontiff tends to be chosen from within the College of Cardinals.[9]

Benedict IX was another layman when he became Pope in 1032, and his private life was to cause scandals and rioting. He would be replaced in January 1045, but by March 1045 he was back again, although his grip on power was weak, and he abdicated in May of the same year in favour of his godfather who then reigned for a year. In 1047 Benedict returned for a third time, and lasted another year before again being ejected in July 1048. Though he had become notorious for 'rapes, orgies, and other unspeakable acts... a routine of sodomy and bestiality', after he finally left in 1048 he got married![10]

After the death of Nicholas IV (Girolamo Masci) in 1292, the papacy was vacant for two years, as the candidates were equally divided between the opposing Orsini and Colonna families, while a brief civil war flared up in Rome.

Clement V became Pope in 1305 and became known for the most unedifying period of all, when successive popes left Rome altogether to live at Avignon – the 'Great Schism'. Other popes established themselves at Orvieto just outside Rome at the same time, claiming the legitimacy of their own rule, which resulted in the farcical situation of having two popes at once, with division as to which were 'real' and which were 'antipopes'. Clement made five of his family into cardinals (in a foretaste of the later Renaissance habit), complete with substantial grants of money to fund luxurious lifestyles, so that the financial problems started again. The old bugbear, the immense temptation of money, would resurface again and again until culminating in the banking scandals of the 1970s.[11]

On the face of it, the nineteenth century appeared more circumspect, giving the world Pope Pius IX (Giovanni Maria Mastai-Ferretti who died in 1878) who was to become the then longest serving pope with a reign of over thirty years. Towards the end of his life, in 1870, he promulgated the Dogma of Infallibility. Though this was only intended to be in respect of papal decisions on religion, it caused the Pope to be described by one observer as 'warm of heart, weak of head, and utterly lacking in any common sense'.

In the light of the onslaught of new scientific and archaelogical discoveries, the church began to equip its own scholars with the ability to confound their adversaries. Thus began the 'Catholic Modernist' movement. This was to come to an abrupt end when it was realised that one of the most prestigious Modernist scholars was encouraging his followers to openly question church dogma. Known as the 'Father of Catholic Modernism', Alfred Loisy (1857–1940) observed that 'Jesus came preaching the Kingdom, and what arrived was the church!' He would further argue that many points of doctrine could not be regarded as immutable truths, 'such as the virgin birth and the divinity of Jesus' and said that these tenets were 'no longer tenable'. By 1902, just before the death of Pope Leo XIII, the Pontifical Bibilical Commission was created to monitor Catholic scholarship and in 1904, the new Pope, Pius X, put Loisy's work on the List of Forbidden Books, and all modernist teachers were dismissed from their posts, as the new thinking was no longer to be tolerated, let alone encouraged.[12]

Of course, alongside all the political and financial scandals, and the struggle for power, winding its tentacles into the very core of the Vatican, was the perennial problem of women.[13] All kinds of women inhabit Rome and always have, ranging from respectable wives and mothers, sisters and religious sisters, to disreputable females of all kinds. The pope's city cannot be immune to the invasion of femininity. It is important to remember the fact that in the early church priests were allowed to marry. The Second Lateran Council in 1139 promulgated the rule of celibacy for the priesthood and the Council of Trent in 156 reaffirmed the church's stance on the subject. Even now, the issue of celibacy is considered to be a 'discipline' rather than a point of doctrine.

For generations, however, the church has been obliged to turn a blind eye to close associations with women, though many attempts have been made to claim that such relationships are purely platonic – and to be fair, some may well have been. But natural affection between the sexes springs up, very often whether the parties concerned actually intend to become involved or not, and there are many cases of these close relationships lasting for many years, bringing comfort and support to both sides.

This is not to attempt to equate an innocent friendship with the excesses of some of the pontiffs, who in the past gloried in parading their women and provided lavishly for their bastards, particularly in granting church offices and benefices to illegitimate sons, sometimes at ridiculously young ages. (These were said to intend to allow for the support and education of the child, in line with a future career in the Church.) Daughters were also useful, in particular during the Renaissance, when illegitimacy was no bar to a girl making a high-status marriage which brought her new in-laws into the pope's circle, to their mutual benefit.[14]

Some popes had female relatives who became enormously powerful in their own right, for example Felice della Rovere, the daughter of Julius II; Olimpia Maidalchini Pamphilj the sister-in-law of Innocent X and the supreme example of female achievement Catherine de' Medici, the niece of Clement VII, who became the all-powerful Queen Regent of France.[15]

As well as these well-known women, there were many others involved with the Vatican and with the popes who offered comfort and basic companionship of one kind or another, to men whose lives would otherwise have been bereft of any normal affection owing to their unique position; it has truthfully been said that the position of pope can be the loneliest job there is. Many men live well enough without women, but others cannot. They need the presence of females as an adjunct of their own lives and heavy responsibilities, whether this means loving mothers and sisters, or mistresses and daughters, who can provide the balm of femininity and the benefit of a different perspective.

Likewise, many men find that, despite taking vows, they cannot live happily without some form of sex and their subsequent affairs (whether with male or female) become a necessary, if secret, part of their lives. Certainly, for Renaissance popes, it was a belief in the trustworthiness of the family one already had, or could produce, that won out over the supposed sanctity of the vows they had taken and created the nepotism that popes often became famous for. Although trying to establish a support network and powerbase drawn from blood relatives was repeatedly shown to be a fallacy, and those people raised to power often proved themselves to be neither trustworthy nor capable, it was still considered to be slightly less dangerous than putting one's trust in outsiders one had been obliged to bribe.[16]

The church had always had an ambivalent attitude towards sex, even among the laity. It was seen as a necessary evil for the procreation of children, and therefore a given that most people would need to marry, but there was also the problem of fornication, which marriage was supposed to solve. It was never considered an ideal, and celibacy, for those people who could manage it, was far preferable.

Augustine, like many of the church fathers, felt that the very act of intercourse was disgusting. Arnobius called it 'filthy and degrading' and in the Garden of Eden humans were supposed to have controlled their impulses, experiencing uncontrollable lust for each other only when they 'fell into sin'. It was this feared impulse that could not be understood or approved of, ignoring it as a natural requirement for the propagation of the species. Naturally, women were blamed for tempting men, even holy priests. Women were considered intemperate creatures, always ready to indulge in sex with just about anyone, forever leading men on, and this was a very useful card for the man to play when he did something he should not, and then regretted the outcome. He could always say, as Adam did, 'the woman tempted me' and be sure of being understood.[17]

It was this atmosphere that allowed only marital sex, considering every other relationship to be sinful, particularly if some attempt at contraception was made. It was even considered to be sinful if one lusted after one's wife – 'If the man would want that woman, even if she were not his wife' – reducing the most honest human desire into nothing more than a duty for both parties. The use of contraception was even worse – was that another reason why churchmen had families, because they feared to compound their error in something even more sinful than the act itself? A penitential of the ninth century seems to indicate that an act of abortion, before the fortieth day of conception, (when the conceived child was considered to have acquired a human soul), was marginally less sinful than having used some form of contraception in the first place. The whole question was confused and the best course seemed to be simply to obey your priest and resist all forms of temptation.[18]

Sexual purity had always neutralised all other sins, so that a mean-minded and spiteful woman, or a cruel and vengeful man, could still be considered righteous, provided they were sexually pure. The 'tart with a heart' was still a whore, however kind or charming she may otherwise have been. The result of this attempted control over natural impulses was the rise of guilt, upon which the church fed. It is a supreme irony that the peasant, fancying a woman in his local village, was known to be sinful and shameful, yet the pope himself could – and often did – not only keep mistresses but advanced in every way the results of his affairs, even allowing women of his choice to have wealth and power far beyond the norm, purely on the basis of their relationship.[19]

That many of the women considered here were also intelligent and independent of mind shows that, unfortunately for them, they still needed a man's agreement and encouragement to achieve what they did. Except for a very few examples, women were still meant to be subservient creatures, useful for procreation or even pleasure, but not expected to be able to do much without the guidance of a man.

Even Caterina Sforza, surely a prime example of a woman able to command, first had to be led, being married to a man of her father's choosing at a frighteningly young age. She made the best of it, and it was only later, when she was able to choose her course for herself, that she found herself at odds not only with the feminine ideal of womanhood but with the pope. She had been expected to acquiesce, and her laudable attempts to protect herself and her children put her outside the mould of what was acceptable. This, in turn, left her exposed to abuse by men, particularly the 'control' rapes of Cesare Borgia.[20]

Cesare's own sister, Lucrezia, was a far more traditional female. Despite being the daughter of the pope, she was still subject to her men, marrying husbands chosen for her, bearing their children, and later in life performing good works as Duchess of Ferrara.[21] Her treatment at the Pope's hands was different from that of his mistress Giulia Farnese. Lucrezia was married off to whoever her father chose for her, but she accepted his choices, and consequently was loved and protected by him. La Bella Giulia, though in some ways beloved, was still a woman trying to make her own way, and she would find that her influence over the Pope had its limits and his attentions towards her were not exclusive.

Into modern times there have been obvious changes, and popes no longer create open scandals with their bastards, or enrich the families of their lovers. However, things still happened that the average person remained unaware of until much later and being given edited details, after the event, often increases speculation rather than dampening it.[22]

The sudden death of Pope John-Paul I, after such a short a reign fuelled conspiracy theories and these continue despite denials. John-Paul (Albino Luciani) was a reluctant pope. During the Conclave, when others told him he would make an excellent 'pastoral' pope due to his warm nature, he declared that if offered the pontificate, he would refuse it.

Pope Paul VI died at Castel Gandolfo in August of 1978 leaving behind scandals of his own. The main problem was the appalling mismanagement of the I.O.R. (Vatican Bank) he had founded, but he was also rumoured to have been involved with the Italian television and film actor Paolo Carlini, and the newspaper *La Repubblica* had openly declared that he had been blackmailed because of his affair, resulting in the appointment of many other homosexual men to Vatican jobs. One article publicly referred to 'his husband Paolo Carlini'. The Conclave following his death was held after twenty days (the limit is twenty-one days). In one day it had elected Cardinal Luciani, the Patriarch of Venice. Despite his reservations, when chosen he felt obligated to accept, and as he had not previously been considered *papabile*, his rise was all the more surprising.[23] He is reported as saying 'May God forgive you for what you have done.'

It has been suggested that he was chosen as a 'malleable' pope, likely to concentrate on his pastoral role and not rock any boats. However, he made it clear that he intended not only to 'promote dialogue' to revise canon law and work towards unity, but that he held many very strong views on matters such as divorce, contraception and women's issues. He was a man of great warmth and kindness, eager to please and to befriend, but he had always been most eager to help the poor, and had witnessed the struggle of his brother Eduardo, attempting to support his wife and ten children in poverty. He had already written a paper on the advisability of allowing contraception to Catholic families. He was immediately perceived as being dangerous, and was isolated in the Vatican (which he never left from his election to his death) where the sisters Vincenza and Margherita, who cared for him, saw him as a lonely figure, and often spoke Venetian dialect with him to make him feel more at home.

He was keen to humanise the papacy, to face modern problems, but found that his most pressing and difficult one was the I.O.R. Officials were notoriously secretive, even devious, about the way this worked. These officials had frequently taken key decisions without the knowledge or approval of the then pope, resulting in disgraceful financial scandals. It had originally been set up to help religious foundations dispense much needed funds throughout the world, but under the directorship of Archbishop Marcinkus had become embroiled with criminals and the Mafia.

Archbishop Marcinkus was questioned in April 1973 about his involvement in the delivery of US$14.5m worth of counterfeit bonds to the Vatican in 1971. These were part of a total intended consignment of $950m, as was stated in a letter written on Vatican headed notepaper. He was questioned by the Organised Crime and Racketeering Section of the US Department of Justice about his unsavoury contacts in Chicago. He was also deeply involved with the Chairman of the Banco Ambrosiano Chairman, Roberto Calvi, and with Michele Sindona, who also had Mafia links. Illicit money was being laundered through the Vatican Bank and, after being manipulated into a huge fraud, Roberto Calvi fled to London, where he was found hanging under Blackfriars Bridge in 1982 with his pockets full of stones, along with $15,000 in cash.

Pope John-Paul I was certainly not connected to these crimes, and was determined to expose them but the realisation of their scale, and the length of time they had been going on, caused him great stress. This either contributed to the heart attack he allegedly died of, or perhaps led to his death by other means, once it became clear to the perpetrators that full exposure was his avowed intention. His demands for honesty and transparency in Vatican finances caused great consternation to those to whom such concepts were anathema.[24] The whispering campaign had started immediately after John-Paul I's election, when one Vatican official remarked 'They have elected Peter Sellers,' referring to the famous comedy actor.

John-Paul I had faced the challenge ahead of him with courage, but his sudden and inexplicable death prevented the implementation of the reforms he had intended. When found dead in his bed by Sister Vincenza the timing of his death was suspect, and she reported officially that at 5.15 am 'he was already cold, and his fingernails were strangely dark.'[25] After his sudden death, all his controversial opinions were airbrushed away, and it was declared that he had been happy to follow the Vatican's 'official' line on all the subjects which had been of most concern to him.

Josef Ratzinger, who became Pope Benedict XVI in 2005, resigned his position in 2013 citing ill health, but he had acquired immense power during the reign of his predecessor John-Paul II (Karol Wojtyla), when that Pope developed Parkinson's Disease. There was some suggestion that John Paul II had been euthanised to prevent further suffering (the considered opinion of Dr Lina Paverelli), in direct contravention of the Vatican stance on the matter. Ratzinger's claim to ill health as a reason for his abdication was widely disbelieved, (he is still at the time of writing going strong in the Casa Santa Marta, where he lives alongside Pope

Francis), but he had been criticised widely for the way he had dealt (or not dealt) with the issue of paedophile priests, plus suggestions of further financial scandals ahead.[26]

The present Pope Francis (Jorge Mario Bergoglio), elected in 2013, led the Argentine church during the December riots of 2001. He is concerned with humility, the fate of the poor, and is personally lacking in ostentation. He declined the use of the magnificent papal apartments and also lives at the Casa Santa Marta, within the Vatican precinct.

He had already faced criticism from theological conservatives on the questions of divorce and sexual abuse by the clergy. He openly described the papal court as 'narcissistic and self-referential', as 'the leprosy of the papacy'. Dominated as it still is by the same infighting cliques that have always marred its peace, along with ever-present financial upsets, it is not the ideal place for any reformer, however mild.[27] It is indisputable that Ratzinger's resignation made the papacy more vulnerable, as having two living popes is nearly as bad as the schism of the old days. If Pope Francis should decide to abdicate (as some authorities suggest) the papacy might be faced with having three popes living at the same time, which begins to take on an aspect of farce. Many writers prefer to concentrate on the question of whether Pope Francis can succeed where others have failed.[28]

To return to the female aspect, we need to look back on Pope John-Paul II (Karol Wojtyla 1978–2005). He was the first non-Italian pope for 450 years and an inspirational figure. He was a popular and well-travelled Pope, yet he, too, had his secret, or not so secret, relationship. Anna-Teresa Tymieniecka was a close personal friend for thirty-two years and a treasured companion of his many adventurous holidays. Their obvious affection for, and devotion towards, each other appeared to benefit them both, confirming that even a pope may need some emotional support; not merely the deferential service of the nuns who wait on him, but a definite, close and personal bond between male and female.

Anna-Teresa's friendship with Karol Wojtyla began in 1973, and in 2008 her archive of their personal correspondence was sold to the National Library in Poland. This included over 350 letters and notes written by him to her over three decades. The only break in their relationship was due to the book they wrote together, when the Vatican wished to write out her part in its production. Wojtyla did not defend her position at that time, perhaps feeling it was still too early for him to insist on protecting a female friend, but his lack of defence of her work caused a breach between them. She said later 'My friend Wojtyla, the Cardinal, now the Pope, has betrayed me.'[29] Their estrangement was ended when he was shot in 1981 and she dropped everything to hurry to be close to him. Though there is no evidence that he broke his vows, it is certain that he cherished the close relationship with her and had no intention of ending it.[30] Eamon Duffy, Emeritus Professor of the History of Christianity at Cambridge said, 'It is not surprising that he should invest this, one of the most important relationships of his life, with that kind of significance.'

The history of the popes and the women (and sometimes men) with whom they shared their private lives, is a fascinating one. Not all the relationships were either lasting or happy, but many were and were only ended by death. They range from devotion and mutual admiration to irritation and exasperation, but all show in their own way that whatever the obstacles in the way, whatever the prejudice against such 'occasions of sin', men and women have a real need of each other; not merely for sex, though it has its place, but for the comfort of shared interests in a special companionship, and that they will continue to flout 'acceptable' behaviour patterns to fulfil that need. If that need to feel special to another person is not satisfied, it can be expended in other ways, becoming promiscuity or even cruelty, greed for money or power, or sheer selfishness.

When it is satisfied, often in contravention of accepted mores, then it can produce feelings of guilt, despair, wrong-doing, and fear that people will not fully understand the need that drove, which is, after all, the most basic human need. The church's insistence on separation of the sexes over the centuries created an atmosphere of sin which pervaded even the most innocent and praiseworthy relationships and prevented people from interacting together without false modesty. It deprived many of the company of others with similar interests, replacing the natural balance and warmth with embarrassment and shame.

Humans are naturally social creatures, who often live unhappy and deprived lives if alone. Healthier and happier if not isolated, they are not designed for too much solitude, which breeds introspection, nor are they intended to smother every natural emotion under a cloak of indifference. We are meant to support each other, and humans who have to live without close contacts become less human than they ought to be, and often more judgemental and severe, less understanding of and sympathetic to the struggles of others.

We now have a generally more civilised approach to religion, more of a nod towards public condemnation of obvious lapses and scandalous private lives, but there is still a continued secrecy at the Vatican, a refusal to listen to the voices of people who are living in a changing world. There is also no voice at all for the still disenfranchised female half of the world's population, unless they fulfil the traditional roles of mother, sister, nuns, servants or whores, and whose needs are often brushed under the carpet in the hope that somebody else, sometime, may deal with them.

John-Paul I wanted open discussion on such issues, but his lone voice was immediately stilled, even at a time when the church was taking the profits of the manufacture of the contraceptive pill, while denying it to the faithful. The church loses members daily due to these matters not being addressed and its inability to see the need and to give help to the truly vulnerable, losses which cannot easily be replaced. As each generation becomes more distant, the church risks becoming less of a leading religious force and more of a tourist attraction, interesting and photogenic, but increasingly separate from real life.

The question 'Is there anything new?' after careful consideration, has regretfully to be answered with 'Perhaps not as much as there should be.'

A Note On Medieval Coinage

SCUDO/SCUDI

This was a silver coin used in Italy and Sicily, and its name derived from the Latin for 'shield'. From the sixteenth century the name referred to large silver coins, varying slightly in size and value, depending on the country of issue. These were usually worth approximately four shillings sterling.

DUCAT/DUCATI

This was a gold or silver coin, which continued in use from the late Middle Ages to the early twentieth century. There were different types, each with a different metallic content and different value. The Great Council of Venice (which previously used Byzantine gold coins) began to issue their own coinage in 1284, but even as early as 1252 the gold florins of Florence and Genoa had already become standard. In the fifteenth century the value of the ducat, in terms of silver money, was stable at 124 Venetian soldi.

In the sixteenth century the price of gold increased, and the coin became known as the ducat di zecca (ducat of the mint). This name was later shortened to zecchino, which was the origin of the word 'sequin'. Sequins were originally a small gold coin, sometimes sewn onto clothing. The Venetian ducat had 3.545 grams of 99.47% pure gold, which was the highest purity that the medieval metallurgists could produce. In 1913 the gold ducat was worth nine shillings and four pence sterling. The silver ducat was then worth approximately half that value.

One ducat was made up of six or seven lira and each of these was in turn made up of twenty soldi. In the fifteenth century a labourer would be lucky to earn one ducat a year.

(From the *Oxford Encyclopaedia of Economic History*.)

Notes

Chapter 1
1. 'Chronicle of the Popes' by P.G. Maxwell-Stuart
2. 'Catholic Encyclopaedia' Vol 11. (Saints of 31 May)
3. 'Storia degli Scavidi Roma' (Vol 1) by Roberto Lancia, taken from Roberto Weiss in 'The Renaissance Discovery of Classical Antiquity'
4. 'Martyrologium Hieronymianum' (The Martyrology of St Jerome) by De Rossi and Duschene
5. 'The Gnostic Gospels' edited by Alan Jacobs
6. 'Holy Blood and Holy Grail' by Baigent, Leigh and Lincoln. Also 'Jesus the Man' by Barbara Theiling.
7. 'The Gnostic Gospels'
8. 'Sex Lives of the Popes' by Nigel Cawthorne
9. 'Roman Women' by J.P.V.D. Balsden
10. 'Emperors of Rome' by David Potter
11. 'Vita Claudii' from The Twelve Caesars by Suetonius.
12. 'From the Gracchi to Nero – a History of Rome 133 BC to 68 AD' by H.H. Scullard
13. 'Saints and Sinners' by Eamon Duffy
14. Ibid
15. Article by Nick Squires in the *Daily Telegraph* of 11 September 2017.
16. Lucius Caecilius Firmianus Lactantius was an early Christian author who died in Gaul in AD 320
17. Quintus Septimus Florens Tertullianus was a Christian theologian who was born in either 155 or 160 in Carthage
18. 'Temples of the Last Pharoahs' by Arnold Dieter
19. 'Saints and Sinners'
20. 'Chronicle of the Popes' – Pope Fabian was a formidable man but the Decian persecutions were equally determined. Although Fabian ruled for fourteen years he was one of the first to die, having refused to offer to the Roman gods. Many Christians were put to work in the quarries and a few were beheaded, though very few of them actually suffered in the arena.

So far as is known, and contrary to popular opinion, the Colosseum was not generally used as a place of martyrdom for religious dissidents.

21. 'Chronicle of the Popes'. It was more usual at that time to perform an immediate beheading, rather than have the victim wait for a 'show' execution.

22. 'Chronicle of the Popes'. As Damasus was already in his sixties when he became Pope, it may have been true that he used his famous charm to convert women, rather than to seduce. However, many men of similar age were perfectly capable of charming the ladies for other reasons.

23. 'History of the Popes' by Michael Walsh. The vow of celibacy for widows was continued throughout the medieval period. It prevented an otherwise eligible widow from being pressured into remarriage against her will.

24. Ammianus Marcellinus (330–400) was a soldier and historian who wrote the 'Ges Restae' which chronicled the history of Rome from the Emperor Nerva to the death of Valens in 378. His surviving work covers the period of 353 to 378, though much of it is unfortunately now lost.

25. 'The secret history of the court of Justinian' by Procopius

26. 'The life and times of Theodora' by Carlo Maria Franzero

27. 'Chronicle of the Popes'

28. The 'Universi Dominici Gregis', which means 'The Lord's whole flock', is now specifically designed to disallow both papal election by compromise or by proclamation. Therefore the secret ballot is now the only valid method of electing a pope. (Issued by John Paul II in 1996.) However, originally, the Universi Dominici Gregis did allow for a pope to be elected by a simple majority, if the usual requirement of a two-thirds 'super' majority could not be reached, after thirty-four ballots had already been completed. On 1 June 2007 Pope Benedict XVI issued a 'moto proprio' which now requires a two-thirds majority, regardless of the number of ballots needed to elect a pope. 'Moto Proprio' is Latin for 'on his own impulse' and refers to an official act taken without any formal request having been made by any other party. In Catholic canon law, it means a document issued by the pope, on his own initiative, which is personally signed by him.

29. 'The Cathars' by Sean Martin

30. 'The Inquisition, the hammer of heresy, a history and legacy of the Holy Office' by Edward Burman.

31. Benedetto Caetoni was Pope from the end of 1294 to his death in 1303.

32. 'The Templars' by Piers Paul Read

Chapter 2

1. 'Journal of a Soul,' the autobiography of Pope John XXIII

2. 'City of God' (De Civitate Dei) by St Augustine of Hippo. (VIII/S)

3. 'The origins of clerical celibacy in the Western church' by Charles A. Frazee

4. 'Sex Lives of the Popes' by Nigel Cawthorne

5. 'Galla Placidia – the last Roman Empress' by Hagith Sivan from 'Women in Antiquity'

6. 'The Myth of Pope Joan' by Alain Boureau

7. 'Chronicle of the Popes'

8. Ibid
9. 'Mistresses, a history of the Other Woman' by Elizabeth Abbott
10. 'The Popes – a history' by John Julius Norwich
11. 'Sex Lives of the Popes'
12. Cardinal Cesare Baronius (1538-1607) was author of the 'Annales Ecclesiastici' or Ecclesiastical Annals, in 12 volumes written from 1588 to 1607. He was Cardinal Priest of Santi-Nereo e Achillio and was also librarian of the Vatican Library. He was awarded the title of 'Venerable' by Pope Benedict XIV.
13. Liudprant of Cremona (958-962) was a bishop, an historian and a diplomat. He was the writer of the 'Antapodosis Seu Rerumper Europam Gestaerum Libri VI' which was an historical narrative relating to events from 887 to 949.
14. 'Mistresses, a history of the Other Woman'
15. 'Chronicle of the Popes'
16. 'Torture' by Edward Peters
17. 'Chronicle of the Popes'
18. The Castel Sant'Angelo was to become a place of refuge for the popes for centuries to come. The Pasetto di Borgo, which is a defensible passageway, now connects the Vatican to Sant'Angelo and this escape route was first created by Pope Nicholas III who reigned from 1277–1280.
19. 'Sex Lives of the Popes'
20. Ibid
21. Ibid
22. Cardinal Cesare Baronius

Chapter 3

1. 'Joanna, the notorious Queen of Naples, Jerusalem and Sicily' by Nancy Goldstone
2. 'Four Queens – the Provencal Sisters who ruled Europe' by Nancy Goldstone
3. 'Robert the Wise and his heirs (1278–1352)' by St Clair Baddeley
4. 'The story of Naples' by Cecil Headlam
5. 'Joanna, the notorious Queen of Naples...'
6. 'Queen Sancia of Naples' by Ronald G. Musto in 'Women of the Medieval World'
7. 'Joanna, the notorious Queen of Naples...'
8. 'The Fates of Illustrious Men' by Giovanni Boccaccio. Translated by L.B. Hall
9. Ibid
10. 'Joanna, the Notorious Queen of Naples...'
11. Ibid
12. 'Robert the Wise and his heirs'
13. Ibid
14. Ibid
15. 'Queens and queenship in medieval Europe', edited by Anne Duggan
16. The 1340s saw the crash of the medieval banking families of Peruzzi and of Bardi. These 'Lombard' companies had grown immensely wealthy by offering to replace the Jewish international moneylenders. The Italian banking skills

included the introduction of double-entry book-keeping and the families involved in the businesses became enormously powerful. The Peruzzi family business went bankrupt in 1343 and the Bardi in 1346, while smaller companies managed to survive the financial difficulties of those years and gradually took over. These successors would include the Pazzi, the Strozzi, the Rucelli, and the Medici, although they would never achieve quite the vast capital assets of the businesses that had perished in the 1340s.

17. 'Robert the Wise and his heirs'
18. The Pipini Brothers had been jailed by Robert the Wise for their participation in the civil unrest of 1338. They had very little respect for law and none at all for the general populace, and had started such a vendetta against their several enemies that they were called 'the scourge of Apulia'. It had taken a small army to make them capitulate and they were brought to trial in 1341 for murder, rape, pillage, arson and treason, 'kindling civil war' and other crimes. They had been intended for execution, but their mother had pleaded with Queen Sancia to have the sentences commuted to life imprisonment.
19. 'Joanna, the notorious Queen of Naples...'
20. Ibid
21. The couple shared a living room and balcony, but had separate sleeping rooms within their joint apartment.
22. 'Robert the Wise and his heirs'
23. A 'papal interdict' is a censure withdrawing the sacraments, and which may be applied to a person, or to a whole country. It implies the most harsh level of criticism and was often used against recalcitrant monarchs in an attempt to force obedience to papal control.
24. 'Letters on Familiar Matters' by Francesco Petrarch. (I-XXIV) translated by Aldo S. Bernardo in three volumes.
25. 'Joanna, the notorious Queen of Naples...'
26. 'Famous Women' by Giovanni Boccaccio
27. 'Joanna, the notorious Queen of Naples...'
28. Ibid
29. 'Memoirs of a Renaissance Pope' by Aeneus Silvius Piccolomini (Pope Pius II)
30. Ibid
31. 'History of Rome in the Middle Ages' by Gregorovius
32. 'Sex Lives of the Popes'
33. 'The Bosnian Church, its place in State and Society, in the Fifteenth Century' by John Van Antwerp Fine.
34. 'Cyprus' by Charles Cawley
35. 'Chronicle of the Popes' Maxwell-Stuart
36. 'The Popes' by John Julius Norwich
37. 'Chronicle of the Popes' Maxwell-Stuart
38. 'Diary of the City of Rome' by Stefano Infessura. Infessura (1435–1500) was for many years the Secretary to the Roman Senate.

Chapter 4

1. 'The Tigress of Forli' by Elizabeth Lev
2. 'The story of the Sforzas' by Collinson-Morley

3. 'Joanna, the notorious Queen of Naples...'
4. 'The Tigress of Forli' by Elizabeth Lev
5. 'Magnifico' by Miles J. Unger
6. Galeazzo Maria's second wife, Bona of Savoy, was the daughter of Louis, Duke of Savoy. One of her sisters, Charlotte of Savoy, married King Louis XI of France, becoming his second wife.
7. 'The Tigress of Forli'
8. 'Florentine Histories' by Machiavelli
9. Riario's demand to sleep with the eleven-year old girl was less an indication of personal desire than concern that the marriage could have been cancelled at a future date, if the consummation had not taken place. By insisting on deflowering the girl immediately, Riario was seeking security within the union, which he might not have if he had had to wait a further four years for his bride with the agreement only. Consummation was the key to marital legality.
10. Letter of 23 January 1473 in Milan State Archives.
11. 'History of Milan under the Sforzas' by Cecilia Ady
12. 'The Tigress of Forli'
13. Caterina's first ceremony was intended to be a betrothal, and Girolamo's insistence on the consummation was not only slightly unusual but not strictly legal. However, being aware that carnal union was everything within the law, Caterina was given to him. Perhaps due to the strict letter of the law not having been carried out on the first occasion, the Pope preferred to clarify the matter by requiring a further proxy wedding. (In contrast to the bridegroom's eagerness the first time, he did not attend the second ceremony.) This made the union between them doubly inviolate legally, and Caterina would then be obliged to look to her husband for her future support, particularly after her father's death.
14. 'Donne Celebri Caterina to Chiara' (3 May 1477) in Milan State Archives.
15. Giuliano della Rovere would become Pope Julius II in 1503. In his nine-year reign his military and diplomatic interventions would avert a takeover of the Italian states by France and would also stop Venetian expansion.
16. The Ponte Sisto across the River Tiber was built by Sixtus IV between 1473 and 1479 taking the name of the Pope. It was built of re-used foundation stones from the Roman Pons Aurelius, which had been destroyed in the early middle ages. The Ponte Sisto was designed with an 'Ocular' or circular 'eye' in its centre, which diminishes the pressure in the centre of the bridge in the event of the Tiber flooding.
17. 'The Tigress of Forli'
18. Francesco Salviati, Archbishop of Pisa, had been an enemy of the Medici and had joined the conspiracy hoping to end their rule in Florence. He had already fostered anti-Medici support among the students at the University of Pisa and the Medici had prevented him from taking up his diocese for three years. However, as he had been appointed by the Pope, his execution might be expected to cause further problems, and the Medici held Raffaelo Riario as a hostage, detaining him for six weeks until the situation became more settled.
19. Even in Ancient Rome this problem was recognised and there was a distinct reluctance for very young women to bear children, either too soon or too frequently. This concern was not only for the welfare of the mother, but for the

quality of the children to be born, fearing that they may have been sickly and less likely to live to maturity and breed in their turn. Caterina Sforza was lucky to escape these dangers and produce a viable family without obvious difficulty.

20. The Riario Palace (the present Palazzo della Cancelleria) now takes its name from the Apostolic Chancellery of the Pope. It is situated close to the Campo di Fiori and was built by Cardinal Raffaelo Riario who was then Camerlengo of the Church. The Camerlengo is the administrator of the properties and revenues of the Holy See and also arranges the Conclaves which elect a new pope.

21. Bona of Savoy lost her regency to her brother-in-law Ludovico Maria Sforza, who was known as 'The Moor'.

22. Venice controlled the salt marshes on the Adriatic coast but Ferrara began to extract salt from Comacchio, which was a territory they at that time leased from Venice! The Venetians forbade them to take part in the rich trade, and a war began in 1482.

23. 'The Tigress of Forli'

24. The della Rovere family came from Liguria and while not living in poverty, were certainly not one of the noble families. The nepotism of the Pope advanced both the della Rovere and the Riario families. He arranged for them a series of ambitious marriages, as well as promoting several relatives to the cardinalate. One of these, Giuliano della Rovere, would later become Pope Julius II and would also install more relatives as cardinals. The commissions of the della Rovere popes were instrumental in making Rome one of Europe's greatest cities.

25. The Castel Sant'Angelo was Roman, being originally the family mausoleum of the Emperor Hadrian in the second century. Its strategic position across the Tiber from the main part of the city, as well as its proximity to the Vatican, made it the perfect defensive structure and it would become the usual bolt-hole for popes during the later medieval period. Once the Pasetto di Borgo was built, it could control the entire Borgo area.

26. These are her first recorded words. Vespucci to Lorenzo de'Medici, in Florence State Archives, 18 August 1484.

27. Elizabeth Lev, quoting Pier Desiderio Pasolini's 'Caterina Sforza'

28. 'The Tigress of Forli'

29. Melchiorre Zaccheo, a relative but distrusted by Caterina, had turned up in Forli when Girolamo was desperate for money. In return for loans, he had demanded to be made castellan of Ravaldino, but that would give him control of the city and his loyalty was suspect. Caterina was determined to remove him,

30. Elizabeth Lev, quoting from Stefano Infessura's 'Il diario di Stefano Infessura'

31. Leone Frieda, 'The Deadly Sisterhood'

32. The remarks Caterina made at Ravaldino were widely reported, but the most famous version was written by Giovanni Corbezi to Lorenzo de' Medici on the day the events took place. Subsequently, Lorenzo Giustiniani, in writing to the Venetian ambassador, called Caterina 'a tigress', which was reprinted in Marino Sanuto's 'I Diarii'.

33. Niccolo Machievelli 'Discourses on the first ten books of Titus Livius'

34. Lorenzo Giustiniani to the Venetian Ambassador, in Sanuto's 'Diarii'

35. Corbizi to Lorenzo de' Medici, 17 April 1488. Manfredo to Lorenzo de' Medici and Migliore Cresci to Lorenzo de' Medici 17 April 1488. Florence State Archives.
36. Leone Corbelli, 'Cronache Forlivesi della Fondazione della Citta, fino al 1498. Translated by Elizabeth Lev in 'The Tigress of Forli'.
37. Elizabeth Lev, 'The Tigress of Forli'
38. The sacking of captured or recaptured towns was commonplace, even when the soldiers concerned had done little, as in this case. Caterina did not want her son's inheritance further destroyed as the Riario property had already been.
39. The Jewish moneylenders, like the town's maidens, were always first to be pillaged when a town was taken.
40. Leone Corbelli, 'Cronache Forlivesi della Fondazione della Citta fino al 1498'
41. Andrea Bernardi, 'Cronache Forlivesi dal 1476 al 1517'. Bernardi gives the best description of Feo becoming Caterina's lover (the fact that they had had a secret marriage was not known until her death). However, his legal status as her actual husband caused him to act with arrogance and made him hated, even by her children.
42. Florence State Archives
43. Nigel Cawthorne, 'Sex lives of the Popes'. His reign was known as 'The Golden Age of Bastards'.
44. Giuliano della Rovere was an opponent of Rodrigo Borgia. At Borgia's election to the papacy, he complained that the new pope had bought all his votes by bribing with cartloads of silver. It was true, but della Rovere had done the same, except that his own campaign had been unsuccessful.
45. Elizabeth Lev, 'The Tigress of Forli'
46. Leone Corbelli, 'Chronache Forlivesi della Fondazione della Citta'
47. Andrea Bernardi, 'Chronache Forlivesi...'
48. The punishments given in Dante's 'Inferno' were intended to fit the crime, hence the violence of the executions.
49. Francesco Tranchedini to Duke Ludovico. Milan State Archives
50. Ibid
51. Elizabeth Lev, 'The Tigress of Forli'
52. Letter of 21 March 1496. Milan State Archives
53. Marquis Giovanni Francesco Gonzaga of Mantua ruled a state traditionally allied to Milan.
54. Savonarola (1452–1498) was a Dominican friar and preacher. He denounced corruption, despotic rule and the exploitation of the poor. He was summoned to Rome by Pope Alexander VI in 1495 after Florence refused to join the Pope's Holy League. He was excommunicated in 1497 and eventually popular opinion turned against him and in 1498 he was hanged and burned in the main piazza in Florence.
55. Caterina Sforza to the Duke of Milan, August 1498. Milan State Archives
56. Florence State Archives
57. Ibid
58. Mantua State Archives
59. Elizabeth Lev, 'The Tigress of Forli'
60. 'Chronica di Antonio Grumello'. Reprinted in Pasolino's 'Caterina Sforza'

61. Marino Sanuto, 'I Diarii'
62. Bernardi. Referring to Caterina's luxurious quarters at the fortress being known as 'Paradise'.
63. Bernardi 'Chronache Forlivesi...'
64. Mantua State papers, reprinted in Pasolini's 'Caterina Sforza'
65. Francesco Fortunati, dated 8 July 1501. Florence State Archives
66. 23 October 1503. Florence State Archives

Chapter 5

1. Mary Hollingsworth, 'The Borgias'
2. *Papabile* refers to the cardinals considered 'front-runners' in the papal election. In medieval Rome votes were actively touted for, and often involved huge bribes. There was still often disappointment and there was a saying that 'he who enters the conclave as a pope, often leaves it as a cardinal,' referring to failed expectations. Very young men were sometimes elected but in the twenty-first century there are rules limiting the ages of candidates. The minimum age is thirty-five and the maximum is eighty. If the man chosen is not already a bishop, then he must be ordained immediately after his election. He must also hold a doctorate, or be at least a licentiate in ancient scripture, theology or canon law, from an institute of higher studies approved by the Apostolic See. Typically, it would only be a bishop who is promoted to the cardinalate, but canon law still allows for any ordained priest to be elevated on personal merit. It is also still possible, technically, for an outsider to be elected 'by acclamation'.
3. Mary Hollingsworth, 'The Borgias'
4. P.G. Maxwell-Stuart, 'Chronicle of the Popes'
5. James McCaffrey, 'Pope Callixtus III' Catholic Encyclopaedia vol 3
6. Michael Mallett 'The Borgias'
7. Enea Piccolomini 'Memoirs of a Renaissance Pope'
8. Ibid
9. Mary Hollingsworth, 'The Borgias'
10. Ibid
11. The preference for elderly popes had always been a feature. Not only did the pope need to be a man of experience and authority, but it was necessary to ensure that his reign did not drag on for decades, in case his person or policies proved unpopular. It also gave other cardinals their chance to try for the Supreme Office.
12. Piccolomini, 'Memoirs of a Renaissance Pope'
13. Ibid
14. Marion Johnson, 'The Borgias'
15. Nigel Cawthorne, 'Sex Lives of the Popes'
16. Marion Johnson, 'The Borgias'
17. Mary Hollingsworth, 'The Borgias'
18. Ibid
19. Sarah Bradford, 'Lucrezia Borgia'
20. Francesco Guicciardini, 'The History of Italy'. Guicciardini (1483–1540) was an historian and statesman and a friend of Niccolo Machiavelli. One of the major political writers of his day, 'The History of Italy' was his masterpiece, written during the last years of his life and intended for posterity.

21. Johannes Burchard, 'Pope Alexander and his Court, extracts from the Latin diary of Johannus Burchardus'. Burchard was a priest and chronicler who served as papal master of ceremonies. He spent his entire career at court during the reigns of Sixtus IV, Innocent VIII, Alexander VI, Pius III and Julius II. His diary extracts give valuable insight into the running of the papal court and the lives of the popes.
22. Ibid
23. Ludwig von Pastor, 'History of the Popes'. Pastor (1854–1928) was nominated six times for the Nobel Prize for Literature and was an important Catholic historian.
24. Juan (second Duke of Gandia after the death of his elder brother Pedro Luiz) married Maria Enriquez de Luna who had originally been betrothed to Pedro Luiz. She was first cousin to Isabella of Castile and Ferdinand of Aragon. She was to bear Juan Borgia three children, the twins Juan and Francesca, and Isabel Borgia.
25. Mary Hollingsworth, 'The Borgias'
26. Ibid
27. Burchard. He ended his report on the escape and the mules carrying empty chests with the words, 'I don't believe it,' but he probably knew Cesare well enough to believe that he could, and would, do exactly that.
28. Ibid
29. Ibid
30. Mary Hollingsworth, 'The Borgias'
31. Michael Mallett, 'The Borgias'
32. Sarah Bradford, 'Lucrezia Borgia'
33. Michael Mallett, 'The Borgias'
34. Johannes Burchard, 'Diary of Alexander VI and his court'
35. Ibid
36. Ibid
37. Letter from Giuliano della Rovere to Alexander VI, 18 January 1499
38. Johannes Burchard, 'Diary of Alexander VI and his court'
39. Sarah Bradford, 'Cesare Borgia'
40. Sarah Bradford, 'Lucrezia Borgia'
41. Marino Sanuto, 'I Diarii'
42. Sarah Bradford, 'Lucrezia Borgia'
43. Marion Johnson, 'The Borgias'
44. F. Matarazzo, 'Cronica della citta di Perugia dal 1492 al 1503'
45. Johannes Burchard, 'Diary of Alexander VI'
46. Ibid
47. Ibid
48. Mary Hollingsworth, 'The Borgias'
49. Bernadino Zambotti, 'Diario Ferrarese dal 1476 al 1504'
50. Michael Mallett, 'The Borgias'
51. Rachel Erlanger, 'Lucrezia Borgia'
52. Ferdinand Gregorovius, 'History of Rome in the Middle Ages'
53. Sarah Bradford, 'Cesare Borgia'
54. Rachel Erlanger, 'Lucrezia Borgia'
55. Ibid

56. Jeronimo Zurita, 'Historia del Rey Don Hernando el Catolico'
57. Edmund G. Gardner, 'Dukes and Poets at Ferrara'
58. Tobias Jones, 'The Dark Heart of Italy'
59. Rachel Erlanger, 'Lucrezia Borgia'
60. Francesco Guicciardini, 'History of Italy'
61. Alessandro Luzio, 'Isabella d'Este e I Borgia' Archivio Storico Lombardo' volumes 1 and II
62. John Julius Norwich 'A history of Venice'
63. Alessandro Luzio 'Isabella d'Este e I Borgia'
64. Ibid
65. Ibid
66. Maria Bellonci 'The life and times of Lucrezia Borgia' (Lucrezia Borgia la sua vita e I suo tempi) edited by Arnoldo Mondadori. Translated by Bernard and Barbara Wall.
67. Alessandro Luzio 'Isabella d'Este e I Borgia'
68. Ibid
69. Maria Bellonci 'The life and times of Lucrezia Borgia'
70. Ferdinand Gregorovius 'History of Rome in the Middle Ages'
71. Rachel Erlanger 'Lucrezia Borgia'
72. Ferdinand Gregorovius 'History of Rome in the Middle Ages'

Chapter 6

1. Painted by Melozzo da Forli in 1480, commissioned by Sixtus IV. It shows the Pope seated on the right with his brother Giovanni alongside. Kneeling before the Pope is his librarian and on the left Giuliano's cousins Girolamo and Raffaelo Riario.
2. Christine Shaw. 'Julius II, the warrior pope'
3. Desiderio Erasmus 'Julius Exclusus'
4. Stefano Infessura 'Diary of the city of Rome'
5. Reay Tannahill 'Sex in history'
6. Caroline P.Murphy 'The Pope's daughter'
7. Ibid
8. Sergio Bosticco 'Piazza Navona, Isola dei Pamphilj'
9. Francesco Albertini 'De Mirabilibus'
10. Richard Krautheimer 'Rome, profile of a city'
11. Ibid
12. P.G. Maxwell-Stuart 'Chronicle of the Popes'
13. John Julius Norwich 'The Popes'
14. Ludwig von Pastor 'History of the Popes'
15. Elizabeth Lev 'The Tigress of Forli'
16. Christine Shaw 'Julius II, the warrior pope'
17. Caroline P.Murphy 'The Pope's daughter'
18. Ibid
19. Ludwig von Pastor 'History of the Popes'
20. Ibid
21. P.G.Maxwell-Stuart 'Chronicle of the Popes'
22. Desiderio Erasmus 'Julius Exclusus'

23. Marino Sanuto 'I Diarii di Marino Sanuto'
24. Ibid
25. Caroline P.Murphy 'The Pope's daughter'
26. Marino Sanuto 'I Diarii di Marino Sanuto'
27. Antonio Giustiniani 'Dispacci di Antonia Giustiniani'
28. Ibid
29. The Cortile del Belvedere was designed by Donato Bramante and connected the Vatican with the Villa Belvedere by a series of terraces and stairs. By the end of the sixteenth century a building was erected across the court, dividing it into two. The original design is commemorated in a fresco in the Castel Sant' Angelo.
30. Letter of Emilia Pia to the niece of the Duchess of Urbino, quoted in 'The Pope's daughter' by Caroline P.Murphy
31. Antonio Giustiniani, reporting arrangements for the Colonna marriage.
32. Antonio Giustiniani, letter from the Venetian ambassador 28th Januaryn 1505.
33. Antonio Giustiniani, letter from the Venetian ambassador 10th February 1505
34. Being a widow was the only way a young woman could be considered respectable if living alone or managing her own money. Felice's father seemed eager to get her off his hands, rather than showing concern for her future happiness. Her illegitimacy heightened her marginalisation.
35. Agnolo Firenzuola. 'Epistola a Claudio Tolomei'
36. Baldassare Castiliglione. 'The Book of the Courtier' (Il Cortegiano)
37. Christine Shaw. 'Julius II, the warrior pope'
38. Francesco Sansovino. 'L'historia di Casa Orsini'
39. Marino Sanuto 'I Diarii di Marino Sanuto'
40. This palace, then known as the Cancellaria, or chancellory, is now the Palazzo Sforza Cesarini.
41. Caroline P. Murphy 'The Pope's daughter'
42. Ibid
43. The marriage bargain depended on vows taken before witnesses followed by carnal knowledge. This validated the contract and why Caterina Sforza'a marriage was consummated when she was only nine years old.
44. Reay Tannahill, 'Sex in history'
45. Marino Sanuto, 'Il Diarii di Marino Sanuto'
46. Caroline P. Murphy, 'The Pope's daughter'
47. George Dennis, 'The cities and cemeteries of Etruria'
48. Marino Sanuto, 'Il Diarii di Marino Sanuto'
49. Christine Shaw, 'Julius II, the warrior pope'
50. Marino Sanuto, 'Il Diarii di Marino Sanuto'
51. Ludwig von Pastor, 'History of the Popes'
52. Marino Sanuto, 'Il Diarii di Marino Sanuto'
53. Ibid
54. Letter of Mantuan emissary to Isabella d'Este of April 1511.
55. Alessandro Luzio, 'Isabella d'Este di fronte a Giulio II negli ultimi tre anni del suo Pontificato' (Isabella d'Este in front of Julius II in the last three years of his Pontificate)
56. G.M. Moncallero, 'Epistolario di Bernardo Douizi da Babbiena'
57. Alessandro Luzio, 'Isabella d'Este di fronto a Giulio II etc'
58. Marino Sanuto, 'Il Diarii di Marino Sanuto'

59. Alessandro Luzio, 'Isabella d'Este di fronto a Giulio II etc'
60. Gonzaga Archives, Mantua.
61. Ibid
62. Ibid
63. Ibid
64. P.G. Maxwell-Stuart, 'Chronicle of the Popes'
65. Caroline P. Murphy, 'The Pope's daughter'
66. Ibid
67. Ibid
68. Archivio Orsini
69. Archivio Santa Croce
70. Archivio Orsini
71. Ibid
72. Archivio Santa Croce. Several copies of the Inventory are in existence.
73. Caroline P. Murphy, 'The Pope's daughter'
74. Archivio Orsini
75. These buildings are now in an urban area, but in the sixteenth century were on open land used for vineyards. The Spanish Steps ascending the hill were not built until the eighteenth century and Felice built a road up the steep hill to improve access. Part of her palace there is now the Villa Malta, in a public park.
76. Marino Sanuto, 'Il Diarii di Marino Sanuto'
77. Archivo di Stato di Firenze
78. Ibid
79. Orsini Archives, UCLA.
80. Lynda Telford, 'Tudor Victims of the Reformation'
81. Archivio Orsini
82. Caroline P. Murphy, 'The Pope's daughter'
83. Archivio Orsini
84. Christine Shaw, 'Julius II, the warrior pope'
85. Caroline P.Murphy, 'The Pope's daughter'
86. Archivio Orsini
87. Ibid
88. Ibid
89. Ibid
90. P.G. Maxwell-Stuart, 'Chronicle of the Popes'
91. Archivio Orsini
92. Matthew Kneale, 'Rome – a history in seven sackings'
93. E. R. Chamberlin, 'The Bad Popes'
94. Catherine Fletcher, 'The Black Prince of Florence'
95. Francesco Guicciardini, 'Storia di Italia'
96. Leone Frieda, 'Catherine de'Medici'
97. Lynda Telford, 'Tudor Victims of the Reformation'
98. Emmanual Pierre Rodoconachi (1859-1934). He was a French writer of several books concerning the history of Rome through the ages.
99. George L. Williams, 'Papal Geneology – the families and descendants of the Popes'
100. Michael Walsh, 'History of the Popes'

101. 'The Index of Forbidden Books' is a list of publications considered heretical, thus Catholics were not allowed to read them. The 'Pauline Index' was promulgated in 1559 and replaced in 1560 by the 'Tridentine Index', so called because it was authorised by the Council of Trent. The aim was to protect morals and religious faith by prohibiting disruptive material. This would include the work of Copernicus and other philosophers and astronomers, together with rules allowing books not actually approved by the church also to be banned.

Chapter 7

1. Rudolph M. Bell, 'How to do it – guides to good living for Renaissance Italians'
2. Eleanor Herman, 'Mistress of the Vatican'
3. Lynda Telford, 'Women in Medieval England'
4. Gregorio Leti, 'History of Donna Olimpia Maidalchini'
5. 'Conclave' comes from the Latin 'cum clave' or 'with a key' this was because the cardinals were locked away to make their choice of the next pope.
6. P.G. Maxwell-Stuart, 'Chronicles of the Popes'
7. Mario Mazzuchelli, 'The Nun of Monza'
8. Eleanor Herman, 'Mistress of the Vatican'
9. Ibid
10. At the time, the northern countries who had converted to Protestantism tended to look down on the Catholic heartlands as being out of date. The practice of pressuring girls to enter convents was considered despicable. Bishop Girolamo Matteucci did not allow Olimpia to win against him because he sympathised with her, though he could not permit the rules of the Council of Trent to be openly flouted. She had caused an open scandal and he feared she might prove more trouble than she was worth.
11. The Council of Trent, held at intervals between 1545 and 1563 (in twenty-five sessions) was important to the Catholic Reformation. It met at the church of Santa Maria Maggiore, in Trento, not only to condemn heresies but also to attempt to reform some abuses. Popes Paul III, Julius III and Pius IV oversaw the sessions over the years. Deliberations included the minimum age for entry into convents (sixteen years), and the banning of coercion.
12. Eleanor Harman, 'Mistress of the Vatican'
13. The results of taking up celibacy for women who had been accustomed to a sex life was much discussed up to Victorian times. Various remedies were prescribed, even 'fine, gentle massage of the female sex organs', preferably by a doctor. Electric treatments of various kinds also became popular during Victorian times, even the production of early vibrators. This was considered a health measure, not for sexual pleasure.
14. Alfeo Cavoli, 'La Popessa Olimpia'
15. Ancient Roman houses always had shops or bars at ground level and later Roman houses followed that tradition. The private apartments above would be accessed through courtyards to keep the family rooms private from the streets.
16. Gregorio Leti, 'History of Donna Olimpia Maidalchini'
17. The remains of the 'Hercules' statue are still on the same site, and still used as a place to leave messages, verses, and satirical comments.

18. Flood banks were not built until 1875. Until that time, people living in the low-lying areas were often killed. The city could be flooded several feet deep within hours when the Tiber burst its banks. The Jewish area suffered the most, as it was in the lowest area by the river, by Papal Decree.

19. In 1499 the ceiling of the Vatican audience chamber fell down onto Pope Alexander VI. The man standing next to the Pope was killed instantly, and the Pope was knocked unconscious. His life was saved by the canopy over his throne, which took the brunt of the weight of fallen masonry.

20. This resembled the bevy of 'clients' following the ancient Roman nobleman. They would be eager for some sign of recognition from him, or even to be seen in his company. The size of the crowd denoted his standing and popularity, but it could disappear overnight if his popularity suffered a decline.

21. The Easter Duty was mandated by the Council of Trent, ensuring that Catholics confessed and received Communion at least once a year. Many, after abstinence, did this on the Thursday before Easter, and Easter had always been the most important festival of the Christian year.

22. However small the rent, it was still an admission that sovereignty still lay with the Pope and that Naples still, technically, belonged to the papacy, not Spain. These 'peppercorn' rents, which could consist of anything from a real peppercorn to a red rose proffered once a year, were a means of establishing title to satisfy the requirements of a legal contract.

23. Archivio Doria Pamphilj

24. Ibid

25. Gregorio Leti, 'History of Donna Olimpia Maidalchini'

26. Ibid

27. Archivio Doria Pamphilj

28. Ibid

29. Archivio di Stata di Venezia

30. P. Sforza Pallavacino, 'Della vita di Alessandro VI'

31. Gustavo Brigante Calonna. 'Olimpia Pamphilj – Cardinal padrone'

32. P.G. Maxwell-Stuart, 'Chronicle of the Popes'

33. Archivio Doria Pamphilj

34. Gregorio Leti, 'History of Donna Olimpia Maidalchini'

35. Donata Chiomenti Vassalli, 'Donna Olimpia, o del nepotismo nel seicento'

36. This new title led to the princes demanding to be called 'highness' instead of 'excellency' and after some argument this became accepted.

37. The 'congregations' were ruling committees. Men appointed for political or family reasons might be given a job dealing with unimportant matters, where they could do little harm.

38. Created by Pope Paul III in 1542.

39. Gregorio Leti, 'History of Donna Olimpia Maidalchini'

40. The Pamphilj property on the Piazza Navona is now the Brazilian Embassy, though part of the interior decoration still carries the Pamphilj emblem of the dove and the olive branch.

41. Archivio Doria Pamphilj

42. Donata Chiomenti Vassalli, 'Donna Olimpia o del nepotismo nel seicento'

43. Gregorio Leti, 'History of Donna Olimpia Maidalchini'

44. Teodoro Amayden, 'Storia delle familigie Romanae'
45. Ibid
46. Gustavo Brigante Colonna, 'Olimpia Pamphilj – cardinal padrone'
47. Gregorio Leti, 'History of Donna Olimpia Pamphilj'
48. Security at Conclave was always lax, until Pope Pius X enforced absolute secrecy in 1904.
49. Mazarin – Cardinal Giulio Mazzarino (1602–1661) had worked his way to the top in France, supposedly by becoming the lover of the widowed Queen Mother, Anne of Austria. He held absolute power for many years, during the minority of King Louis XIV.
50. Gregorio Leti, 'History of Donna Olimpia Maidalchini'
51. Donata Chiomenti Vassalli, 'Donna Olimpia o del nepotismo nel seicento'
52. Giacinto Gigli, 'Diario di Roma (1608-1670)
53. Gregorio Leti, 'History of Donna Olimpia Maidalchini'
54. Eleanor Herman, 'Mistress of the Vatican'
55. Gregorio Leti, 'History of Donna Olimpia Maidalchini'
56. Donato Chiomenti Vassalli, 'Donna Olimpia o del nepotismo nel seicento'
57. P. Sforza Pallavacini, 'Della vita di Alessandro VI'
58. Donata Chiomenti Vassalli, 'Donna Olimpia o del nepotismo nel seicento'
59. Teodoro Amayden, a Vatican lawyer who wrote weekly 'advisaries' to Spain and Spanish embassies in Europe.
60. Donata Chiomenti Vassalli, 'Donna Olimpia o del nepotismo nel seicento'
61. Eleanor Herman, 'Mistress of the Vatican'
62. Olimpia Aldobrandini was related to Pope Paul III and was cousin to the Duke of Parma. She was also great-grand niece of Pope Clement VIII who left all his wealth to his relative Ippolito Aldobrandini, which was inherited by Olimpia when she was fifteen. In 1646 her husband, Prince Paolo Borghese, died but she needed a second son to acquire her uncle's Aldobrandini fortune. She needed to marry again.
63. Gregorio Leti, 'History of Donna Olimpia Pamphilj'
64. Donata Chiomenti Vassalli, 'Donna Olimpia o del nepotismo nel seicento'
65. Giacinto Gigli, 'Diario di Roma'
66. Ibid
67. Eleanor Harman, 'Mistress of the Vatican'
68. There were then 355 churches in Rome, but the four 'Jubilee' churches were St Peter's, St John Lateran, St Mary Major and St Paul's Outside the Walls.
69. Giacinto Gigli, 'Diario di Roma'
70. Ignazio Ciampi, 'Innocenzo X e la sue corte – storia di Roma dal 1644 al 1655'
71. Giacinto Gigli, 'Diario di Roma'
72. Gustavo Brigante Colonna, 'Olimpia Pamphilj – cardinal padrone'
73. Donata Chiomenti Vassalli, 'Donna Olimipia o del nepotismo nel seicento'
74. Eleanor Herman, 'Mistress of the Vatican'
75. Donata Chiomenti Vassalli, 'Donna Olimpia o del nepotismo nel seicento'
76. Cardinal Fabio Chigi would become Pope Alexander VII on 7 April 1655 and would reign until 1667.
77. Eleanor Harman, 'Mistress of the Vatican'

78. Ibid
79. Archivio Gonzaga di Mantova
80. Giacinto Gigli, 'Diario di Roma'
81. Gustavo Brigante Colonna, 'Olimpia Pamphilj – cardinal padrone'
82. Cardinal Decio Azzolino (1623–1689) and Cardinal Carlo Gualterio, along with five others, were elevated, bringing the College of Cardinals up to its limit of seventy members. The list was written out by Olimpia.
83. Eleanor Herman, 'Mistress of the Vatican'
84. According to the duties laid out in the 'Relatione della Corte di Roma' of 1650, which detailed the etiquette to be followed if possible.
85. Giacinto Gigli, 'Diario di Roma'
86. Gregorio Leti, 'History of Donna Olimpia Maidalchini'
87. Ibid
88. Pope Innocent X was later buried in the Chiesa di Santa Agnese in Agone, next to the Palazzo Pamphilj on the Piazza Navona, as he had wished, in 1677. A large bronze statue of him was made by Alessandro Algardi (1598–1654) but a painting in the Capuchin Chuch in Rome shows St Michael trampling on a Satan who bears the features of Pope Innocent X. That Pope's circumstances also inspired the 'Screaming Pope' painting by Francis Bacon in 1953 (taken from the Velaquez portrait of around 1650). The Bacon version shows the Pope trapped and screaming, representing his humiliation and lack of personal power.
89. Gregorio Leti, 'History of Donna Olimpia Maidalchini'
90. Ibid
91. Eleanor Harman, 'Mistress of the Vatican'
92. Gregorio Leti, 'History of Donna Olimpia Maidalchini'
93. Eleanor Harman, 'Mistress of the Vatican'
94. Archivio Doria Pamphilj

Chapter 8

1. The causes of CAH are described in 'Christina of Sweden' by Veronica Buckley. Information provided by UK Adrenal Hyperplasia Network.
2. Carl-Herman Hjortsjo, 'Queen Christina of Sweden, a medical-anthropological investigation of her remains in Rome'
3. Veronica Buckley, 'Christina of Sweden'
4. Ibid
5. Ibid
6. Francoise Kermina, 'Christina de Suede'
7. Veronica Buckley, 'Christina of Sweden' quoting Bulstrode Whitelock's 'Journal of the Swedish Embassy 1653-1654'
8. Sforza Pallavicino, 'Descrizione del Primo Viaggio fatto a Roma della Regina di Svezia, Cristina Maria'
9. The Palazzo Farnese was built by Cardinal Alessandro Farnese, later PopePaul III, (known as the Petticoat Cardinal). It passed through the hands of a series of architects before its completion, including Michaelangelo. Since 1875 it has housed the French Embassy.

10. Gregorio Leti, 'Il nepotismo di Roma'
11. Letter from Charles Longland in Livorno to John Thurloe in London, 14 April 1656.
12. Jacques Castelnau, 'La Reine Christine'
13. Quoted by Gobry in 'La Reine Christine'
14. Mme de Montpensier, 'Memoirs'
15. Letter from Lascaris to Azzolino of 28 December 1656, quoted by Neumann in 'The Life of Christina of Sweden'
16. Count Grigorii Orlov, 'Reflection de la mort du Marquis Monaldeschi'
17. Ibid
18. Ibid
19. Ibid
20. Veronica Buckley, 'Christina of Sweden'
21. This is now the Palazzo Corsini on the Via della Lungara. It was extensively rebuilt during the eighteenth century. It now houses the Academy of Science and the Botanical Gardens.
22. Veronica Buckley, 'Christina of Sweden'
23. Georgina Masson, 'Queen Christina'
24. Letter from Christina to Azzolino dated 15 June 1667.
25. Letter from Christina to Azzolino dated 23 June 1666.
26. Letter from Azzolino to Christina dated December 1679.
27. Modern opinion is that Christina suffered from diabetes mellitus and by April 1689 had contracted the streptococcal infection erysipelas, later developing pneumonia.
28. Marie-Louise Rodan, 'The Burial of Queen Christina' quoting letter from Azzolino to Cardinal Cibo dated 19 April 1689 – in his confusion Cardinal Azzolino had dated this letter wrongly as 28 April.
29. Marie-Louise Rodan 'Church Politics in 17th-century Rome' quoting a letter from Azzolino to his cousin Francesco.
30. Marie-Louise Rodan 'Church Politics in 17th-century Rome' quoting letter from Azzolino to Giovanni Mattia del Monte dated 30 April 1689.

Chapter 9

1. Charles Theodore Murr, 'The Godmother, Madre Pascalina, a feminine Tour de Force'
2. Paul I. Murphy, 'La Popessa'
3. The Pacelli family were members of the 'Black Nobility' who had supported the pope when the Papal States were seized by the Government in 1870. The papacy retired within the walls of the Vatican for the next fifty-nine years, and those members of the aristocracy who had received titles from the pope closed their own doors in mourning. This earned them the title of 'Black Nobility'
4. Paul I.Murphy, 'La Popessa'
5. Pascalina Lehnert, 'His Humble Servant – memoirs of her years in service to Eugenio Pacelli, Pope Pius XII'
6. Paul I.Murphy, 'La Popessa'
7. Pacelli would later intervene to save Ludendorff, who was to back Hitler in the unsuccessful Munich putsch of 1923. After that Ludendorff was threatened with trial for his alleged war crimes.

8. John Cornwell, 'Hitler's Pope – the secret history of Pius XII'

9. Pascalina Lehnert, 'His Humble Servant'

10. Ibid

11. The Vatican wanted no more attacks from the dictator, and for Catholicism to be recognised as Italy's official religion. All marriages were to be made within a church and divorce was to be banned. Tax exemptions for all church property, mandatory religious instruction for children, and church-appointed teachers were also required. Also, crucially, the Vatican was to be recognised as a Sovereign State with the Pope as its ruler, and it should receive the sum of one hundred million dollars in compensation for property seized by the government in 1870.

12. Pascalina Lehnert, 'His Humble Servant'

13. The importance of the office of Secretary of State within the Vatican cannot be over-emphasised. He is the Prime Minister of the Vatican State and second only to the pope. He has constant access to the pontiff and often knows more of what is going on than the pope himself. He is the head of the Curia, and controller of the Vatican's diplomatic wing.

14. Paul I.Murphy, 'La Popessa'

15. To increase revenues after the near bankruptcy of the Vatican, the money 'awarded' by Mussolini was invested in many profitable but often dubious ventures. After thirty years of controlling the finances, Bernadino Nogera had vastly increased the surplus, and in his own reign Pacelli (Pius XII) would appoint a nephew, Giulio Pacelli, to be chairman of the board of a company making birth control pills.

16. The one pope who was determined to 'clean up' the embarrassing financial situation at the Vatican was John Paul I. (Albino Luciani 1912–1978). He would unfortunately reign for only thirty-three days.

17. Pascalina Lehnert, 'His Humble Servant'

18. Giovanni Montini (1897–1978) became Pope Paul VI in June 1963. He was the first pope in history to actually publicly deny accusations of homosexuality. These had been made by Roger Peyrofitte, who had written two books claiming that the Pope had a long-term homosexual relationship. This was repeated in a gay magazine, which named his partner as the actor Paolo Carlini. In 1994 the Vatican newspaper *L'Osservatore Romano* alleged in addition that Pope Paul VI had been blackmailed and had, as a result of this, promoted several other gay men into powerful positions within the Vatican. (From 'Controvita di un Papa' by Franco Bellegrandi. 1994.)

19. The staff of the Secretariat were concerned with diplomatic assignments, where cardinals, archbishops, and bishops (known as Nuncios or Apostolic Delegates) were sent abroad to represent the Vatican in dealings with foreign governments.

20. The Camerlengo (Chamberlain) is a far more important position than its name might suggest. The Camerlengo administers the property and revenues of the Holy See. He is the pope's treasurer and financial secretary. When a pope dies it is the duty of the Camerlengo to take possession of the Fisherman's Ring, always worn by the pope, and cut it in half. This signifies the end of that pope's reign, but it also prevents the ring being used to seal documents after the pope's death, thereby avoiding forgery. The Camerlengo also serves as

Acting Sovereign of the Vatican State until a new pope is elected, in order to keep church institutions operating, but he does not have the power to make any new decisions. He then takes responsibility for the Conclave gathered to elect the new pope. The powers of the position were changed in 1996, some being confirmed and others curtailed, by the 'Universi Dominici Gregis'

21. Charles Theodore Murr, 'The Godmother'
22. Corrado Pallenberg, 'Inside the Vatican'
23. Cardinal Eugene Tisserant (1884–1972) was a fiercely anti-Nazi and worked with Catholic networks during the Second World War to protect the Jewish population. He was an opponent of Mother Pascalina, and deeply resented her closeness with Pope Pius XII.
24. John Cornwell, 'Hitler's Pope'
25. Charles Theodore Murr, 'The Godmother'
26. Paul I. Murphy, 'La Popessa'
27. Pascalina Lehnert, 'His Humble Servant'
28. Paul I.Murphy, 'La Popessa'
29. Pascalina Lehnert, 'His Humble Servant'
30. David A. Yallop, 'In God's Name'
31. Paul I. Murphy, 'La Popessa'
32. Pascalina Lehnert, 'His Humble Servant'
33. Pope Pius XII had been seriously ill with gastritis intermittently since 1953. He underwent cellular rejuvenation treatment, but the side effects of this caused terrible nightmares and even hallucinations. Some people believed that his two 'visions' during the final year of his life were connected to this treatment and its after-effects, rather than being the miracles he claimed them to be. It was the first time since St Peter that any living pope had claimed to have actually seen Christ.
34. Paul. I.Murphy, 'La Popessa'
35. Monsignor Giovanni Montini's main fault was that he was a colleague of Tisserant and though his removal was advertised as 'a promotion' everyone knew that it meant the end of any possibility of him becoming a pope. However, in this case the prophecies proved to be wrong, and eight years later hebecame Pope Paul VI.
36. Paul I. Murphy, 'La Popessa'
37. David A. Yallop, 'The Power and the Glory'
38. 'Catholics for Choice' in 1998 stated that 98% of Catholic women had at some point used artificial contraception, despite the ruling of the church. A nationwide poll online in September of 2005 by Harris Interactive stated that 90% of US Catholics supported the use of birth control.
39. David A. Yallop, 'In God's Name'
40. Ibid
41. Ibid
42. John Follain, 'City of Secrets – the truth behind the murders at the Vatican'
43. David A.Yallop, 'The Power and the Glory'
44. Ed Stourton for BBC Panorama Report of 15 February 2016, 'Secret Letters of John-Paul II'
45. Dr. Mark Lesota, specialist in The Communist Records at the Institute of National Remembrance in Krakow.

46. Ed Stourton, 'Secret Letters of John-Paul II'
47. Lord Longford, 'Pope John-Paul II'
48. Letter of Pope John-Paul II to 'Every Woman' dated 10 July 1995.
49. Ed Stourton, 'Secret Letters of John-Paul II'
50. Carl Bernstein and Marco Politi, 'His Holiness and the Hidden History of our Time'

Chapter 10

1. E.R. Chamberlin, 'The Bad Popes'
2. P.G. Maxwell-Stuart, 'Chronicle of the Popes'
3. Nigel Cawthorne, 'Sex Lives of the Popes'
4. Terence Wise, '1066 – Year of Destiny'
5. Dante Alighieri, 'Divine Comedy'
6. John Julius Norwich, 'The Popes'
7. Donald F. Logan, 'History of the church in the Middle Ages'
8. David A. Yallop, 'The Power and the Glory – inside the dark heart of Pope John-Paul II's Vatican.'
9. Frederic J. Baumgartner, 'Behind Locked Doors.'
10. Oscar E. Feught. 'Sex in the Church'
11. Richard P. McBrian, 'Lives of the Popes – the Pontiffs from St.Peter to Pope Benedict XVI'
12. John Julius Norwich, 'The Popes – A History'
13. Charles A. Frazee, 'The origins of clerical celibacy in the Western Church'
14. Elizabeth Abbott, 'Mistresses, the History of the Other Woman'
15. Paul Hofmann, 'The Vatican's Women – female influence at the Holy See'
16. Garry Wills, 'Papal Sin –Structures of Deceit'
17. Oscar E. Feught, 'Sex in the Church'
18. Lynda Telford, 'Women in Medieval England'
19. Paul Hofmann, 'The Vatican's Women'
20. Elizabeth Lev, 'The Tigress of Forli'
21. Emma Lucas, 'Lucrezia Borgia'
22. Elizabeth Abbott, 'Mistresses – The history of the Other Woman'
23. David A. Yallop, 'In God's Name'
24. Gerald Posner, 'God's Bankers – a history of the money and power at the Vatican'
25. David A. Yallop, 'In God's Name'
26. David A. Yallop, 'The Power and the Glory'
27. Mark Dowd, 'The Report' BBC Radio 4, Thursday 28 November 2013.
28. Gerald Posner, 'God's Bankers'
29. Ed Stourton, 'Secret Letters of Pope John-Paul II' Panorama report. BBC News, 15 February 2016.
30. Carl Bernstein and Marco Politi, 'His Holiness John-Paul II and the Hidden History of our Time.'

Bibliography

Primary Sources

ARCHIVIO AZZOLINO in Biblioteca Communale, Piazza Angelo. Colocci.

ARCHIVIO DORIA PAMPHILJ (records for the Pamphilj, Maidalchini and Facchinetti families) Via del Corso, Roma.

ARCHIVIO di STATO di FIRENZE

ARCHIVIO GONZAGA di MANTOVA

ARCHIVIO ORSINI. University of California Special Collection.

ARCHIVIO CENTRALE della STATO, Roma

ARCHIVIO DELLA STATO, Roma

ARCHIVIO di STATO di SIENA

ARCHIVIO di STATO di MILANO

ARCHIVIO SEGRETO di VATICANO. (Borgia family letters).

(A.A.Arm. 1-XVIII 5027 Vol 9

A.A.Arm. 1-XVIII 5024 Vol 2

A.A.Arm. XXXIX Vol 9)

ARCHIVIO STATO di VENEZIA

NATIONAL ARCHIVE of STOCKHOLM (official correspondence of Queen Christina)

ARCHIVIO SEGRETO ESTENSE (Documenti spettanti alla familgia Borgia)

VATICAN ARCHIVES ('I Diario Romani' – Registri Garampi 1435–1505)

ROYAL ARMOURY of STOCKHOLM (The Azzolino Collection – letters of Queen Christina to Cardinal Decio Azzolino 1666–1668)

ALBERTINI Francesco. 'Oposculum de Mirabilius – novae et veteris urbis Romanae'

AMAYDEN Teodoro. 'Storia delle Familie Romanae'

BERNARDINI Andrea. 'Cronache Forlivesi dal 1476 al 1517'. Trans. Elizabeth Lev.

BOCCACCIO Giovanni. 'Famous Women' (1362) Trans. Virginia Brown.

BOCCACCIO Giovanni. 'The Fates of Illustrious Men' Trans. Louis Brewer Hall.

BURCHARDUS Johannes. 'Pope Alexander VI and his Court – Diary of Johannes Burchardis 1450-1506'

'CRONACHE FORLIVESI dal 1476 al 1517'. Trans. Elizabeth Lev. La Deputazione Storia per la Romagna.

CASTIGLIONE Baldassare. 'The Book of the Courtier'. Trans. Chas. S. Singleton

COBELLI Leone. 'Cronache della Citta fino al 1498'. Trans. Elizabeth Lev

CORIO Bernardino. 'Storia di Milano' 1503

ERASMUS Desiderio. 'Julius Exclusus'. Trans. Paul Pascal.

GIUSTINIANI Antonio. 'Dispacci di Antonio Giustiniani.'

GNOSTIC GOSPELS. Ed. Alan Jacobs.

GUICCIARDINI Francesco. 'The History of Italy' 1560. Ed. Sidney Alexander

INFESSURA Stefano. 'I Diario di Stefano Infessura' Trans. Elizabeth Lev.

LETI Gregorio. 'History of Donna Olimpia Maidalchini' 1666.

LETI Gregorio. 'Il Nepotismo di Roma' (History of the Popes Nephews, from the time of Sixtus IV anno 1471 to the death of the late Pope Alexander VII anno 1667)

LIBER PONTIFICALIS. Ed. Louise Ropes Loomis

MACHIAVELLI Niccolo. 'Il Principe'. First printed 1532. Earlier distributed as 'De Principatibus' in 1513.

MACHIAVELLI Niccolo. 'Discourses on the first books of Titus Livius.' Book 3. Originally published 1531.

MATARAZZO Francesco. 'Croniche della Citta di Perugia – dal 1492 al 1503' Trans. E.S.Morgan. Edited A. Fabretti.

PETRARCH Francesco. 'Letters on familiar matters' Trans. Aldo S. Bernardo.

PROCOPIUS of CAESARIA 'The Secret History of the Court of Justinian'

SANUTO Marino. 'I Diarii – (1493-1530)'. Ed. Federico Visentini.

WHITELOCK Bulstrode. 'Journal of the Swedish Embassy in the years 1653–1654)

ZAMBOTTI Bernardino. 'Diario Ferrarese dal anno 1476 sino al 1504'

ZURITA. Geronimo. 'Historia del Rey Don Hernando el Catolica.' 1610.

Secondary Sources

ABBOTT Elizabeth. 'Mistresses – the history of the Other Women' Pub. Clearway Logistics 2011

ADY Cecilia Mary 'A History of Milan under the Sforzas' (1907) Pub. Forgotten Books Reprint 2017.

ALIGHIERI Dante 'Divine Comedy' Pub. Berkeley Books 2007

AMBROSINI Maria Luisa and WILLIS Mary. 'The Secret Archives of the Vatican' Pub. Little, Brown. 1969.

BADDELEY. St Clair. 'Robert the Wise and his Heirs – 1278 – 1352' Heineman.1893

BALSDON J.P.V.D. 'Roman Women' Pub. Bodley Head. 1962

BARRACLOUGH Geoffrey. 'The Medieval Papacy' Pub. Thomas Hudson. 1968

BARTON John. 'A History of the Bible: The Book and its Faiths' Pub Allen Lane 2019

BAUMGARTNER Frederic J. 'Behind locked doors – A history of the Papal elections' Pub. Palgrave McMillan 2003

BELL Rudolph M. 'How to do it – Guides for good living for Renaissance Italians' Pub. University of Chicago Press. 1991.

BELLONCI Maria. 'The life and times of Lucrezia Borgia' Trans. Bernard and Barbara Wall. Edited by Arnoldo Mandadori. 1967

BERNSTEIN Carl and POLITI Mario 'His Holiness John Paul II and the hidden history of our Time.' Pub. Pastime Books 1997

BILDT. C.D.N. Baron de... 'Letters of Christina of Sweden and Cardinal Azzolino – 1666 to 1668' Pub. Paris 1899

Bibliography

BOUREAU Alain. 'The Myth of Pope Joan' Trans. Lydia G. Cochrane. Pub. University of Chicago Press. 2001

BOSTICCO Sergio. 'Piazza Navona, Isola dei Pamphilj' Pub. Rome 1978

BUCKLEY Veronica. 'Christine, Queen of Sweden – the restless life of a European Eccentric' Pub. Harper Collins. 2005

BURMAN Edward. 'The Inquisition – the Hammer of Heresy (History and legacy of the Holy Office)' Pub. History Press. 2004

BRADFORD Sarah. 'Cesare Borgia' Pub. Weidenfeld and Nicolson. 1976.

BRADFORD Sarah. 'Lucrezia Borgia' Pub. Viking 2004

BRENTANO Robert. 'Rome before Avignon. A social history of thirteenth century Rome' Pub. University of California Press. 1992

CATHOLIC ENCYCLOPAEDIA Pub. Catholic University of America. 2002

CARPEGNA-FALCONIERI Tommaso. 'Marozia – Dizionario biografica degli Italiani' 2008

CASTEEN Elizabeth. 'Sex and Politics in Naples – the Regent Queen Joanna I' Pub. Journal of Historical Society. Malden. USA. June 2011

CASTELNAU Jacques. 'Le Reine Christine' (1626-1689) Pub. Payot, Paris. 1981. (First published as 'Christine de Suede' by Hatchett 1944)

CAVOLI Alfio. 'La Papessa Olimpia' Pub. Scipione, Roma. 1992

CAWTHORNE Nigel. 'Sex Lives of the Popes' Pub. Prion. 1996

CHAMBERS D.S. 'Renaissance cardinals and their worldly problems' Pub. Aldershot Viriarium. 1997

CHAMBERLIN E.R. 'The Bad Popes' Pub. Dorset Press. 1969

CHAMBERLIN E.R. 'The Sack of Rome' Pub. Batsford. 1979

CIAMPI Ignazio. 'Innocento X e le sue corte' (Storia di Roma dal 1644 al 1655) 1878

COLLINS Roger. 'Keepers of the keys of Heaven' (A history of the Papacy) Pub. Basic Books 2009

COLLINSON-MORLEY Lacy 'The story of the Sforzas' Pub. Dutton. 1934

COLONNA Gustavo-Brigante. 'Olimpia Pamphilj, Cardinal Padrone – 1594-1657' Ed. by A.Mondadori. Pub Verona. 1941

CORNWELL John. 'Hitler's Pope – the secret history of Pius XII' Pub. Viking 1999

DEAN Trevor and LOWE K.J.P. 'Marriage in Italy 1300-1650' Pub. Cambridge University Press. 1998

DENNIS George. 'The Cities and cemeteries of Etruria' London 1848

De ROSA Peter. 'Vicars of Christ – the dark side of the Papacy' Pub. Poolbeg. 2000

De ROSSI Giovanni Battista and DUCHENE Louis. 'Martyrology Hieronymianus' 1894

DIETER Arnold. 'Temples of the Last Pharoahs' Pub. Oxford University Press. 1999

DUFFY Eamon. 'Saints and Sinners' Pub.Yale. 1987/2006

DUGGAN Anne J. (Editor) 'Queens and Queenship in Medieval Europe' Boydell Press, proceedings of a conference held at King's College, London. April 1995

ERLANGER Rachel. 'Lucrezia Borgia' Pub. Michael Joseph. 1979.

FALCONI Carlo. 'The Popes in the Twentieth Century – Pius X to John XXII' Trans. Muriel Grindrod. Pub. Weidenfeld and Nicholson. 1967

FEUGHT Oscar E. 'Sex in the Church' Pub. Concordia. 1961

FLETCHER Catherine. 'The Black Prince of Florence – the spectacular life and treacherous death of Alessandro de' Medici' Pub. Bodley Head. 2016

FOLLAIN John. 'City of Secrets – the truth behind the murders at the Vatican' Pub. Harper Collins. 2003

FRANZERO Carlo Maria. 'The life and times of Theodora' Pub. Alvin Redman. 1961

FRASER Antonia. 'The Warrior Queens' Pub. Weidenfeld and Nicholson. 1988

FRAZEE Charles A. 'The origins of clerical celibacy in the Western Church' Journal of Church History vol 57. Issue S1. March 1988.

FRIEDA Leone 'Catherine de' Medici' Pub. Phoenix 2005

FRIEDA Leone 'The Deadly Sisterhood – a story of women, power, and intrigue in the Italian Renaissance' Pub. Weidenfeld and Nicholson. 2012

FREIDLANDER Saul. 'Pius XII and the Third Reich' Pub. Knopf. 1966

GARDNER Edmund G. 'Dukes and Poets of Ferrara' Pub. Dutton. 1903

GIGLI Giacinto. 'Diario di Roma – 1608-1670' 2 vols. Editore Columba, Roma. 1994

GIUSTINIANI Antonio. 'Dispacci' Vols I and II. Pub.Florence 1876.

GOBRY Ivan. 'La Reine Christine' Pub. Pygmalion/Gerard Watelet. 2001

GOLDSMITH Margaret. 'Christina of Sweden – a psychological biography' Pub. Doubleday, Doran and Co. 1935

GOLDSTONE Nancy. 'Four Queens – the Provencal sisters who ruled Europe' Pub. Viking. 2007

GOLDSTONE Nancy. 'Joanna, the Notorious Queen, of Naples, Jerusalem and Sicily' Pub. Phoenix. 2011

GRAGG Florence A. (Translator) 'Secret Memoirs of a Renaissance Pope' (Commentaries of Aeneus Silvius Piccolomini – Pope Pius II) Pub. Folio Society. 1961

GRAMICK Jeannine (Editor) 'Homosexuality in the Priesthood and the religious life' Pub. Crossroads. 1989

GRAVES Robert. 'Suetonius – The Twelve Caesars' Pub. Penguin 1957/1987

GREGOROVIUS Ferdinand. 'History of Rome in the middle ages' Trans. Annie Hamilton. Pub. Bell and Sons. 1894

GRIBBLE Francis. 'The Court of Christina of Sweden, and the later adventures of the Queen in exile.' Pub 1913. Forgotten Books Edition 2013

HEADLAM Cecil. 'The story of Naples' Pub. Dent and Sons. 1927

HEBBLETHWAITE Peter. 'The Year of the Three Popes' Pub. Collins. 1979

HEBBLETHWAITE Peter. 'In the Vatican' Pub. Sidgwick and Jackson. 1986

HERMAN Eleanor. 'Mistress of the Vatican – the true story of Olimpia Maidalchini' Pub. Harper Collins. 2008

HJORTSO Carl Herman. 'Queen Christina of Sweden – a medical/anthropological investigation of her remains in Rome' Pub. Lund, Gleerup (in English). 1966

HOLLINGSWORTH Mary. 'The Borgias' (History's most notorious Dynasty' Pub. Quercus 2011

HOFMAN Paul. 'The Vatican's Women – Female influence at the Holy See' Pub. St.Martin's Press. New York. 2002

HOOK Judith. 'The Sack of Rome' Pub. Palgrave McMillan. 1972

HUNT Edwin S. 'The Medieval Supercompanies – a Study of the Peruzzi Company of Florence' Cambridge University Press. 1994

Bibliography

HUTCHINSON Robert. 'Their Kingdom Come – Inside the secret world of Opus Dei' Pub. Corgi. 2012

JAKI Stanley. 'God and the Sun at Fatima' Pub. Real View Books. Michigan. 1999

JOHNSON Marian. 'The Borgias' Pub. MacDonald 1981

JONES Tobias. 'The Dark Heart of Italy' Pub. Faber and Faber. 2004

KERMINA Francoise. 'Christine from Sweden' Pub. Perrin. 1995

KNEALE Matthew. 'Rome – a History in Seven Sackings – from the Gauls to the Nazis' Pub. Atlantic Books. 2017

KNOWLES Dom David. 'Bare Ruined Choirs' Cambridge University Press. 1976

KRAUTHEIMER Richard. 'Rome – Profile of a City 312-1380' Pub. Princeton. 1980

LANCIANI Roberto. 'Storia degli Scavi di Roma' Vol 1. Pub. in 'Renaissance Discovery of Classical Antiquity' 1969

LEHNERT Pascalina.'His Humble Servant' (Sister Pascalina Lehnert's memoirs of her years of service to Eugenio Pacelli, Pope Pius XII) Pub. St.Augustine Press. 2014

LEHNERT Pascalina. 'La Giornato del Pontefice Pio XII' Pub. L'Osservatore Romano. Article dated 22nd March 1952.

LEHNERT Pascalina. (1894-1983) 'Women in World History – a Biographical Encyclopaedia.' Retrieved 28th November 2018

LUCAS Emma. 'Lucrezia Borgia' Pub. New World City. 2014

LUZIO   Alessandro. 'Isabella d'Este a fronte a Giulio II ultimi tue anni del suo Pontificato' Pub. Milan. 1912

LUZIO Alessandro. 'Isabella d'Este e i Borgia' Archivio Storico Lombardo. Serie Quinta. Vols I and II. Pub. Milan. 1916

LEV Elizabeth. 'The Tigress of Forli' (Renaissance Italy's most courageous and notorious Countess – Caterina Riario Sforza de' Medici' Pub. Head of Zeus Books. 2012

LOGAN F.Donald. 'History of the Church in the Middle Ages' Pub. Psychology Press. 2002. Pub Routledge 2012.

LONGFORD Earl of... (a.k.a Frank Pakenham). 'Pope John Paul II' Pub. Michael Joseph. 1981

LUBKIN Gregory. 'A Renaissance Court. – Milan under Galeazzo Maria Sforza' Pub. University of California Press. 1994

MALLETT Michael. 'The Borgias – the Rise and Fall of a Renaissance Dynasty' Pub. Paladin 1969.

MARTIN Sean. 'The Cathars – Rise and Fall of the Great Heresy' Pub. Oldcastle 2005

MARTINES Lauro. 'April Blood – Florence and the Plot against the Medici' Pub Oxford University Press. 2002

MASSON Georgina. 'Queen Christina' Secker and Warburg. 1968

MAXWELL-STUART P.G. 'Chronicle of the Popes' Pub. Thames Hudson. 1997

MAZZUCHELLI Mario. 'The Nun of Monza' Trans.Evelyn Gendel. Pub Hamish Hamilton. 1963

McBRIAN Richard P. 'Lives of the Popes – the Pontiffs from St.Peter to Benedict XVI' Pub. Harper Collins 1997

MacCAFFREY James "Pope Calixtus III" Pub. Appleton. 1908

McCULLOCH John M. 'Martyrology' in 'Dictionary Of The Middle Ages'. Pub. Strayer. 1989

MICHAEL (Brother of the Holy Trinity) 'The Third Secret of Fatima' Pub. Tan Books. 1991

MOLLAT Guillaume. 'The Popes at Avignon 1305-1378' Pub. Nelson and Sons. 1949

MURR Charles Theodore. 'The Godmother – Madre Pascalina, a feminine tour de force' Pub. Create Space Independent. 2017

MURPHY Caroline P. 'The Pope's Daughter – Felice della Rovere' Pub. Faber 2004

MURPHY Paul I. 'La Popessa' Pub Warner 1983

MUSTO Ronald G. 'Queen Sancia of Naples and the Spiritual Franciscans' Pub in 'Women in the Medieval World' by Blackwell. 1985

MUSTO Ronald G. 'Medieval Naples – a documentary history 400-1400' Pub Italica, New York. 2013

NEUMANN Alfred. 'The Life of Christina of Sweden' Pub. Hutchinson. 1936

NORWICH John Julius. 'A History of Venice' Pub Vintage. 1989

NORWICH John Julius 'Absolute Monarchs – a history of the Papacy' Pub Randon House. 2011

NORWICH John Julius. 'The Popes' Pub Vintage. 2012

NOGUERES Henri. 'The Massacre of Saint Bartholomew' Pub Allen and Unwin. 1962

ORMROD W.M. 'The Reign of Edward III' Pub. Tempus. 2000

PALLENBERG Corrado. 'Inside the Vatican' Pub Hawthorn. 1960

PALLAVACINO P.Sforza. 'Descrizione del primo viaggio della Regina di Svezia Cristina Maria' Pub. Salvicci. Roma. 1838

PALLAVACINO P.Sforza. 'Della Vita di Alessandro VII' Pub Prato. Italia. 1839

PARTNER Peter. 'Renaissance Rome, 1500-1555' Pub. Berkeley 1976. Pub University of California Press 1992

PARTNER Peter. 'The Pope's Men – Papal Civil Service in the Renaissance' Pub Oxford University Press/University of Michigan. 1980

PASOLINI Pier Desiderio. 'Caterina Sforza' Three volumes. Pub.Loescher. Rome. 1897

PASTOR Ludwig von 'History of the Popes' Ed.Frederick Ignatius. Pub Scholar's Choice. 2015

PETERS Edward. 'Torture' Pub Blackwell 1985. Pub Penn Press 1996

POSNER Gerald. 'God's Bankers – a History of money and power at the Vatican' Pub Simon and Schuster. 2015

POTTER David. 'Emperors of Rome' Pub Quercus 2008

POWER Eileen. 'Medieval People' Pub Biblio Life. 2008

QUIGLEY Isabel. (Trans.) 'Letters of John Paul I' Pub Gracewing. 2001

RANKE HEINEMAN Uta. 'Eunuchs for the Kingdom of Heaven – the Catholic Church and Sexuality' Pub Doubleday/Penguin 1990

READ Piers Paul. 'The Templars' Pub Pheonix. 2002

REARDON Wendy J. 'The Deaths of the Popes' Pub McFarland. 2012

REIBLING Mark. 'Church of Spies – the Pope's secret war against Hitler' Pub Scribe 2015

REESE Thomas J. 'Inside the Vatican' Pub Harvard 1996

RODEN Marie-Louise. (Editor) 'The Burial of Queen Christina of Sweden in St.Peter's Church' Pub Scandinavian Journal of History. 12/1 1987.

Bibliography

RODEN Marie-Louise. 'Church Politics in Seventeenth Century Rome.' (Cardinal Decio Azzolino, Queen Christina and the Squadron Volante). Pub. Almquist and Wiksell Int. Stockholm. 2000

ROLFE F.W. 'Chronicles of the House of Borgia' Pub Dover, New York. 1962

SABATINI Raphael. 'The Life of Cesare Borgia' Pub Stanley Paul and Co. 1912

SCULLARD H.H. 'From the Gracchi to Nero – History of Rome 133 BC to 68 AD' Pub Routledge 1998.

SHAW Christine. 'Julius II – the Warrior Pope' Pub Blackwell. 1993

SIGNOROTTO Gian Vittorio and VISCEGLIA Maria Antonietta (Editors) 'Court and Politics in Papal Rome, 1492-1700' Pub Cambridge University Press. 2002

SIPE A.W. Richard. 'A secret world – Sexuality and the Search for Celibacy' Pub Brunner-Mazel New York. 1990

SMITH Dennis Mack. 'A History of Sicily – Medieval Sicily 800-1713' Pub Viking. 1968

STEWART James Alan. 'Empress Theodora' Pub University of Texas Press. 2003

STOURTON Ed. 'Secret Letters of John Paul II' BBC Panorama Report 15th February 2016

TELFORD Lynda. 'Tudor Victims of the Reformation' Pub Pen and Sword. 2016.

TELFORD Lynda. 'Women of Medieval England' Pub Amberley. 2018.

THEILING Barbara. 'Jesus the Man – a new interpretation from the Dead Sea Scrolls' Pub Corgi. 1993

TOMAS Natalie. 'The Medici Women – gender and power in Renaissance Florence' Pub Burlington. 2003

UNGER Miles J. 'Magnifico – the brilliant life and violent times of Lorenzo de'Medici' Pub Simon and Schuster. 2008

VASSILI Donata Chiomenti. 'Donna Olimpia o del nepotismo nel Seicento' Pub Milan-Mursia. 1979

WALSH Michael. 'History of the Popes' Pub. Marshall Cavendish. 1980

WARD Jennifer. 'Women in Medieval Europe1200-1500' Pub Longman. 2002

WEISS Rene. 'The Yellow Cross – the Last Cathars 1290-1329' Pub Viking 2006

WEISS Roberto. 'The Renaissance Discovery of Classical Antiquity' Pub Wiley-Blackwell 1973

WEST Nigel. 'The Third Secret' Pub Harper Collins. 2000

WETTERBURG Gunnar. 'Chancellor Axel Oxenstierna in his Time' Pub Atlantis-Stockholm. 2002

WILLS Garry. 'Papal Sin – Structures of Deceit' Pub Doubleday. 2000

WILLIAMS George L. 'Papal Geneology – the families and descendants of the Popes' Pub Jefferson/MacFarland 1998.

WILLIAMSON Hugh Ross. 'Catherine de'Medici' Pub Michael Joseph. 1973

WILLIAMSON Hugh Ross. 'Lorenzo the Magnificent' Pub Michael Joseph. 1974

WISE Terence. '1066 – the Year of Destiny' Pub Osprey. 1979

YALLOP David Anthony. 'In God's Name – an Investigation of the murder of Pope John-Paul I' Pub. Bantam. 1983

YALLOP David Anthony. 'The Power and the Glory – Inside the dark heart of Pope John-Paul II's Vatican' Pub Constable. 2007

ZERBINATI Giovanni Maria. 'Chronicle di Ferrara' Pub Ferrara 1989.

Index

Index

Index